The Social Fabric

THE SOCIAL FABRIC

American Life from 1607 to the Civil War

THIRD EDITION

Editors

JOHN H. CARY   *Cleveland State University*

JULIUS WEINBERG   *Cleveland State University*

LITTLE, BROWN AND COMPANY   *Boston   Toronto*

Dedicated with love to

Kathryn Ditter Cary

and to Sean, Paul, Kenneth, and Carolyn

LIBRARY OF CONGRESS CATALOG CARD NO. 80-82172
ISBN 0-316-130788

9 8 7 6 5 4 3 2 1

ALP

Published simultaneously in Canada
by Little, Brown & Company (Canada) Limited

PRINTED IN THE UNITED STATES OF AMERICA

Preface

> I know histhry isn't thrue Hinnessy, because it ain't like what I see ivry day
> in Halsted Sthreet. If any wan comes along with a histhry iv Greece or Rome
> that'll show me th' people fightin,' gettin' dhrunk, makin' love, gettin' mar-
> ried, owin' the grocery man an' bein' without hard-coal, I'll believe they was
> a Greece or Rome, but not befure.

The sentiment of Mr. Dooley, Finley Peter Dunne's comic Irish philosopher,
expresses the attitude of many people toward history. Young Americans,
especially, question the relevance of a history that deals only with politics,
diplomacy, governments, and famous leaders, and ignores the daily life of
average men and women. Two recent trends, however, are doing much to
remedy this neglect. One is increased popular interest in the forgotten mass
of men and women who tilled our fields, built our cities, and fought our
wars, but who achieved no particular fame and left very little record of their
lives and thought. The second development is the renewed concern of historians with social history.

This kind of history has more meaning for us, and touches our lives more
directly, than any other aspect of our past. In an age seeking "relevance"
nothing is more relevant than American social history. Each of us has direct
experience, or an intimate awareness, of being part of a family, of falling in
love and marrying, of poverty and pain, of suffering in war, of earning a living, of social oppression and reform. By understanding the social life of an
earlier age, we can gain an understanding of ourselves and of others, in
whatever time or place they lived.

This is an anthology of American social history for college history courses.
It began with our belief that college students would find more meaning in
the kind of history described by Mr. Dooley than in political, diplomatic,
or constitutional history. This and the companion volume of *The Social*

Fabric, which covers the period from 1865 to the present, touch upon marrying and making love, fighting and getting drunk, owing the grocer, and going without heat. Covering the time from the earliest settlement of America to the Civil War, it contains descriptions of what it was like to cross the ocean in an immigrant ship and the Great Plains in a covered wagon, what marriage and the family were like in the eighteenth century and what sex was like in the nineteenth, what life was like for women workers in New England factories and for slaves on southern plantations, and how people behaved in a frontier revival meeting or in an austere Shaker community.

No single book can treat every aspect of our history, but these volumes examine American life in much of its diversity. There are essays on women as well as men; on Indians and blacks as well as whites; and on the poor and the oppressed as well as the rich and the powerful. The sectional, class, racial, and religious differences among our heterogeneous people have created serious strains that at times threatened to tear the nation apart. But with all their diversity, the American people have also shared many common attitudes and traditions that provided a common social fabric to bind them together.

We have selected the readings from some of the most interesting writing on the American past. We have prefaced each reading with an introductory note, explaining the relation of the subject to broader developments in American history of the period. Each selection is also accompanied by an illustration, which provides a visual commentary on the topic under consideration. The study guide that follows the selection will help you review the special aspects of the reading, and may suggest issues for class discussion. The bibliographical note will help you find further material, should you wish to read more on the topic.

This third edition of volume I of *The Social Fabric* retains many of the best readings of earlier editions, with six entirely new selections. The first is a description of one of the most celebrated episodes in American history — the famous Salem witchcraft craze. The second is a charming essay on an early American inventor, who did much to lay the foundations of modern American industrialism. The third new essay is on the creation of institutions for incarcerating juvenile delinquents and homeless children during the Jacksonian period. An extraordinary number of fine books have been published in recent years in the fields of black and women's history, and new articles on these subjects have been substituted for the selections used in earlier editions of *The Social Fabric.* The sixth new selection is a graphic account of the tribulations of the Donner Party on the trail to California.

The response of students and teachers in both four-year colleges and community colleges to this anthology has been most gratifying. A number of teachers who used the earlier editions of *The Social Fabric* in introductory courses have indicated that these volumes rank with the most successful supplementary materials they have ever used. Many of them contributed suggestions, as have a number of students, which have been incorporated in this new edition. We have appreciated the comments that students have made on the evaluation form that appears as the last page of each volume.

J.C.
J.W.

Contents

The Social Fabric

I ORIGINS OF THE AMERICAN PEOPLE

The migration of peoples from Europe, Africa, and the Far East to the Western Hemisphere is one of the great stories in all of human history. Though the full force of immigration did not hit these shores until the nineteenth and twentieth centuries, the age of exploration and settlement in the seventeenth and eighteenth centuries saw some of the most important developments in the history of the Western world.

In 1600, the land we know as the United States was inhabited by at least 500,000 and perhaps as many as a million and a half Indians, thinly scattered in small tribes from the warlike Iroquois hunters of the Northeast to the pueblo dwellers of the Southwest. These people, who had crossed from Asia to Alaska perhaps 20,000 years earlier, had used the land and its resources well. Killing only for food, traveling by water and forest paths, making their weapons and tools from stone and wood, and using animal skins and bark for their shelters, they had left a beautiful, virgin landscape relatively untouched.

In 1607, the first permanent settlement of Englishmen was established at Jamestown, Virginia, and the first Africans arrived there just twelve years later. The encounter of these three peoples, one a hunting society that depended on game for its existence, the second an agricultural people who cleared the forests for planting, and the third an enslaved labor force, was often tragic and sometimes brutal. By 1790, when the first census of the American republic was taken, the Atlantic seaboard that the Indian had known was scarcely recognizable. Vast forest regions had been cleared, intercolonial roads were being built, the port towns were developing into bustling cities, and a growing number of adventurers were passing through the mountain gaps to settle the Ohio Valley. Excluding Indians, nearly four million men, women, and children, all reflecting an extraordinary ethnic diversity, lived in the new United States.

This section treats three of the earliest inhabitants of the New World — the American Indian, the African slave, and the English colonist. The first selection depicts the life and culture of the Seneca Indians in the eighteenth century, by which time all of the eastern Indian tribes had suffered serious consequences from the European invasion of their lands. The second reading describes one pattern of social organization that the colonists established, the New England town, which should be compared with other forms, such as the southern county, that are described in your textbook or other course reading. The third depicts the conditions of slavery in eighteenth-century Virginia and the complex relationship that existed between master and slave. Together, these first readings introduce us to three distinct racial groups — red, white, and black — whose conflicts and contributions go far to explain the special character of American society today.

Bertoli's 1796 portrait of Cornplanter (Ki-on-twog-ky) reflects European influence on the clothing and weapons of the Seneca.

1

ANTHONY F. C. WALLACE

Indian Life and Culture

In order to understand the history of the United States, we must look to two remote cultures — the European world in the fifteenth century, on the eve of the discovery of the Western Hemisphere, and the ancient Indian culture that existed on this side of the Atlantic. The red man has lived on this continent for about 20,000 years and has been in contact with Europeans and Africans for nearly five hundred years. Yet most Americans know little about Indian life and culture. The movie image of a treacherous savage and the trinket purchased at a souvenir shop have left the real character of the Indian as invisible to the white majority as that of the black man has been for more than three hundred years.

Oliver La Farge has suggested that the Indian has always been unknown to his more recently arrived fellow countrymen, because of a number of myths that white men found convenient to believe in. The earliest of these myths — picturing the Indian as a noble, uncorrupted child of nature — survived in distant Europe longer than it did in the British colonies. Here, as settlers pushed inland and came into conflict with the Indian over land, the more convenient myth of the brutal, treacherous savage supplanted it. Eventually, as industrialized America pushed the Indian tribes onto reservations, a third myth, that of a drunken, irresponsible dependent, became popular.

Anthropologists and historians have been devoting serious attention to the American Indian since Lewis Henry Morgan published a path-breaking study of the Iroquois in 1851. Yet, much of the writing has necessarily been based on a record left by whites, has dealt mostly with Indian-white relations, and leaves one wondering what Indian life looked like from the inside. In fact, Indian life was somewhat different in different historical periods, and it varied considerably from the culture of the war-like tribes of the Northeast to the buffalo hunters of the Plains and the pueblo peoples of the Southwest.

Anthony F. C. Wallace is one of the leading students of the Iroquois. His book, *The Death and Rebirth of the Seneca,* is a remarkable study of the devastating effects of European influences on this Iroquois tribe and of the attempt of the prophet Handsome Lake to renew the spirit of his people. The following selection is a general introduction to the Seneca in the eighteenth century. Wallace describes their farming, hunting, warfare, marriage, and training of children, and thus conveys a sense of the fierce independence and loyalty of these earliest Americans.

. . . The traditional Iroquois dwelling unit was called a longhouse. It was a dark, noisy, smoke-filled family barracks; a rectangular, gable-roofed structure anywhere from fifty to seventy-five feet in length, constructed of sheets of elm bark lashed on stout poles, housing up to fifty or sixty people. The roof was slotted (sometimes with a sliding panel for rainy days) to let out some of the smoke that eddied about the ceiling. There was only one entrance, sometimes fitted with a wooden or bark door on wooden hinges, and sometimes merely curtained by a bearskin robe. Entering, one gazed in the half-light down a long, broad corridor or alleyway, in the center of which, every twelve or fifteen feet, smoldered a small fire. On opposite sides of each fire, facing one another, were double-decker bunks, six feet wide and about twelve feet long. An entire family — mother, father, children, and various other relatives — might occupy one or two of these compartments. They slept on soft furs in the lower bunks. Guns, masks, moccasins, clothing, cosmetic paint, wampum, knives, hatchet, food, and the rest of a Seneca family's paraphernalia were slung on the walls and on the upper bunk. Kettles, braided corn, and other suspendable items hung from the joists, which also supported pots over the fire. Each family had about as much room for permanent quarters as might be needed for all of them to lie down and sleep, cook their meals, and stow their gear. Privacy was not easily secured because other families lived in the longhouse; people were always coming and going, and the fires glowed all night. In cold or wet weather or when the snow lay two or three feet deep outside, doors and roof vents had to be closed, and the longhouses became intolerably stuffy — acrid with smoke and the reeking odors of leftover food and sweating flesh. Eyes burned and throats choked. But the people were nonetheless tolerably warm, dry, and (so it is said) cheerful.

The inhabitants of a longhouse were usually kinfolk. A multifamily long-house was, theoretically, the residence of a maternal lineage: an old woman and her female descendants, together with unmarried sons, and the husbands and children of her married daughters. The totem animal of the clan to which the lineage belonged — Deer, Bear, Wolf, Snipe, or whatever it might be — was carved above the door and painted red. In this way directions were easier to give, and the stranger knew where to seek hospitality or aid. But often — especially in the middle of the eighteenth century — individual families chose to live by themselves in smaller cabins, only eighteen by twenty feet or so in size, with just one fire. As time went on, the old longhouses disintegrated and were abandoned, and by the middle of the century the Iroquois were making their houses of logs.

Around and among the houses lay the cornfields. Corn was a main food. Dried and pounded into meal and then boiled into a hot mush, baked into dumplings, or cooked in whole kernels together with beans and squash and pieces of meat in the thick soups that always hung in kettles over the fires, it kept the people fed. In season, meats, fresh fruits, herb teas, fried grasshoppers, and other delicacies added spice and flavor to the diet. But the Iroquois were a cornfed people. They consumed corn when it was fresh and stored it underground for the lean winter months. The Seneca nation alone raised as much as a million bushels of corn each year; the cornfields around a large village might stretch for miles, and even scattered clearings in the woods were cultivated. Squash, beans, and tobacco were raised in quantity, too. Domesticated animals were few, even after the middle of the century: some pigs, a few chickens, not many horses or cattle. The responsibility for carrying on this extensive agricultural establishment rested almost entirely on the women. Armed with crude wooden hoes and digging-sticks, they swarmed over the fields in gay, chattering work bees, proceeding from field to field to hoe, to plant, to weed, and to harvest. An individual woman might, if she wished, "own" a patch of corn, or an apple or peach orchard, but there was little reason for insisting on private tenure: the work was more happily done communally, and in the absence of a regular market, a surplus was of little personal advantage, especially if the winter were hard and other families needed corn. In such circumstances hoarding led only to hard feelings and strained relations as well as the possibility of future difficulty in getting corn for oneself and one's family. All land was national land; an individual could occupy and use a portion of it and maintain as much privacy in the tenure as he wished, but this usufruct title reverted to the nation when the land was abandoned. There was little reason to bother about individual ownership of real estate anyway: there was plenty of land. Economic security for both men and women lay in a proper recognition of one's obligation to family, clan, community, and nation, and in efficient and cooperative performance on team activities, such as working bees, war parties, and diplomatic missions.

If the clearing with its cornfields bounded the world of women, the forest was the realm of men. Most of the men hunted extensively, not only for deer, elk, and small game to use for food and clothing and miscellaneous household items, but for beaver, mink, and otter, the prime trade furs. Pelts were the gold of the woods. With them a man could buy guns, powder, lead, knives, hatchets, axes, needles and awls, scissors, kettles, traps, cloth, ready-made shirts, blankets, paint (for cosmetic purposes), and various notions: steel springs to pluck out disfiguring beard, scalp, and body hair; silver bracelets and armbands and tubes for coiling hair; rings to hang from nose and ears; mirrors; tinkling bells. Sometimes a tipsy hunter would give away his peltries for a keg of rum, treat his friends to a debauch, and wake up with a scolding wife and hungry children calling him a fool; another might, with equal improvidence, invest in a violin, or a horse, or a gaudy military uniform. But by and large, the products of the commercial hunt — generally conducted in the winter and often hundreds of miles from the home village, in the Ohio country or down the Susquehanna River — were exchanged for a limited range of European consumer goods, which had become, after five generations of contact with beaver-hungry French, Dutch, and English traders, economic necessities. Many of these goods were, indeed, designed to Indian specifications and manufactured solely for the Indian trade. An Iroquois man dressed in a linen breechcloth and calico shirt, with a woolen blanket over his shoulders, bedaubed with trade paint and adorned with trade armbands and earrings, carrying a steel knife, a steel hatchet, a clay pipe, and a rifled gun felt himself in no wise contaminated nor less an Indian than his stone-equipped great-great-grandfather. Iroquois culture had reached out and incorporated these things that Iroquois Indians wanted while at the same time Iroquois warriors chased off European missionaries, battled European soldiers to a standstill, and made obscene gestures when anyone suggested that they should emulate white society (made up, according to their information and experience, of slaves, cheating lawyers with pen and paper and ink, verbose politicians, hypocritical Christians, stingy tavern keepers, and thieving peddlers).

Behavior was governed not by published laws enforced by police, courts, and jails, but by oral tradition supported by a sense of duty, a fear of gossip, and a dread of retaliatory witchcraft. Theft, vandalism, armed robbery, were almost unknown. Public opinion, gently exercised, was sufficient to deter most persons from property crimes, for public opinion went straight to the heart of the matter: the *weakness* of the criminal. A young warrior steals someone else's cow — probably captured during a raid on a white settlement — and slaughters it to feed his hungry family. He does this at a time when other men are out fighting. No prosecution follows, no investigation, no sentence: the unhappy man is nonetheless severely punished, for the nickname "Cow-killer" is pinned to him, and he must drag it rattling behind him wherever he goes. People call him a coward behind his back and snicker when they tell white men, in his presence, a story of an unnamed Indian who killed cows when he should have been killing men. Such a curse was not generalized to the point of ostracism, however. The celebrated Red Jacket, about whom the "Cow-killer" story was told, vindicated his courage in later wars, became the principal spokesman for his nation, and was widely respected and revered. But he never lost the nickname.

Disputes between people rarely developed over property. Marital difficulties centering around infidelity, lack of support, or personal incompatibility were settled by mutual agreement. Commonly, in case of difficulty, the man left and the woman, with her children, remained with her mother. A few couples remained together for a lifetime; most had several marriages; a few changed mates almost with the season. Men might come to blows during drunken arguments over real or fancied slights to their masculine honor, over politics, or over the alleged mistreatment of their kinfolk. Such quarrels led at times to killings or to accusations of witchcraft. A murder (or its equivalent, the practice of witchcraft) was something to be settled by the victim's kinfolk; if they wished, they might kill the murderer or suspected witch without fear of retaliation from his family (provided that family agreed on his guilt). But usually a known killer would come to his senses, admit himself wrong, repent, and offer retribution in goods or services to the mourning family, who unless exceptionally embittered by an unprovoked and brutal killing were then expected to accept the blood money and end the matter.

Drunkenness was perhaps the most serious social problem. Two Moravian missionaries who visited the Iroquois country in 1750 had the misfortune to reach the Seneca towns at the end of June, when the men were just returning from Oswego, where they had sold their winter's furs, and were beginning to celebrate the start of summer leisure. Hard liquor was dissolving winter's inhibitions and regrets. At Canandaigua, the missionaries, who were guests at the house of a prominent warrior, had just explained the friendly nature of their errand when the rum arrived. "All the town was in a state of intoxication, and frequently rushed into our hut in this condition," complained the white men. "There was every reason to think that fighting might ensue, as there were many warriors among those who were perfectly mad with drink." After a sleepless night the missionaries traveled on, reaching the outskirts of Geneseo on the second of July. "The village," said the observers in surprise, "consisted of 40 or more large huts, and lies in a beautiful and pleasant region. A fine large plain, several miles in length and breadth, stretches out behind the village." But the kegs of rum had anticipated them. "When we caught sight of the town we heard a great noise of shouting and quarreling, from which we could infer that many of the inhabitants were intoxicated, and that we might expect to have an uncomfortable time. On entering the town we saw many drunken Indians, who looked mad with drink. . . ."

Alas, poor Christians! They had to hide in a stuffy garret, without food or water. David, their devoted Indian convert and servant, stole out toward evening with a kettle to fetch his masters some water and was seen. "A troop of drunken women came rushing madly toward him. Some of them were naked, and others nearly so. In order to drive them away he was obliged to use his fists, and deal blows to the right and left. He climbed up a ladder, but when he had scarcely reached the top they seized it and tore it from under his feet." David barely managed to escape "in safety" from these playful Amazons. The missionaries decided not to wait the two days until the liquor ran out to meet the chiefs in council; they bent their prayers to an early departure. They finally managed to escape at dawn by jumping down from an opening in the gable and tiptoeing away. "The Lord watched over us in such a manner that all the drunken savages were in their huts, not a creature to be seen. Even the dogs, numbering nearly 100 in the whole village, were all quiet, wonderful to relate, and not a sound was heard. A dense fog covered the town, so that we could not see 20 steps before us. A squaw stood at the door of the last hut, but she was sober and returned our greeting quietly."

But such drunken debauches were only occasional rents in a fabric of polite social behavior. Other missionaries were more favorably impressed than the Moravians. The Seneca, said a Quaker scribe, "appear to be naturally as well calculated for social and rational enjoyment, as any people. They frequently visit each other in their houses, and spend much of their time in friendly intercourse. They are also mild and hospitable, not only among themselves, but to strangers, and good natured in the extreme, except when their natures are perverted by the inflammatory influence of spirituous liquors. In their social interviews, as well as public councils, they are careful not to interrupt one another in conversation, and generally make short speeches. This truly laudable mark of good manners, enables them to transact all their public business with decorum and regularity, and more strongly impresses on their mind and memory, the result of their deliberations."

During the seventeenth and eighteenth centuries Iroquois men earned a reputation among the French and English colonists for being the most astute diplomatically and most dangerous militarily of all the Indians of the Northeast. Yet at the same time the Iroquois were famous for the "matriarchal" nature of their economic and social institutions. After the colonial era came to an end with the victory of the United States in the Revolutionary War, the traditional diplomatic and military role of the Iroquois men was sharply limited by the circumstances of reservation life. Simultaneously, the "matriarchal" character of certain of their economic, kinship, and political institutions was drastically diminished. These changes were codified by the prophet Handsome Lake. As we shall see later in more detail, the changes in kinship behavior that he recommended, and which to a considerable degree were carried out by his followers, amounted to a shift in dominance from the mother-daughter relationship to that of the husband-wife. Handsome Lake's reforms thus were a sentence of doom upon the traditional quasi-matriarchal system of the Iroquois.

The Iroquois were described as matriarchal because of the important role women played in the formal political organization. The men were responsible for hunting, for warfare, and for diplomacy, all of which kept them away from their households for long periods of time, and all of which were essential to the survival of Iroquois society. An expedition of any kind was apt to take months or even years, for the fifteen thousand or so Iroquois in the seventeenth and eighteenth centuries ranged over an area of about a million square miles. It is not an exaggeration to say that the full-time business of an Iroquois man was travel, in order to hunt, trade, fight, and talk in council. But the women stayed at home. Thus, an Iroquois village might be regarded as a collection of strings, hundreds of years old, of successive generations of women, always domiciled in their longhouses near their cornfields in a clearing while their sons and husbands traveled in the forest on supportive errands of hunting and trapping, of trade, of war, and of diplomacy.

The women exercised political power in three main circumstances. First, whenever one of the forty-nine chiefs of the great intertribal League of the Iroquois died, the senior women of his lineage nominated his successor. Second, when tribal or village decisions had to be made, both men and women attended a kind of town meeting, and while men were the chiefs and normally did the public speaking, the women caucused behind the scenes and lobbied with the spokesmen. Third, a woman was entitled to demand publicly that a murdered kinsman or kinswoman be replaced by a captive from a non-Iroquois tribe, and her male relatives, particularly lineage kinsmen, were morally obligated to go out in a war party to secure captives, whom the bereaved woman might either adopt or consign to torture and death. Adoption was so frequent during the bloody centuries of the beaver wars and the colonial wars that some Iroquois villages were preponderantly composed of formally adopted war captives. In sum, Iroquois women were entitled formally to select chiefs, to participate in consensual politics, and to start wars.

Thus the Iroquois during the two centuries of the colonial period were a population divided, in effect, into two parts: sedentary females and nomadic males. The men were frequently absent in small or large groups for prolonged periods of time on hunting, trading, war, and diplomatic expeditions, simultaneously protecting the women from foreign attack and producing a cash crop of skins, furs, and scalps, which they exchanged for hardware and dry goods. These activities, peripheral in a geographical sense, were central to the economic and political welfare of the Six Nations. The preoccupation of Iroquois men with these tasks and the pride they took in their successful pursuit cannot be overestimated. But the system depended on a complementary role for women. They had to be economically self-sufficient through horticulture during the prolonged absences of men, and they maintained genealogical and political continuity in a matrilineal system in which the primary kin relationship (not necessarily the primary social relationship) was the one between mother and daughter.

Such a quasi-matriarchy, of course, had a certain validity in a situation where the division of labor between the sexes required that men be geographically peripheral to the households that they helped to support and did defend. Given the technological, economic, and military circumstances of the time, such an arrangement was a practical one. But it did have an incidental consequence: It made the relationship between husband and wife an extremely precarious one. Under these conditions it was convenient for the marital system to be based on virtually free sexual choice, the mutual satisfaction of spouses, and easy separation. Couples chose one another for personal reasons; free choice was limited, in effect, only by the prohibition of intraclan marriage. Marriages were apt to fray when a husband traveled too far, too frequently, for too long. On his return, drunken quarreling, spiteful gossip, parental irresponsibility, and flagrant infidelity might lead rapidly to the end of the relationship. The husband, away from the household for long periods of time, was apt in his travels to establish a liaison with a woman whose husband was also away. The wife, temporarily abandoned, might for the sake of comfort and economic convenience take up with a locally available man. Since such relationships were, in effect, in the interest of everyone in the longhouse, they readily tended to become recognized marriages. The emotional complications introduced by these serial marriages were supposed to be resolved peacefully by the people concerned. The traveling husband who returned to find his wife living with someone else might try to recover her; if she preferred to remain with her new husband, however, he was not entitled to punish her or her new lover, but instead was encouraged to find another wife among the unmarried girls or wives with currently absent husbands.

The basic ideal of manhood was that of "the good hunter." Such a man was self-disciplined, autonomous, responsible. He was a patient and efficient huntsman, a generous provider to his family and nation, and a loyal and thoughtful friend and clansman. He was also a stern and ruthless warrior in avenging any injury done to those under his care. And he was always stoical and indifferent to privation, pain, and even death. Special prominence could be achieved by those who, while adequate in all respects, were out-standing in one or another dimension of this ideal. The patient and thought-ful man with a skin "seven thumbs thick" (to make him indifferent to spite-ful gossip, barbed wit, and social pressures generally) might become a sachem or a "distinguished name" — a "Pine Tree" chief. An eloquent man with a good memory and indestructible poise might be a council speaker and represent clan, nation, even the confederacy in far-flung diplomatic ventures. And the stern and ruthless warrior (always fighting, at least accord-ing to the theory, to avenge the death or insult of a blood relative or pub-licly avowed friend) might become a noted war-captain or an official war-chief. The war-captain ideal, open as it was to all youths, irrespective of clan and lineage or of special intellectual qualifications, was perhaps the most emulated.

In the seventeenth century an Onondaga war-captain named Aharihon bore the reputation of being the greatest warrior of the country. He realized the ideal of autonomous responsibility to virtually pathological perfection. Let us note what is told of Aharihon in the *Jesuit Relations.*

Aharihon was a man of dignified appearance and imposing carriage, grave, polished in manner, and self-contained. His brother had been killed about 1654 in the wars with the Erie, a tribe westward of the Iroquois. As clansman and close relative, he was entitled — indeed obligated — either to avenge his brother's death by killing some Erie people or by adopting a war captive to take his place. Aharihon within a few years captured or had pre-sented to him for adoption forty men. Each of them he burned to death over a slow fire, because, as he said, "he did not believe that there was any one worthy to occupy his [brother's] place." Father Lalemant was present when another young man, newly captured, was given to Aharihon as a substitute for the deceased brother. Aharihon let the young man believe that he was adopted and need have no further fear, and "presented to him four dogs, upon which to hold his feast of adoption. In the middle of the feast, while he was rejoicing and singing to entertain the guests, Aharihon arose, and told the company that this man too must die in atonement for his brother's death. The poor lad was astounded at this, and turned toward the door to make his escape, but was stopped by two men who had orders to burn him. On the fourteenth of February, in the evening, they began with his feet, intending to roast him, at a slow fire, as far up as the waist, during the greater part of the night. After midnight, they were to let him rally his strength and sleep a little until daybreak, when they were to finish this fatal tragedy. In his torture, the poor man made the whole village resound with his cries and groans. He shed great tears, contrary to the usual custom, the victim commonly glorying to be burned limb by limb, and opening his lips only to sing; but, as this one had not expected death, he wept and cried in a way that touched even these Barbarians. One of Aharihon's relatives was so moved with pity, that he advised ending the sufferer's torments by plunging a knife into his breast — which would have been a deed of mercy, had the stab been mortal. However, they were induced to continue the burning without interruption, so that before day he ended both his sufferings and his life." Aharihon's career of death continued without interruption, and by 1663 he was able to boast that he had killed sixty men with his own hand and had burned fully eighty men over slow fire. He kept count by tattooing a mark on his thigh for each successive victim. He was known then as the Captain General of the Iroquois and was nicknamed Nero by the Frenchmen at Montreal because of his cruelty.

The French finally captured him near Montreal, but even in captivity his manner was impressive. "This man," commented Father Lalemant, "commonly has nine slaves with him, five boys and four girls. He is a captain of dignified appearance and imposing carriage, and of such equanimity and presence of mind that, upon seeing himself surrounded by armed men, he showed no more surprise than if he had been alone; and when asked whether he would like to accompany us to Quebec, he deigned only to answer coldly that that was not a question to ask him, since he was in our power. Accordingly he was made to come aboard our Vessel, where I took pleasure in studying his disposition as well as that of an Algonquin in our company, who bore the scalp of an Iroquois but recently slain by him in war. These two men, although hostile enough to eat each other, chatted and laughed on board that Vessel with great familiarity, it being very hard to decide which of the two was more skillful in masking his feelings. I had Nero placed near me at table, where he bore himself with a gravity, a self-control, and a propriety, which showed nothing of his Barbarian origin; but during the rest of the time he was constantly eating, so that he fasted only when he was at table."

But this voracious captain was not renowned among the Onondaga as a killer only. He was, on the contrary, also a trusted ambassador, dispatched on occasion to Montreal on missions of peace. He was, in a word, a noted man. He was a killer, but he was not an indiscriminate killer; he killed only those whom it was his right to kill, tortured only those whom he had the privilege of torturing, always as an expression of respect for his dead brother. And although his kinfolk sometimes felt he was a little extreme in his stern devotion to his brother's memory, they did not feel that he was any the less a fine man, or that they had a right to interfere with his impulses; they were willing to entrust the business of peace, as well as war, to his hand.

A century and a half later Mary Jemison, the captive white woman who lived for most of her life among the Seneca on the Genesee River, described her Indian husband in not dissimilar terms. "During the term of nearly fifty years that I lived with him," she recalled, "I received, according to Indian custom, all the kindness and attention that was my due as his wife. — Although war was his trade from his youth till old age and decrepitude stopt his career, he uniformly treated me with tenderness, and never offered an insult. . . . He was a man of tender feelings to his friends, ready and willing to assist them in distress, yet, as a warrior, his cruelties to his enemies perhaps were unparalleled. . . . In early life, Hiokatoo showed signs of thirst for blood, by attending only to the art of war, in the use of the tomahawk and scalping knife; and in practising cruelties upon every thing that chanced to fall into his hands, which was susceptible of pain. In that way he learned to use his implements of war effectually, and at the same time blunted all those fine feelings and tender sympathies that are naturally excited, by hearing or seeing, a fellow being in distress. He could inflict the most excruciating tortures upon his enemies, and prided himself upon his forti- tude, in having performed the most barbarous ceremonies and tortures, without the least degree of pity or remorse. . . . In those battles he took a number of Indians prisoners, whom he killed by tying them to trees and then setting small Indian boys to shooting at them with arrows, till death finished the misery of the sufferers; a process that frequently took two days for its completion! . . . At Braddock's defeat he took two white prisoners, and burnt them alive in a fire of his own kindling. . . ."

With this sort of man serving as an ego-ideal, held up by sanction and by praise to youthful eyes, it is not remarkable that young men were ambitious to begin the practice of war. All had seen captives tortured to death; all had known relatives lost in war whose death demanded revenge or replacement. The young men went out on practice missions as soon as they were big enough to handle firearms; "infantile bands, armed with hatchets and guns which they can hardly carry, do not fail to spread fear and horror every- where." Even as late as the middle of the eighteenth century, Handsome Lake and his brothers and nephews were still busy at the old business of war for the sake of war. Cornplanter became a noted war-captain; Blacksnake, his nephew, was one of the official war-chiefs of the Seneca nation; and Handsome Lake himself took part in the scalping-party pattern as a young man. But Handsome Lake became a sachem and later a prophet, and he never gloried in the numbers of men he killed as his brother Cornplanter (somewhat guiltily) did. "While I was in the use of arms I killed seven persons and took three and saved their lives," said Cornplanter. And Black- snake, in later life, told with relish of his exploits as a warrior. "We had a good fight there," he would say. "I have killed how many I could not tell, for I pay no attention to or kept [no] account of it, it was great many, for I never have it at all my Battles to think about kepting account what I'd killed at one time. . . ."

The cultivation of the ideal of autonomous responsibility — and the sup- pression of its antinomy, dependency — began early in life. Iroquois children were carefully trained to think for themselves but to act for others. Parents were protective, permissive, and sparing of punishment; they encouraged children to play at imitating adult behavior but did not criticize or con- demn fumbling early efforts; they maintained a cool detachment, both physically and verbally, avoiding the intense confrontations of love and anger between parent and child to which Europeans were accustomed. Children did not so much live in a child's world as grow up freely in the interstices of an adult culture. The gain was an early self-reliance and enjoyment of responsibility; the cost, perhaps, was a lifelong difficulty in handling feelings of dependency.

The Seneca mother gave birth to her child in the privacy of the woods, where she retired for a few hours when her time came, either alone or in the company of an older woman who served as midwife and, if the weather was cold, built and tended a fire. She had prepared for this event by eating sparingly and exercising freely, which were believed (probably with good reason) to make the child stronger and the birth easier. The newborn infant was washed in cold water, or even in snow, immediately after parturition and then wrapped in skins or a blanket. If the birth were a normal one, the mother walked back to the village with her infant a few hours afterwards to take up the duties of housewife. The event was treated as the consummation of a healthful process rather than as an illness. The infant spent much of its first nine months swaddled from chin to toe and lashed to a cradle-board. The child's feet rested against a footboard; a block of wood was placed between the heels of a girl to mold her feet to an inward turn. Over its head stretched a hoop, which could be draped with a thin cloth to keep away flies or to protect the child from the cold. The board and its wrappings were often lavishly decorated with silver trinkets and beadwork embroidery. The mother was able to carry the child in the board, suspended against her back, by a tumpline around her forehead; the board could be hung from the limb of a tree while she hoed corn; and it could be converted into a crib by suspending it on a rack of poles laid horizontally on forks stuck in the ground. The mother was solicitous of the child's comfort, nursed it whenever it cried, and loosened it from the board several times a day to change the moss that served as a diaper and to give it a chance to romp. The children, however, tended to cry when released from the board, and their tranquility could often be restored only by putting them back. Babies were seldom heard crying.

The mother's feeling for her children was intense; indeed, to one early observer it appeared that "Parental Tenderness" was carried to a "dangerous Indulgence." Another early writer remarked, "The mothers love their children with an extreme passion, and although they do not reveal this in caresses, it is nevertheless real." Mothers were quick to express resentment of any restraint or injury or insult offered to the child by an outsider. During the first few years the child stayed almost constantly with the mother, in the house, in the fields, or on the trail, playing and performing small tasks under her direction. The mother's chief concern during this time was to provide for the child and to protect it, to "harden" it by baths in cold water, but not to punish. Weaning was not normally attempted until the age of three or four, and such control as the child obtained over its excretory functions was achieved voluntarily, not as a result of consistent punishment for mistakes. Early sexual curiosity and experimentation were regarded as a natural childish way of behaving, out of which it would, in due time, grow. Grandparents might complain that small children got into everything, but the small child was free to romp, to pry into things, to demand what it wanted, and to assault its parents, without more hazard of punishment than the exasperated mother's occasionally blowing water in its face or dunking it in a convenient river.

The years between about eight or nine and the onset of puberty were a time of easy and gradual learning. At the beginning of this period the beginnings of the differentiation of the roles of boys and girls were laid down. The girls were kept around the house, under the guidance of their mothers, and assigned to the lighter household duties and to helping in the fields. Boys were allowed to roam in gangs, playing at war, hunting with bows and arrows and toy hatchets, and competing at races, wrestling, and lacrosse. The first successes at hunting were greeted with praise and boasts of future greatness. Sometimes these roaming gangs spent days at a time away from the village, sleeping in the bush, eating wild roots and fruits, and hunting such small game as could be brought down by bow and arrow, blowgun, or snare. These gangs developed into war parties after the boys reached puberty. Among themselves, both in gangs and among siblings of the same family, the children's playgroups were not constantly supervised by parents and teachers, and the children governed themselves in good harmony. Said one close observer, "Children of the same family show strong attachments to each other, and are less liable to quarrel in their youthful days than is generally the case with white children."

The parents usually tried to maintain a calm moderation of behavior in dealing with their children, a lofty indifference alike to childish tantrums and seductive appeals for love. Hardihood, self-reliance, and independence of spirit were sedulously inculcated. When occasion presented itself, fathers, uncles, or other elder kinfolk instructed their sons in the techniques of travel, firemaking, the chase, war, and other essential arts of manhood, and the mothers correspondingly taught their daughters the way to hoe and plant the cornfields, how to butcher the meat, cook, braid corn, and other household tasks. But this instruction was presented, rather than enforced, as an opportunity rather than as a duty. On occasion the parent or other responsible adult talked to the child at length, "endeavoring," as a Quaker scribe gently put it, "to impress on its mind what it ought to do, and what to leave undone." If exhortation seemed inadequate in its effect, the mentor might ridicule the child for doing wrong, or gravely point out the folly of a certain course of action, or even warn him that he courted the rage of offended supernatural beings. Obedience as such was no virtue, however, and blows, whippings, or restraints of any kind, such as restriction to quarters, were rarely imposed, the faults of the child being left to his own reason and conscience to correct as he grew mature. With delicate perception the adults noted that childish faults "cannot be very great, before reason arrives at some degree of maturity."

Direct confrontation with the child was avoided, but when things got seriously out of hand, parents sometimes turned older children over to the gods for punishment. A troublesome child might be sent out into the dusk to meet Longnose, the legendary Seneca bogeyman. Longnose might even be impersonated in the flesh by a distraught parent. Longnose was a hungry cannibal who chased bad children when their parents were sleeping. He mimicked the child, crying loudly as he ran, but the parents would not wake up because Longnose had bewitched them. A child might be chased all night until he submitted and promised to behave. Theoretically, if a child remained stubborn, Longnose finally caught him and took him away in a huge pack-basket for a leisurely meal. And — although parents were not supposed to do this — an unusually stubborn infant *could* be threatened with punishment by the great False Faces themselves, who, when invoked for this purpose, might "poison" a child or "spoil his face." "I remember," recalled a Cayuga woman of her childhood, "how scared I was of the False-faces; I didn't know what they were. They are to scare away disease. They used to come into the house and up the stairs and I used to hide away under the covers. They even crawled under the bed and they made that awful sound. When I was bad my mother used to say the False-faces would get me. Once, I must have been only 4 or 5, because I was very little when I left Canada, but I remember it so well that when I think of it I can hear that cry now, and I was going along a road from my grandfather's; it was a straight road and I couldn't lose my way, but it was almost dark, and I had to pass through some timber and I heard that cry and that rattle. I ran like a flash of lightning and I can hear it yet."

At puberty some of the boys retired to the woods under the stewardship of an old man, where they fasted, abstained from any sort of sexual activity (which they had been free to indulge, to the limit of their powers, before), covered themselves with dirt, mortified the flesh in various ways, such as bathing in ice water and bruising and gashing the shinbones with rocks. Dreams experienced during such periods of self-trial were apt to be regarded as visitations from supernatural spirits who might grant *orenda,* or magical power, to the dreamer, and who would maintain a special sort of guardian-ship over him. The person's connection with this supernatural being was maintained through a charm — such as a knife, a queerly shaped stone, or a bit of bone — which was connected with the dream through some association significant to the dreamer. Unlike many other tribes, however, the Iroquois apparently did not require these guardian-spirit visions for pubescent youths. Many youths were said not to have had their first vision until just before their first war party. Furthermore, any man could have a significant dream or vision at any time. Girls too went through a mild puberty ritual, retiring into the woods at first menstruation and paying particular attention to their dreams. With the termination of the menstrual period the girl returned to the household; but hereafter, whenever she menstruated, she would have to live apart in a hut, avoiding people, and being careful not to step on a path, or to cook and serve anyone's food, or (especially) to touch medicines, which would immediately lose their potency if she handled them.

The Europeans who observed this pattern of child experience were by no means unfavorably impressed although they were sometimes amazed. They commented, however, almost to a man, from early Jesuit to latter-day Quaker, on a consequence that stood out dramatically as they compared this "savage" maturation with "civilized." "There is nothing," wrote the Jesuit chronicler of the Iroquois mission in 1657, "for which these peoples have a greater horror than restraint. The very children cannot endure it, and live as they please in the houses of their parents, without fear of reprimand or chastisement." One hundred and fifty years later, the Quaker Halliday Jackson observed that "being indulged in most of their wishes, as they grow up, liberty, in its fullest extent, becomes their ruling passion." The Iroquois themselves recognized the intensity of their children's resentment at parental interference. "Some Savages," reported Le Mercier of the Huron, "told us that one of the principal reasons why they showed so much indulgence toward their children, was that when the children saw themselves treated by their parents with some severity, they usually resorted to extreme measures and hanged themselves, or ate of a certain root they call *Audachienrra,* which is a very quick poison." The same fear was recorded among the Iroquois, including the Seneca, in 1657. And while suicides by frustrated children were not actually frequent, there are nevertheless a number of recorded cases of suicide where parental interference was the avowed cause. And *mutatis mutandis,* there was another rationalization for a policy of permissiveness: that the child who was harshly disciplined might grow up, some day, to mistreat his parents in revenge.

This theory of child raising was not taken for granted by the Seneca; on the contrary, it was very explicitly recognized, discussed, and pondered. Handsome Lake himself, in later years, insisted that parents love and indulge their children.

STUDY GUIDE

1. Be prepared to discuss European influences on Indian social life, housing, clothing, weapons, and values.

2. What was the role of the Seneca woman in the family, economic life, and government affairs, and how was her position different from that of a European or American woman?

3. Review the introduction to this selection, in which certain myths held by Europeans are discussed. Considering Seneca government, the personality of the Iroquois, and attitudes toward loyalty and war, how does the picture presented by Wallace differ from the myths La Farge noted?

4. Different societies have varied views on childrearing, marriage, and divorce, and have different ways of controlling such antisocial behavior as crime. How did Seneca practices in each of these areas differ from the patterns in modern America?

BIBLIOGRAPHY

One should keep in mind that in this selection Wallace is portraying only one of many Indian societies. Generally, we have tended to see Indian culture as a monolithic system and to ignore important differences among the various tribes. Many people think of all Indians as wearing colorful headdresses, living in tepees, using horses and canoes for transportation, and depending on the bow and arrow for their livelihood. Dress, housing, economy, marital customs, burial rites, and agricultural patterns varied in different regions. Your library may have some of the specialized studies of these aspects of Indian life or books on individual tribes through which you can extend your knowledge of these first Americans.

Wallace's essay on the Iroquois replaces an essay by the distinguished anthropologist Ruth Underhill on the Southeastern tribes that was used in the first edition of this volume. Her book, *Red Man's America* * (Chicago, 1953), is one of the best general studies of the various Indian societies. Another very well written, general study of most tribes is Peter Farb, *Man's Rise to Civilization as Shown by the Indians of North America from Primeval Times to the Coming of the Industrial State* * (New York, 1968). The following are also excellent studies, utilizing both anthropological and historical knowledge: Harold E. Driver, *The Indians of North America,* * 2nd ed. (Chicago, 1969); William T. Hagan, *American Indians* * (Chicago, 1961); Alvin M. Josephy, Jr., *The Indian Heritage of America* * (New York, 1968); and Clark Wissler, *Indians of the United States,* * rev. ed. (Garden City, N.Y., 1966).

In much historical writing, the American Indian has been treated merely as a "problem" or an obstacle in the path of the more highly advanced civilization of Europe. A very different perspective is given in Francis Jennings, *The Invasion of America: Indians, Colonialism, and the Cant of Conquest* * (Chapel Hill, N.C., 1975), which treats the European colonists as invaders. Another work which gives a more balanced, and less European-oriented, view of early American history is Gary B. Nash, *Red, White, and Black: The Peoples of Early America* * (Englewood Cliffs, N.J., 1974).

* Asterisk indicates book is available in a paperback edition.

Plimoth Plantation

This photo of Plimoth Plantation suggests the closely knit quality of New England community life.

2

THOMAS J. WERTENBAKER

The New England Town

Two features of modern life are the extraordinary degree of organization of every aspect of human existence and the almost limitless regulation of our conduct and even our thought. Our jobs, our politics, our social and religious life, our education and recreation, even our birth and death, have been bureaucratized by various giant organizations. We have footprints taken at birth, identification numbers given as we enter the job force, and we cannot be buried without the ministrations of the undertakers' lobby. So dependent have we become, that most men have to pay others to cut down a tree in their own backyards, and a great many women would be helpless if they had to bake a loaf of bread or make their own clothes.

Our highly organized, industrial society has brought with it great advantages — convenience, a higher standard of living, and many others. But it has also undermined man's self-sufficiency and severely restricted his ability to determine his own fate. Increasingly, he has come to feel as helpless in trying to influence his union as in influencing corporations or government. Yet, when we glorify and romanticize the simple life and pleasures of an earlier age, we often ignore the problems such a society faced and fail to recognize that even in the earliest colonial settlements there was a degree of interdependence.

In the following selection from *The Puritan Oligarchy*, Professor Thomas J. Wertenbaker describes how New England pioneers transformed a wilderness into a settled community. Unlike the pattern of dispersed settlement in the South, which led to reliance on the county as the unit of local government, the pattern of communal settlement within a small area led New

23

Englanders to adapt the English town and manor to their needs.

The town, or township, coupled with the church, the family, and other traditional institutions of their agricultural background, served them well here, though these institutions necessarily underwent modifications on this side of the Atlantic. In England they had had cleared fields, long experience with crops and their cultivation, gristmills and sawmills near at hand, and accessibility to such essential craftsmen as blacksmiths. In America they faced endless forests, new crops and crop diseases, and a scarcity of professional craftsmen to assist them in building their houses, grinding their grain, and making their implements. What was true of their farming was equally true of their social life, their law and their public works, their places of worship and their marketing of goods. In each of these fields they brought a long and settled tradition with them, but they brought it to a new and quite unsettled world.

When the group of settlers had perfected their plans and received their instructions, they gathered their belongings around them, said good-bye to their friends and set out through the wilderness. To guide them along the forest trails they often had a trusted Indian. Trudging behind him came the men and women, driving before them the cows, sheep, swine and other domestic animals upon which they must in part depend for sustenance during the first year of the settlement; the children, together with household utensils and farm implements, in the crude carts that they had brought from England in separate parts and put together at the port.

It was with mixed emotions that they arrived at the site of their future home — dismay at the wildness of the country, the huge trees, the dense undergrowth, the lack of all facilities for civilized life; hope at the thought that the land was theirs, hundreds of acres of land, which their labor could convert into fields of waving Indian corn, or wheat or rye; sadness at the memory of England with its comfortable houses, its fertile farms, its villages and towns. But it was not a time for repining, for there was work to be done and without delay. . . .

. . . The first act of the freemen was to gather, perhaps in some open space in the woods, in order to elect a committee to decide upon the lo-

Reprinted by permission of Charles Scribner's Sons from *The Puritan Oligarchy* by Thomas Jefferson Wertenbaker. Copyright 1947 by Charles Scribner's Sons.

cation of the village, to plot its streets and lots, to supervise the sur-
veying and to conduct the division of land. There must have been prolonged discussions as to where to place the village, since it was to be
the center of religious, political and economic activities. If there were
a body of navigable water at hand, some spot along its shores was usually
chosen, so that transportation would be convenient and cheap. The village of Enfield was built on the east bank of the Connecticut; Cambridge,
as near to the Charles as the marshy banks permitted; Milford, on the
Mill and West rivers. In case navigable water was lacking, the village
was usually laid out in the center of the town, so that as much of the
surrounding arable, woodland and pasturage as possible would be within
a short compass. It was of the utmost importance that the distance
from residence to field be not too great for the owner to go out in
the morning with his hoe or his ox team and return at the close of
the work day.

In planning the village it was customary, if the lay of the land
permitted, to have one long main street, with long, narrow home lots
which abutted upon it on either side. The motorist who today passes
through the quaint New England village with its old houses seldom
realizes that the lots on which they are built formerly often stretched
out behind for a mile or more. Thus the Enfield home lots, which had
a frontage of 198 feet, were 1,920 feet in length. They constituted
what must have seemed to their proprietors little farms in themselves,
with ample space, not only for a residence, a barn, an orchard and a vege-
table garden, but for fields of Indian corn or of English grain. In many
cases the settlers contented themselves with their home lots for several
years, before asking for additional land lying beyond.

In the distribution of lots, the settlers displayed a decided leaning
toward economic democracy. There must be no aristocracy of wealth to
vie with the aristocracy of religion, to dispute its authority and magnify
the things of this world in comparison with the things of the next. In
the words of Urian Oakes they hoped never to see the day when
"houses and lands, lots and farms and outward accommodations are
of more value . . . than the Gospel and Gospel ordinances. . . . Sure there
were other and better things the People of God came hither for than the
best spot of ground, the richest soil." So the leaders not only were very
temperate in demanding land for themselves, but they would not permit others to monopolize the choice spots or to hold large areas for
speculative purpose or to build up great estates. There should be no
landed aristocracy in New England if they could prevent [it,] no Van
Rensselaers, no Dulaneys, no "King" Carters.

Yet the Puritans did not carry economic democracy to the extreme of
making every lot exactly equal in size and value so that no man
would have any advantage over his neighbor. In Milford, for instance,

they determined each man's share of the common land by "the rule of persons and estates," by which was understood the relative amount of a man's property and of his contributions to the undertaking, the size of his family and his powers of leadership. But inequalities were never carried to an extreme, and always great care was taken that injustice be done no man. In Enfield the Committee was empowered to determine "where and in what order men's lots and land" should lie; "the Committee laboring the best they can to suit and accommodate . . . and when a man lies bad in the first field to endeavor to mend him in the next."

Once the proud owner had taken possession of his home lot, he faced the arduous tasks, not only of erecting his house and barn, setting out his orchard and planting grain and vegetables, but of clearing away the trees and underbrush. In Enfield it was ordered "that every man cut up and clear the brush and bushes in the highway . . . all the breadth of his home lot from front of it for the one half of the highway or street." Time-consuming also, was the constructing of a fence around his lot to protect the precious crops from the depredations of cattle and swine. In some cases the fence was made of rails closely spaced, in others of paling. The Boston common was paled, each of forty-two persons erecting and keeping up his share.

Had one been able to fly over a New England village of three centuries ago, an interesting view would have presented itself. On either side of the main street were the houses of the freeholders, with the barns, the orchards and the gardens behind them. Here was the meeting-house, its simple lines and the absence of a steeple giving it more the appearance of a large residence than a church. Here was the gristmill, its fans spread to catch the breeze; here the schoolhouse; here the smithy; here the sawmill. Stretching out on all sides were the fields; the strips, planted some in Indian corn, some in wheat, some in rye, some in barley, giving the appearance of a crazy quilt. The broad bands of green on either bank of a small stream one recognized as the common pasture. And in the distance were the woods, awaiting the day when a new division would bring them under the axe.

The town imitated the manor, not only in its agricultural life, but in its economic semi-independence. It is true that the typical town was by no means completely cut off fom the rest of the world; it shipped out its surplus of Indian corn, wheat, rye, hides, etc., and received in return the finer grade of manufactured goods — clothing, firearms, household utensils, farm implements. But many of the articles of everyday use were made in the village itself by the local shoemaker, carpenter, cooper, weaver or blacksmith. There was no need to train artisans to serve the infant community, for there were many skilled workers among the immigrants. These men brought their tools with them and had only to begin in their new homes where they left off in the old. The "mystery" of their trade, as it was customary to call it, they passed on to their sons or to apprentices. . . .

In New England the social, as well as religious and political, unit was the village. The people of the little community knew each other's virtues, weaknesses, habits. Every woman in town could tell just how many gowns Goodwife Collins had in her chest, just how many dishes in her kitchen, how many feather beds she inherited from her father, shook her head when word went around that she had lost her temper when the cow kicked over the milk. And when she became ill it was the neighbors who sat beside her bed or did her chores for her. For the minister and congregation to admit one to the communion was an event of first importance to the villagers. The people passed each other on the street every day, they met several times a week for religious services, they stopped at the town pump to gossip or to pass the time of day, they saw each other at the mill or the smithy or at the shoemaker's shop. As in tidewater and piedmont Virginia and Maryland the key to social life was isolation, so in early New England it was concentration, but concentration chiefly in little units which themselves were isolated. . . .

The satisfaction which came with the ownership of land was tempered for the Puritans by the costliness of fencing it in. It was the custom to make the owner of every home lot responsible for the fence, and many were the regulations requiring it to be "good and sufficient" with five rails or "double rail and poles," etc. Yet it was frequently a strain upon "brotherly sweetness," when Deacon Smith's cows got into Master Jones' lot and trampled his wheat. Such a serious case might even come before the Selectmen. So it was a saving in labor as well as in tempers when it was ordered that for the common fields the whole, and not the lots of which it was composed, should be fenced. Of the common fence each man took his share both in its construction and maintenance. At Enfield the proprietors of each field met to "appoint men amongst themselves to see that each man's proportion of fence be done and made according to order." Should one dispute their decision or plead that they had assigned him a greater part than his just share, he could bring the matter before the Selectmen. It was a temptation to allow the fence to fall into disrepair at times, but once a rail was broken or a post began to rot, the negligent owner was certain to be called to account by the town fence viewers. . . .

The settlers were delighted to find that many of the fruits and vegetables, the seed of which they had brought with them, throve in the New England soil, and that they could make good use of others indigenous to the country. "Our turnips, parsnips and carrots are here both bigger and sweeter than is ordinary to be found in England," wrote Francis Higginson. "Here are stores of pumpions [pumpkins], cucumbers and other things of [what] nature I know not. Plenty of strawberries in their time, and penny-royal, winter savory, carvell and water-cresses, also leeks and onions." So every man laid out his garden in his home lot, perhaps back of his residence, and planted it with the pumpkins, beans, squashes, cabbages, turnips, onions, radishes, beets, spinach, and other vegetables which contributed so greatly to the health and enjoyment of his family.

Nearby was the orchard. "Our fruit trees prosper abundantly," John Josselyn reported. "Apple trees, pear trees, quince trees, cherry trees, plum trees, barberry trees. I have observed with admiration that the kernels on suckers planted produce as fair and good fruit, without grafting, as the tree from whence they were taken. The country is replenished with fair and large orchards." The apple tree especially prospered so greatly in New England soil that it became very important in the economy of the people and was a source not only of food but of drink as well. Especial inducements were held out for the erection of cider mills, and in Woodbury the town fathers went so far as to give permission to a certain Matthew Minor to set up one in the highway.

The English were prompt in making Indian corn their most important crop. No doubt they deemed it prudent to trust to a grain which had proved itself by experience, yielded more per acre than the European grains, gave a more uniform return, ripened early and was more hardy in resisting sudden changes of weather. A glimpse in the barn or perhaps in the loft of the typical settler would have revealed, side by side with a few bushels of oats or rye or wheat, a bountiful supply of maize, while a visit to his lots in the common fields would have shown acre after acre devoted to this staple. Yet the settlers were by no means negligent of the grain to which they and their fathers before them had been accustomed, bringing with them wheat, rye, oats and barley for a trial in the New England soil. When the first wheat crop proved a failure in the sandy soil of Plymouth, the Pilgrims were dismayed at the prospect of doing without English bread. But trials elsewhere proved more successful, so wheat soon attained an importance in the farm economy second only to that of Indian corn. Even when the blast visited New England to destroy whole fields of wheat and force the people to increase their acreage of rye, wheat continued an important part of the food supply. Barley was grown for beer, which was a standard drink, and oats for provender for horses. . . .

The settlers continued to use the agricultural implements which they had brought with them from England until they wore out, and then turned to the village blacksmith to fashion others just like them. Yankee inventiveness had not yet applied itself to producing machinery with which to plow, harrow, harvest and thresh, so that the work was done with infinite toil with the aid of hoes, scythes, spades and pitchforks. The Pilgrims had no plow for twelve years after their first landing, while in 1636, so it is stated, there were but thirty plows in all Massachusetts. Not infrequently a town would pay a bounty to a farmer to buy a plow on condition that he use it, not exclusively for his own needs, but for the community as a professional plowman. Crude contrivances these early plows were, whose wooden shares barely scratched the earth despite their four oxen and two drivers.

The settlers brought their cattle with them, for the Indians had none. The ocean voyage, when the animals were penned in a restricted space, where they were bruised and perhaps fatally injured by the tossing of the little vessels, often caused severe losses. If we may believe Captain John Smith, seventy of the two hundred cattle taken on board the Winthrop fleet of 1630 died on the way over. Yet the cattle increased rapidly in New England, so that in a few years all save the poorest family had one or more cows.

Though the arable land was divided among the individual owners, it was the custom to hold the pasture in common. A town meeting in Cambridge in March, 1679, ordered that "all the common land on the south side of the highway leading from Captain Cooke's mill to Watertown . . . be fenced in for a cow common for such as have cow rights recorded in the town book." The fence was to be "done with a stone wall, either a whole wall or a half wall and something of brush upon it and not be less than four foot high." To save the back-breaking labor of erecting walls such as this, the townsmen when possible availed themselves of necks of land, such as Great Neck in Dorchester, or the bend of a river, where the cattle would be confined in part by the water. . . .

If the village, with its home lots, its gardens and orchards, the grain fields, the cow commons, the meadows, formed the visible body of the town, so the congregation constituted its soul. To the settlers the spiritual side of their community was all-important. This it was which had led them into the wilderness, which shaped their characters and their thoughts, which determined the form of their social and economic life. So one of their first steps upon reaching the site of their new homes was to form themselves into a Church. This they did by assembling in some open space, perhaps a long-disused Indian cornfield, to enter into a solemn covenant with God.

The Pilgrims before them had formed such a covenant when they reverently repeated the one sentence: "We covenant with the Lord and with one another and do bind ourselves in the presence of God to walk together in all His ways, according as He is pleased to reveal Himself unto us in His blessed word of truth." The Northampton covenant was more detailed: "Disclaiming all confidence of, or any worthiness in, ourselves either to be in covenant with God or to partake of the least of His mercies, and also all strength of our own to help covenant with Him . . . by relying upon His tender mercy and gracious assistance of the Lord through Jesus Christ, we do promise and covenant in the presence of the Lord, the searcher of all hearts, and before the holy angels and this company, first and chiefly to cleave forever unto God with our whole hearts as our chief, best, yea and only good, and unto Jesus Christ as our only Savior, husband and Lord and only high priest, prophet and king. . . . We promise and engage to observe and maintain . . . all the holy institutions and ordinances which He 'hath appointed for His Church. . . . And as for this particular company and society of saints, we promise . . . that we will cleave one unto another in brotherly love and seek the best spiritual good each of other, by frequent exhortation, seasonable admonition and constant watchfulness according to the rules of the Gospel." . . .

The new congregation next proceeded to elect a minister. Had the settlers brought a minister with them it was nonetheless necessary to elect him, since they did not constitute a Church until they had made a covenant. Thus John Davenport, who led a company of Puritans to Quinnipiac to found the New Haven colony, was not elected pastor until his flock constituted themselves into a congregation some months after their arrival. The election at Salem in July, 1629, was preceded by "a solemn day of humiliation," after which the "company of believers . . . joined together in covenant," chose, by the votes of the male members, Endicott to be their minister.

The election of a minister was followed by the ordination. This, according to the *Platform of Church Discipline,* drawn up in 1646, was merely "the solemn putting a man into his place and office in the Church, whereunto he had right before by election; being like the installing of a magistrate in the commonwealth. . . . Ordination doth not constitute an officer, nor give him the essentials of his office." It was, however, a solemn ceremony, marked by prayer, preaching and the laying on of hands by the elders or by neighboring ministers. "Reverend Mr. Josiah Sherman was ordained pastor of the First Church for Woburn," Reverend Ebenezer Bridge wrote in his diary in 1755. "I began with Prayer. Reverend Mr. Dunbar preached of fellowship. It was a very large assembly." . . .

If the responsibilities of the minister were great, so was his authority, and bold indeed was the person who ignored his frowns or his admonitions. Not only might he become a black sheep, suspected and censured by the elders and the congregation, but he might suffer excommunication, with the loss of the privileges, political as well as religious, which were attached to Church membership. But it must not be forgotten that the minister was not only the moral censor and preceptor for his flock but their loving father as well. It has become too much the custom to regard him as a cold, unrelenting person, who forgot the frailties of the human body in his zeal to save the soul. One has only to become well acquainted with some of these men to discover under the outward cloak of ecclesiastical harshness the devoted husband, the kind father, the sympathetic pastor. But they did not think it kind to condone sin, to temporize with error, or to permit assaults upon what they firmly believed to be God's Church on earth. The men who were instrumental in sending innocent persons to the scaffold as witches or in subjecting the Quakers to cruel persecution acted from a strong sense of duty, were performing a most unpleasant task because they believed with all their hearts that they were carrying out the divine will.

Second to the minister in influence and power were the elders. Under the *Platform of Church Discipline,* the elders were "to open and shut the doors of God's house, by the admission of members approved by the Church, by ordination of officers chosen by the Church and by excommunication of notorious and obstinate offenders"; to call the congregation together, to serve as "guides and leaders," to "prevent and heal such offences in life or in doctrine as might corrupt the Church," to "feed the flock of God with a word of admonition," to "visit and pray over the sick brother." . . .

Discipline in the Church was every man's business. If Master Smith broke the Sabbath, it was the duty of his neighbors to reprove him; if Mistress Peters gossiped about her neighbors, it was certain to be reported to the elders. When one member committed an offense against another, the injured brother was to go to him privately to admonish him, and if this did not suffice, to return in the company of one or two others to renew the attempt. In case the offender still remained stubborn, the matter was brought to the attention of the elders, who were to place it before the Church. Should he now make a public penitent confession, he was declared "recovered and gained," otherwise he might be suspended from the fellowship of the Lord's Supper. Excommunication was reserved for exceptionally serious offenses such as heresy or blasphemy, for it was a severe punishment indeed. Not only was the congregation to refrain from communion with the culprit in spiritual matters, "but also from all familiar communion with him in civil things, further than the necessity of natural, domestical or civil relations do require, and are therefore to forbear to eat and drink with him, that he may be ashamed."

It was fundamental to the congregational conception of a true Church that none but saints be admitted. "By saints we understand such as have not only attained the knowledge of the principles of religion and are free from gross and open scandals, but also do, together with the profession of their faith and repentance, walk in blameless obedience to the Word, so that in charitable discretion they may be accounted saints by calling, though perhaps some or more of them be unsound and hypocrites inwardly." But should hypocrisy be discovered the persons concerned were to be cast out, since their example endangered the sanctity of others and "a little leaven leaveneth the whole lump." "Particular Churches ought to consist of saints and true believers on Christ," Increase Mather declared. "Nothing can be more fatal to the interest of religion than to constitute Churches of unsanctified members."

This high standard was a matter of grave concern to the people, not only because Church membership opened to them the doors to Heaven but also the doors to political freedom. As early as 1631 the General Court passed a law declaring that "to the end the body of the commons may be preserved of honest and good men . . . no man shall be admitted to the freedom of this body politic but such as are members of some of the Churches."

This drastic restriction upon the franchise has been praised by some historians, severely criticized by others. "Not birth, nor wealth, nor learning, nor skill in war was to confer the power, but personal character, goodness of the highest type," wrote J. G. Palfrey. Others have pointed out that to deny any voice in the government to good citizens merely because they were not in full harmony with the established Church was inconsistent with human rights and English traditions. Yet the Massachusetts leaders clung to the law as the cornerstone of their structure, even though it brought upon them the anger of the King and endangered their charter. . . .

Anyone desiring admission [to the Church] had first to satisfy the minister and the elders "and other able brethren" that he was duly qualified. This he must do in a series of conferences, in which he was interrogated upon his beliefs, his understanding of Church doctrines, his personal conduct and his willingness to join in the covenant. "I discourse with David Butterfield about coming into full communion," Reverend Ebenezer Bridge wrote in his diary. Thus the one sure means of enjoying Church fellowship, and also of gaining the right to vote in civil elections, was for the candidate to convince this small group of Church leaders that his life had been "subdued to some hope of godly conversation," and that he was in hearty sympathy with the established order. . . .

The Massachusetts Puritans were severely criticized in England and Scotland for refusing Church membership to so many persons. Thomas Lechford claimed that "here are such confessions and professions required of men and women both in private and public before they are admitted that three parts of the people of the country remain out of the Church." This John Cotton denied. "In the Churches within the Bay we may truly say that for the heads of families those that are admitted are far more in number than the other. . . . Those that are godly they are all admitted to some Church or other." However true this may have been in Cotton's day, the evidence tends to show that before the end of the century the freemen, who alone could vote for governor, deputies and magistrates, had become a minority in every town, while those who were not members of the Churches, but who were in sympathy with the established order, constituted a majority. A third group, consisting at first chiefly of servants and apprentices, but later recruited by newcomers and even the sons and grandsons of ardent Puritans, were hostile to the "theocracy." They it was who protested against their disfranchisement and fomented what Urian Oakes called "jealousies and fears in the minds of men concerning magistrates and ministers" and "false alarms of danger that the people may believe that religion and liberties are at stake and in danger to be lost."

The Puritan leaders made an effort to prevent the "unsanctified" groups from increasing in numbers, by restricting immigration. In 1636 the town of Boston ordered "that no townsmen shall entertain any strangers into their houses for above fourteen days, without leave from those that are appointed to order the town's business." Salem was even less hospitable, for there one Thomas Oliver was employed "to go from house to house about the town once a month to inquire what strangers do come to have privily thrust themselves into the town." To quicken his zeal, he was to be rewarded with the fines imposed on those who defied the ordinances against entertaining newcomers. In 1637 the colonial government itself took this matter in hand by enacting a law making it illegal for a town "to receive any stranger resorting thither with intent to reside" without the consent "of some one of the Council or of two other magistrates."

Despite these regulations the influx of strangers continued. He who succeeded in convincing the authorities that he was of good conduct and orthodox in faith might purchase land from an old inhabitant or he might receive a grant of a home lot from the town committee. He must, however, build upon it within a year, or perhaps two years, or forfeit his claim. Gradually the laws became less rigid, the enforcement less severe. The need for labor made it necessary for the town to admit servants, apprentices and journeymen, and common justice made it difficult to eject them after their terms had expired. The port towns attracted many sailors, some of whom were far indeed from being "saints"; English shipwrights came over in response to the demands of the shipyards; when a town was without a physician, or a blacksmith, or a miller, the Selectmen were not apt to be overscrupulous about religious requirements if one presented himself.

In the first days of the settlement, however, there were few inhabitants who were not freeholders and few freeholders who were not members of the Church. This gave a unity to the town which was gradually lost, but which, while it lasted, was the very cornerstone of the social, political and religious fabric. There was a clear distinction at all times between the congregation and the body politic, but this distinction was largely academic so long as the two bodies had an identic personnel. When the freemen assembled in the meeting-house for a town meeting they might, and usually did, concern themselves with religious as well as civic affairs.

It was the town meeting which determined the minister's salary, erected his house, levied tithes, built the meeting-house and allotted the seats in it. It could at one moment be considering the matter of the common fence around a grain field and the next, if it so chose, convert itself into the congregation without leaving the meeting room, and proceed to discipline wayward brothers or sisters, or elect a deacon, or receive a person to communion.

As the individual Church enjoyed a large degree of independence in ecclesiastical affairs, so the town meeting in local civic affairs was supreme. And like the Church, it drew its vigor as an institution in large part from the agricultural village, for the freemen, dwelling as they did in the shadow of the meeting-house, found it possible to constitute themselves a legislative body without the use of representatives. So, when they had been "warned" by the ringing of the bell or the cry of the watchman, they emerged from their houses, made their way down the street to the meeting-house, took their seats and at the order of the moderator proceeded with business. The election of the town officers was always a matter of great concern — the fence viewers, the treasurer, the field drivers, the hog reeves, the sealer of weights and measures, the town clerk, the constable, the tax assessors, the tithemen, the surveyors, the selectmen. Then Master Goodwin might rise and move that the meeting-house be reshingled, or that a bridge over the creek be repaired, or that a road be opened, or that a new division of arable be authorized, or that fifty acres of land be offered any wheelwright who would settle in the town. . . .

Thus did the English who came to New England found their Wilderness Zion. Although it was a unique experiment, for nothing like it existed in England, the blueprints had been made long before the exodus began. As Winthrop and Cotton and others were the builders, so [the English writers and clergymen] Ames, Parker, Baynes and before them Cartwright and Barrow and Browne were the architects. The semi-independence of congregations, the Church covenant, the fellowship of Churches, the synod, the close relationship of Church and State were not put into operation as afterthoughts; the Puritans came to America for the purpose of putting them into operation.

New England was not the extension of old England across the Atlantic, but rather an English conception which for the first time found its practical application. Even though the settlers brought with them the English language, English institutions, English architecture, continued to read English books, wear English clothes, use English implements, the structure of their society was essentially different from that of England. Nor did they constitute a cross section of the English people, since they came in large part from one part of the kingdom and from one religious group in that part.

They were separated from England, also, by the belief that they were God's chosen people, the especial object of His care and guidance, and that they had come to America in obedience to His direct command. "Hath God brought us into a wilderness and caused us to dwell alone and separated us for a peculiar people to Himself, that we should imitate the nations in their vanities?" asked Urian Oakes in rebuking the people for their "garish attire." "The ministers and Christians, by whom New England was first planted, were a chosen company of men," said Cotton Mather, "picked out of, perhaps, all the counties in England, and this by no human contrivance, but by a strange work of God upon the spirits of men that were, no ways, acquainted with one another — inspiring them as one man to secede into a wilderness, they knew not where." The synod of 1679 declared that "the ways of God towards this His people are in many respects like unto his dealings with Israel of old. It was a great and high undertaking of our fathers when they ventured themselves and their little ones upon the rude waves of the vast ocean, that so they might follow the Lord into this land."

This belief that God had set them apart for His special guidance and blessing pervaded every phase of New England religious and political life and gave to it a purpose and strength lacking in many societies. "In the wilderness we have dwelt in safety alone, being made the subjects of most peculiar mercies and privileges. . . . The Lord hath planted a vine, having cast out the heathen, prepared room for it and caused it to take deep root. . . . We must ascribe all these things, as unto the grace and abundant goodness of the Lord our God, so to His owning a religious design and interest." . . .

As Winthrop, Cotton, Norton, Shepard and the others viewed their Bible commonwealth, it must have seemed to them almost impregnable. Yet its disintegration began almost at once, and within half a century after the settlement of the Bay ministers were bewailing the degeneracy of the times, the laxity of the new generation, and the decay of religion. "He that remembers the good old spirit of those who followed God into this wilderness . . . cannot but easily discern a sad alteration," complained Urian Oakes in 1673. Among the many things of "solemn significance and awful import," in "the decaying and almost dying state of this poor country," only a few held open the door of hope.

Although Oakes and other ministers exaggerated the situation in their efforts to stay the forces of change, they were quite correct in pointing out that the old order was giving way to the new. The religious zeal of the first settlers was less apparent in the second and third generation; the ministers commanded less respect and love; the charter upon which such hopes had been based had been annulled; the unity of Church and State in the towns had been disrupted; despite all the efforts to exclude them, strangers had come in who were out of sympathy with the Church and the government; there were loud demands for the extension of the franchise; in Boston the organization of the Anglican congregation of King's Chapel bore testimony to the break which had been made in the wall of orthodoxy. Before the end of the seventeenth century, although the ideals of the founders still exercised a powerful influence upon the minds and hearts of the people, the experiment of a Bible commonwealth had definitely failed.

STUDY GUIDE

1. The New England agricultural community described by Wertenbaker has been characterized as "Yankee Communism" because of the relative equality and mutual cooperation of the townspeople. What evidence do you find in Wertenbaker's description that would support this characterization

— for example, in land distribution, cooperation in public works and agriculture, and the relative equality among townspeople in making town and church policy?

2. In what areas of town and church life can you detect a respect for authority and for class differences?

3. It would have been difficult, or impossible, in the early New England town for a single man or a separate family to be completely self-sufficient economically, socially, religiously, and in terms of essential services usually provided by government. In each of these categories of human existence, what common institutions and cooperative services did the New Englanders develop to meet their needs?

4. Today we think of a church as primarily a place of religious worship. Describe how the church in the New England town fulfilled the following additional functions: discipline and regulation of conduct in the community; service as a social institution; regulation of popular participation in government.

5. Generally, the initial group that founded a new town had common religious ideals, fairly close social connections, and common agricultural and governmental traditions. What factors contributed to the breaking down of this early unity of spirit and activities?

BIBLIOGRAPHY

The selection you have read is from one of three volumes Professor Wertenbaker wrote on the settling of America's three principal regions. The other two, in his trilogy entitled *The Founding of American Civilization,* are *The Middle Colonies* (New York, 1938) and *The Old South* (New York, 1942). For more than fifty years, following the example set by Herbert Baxter Adams in the late nineteenth century, historians have been investigating the English origins of colonial governmental institutions such as the town and county. Two general studies of the New England town from different angles are: Roy H. Akagi, *The Town Proprietors of the New England Colonies . . . , 1620–1770* (Philadelphia, 1924) and John F. Sly, *Town Government in Massachusetts, 1620–1930* (Cambridge, Mass. 1930).

More recently, historians have examined New England history through case studies of individual towns, trying to determine how the pattern in Sudbury, Dedham, and other towns was influenced by the area of England from which the settlers came, their conceptions of a holy commonwealth, the traditions of the English manor, and so forth. Among the many significant studies of individual towns, the following four are especially fine: Darrett B. Rutman, *Winthrop's Boston: Portrait of a Puritan Town, 1630–1649* * (Chapel Hill, N.C., 1965); Sumner C. Powell, *Puritan Village: The Formation of a New England Town* * (Middletown, Conn., 1963); Philip J. Greven, Jr., *Four Generations: Population, Land and Family in Colonial Andover, Massa-*

chusetts * (Ithaca, N.Y., 1970); and Kenneth A. Lockridge, *A New England Town, The First Hundred Years: Dedham, Massachusetts, 1636–1736* * (New York, 1970).

Ola E. Winslow, *Meetinghouse Hill, 1630–1783* * (New York, 1952) is a study of the founding of a particular congregation and of the role of churches in Puritan society. William B. Weeden, *Economic and Social History of New England, 1620–1789,* 2 vols. (Boston and New York, 1890) is an older work that is quite comprehensive and worth looking into. An easier and, for the beginning student, a somewhat more interesting study is George F. Dow, *Everyday Life in the Massachusetts Bay Colony* (Boston, 1935). There are general surveys of the agriculture of the North and the South, but another book by Rutman that focuses directly on early New England is extremely interesting: *Husbandmen of Plymouth: Farms and Villages in the Old Colony, 1620–1692* (Boston, 1967). If you like a biographical approach to history, the following two books are especially charming and reveal a good deal about the early colony of Massachusetts as well as the men who are studied: Samuel E. Morison, *Builders of the Bay Colony* * (Boston and New York, 1930) and Edmund S. Morgan, *The Puritan Dilemma: The Story of John Winthrop* * (Boston, 1958). James T. Adams, *The Founding of New England* (Boston, 1921) is much less sympathetic to the Puritans than most of the works mentioned. If Wertenbaker's work on the southern colonies is not available, another excellent work on that region is Wesley F. Craven, *The Southern Colonies in the Seventeeth Century, 1607–1689* * (Baton Rouge, La. 1949).

* Asterisk indicates book is available in a paperback edition.

The painting "The Old Plantation" shows a slave wedding and the survival of African culture in customs, headties, and the musical instrument.

3

GERALD W. MULLIN

Life Under Slavery

The attitude of British colonials — and later, of American whites — toward blacks, who first landed at Jamestown in 1619, was shaped by myths and stereotypes. Influenced by sexual anxieties, economic self-interest, physical distinctions, and other factors, white men found it impossible to view blacks unemotionally. The first blacks in Virginia were bound to a limited term of service, just as were white indentured servants, but by the 1660s slave codes provided permanent enslavement of African laborers.

The serious study of black history began well before 1900. A number of circumstances limited such study, even by thoughtful scholars who tried to be objective. Black Americans had left some written records and a substantial oral tradition, but most of the sources from which black history was written were left by whites. An equally important limitation was that historians were most interested in those aspects of black history that shed light upon general American history. Thus, their attention was concentrated on slavery. Some understanding of slavery was essential for studying the history of American agriculture, presidential and congressional politics before the Civil War, westward expansion, or the upsurge of social reform after 1830.

Aspects of black life and culture that were only marginally related to white concerns went unstudied. African influences on American culture, black religion, the slave trade, even the impact of slavery on the American black's personality, received scant attention. With the exception of slavery, black history before the Civil War was not considered worthy of intensive study. The mainstream of American social and cultural life clearly came from Europe, as had the ancestors of most Americans, and little note was taken of the early origins of the Afro-American minority.

Yet many black Americans today can assume that their ancestors were in this country before 1800, and most of them can also be certain that those ancestors came in chains. They were rugged pioneers who cherished freedom, but, like no other people, they suffered harrowing hardships involuntarily, helping to establish the foundations of American agriculture under the lash. Disagreement remains concerning some aspects of slavery, but historians have reached a large measure of agreement concerning the life of the slave. By the use of more representative records and new approaches to the study of slavery, they have drawn a graphic portrait of the slave's family life, housing, food, legal status, rewards and punishments, his work in the fields and in the cities, and his reaction to enslavement.

Gerald W. Mullin's *Flight and Rebellion* is a sensitive study of how African people adapted to, and resisted, enslavement. Mullin deals with slavery in Virginia at the end of the eighteenth century. On one question — whether slaves were contented with their lot or fundamentally rebellious — his work may be more informative than studies of the era just before the Civil War. He writes of a time before the antislavery movement, with its tracts, newspapers, and underground railroad. In the eighteenth century, the slaves reached their own decision. This selection gives a vivid picture of slave life and the determination to gain freedom of a group of our forefathers who happened to be black.

The field slave "is called up in the morning at daybreak, scarcely allowed time to swallow three mouthfuls of homminy," wrote the English traveler J. F. D. Smyth. Brief notations like this in travelers' and plantation accounts and record books must suffice for data on the field slave's material condition. Although the records are sketchy, his diet, although probably adequate in bulk, was scarcely nourishing. "Homminy," Indian corn, was the slaves' staple food.

Random accounts of quantities of corn allotted suggest that provisions were sometimes based on the worker's productivity. During the Revolutionary War, "Councillor" Carter asked that "the stronger Shears [shares] men & women" be given one peck of corn per week, "the Remainder of the Black People they to have ¼ Peck per Week each." By 1787 Carter, who was one of the least oppressive slave masters, increased this slightly. He ordered 44

From *Flight and Rebellion: Slave Resistance in Eighteenth-Century Virginia* by Gerald W. Mullin. Copyright © 1972 by Oxford University Press, Inc. Reprinted by permission. (Footnotes omitted) pecks of shelled Indian corn as two weeks' allowance for 26 slaves, less than a full peck per week per laborer. (One peck equals 14 lbs. of Indian corn.)

Meat was seldom given to slaves. Smyth said slaves ate hoecakes and little else; unless their master "be a man of humanity the slave eats a little fat, skimmed milk, and rusty bacon." La Rochefoucauld-Liancourt said that on large plantations the slave subsisted on corn and sometimes on buttermilk. They were given meat 6 times a year. Robert "Councillor" Carter estimated that the common allowance for wheat per hand per year was 15 bushels for those "negroes, who are not fed with animal food" (e.g., meat). These slaves only received meat on special occasions. Joseph Ball wrote his steward that slaves were to "have ffresh meat when they are sick, if the time of the year will allow it." The cuts were to be the least desirable, although not necessarily the least nutritious. When calves were slaughtered, Ball ordered him to give the field hands the "head and Pluck"; the "ffat backs, necks, and other Coarse pieces" of hogs were also to be reserved for the slaves. James Mercer directed his steward to give the slaves the innards of chickens unless he sold them to the local Negro chicken merchants.

Plantation slaves wore clothing usually cut from a heavy, coarse cloth of flax and tow originally manufactured in Osnabrück, Germany. Following the non-importation agreements of the late 1760's, coarse-textured cotton wool weave, "Virginia plains," "country linen," replaced "Osnabrugs." Unlike the colorful variety of many of the artisan's clothing, the notices for runaways after 1770 indicate that field laborers wore uniform pants and trousers. "They are well clothed in the usual manner for Negroes"; "clothed as usual" and "the usual winter clothing for corn field negroes" are representative descriptions from advertisements of that period.

Black women who worked on the quarter wore clothing of the same weight and texture as the men. They usually dressed in a loose-fitting smock or shift, often tied at the waist; a short waistcoat was fitted over this dress. A Dutch blanket used for a sleeping robe and shoes and stockings completed the plantation Negroes' clothing allowance.

Housing for slaves varied widely. But there are frequent references in travelers' accounts to clusters of slave cabins that looked like small villages, and, in plantation records, numerous directions from masters indicating a concern for warm, dry houses with floors, lofted roofs, and on occasion, fireplaces. Slave quarters, however, may have been a late development. Subscribers who used advertisements to sell plantations frequently mentioned "negro quarters," but usually only in those notices published in the last quarter of the century. The plantation's size, location, and wealth were not factors; nearly all had slave quarters. It is likely that the smaller planter's field hands may have slept in the lofts of barns, in tobacco houses, and other outbuildings before the war. Joseph Ball told his nephew that the slaves "must ly in the Tobacco house" while their quarters, 15 by 20 feet with fireplace and chimney, were "lathed & fitted." However, several planters, including George Washington, used a less substantial, pre-fab arrangement. These shacks were small, temporary, and were moved from quarter to quarter following the seasonal crop.

J. F. D. Smyth was forced to take shelter one evening in a "miserable shell" inhabited by six slaves and their overseer. Unlike many slaves' houses "it was not lathed nor plaistered, neither ceiled nor lofted above . . . one window, but no glass in it, not even a brick chimney, and, as it stood on blocks about a foot above the ground, the hogs lay constantly under the floor, which made it swarm with flies."

On the home plantations, "servants," like the crop hands, usually slept in their own quarters. A planter who moved to the valley in 1781 asked his steward to place the "house Servants for they have been more indulged than the rest" with the overseer and his family, "till Such Time as Warehouses can be provided for them." Slaves evidently rarely slept in the great house. A letter dated 1823, written to Dr. A. D. Galt of Williamsburg, mentioned that the writer's father could not find a house, "and the ones he has seen have not had separate quarters for the servants." They would then "have to stay in the basement or the garret rooms." This, she concluded, "[as] you know cannot be very agreeable to Virginians."

Some idea of a slave's yearly expenses is provided by James Madison's remark to a British visitor earlier in the nineteenth century. "Every negro earns annually, all expenses being deducted, about $257," wrote John Foster. "The expense of a negro including duty, board, clothing, and medicines, he [Madison] estimates from $12–$13."

The lean, spare character of the field slave's material condition was a function of his place in the servile work hierarchy. Most plantation slaves worked in the fields where their tasks were tedious, sometimes strenuous, and usually uninspiring. Although tobacco is a difficult and challenging crop, field laborers — especially the "new Negroes" — were forced into the most routine tasks of transplanting seedlings, weeding, suckering, and worming. Following the harvest their work days extended into the night, when they sorted, bundled, and pressed the tobacco into hogsheads for shipment.

The slave jobber's work assignments were not as routine as the field laborer's chores. Armistead was hired out by his master to "act as a jobber, viz. to cut firewood, go to [the] Mill, work in your garden, and occasionally to work in your Corn-field." Jobbers also mended stone and wood fences, patched and whitewashed the plantation's outbuildings, dug irrigation and drainage ditches, and the like. "Councillor" Carter hired John McKenney to "overlook" his jobbers in 1777. Their agreement read:

> the sd Jobbers to make a Crop of Corn Pumpkins, Irish Potatoes, at my plantation called Dickerson's Mill, that is, a full crop fr about 4 Shares — the sd Jobbers to raise Stone to build a tumbling Dam at Dickerson's Mill, they to make ye dirt Dam sufficient, there, and to do several Jobs at Nomony Hall in the course of this year.

McKenney's wages indicate that this type of work was not well paid: he was "to receive f[o]r his services at the rate of 25s/6 per month, [is] to find himself, Board, lodging, Washing &c."

But jobbers were scarcely better off than the field laborers, because they too did not travel outside the plantation. Nor did their menial tasks spur assimilation and a corresponding change in their view of slavery. Regardless of the specific nature of their tasks, the horizons and expectations of most plantation slaves were sharply limited by the plantation environment.

Their tiresome routines in the meager setting of reserve land, in meadow and woods, monotonous rows of tobacco, and temporary, ramshackle buildings, made the quarter a world of its own. But the isolation and work routines of the quarter provided slaves with a convenient means of expressing their unhappiness, so it was also a constant, nagging source of trouble for the planter. Blacks and whites alike knew that the plantation's efficiency and profitability could be seriously impaired simply by a "little leaning" on the slaves' part. "My people seem to be quite dead hearted, and either cannot or will not work"; "my people are all out of their senses for I cannot get one of them to do a thing as I would have it and as they do it even with their own time they have it to do again immediately." These words are Landon Carter's. A tough and competent man, Carter did not bend easily, but this note of resignation is heard early in his diary.

Accounts of the field slave's performance are rare, but one of the best can be found in Jack P. Greene's fine edition of Landon Carter's Diary which tells a dreary story of the crop laborers' quiet and persistently non-cooperative actions. Slaves reported ill every day but Sunday when there were no complaints because they considered this "a holy day"; men treading wheat slept while their "boys," left to do the job, "neglected" it; the "crop people," forced to stem tobacco in the evening hours, retaliated "under the guise of semi-darkness [by] throwing away a great deal of the saleable tob[acco]"; men whom Carter harassed about weeding a corn patch feigned stupidity and leveled thousands of hills of corn seedlings. Carter's slaves, in fact, were so rebellious that he came to question the profitability of slavery. "It is the same at all my plantations," he complained:

> Although I have many to work and fine land to be tended, I hardly make more than what cloaths them, finds them tools, and pays their Levies. Perhaps a few scrawney hogs may be got in the year to be fattened up here. If these things do not require the greatest caution and frugality in living I am certain nothing can do.

William Strickland, an Englishman who visited colonial America in 1800, concurred. As well as any traveler, he succinctly defined the character of the plantation slaves' rebelliousness in a letter to the Board of Trade:

> Any slave that I have seen at work, does not appear to perform half as much, as a labourer in England; nor does the business under which the master sits

down contented, appear to be half of what we require to be performed by one. . . . If to this be added the slovenly carelessness with which all business is performed by the slave, the great number of useless hands the slave owner is obliged to maintain, the total indifference to, and neglect, not to say the frequent wilful destruction, of whatever is not immediately committed to his case. . . . And also the universal inclination to pilfering shown by them, I cannot do otherwise than acquiesce in the received opinion of the country, that slave labor is much dearer than any other.

Lazy, wasteful, and indifferent work was a chronic problem on eighteenth-century plantations. Slaves understood that there was a great deal of time to waste, and little hope of improving their lot. "It will be better to have more eyes than one over such gangs," Landon Carter noted. Following another inspection he complained, "the old trade, take one hour from any job and it makes a day loss in work." Most plantation slaves desired challenging tasks, but once they had them, they dragged out the job as long as possible. Herdsman Johnny, charged with breaking up the quarter patch at Sabine Hall, "does not intend to finish," Carter wrote, "by contriving that all his lambs should get out of the yard that he may be trifling about after them."

Careful planters habitually spot-checked their slaves' productivity. Planters like Landon Carter and George Washington who demanded from their slaves punctiliousness, order, and a high output, were convenient and effective targets for the slaves' piddling laziness and wasteful procedures. A 1760 entry in Washington's diary noted that four of his sawyers hewed about 120 feet of timber in a day. Dissatisfied with this rate of production, and determined to apply gentle pressure, Washington stood and watched his men. They subsequently fell to work with such energy and enthusiasm that he concluded that one man could do in one day what four had previously accomplished in the same length of time.

How many seemingly routine plantation practices were actually concessions to the unreliability of slave labor? For years Landon Carter refused to introduce plows and carts onto his quarters since he felt that these technological innovations would only serve "to make Overseers and people extremely lazy . . . wherever they are in great abundance there is the least plantation work done."

Feigned illness was another remarkably simple but effective ruse. When a slave asked to "lay-in," his master often suspected he was faking, but could never be certain. Too many had stood helplessly by while a strange and lethal "distemper," or "ague," suddenly swept through their slave quarters and carried off numbers of workers. Plantation records are filled with notes on these epidemics: "The mortalities in ties in my families are increased. . . . The number of my dead is now fifteen working slaves. I thank God I can bear these things with a great deal of resignation," or "a grevious mortality of my familys hath swept away an abundance of my people"; and, "we kept the plantations on James River to try to make Crops, but there broke out a malignant fever amongst the Negroes & swept off most of the able Hands; this threw all into Confusion & there has been little or no thing made since."

Women who feigned illness were usually more effective than men. "As to Sall," James Mercer wrote his steward, "I believe her old complaint is mere deceit, if it is not attended with a fever it must be so unless it is owing to her monthly disorder & then can only last two days, and exercise is a necessary remedy." Washington complained of women who "will lay up a month, at the end of which no visible change in their countenance, nor the loss of an ounce of flesh, is discoverable; and their allowance of provision is going on as if nothing ailed them." Exasperated and uncertain about the health of a black woman, Betty Davis, he explained that "she has a disposition to be one of the most idle creatures on earth, and besides one of the most deceitful." When two of his slave women approached clutching their sides, Landon Carter told them to work or be whipped. He observed that they had no fever (the test of whether or not slaves were ill). "They worked very well with no grunting about pain." But Sarah, one of the women who had pretended to be pregnant for eleven months earlier in the year, soon ran off. When Wilmot used the same stratagem, Carter noted: "it cost me 12 months, before I broke her." This lesson was not satisfactory; for a third woman "fell into the same scheme," and "really carried it to a great length." So Carter whipped her severely; and she was "a good slave ever since only a cursed thief in making her Children milk Cows in the night."

Plantation slaves who "hid out" in the woods and fields as runaways represented a more serious breach of plantation security. They often returned to the quarter in the evening for food and shelter and were an invitation to others to follow their example. But truancy was also inward rebelliousness: it was sporadic, and it was directed toward the plantation or quarter. Unlike the real fugitives, truants had no intention of leaving the immediate neighborhood and attempting to permanently change their status. Truancy was so common that most planters either did not make it a matter of record or simply referred to it in a random manner in their correspondence. "King" Carter actually viewed it as part of his "outlandish" slaves' learning process: "Now that my new negro woman has tasted the hardships of the woods," he observed to an overseer, "she'll stay nearer to home where she can have her belly full." Planters accepted the fact that absenteeism, particularly in the evening hours, was scarcely controllable. In response to Landon Carter's complaint that his pet deer were straying in the Sabine Hall fields, John Tayloe wrote:

Dear Col

. . . Now give me leave to complain to you, That your Patroll do not do their duty, my people are rambleing about every night, . . . my man Billie was out, he says he rode no horse of Master & that he only was at Col. Carter's, by particular invitation, so that the Entertainment was last night at Sabine Hall, & may probably be at Mt Airy this night, if my discoverys do not disconcert the Plan, these things would not be so I think, if the Patrollers did the duty they are paid for.

Plantation slaves probably "rambled" to the "entertainment" in the neighborhood several nights of the week; as long as they reported for work the following day few efforts were made, or could be made, to curtail this practice.

Truants habitually remained very close to the quarter or plantation; but this did not make it much easier for the planter to recapture them. Evidently they were sufficiently clever (and the other plantation slaves were sufficiently secretive) to keep themselves in hiding until they decided to return on their own. Sarah ran off because Carter refused to let her "lie-in" as ill. She spent a week in the woods and ate during the evening hours while visiting the slave quarters. Simon, an ox-carter, also hid beneath the vigilant Carter's very nose. He "lurked" in Johnny's "inner room," and in the "Kitchen Vault."

The outlaw, a far more dangerous type of runaway, used his temporary freedom to inflict punishment on his tormentors. Outlawing a slave was a legal action, placing the runaway beyond the law, making him a public liability, and encouraging his destruction by any citizen. Those who killed outlaws did so without fear of legal prosecution; they also collected a fee from the public treasury and a reward from the slave's owner. The master's advertisements usually did not encourage the slave's preservation: George America was worth forty shillings if taken alive; five pounds if destroyed.

Some slaveowners only threatened to outlaw truants. Recognizing the effective communication between slaves who remained on the quarter and their "outlying" brother, masters used outlawry as a warning for slaves to come in or suffer the consequences. Many did not return, nor were they satisfied with merely "lurking" about and "tasting the hardships of the woods" until hunger brought them back to the quarter. Outlaws destroyed. The omnibus slave codes of the century (four were passed from 1705 to 1797) described these desperate, courageous and "incorrigible" slaves in language which changed only slightly during the ninety years:

> WHEREAS many times slaves run away and lie hid and lurking in swamps, woods, and other obscure places, killing hogs, and committing other injuries to the inhabitants . . . upon intelligence, two justices (*Quorum unus*) can issue a proclamation . . . if the slave does not immediately return, anyone whatsoever may kill or destroy such slaves by such ways and means as he . . . shall think fit. . . . If the slave is apprehended . . . it shall . . . be lawful for the county court, to order such punishment to the said slave, either by dismembering, or in any other way . . . as they in their discretion shall think fit, for the reclaiming any such incorrigible slave, and terrifying others from the like practices.

Newspaper advertisements provide a glimpse of why a few runaways were outlawed: John Smith outlawed Mann because he threatened to burn Smith's house; and John Tayloe's manager at the Occoquan Furnace reported that "Leamon's obstinacy in not delivering himself up when lurking a considerable time about the ironworks, and doing mischief, Induced me to have him outlawed; in which condition he now stands and remains." Other explanations were not as clear as these. Moses and his wife were "harboured" by some "ill disposed" persons in Williamsburg. His master advertised "such notorious offences are not to be borne with any degree of patience." Edward Cary's explanation for outlawing Ben and Alice was even more cryptic. Cary was the chairman of the House of Burgesses committee that reimbursed masters whose slaves were outlawed as public liabilities. "As neither of those slaves have been ill used at my hands, I have had them outlawed in this county and for their bodies without hurt, or a proper certificate of their death, a proper reward will be given."

Some potentially explosive outlaws stayed on the quarters and physically assaulted their overseers. One of Landon Carter's supervisors, Billy Beale, chastised a slave who was weeding a corn patch. Told that his work was "slovenly," the slave replied "a little impudently" and Beale was "obliged to give him a few licks with a switch across his Shoulders"; but the slave fought back, and he and Beale "had a fair box." Subsequently, the laborer was brought before his master; and Carter noted that "it seems nothing scared him." Direct confrontations such as these, between comparatively unassimilated slaves and whites, seem to have been rare; a few, however, are described in detail in the advertisements for runaways. Two fugitives, for example, a husband and wife, were recaptured by an overseer while crossing a field, and were "violently" taken from the overseer and set free by field workers. Another runaway, also a field hand, escaped by "cutting his Overseer in Several Pieces [places?] with a Knife." John Greenhow of Williamsburg lost a slave who "laid violent hands" on him; this man ran off with another field slave who had also beaten his overseer.

Murders, small and unplanned uprisings, and suicides are instances of rebelliousness that was clearly inward-directed in a psychological sense as well as directed against the confines of the plantation. A September 1800 newspaper story graphically illustrates how even the most calculating, courageous, and murderously violent action could be, in a fashion, internalized violence: for after this slave methodically stalked and killed his master he simply "went home."

Captain John Patteson, a tobacco inspector at Horsley's warehouse in Buckingham County, punished his slave for "some misdemeanor"; and from that time, the slave told the court, "he ever after meditated [Patteson's] destruction."

On the evening to which it was effected, my master directed me to set off home . . . and carry a hoe which we used at the place. . . . I concluded to waylay him. . . . after waiting a considerable time, I heard the trampling of horses' feet. . . . I got up and walked forwards — my master soon overtook me, and asked me (it being then dark) who I was: I answered Abram; he said he thought I had gone from town long enough to have been further advanced on the road; I said, I thought not; I spoke short to him, and did not care to irritate him — I walked on however; sometimes by the side of his horse, and sometimes before him. — In the course of our traveling an altercation ensued; I raised my hoe two different times to strike him, as the circumstance of the places suited my purpose, but was intimidated. . . . [W]hen I came to the fatal place, I turned to the side of the road; my master observed it, and stopped; I then turn'd suddenly round, lifted my hoe, and struck him across the breast; the stroke broke the handle of the hoe — he fell — I repeated my blows; the handle of the hoe broke a second time — I heard dogs bark, at a house which we passed, at a small distance; I was alarmed, and ran a little way, and stood behind a tree, 'till the barking ceased; in running, I stumbled and fell — I returned to finish the scene I began, and on my way picked up a stone, which I hurl'd at his head, face, &c. again and again and again, until I thought he was certainly dead — and then I went home.

The most violent reactions to slavery were small, unorganized uprisings. A newspaper account written in 1770 reported a battle between slaves and free men, which suddenly erupted during the Christmas holidays on a small plantation quarter in New Wales, Hanover County. The reporter's explanation for the uprising was a familiar one. "Treated with too much lenity," the plantation slaves became "insolent and unruly." When a young and inexperienced overseer tried to "chastise" one of them by beating him to the ground and whipping him the man picked himself up and "slash[ed] at the overseer with an axe." He missed, but a group of slaves jumped on the white and administered such a severe beating that the "ringleader," the slave whom the overseer had whipped, intervened and saved his life. The overseer ran off in search of reinforcements; and instead of fleeing or arming themselves, the slaves tied up two other whites and "whipped [them] till they were raw from neck to waistband." Twelve armed whites arrived, and the slaves retreated into a barn where they were soon joined by a large body of slaves, "some say forty, some fifty." The whites "tried to prevail by persuasion," but the slaves, "deaf to all, rushed upon them with a desperate fury, armed solely with clubs and staves." Two slaves were shot and killed, five others were wounded, and the remainder fled.

Some slaves took their own lives. The journals of the House of Burgesses contain 55 petitions from slaveowners who sought reimbursement from public funds for slaves who committed suicide. Most of these men were outlawed runaways who, since they feared trial and conviction for capital crimes, hanged or drowned themselves. Since few petitioners reported the circumstances of a slave's death, the journals are not too informative. But one suicide, William Lightfoot's Jasper, was also described in a runaway notice:

> [A] well set Negro Man Slave, much pitted with the Small-pox; he was lately brought from *New-York,* but was either born or lived in the *West-Indies,* by which he has acquired their peculiar Way of speaking, and, seems to frown when he talks; he carried with him different Sorts of Apparel.

If indeed Jasper was a suicide his decision to "dash his brains out against a rock" must have been sudden, for he took a change of clothing with him.

But the field slaves' rebelliousness was not typically violent, self-destructive, or even individualistic. In fact they were much more inclined to attack the plantation in a quietly cooperative and effective way than were the slave artisans. Pilferage was a particularly rewarding and often organized action. "I laughed at the care we experienced in Milk, butter, fat, sugar, plumbs, soap, Candles, etc." wrote Landon Carter. "Not one of these ennumerations lasted my family half the year. All gone, no body knows how . . . thievish servants . . . Butter merely vanishing." Washington estimated that his servants stole two glasses of wine to every one consumed by the planter's visitors. His slaves made a practice of stealing nearly everything they could lay their hands on. Washington had to keep his corn and meat houses locked; apples were picked early, and sheep and pigs carefully watched.

The following offhand comments in records and newspapers indicate that much of this pilferage was not simply to satisfy hunger or anger. "Tell ye overseers to keep the keys of the folk's Cornhouse or else they will sell it, and starve themselves"; "bacon to spare will allow me a preference with the Country People, or rather Nigroes who are the general Chicken merchants"; and, "papermills I believe will answer well there . . . and I am sure the Negroes would supply them with Rags enough for Trifles"; and Washington's order that all dogs belonging to slaves be hanged immediately, because they "aid[ed] them in their night robberies."

The slaves' traffic in stolen goods was extensive, relatively well organized, and carried on virtually with impunity. The problem was of such proportions that by the 1760's it led to several letters to newspaper editors and to a series of laws. "I suppose every family must have so sensibly felt this evil," noted one letter writer to the *Virginia Gazette.* He observed that in every part of the country, henhouses, dairies, barns, granaries, gardens, and even patches and fields were "robbed in every convenient moonshiny night." Another contributor noted that, in his travels about the country, he had heard "frequent and various complaints" of this "pernicious evil." There was "hardly a family that was not full of enjuries they had received from the numerous thefts of servants and slaves."

Many slaves were fences for stolen goods; they had licenses from "over-tender" masters to sell produce. Whites, too, cooperated with the plantation slaves; they were referred to in the newspapers as "common proprietors of orchards," "liquor fellers," and "idle scatter lopping people." One writer made the interesting observation that some slaveowners, with "a modest blush," were so ashamed to sell certain farm products that they gave them to their slaves to dispose of. "Pray why is a fowl more disgraceful," he asked, "in the sale of it at market, than a pig, lamb, a mutton, a veal, a cow or an ox?"

Additional evidence of organized thievery as an outgrowth of the plantation slaves' culture and community is preserved in the Richmond County court records. Between 1710 and 1754 the justices tried and passed sentence in 426 cases. In 1750, although blacks made up 45 per cent of the population and there were nearly twice as many black tithes (1,235) as white (761), only 26 of these 426 actions involved slaves. (It should also be remembered that all slave criminals — with the exception of insurrectionists and murderers who were supposed to be tried by the General Court — were tried by county justices.) Only two trials concerned serious crimes. These were murder trials and both defendants were slave men. One was convicted of stabbing a black woman to death; the other, who later died in jail under very unusual circumstances, was charged with killing his master's young daughter. After his death, the court ordered his body to be quartered and displayed. Most slave crimes in this forty-four year period were petty thefts of the kind described earlier; that is, the charge was nearly always breaking and entering, and the slaves usually took a few shillings' worth of cider, liquor, bacon, cloth, or hogs. One typical case involved a slave who stole five sheets, a fishing line, and a bottle of brandy. Nearly all of these robberies were committed by one person; but the largest theft was conducted by a man and a woman. They took forty gallons of rum and fifty pounds of sugar. Evidently these thefts were well organized; the slaves usually selected such vulnerable targets as the homes of widows, ministers, warehouses, and slave quarters. Only on one occasion did a slave rob his master (who was Landon Carter!). The usual punishment for these crimes was between ten and thirty-nine lashes. For more serious crimes (including a conviction of perjury) slaves lost one or both ears. For capital crimes, slaves were often allowed to plead benefit of clergy.

The plantation slaves' organized burglaries were similar to the rebellious styles of the mobile, comparatively assimilated slaves. These crimes required planning; they took the slaves outside the plantation, and evidently compensated them with money and goods which could be exchanged for articles they needed.

Most field slaves, however, never acquired sufficient literate and occupational skills to move away from the quarter and into the society beyond it. Most were Africans and they remained "new Negroes" all of their lives. There are, then, two possible aspects to the personal dimension of slave life on the quarter. First, from an outsider's point of view, the quarter was a stultifying experience which slowed and restricted the slave's rate of acculturation. Second, from the slave's point of view, life on the quarter was perhaps preferable to daily contact with his captors, because it allowed him to preserve some of his ways.

Household slavery entwined the lives of whites and blacks. In the household more than anywhere else, there were direct and personal encounters that intensified the meaning of slavery for slaves and free alike. For the black servant these situations were often harrowing experiences which threatened to expose a nature sharply divided between enervating fear and aggressive hostility. His inward styles of rebelliousness and such related neurotic symptoms as speech defects were often manifestations of a profound ambiguity about whites and his own "privileged" status. For the white master the intimate presence of so many blacks subtly influenced domestic affairs, particularly his behavior toward his wife and children. The roles developed in household slavery restricted the master's actions toward his servants too. Once a style of discipline and correct order had been established, the master's reactions were often determined by what the slaves had come to expect of him. Highly sensitive to the patriarch's role, servants were quick to exploit any weakness in his performance. If the master was insecure, so were his dependents; but they also kept him that way by their persistent and petty rebelliousness. Household slavery then was the epitome of Professor Tannenbaum's dynamic view of human relationships in slave societies in which slavery was "not merely for blacks, but for the whites [and] . . . Nothing escaped, nothing, and no one."

The greatly enlarged situational (or interpersonal) dimension of slavery in the household is fundamentally important for another reason. Our limited understanding of slave behavior is based almost exclusively on interpretations of these personal encounters. These interpretations, which argue that slaves became the characters they played for whites, that their masters' view of them as infants or Sambos became their self-view, must be used with extreme caution. The interpersonal encounter was only a fragment of slavery's reality for both whites and blacks. When slaves were among their own and using their own resources as fugitives and insurrectionists, it is abundantly clear that much of their true character was concealed or intentionally portrayed in a dissembling manner in the presence of whites.

STUDY GUIDE

1. Differences between black slaves and poor white farmers with respect to freedom are obvious. How would their lives compare with respect to the following: housing; the actual labor they performed; food; health and medical care?

2. What were the various kinds of violent resistance that slaves used to protest enslavement? What were the techniques of "quiet resistance" that they used?

3. How might the following factors have influenced the slave's choice of violent or passive resistance: the master or conditions on the plantation; the slave's personality and character; the slave code and attitudes of a particular region, such as South Carolina as compared to Virginia?

4. How did the household slave's relationship to whites differ from that of the field slave? What were the relative advantages and disadvantages of each position?

5. Though Mullin's selection focuses on the life of the slave, he mentions several times that the institution of slavery influenced every aspect of life in the South for both blacks and whites. How do you think black slavery might have influenced each of the following aspects of southern life: education of whites; relations between whites of different classes; the relative slowness of the South in industrial development; southern politics? Can you think of specific evidence to support your arguments on these points?

BIBLIOGRAPHY

Mullin's book is a study of slavery in eighteenth-century Virginia. The work, the slave code, and the conditions of slave life differed somewhat in other colonies such as New York or South Carolina. Wherever he ended up — on a southern plantation or in a port city, as a farmer or a craftsman — the slave's experience began with his capture and sale to the captain of a slave ship in Africa. The ghastly conditions aboard such vessels is described in Daniel P. Mannix and Malcolm Cowley, *Black Cargoes: A History of the Atlantic Slave Trade* (New York, 1962). Philip D. Curtin, *The Atlantic Slave Trade: A Census* * (Madison, Wis., 1969), is a careful study of the number of slaves brought to various parts of North and South America.

Unlike most Europeans who came to the colonies, the African brought virtually no personal property with him — no jewelry, no utensils, no tools, no musical instruments, no clothes. He did, however, bring his traditions and values — his dances and music, his folklore and religion, and his sense of family and personal relations. Since Melville J. Herskovits published his study of the subject, *The Myth of the Negro Past* * (New York and London, Eng., 1941), scholars have devoted much energy to identifying African influences upon American Negro culture. The first chapter of John Blassingame, *The Slave Community: Plantation Life in the Ante-Bellum South* * (New York, 1972) discusses the cultural shock of enslavement, as well as the question of the survival of African culture in the New World.

Another important question is whether racism or slavery developed first in the British colonies. In the very early seventeenth century, Africans were treated as indentured servants and were freed after a number of years of service. Did

English colonials force Africans into slavery because of white racism, while allowing Europeans to continue in temporary servitude? Or was it the economic advantage of a wageless, hereditary labor force that led to enslavement, with racism following as a rationalization of white guilt? Anyone interested in this question should read Winthrop Jordan's lengthy study *White over Black: American Attitudes toward the Negro, 1550–1812* * (Chapel Hill, N.C., 1968), and Edmund S. Morgan, *American Slavery, American Freedom: The Ordeal of Colonial Virginia* * (New York, 1975).

About half of the people who came to the English colonies in the colonial period were of English descent; Africans were the second largest group, making up nearly twenty percent of the population by 1790. Many other nationalities came in smaller numbers, and your college library is likely to have some of the studies of the Germans, the Scots-Irish, and the other groups that settled the New World. The origins, voyages, and New-World conditions of the European group that most closely paralleled the enslaved African is studied in Abbot E. Smith, *Colonists in Bondage: White Servitude and Convict Labor in America, 1607–1776* * (Chapel Hill, N.C., 1947).

* Asterisk indicates book is available in a paperback edition.

II COLONIAL SOCIETY

Each of the several races and nationalities that sought a new life in the British colonies brought their own traditions and social attitudes with them. People of English descent made up half of the total population, and the colonies were under the English government. Thus, the English influence was naturally predominant in shaping colonial institutions and social life. One must remember, however, that Africans and continental Europeans made up the other half of the population by the late eighteenth century. The language, customs, and culture of these peoples did much to modify English institutions and contributed significantly to the rich variety of American society.

The establishment of English settlements in North America, begun at Jamestown in 1607, continued into the eighteenth century; Georgia, the last colony, was founded in 1732. By 1775, the new civilization had attained the characteristics of a mature social world. Colonial legislatures met in solemn session to make laws for the new land. The thousands of acres that had been cleared supported a flourishing agriculture, as the immigrants learned New-World ways of planting, fertilizing, and harvesting. The rude lean-tos of the earliest settlements had given way to sturdy houses built from the sawn lumber of the endless forests. As a part of a vast English empire that extended from Hudson Bay in Canada around the world to India, the colonies along the Atlantic seaboard were deeply involved in the complex economic world of eighteenth-century mercantilism.

This section has articles that illustrate the changes that took place in colonial life from the late seventeenth century to the American Revolution. The first reading, on the Salem witchcraft affair of 1692, illustrates the powerful influence that European religions, values, and even superstitions continued to exercise upon the British colonies. However, the Old-World values and practices were substantially modified in subsequent decades, and by 1775, family life, politics, and many other facets of living had taken on an American coloration. The second reading describes the importance of women in colonial society, and serves to counterbalance the frequent emphasis upon the pioneers as hardy hunters and yeoman farmers. In the British colonies, there were significant social conflicts almost from the beginning of settlement. The last reading describes the often vicious social war that was fought between Whigs and Tories during the War for Independence.

T. H. Matteson's painting (1855) portrays the anxiety and excitement accompanying George Jacobs's examination on witchcraft charges at Salem.

4

JOHN C. MILLER

The Witchcraft Scare

One of the striking phenomena of the past decade has been widespread interest in witchcraft, the occult, and occurrences beyond normal, sensory perception. Hollywood producers have beaten paths to the bank with the box-office receipts from dozens of films on vampires, ghosts, and satanic possession. Thousands of readers have believed quite as firmly in the reality of supernatural forces haunting the house in Amityville as in the astrological forces in their own lives. One major university has a center for the study of extrasensory perception, and many others offer courses on magic, the devil, and the mystery of evil. If, after all, one believes in God and the forces of good, is it illogical to believe in Satan and the forces of evil?

One might, however, ask why the belief or at least the interest in magic and witchcraft seems to be especially strong in certain periods and to be the subject of skepticism or ridicule at other times. Some scholars have suggested that a society is more likely to turn to supernatural explanations in an especially troubled time and to charge unpopular or deviant members of the society with witchcraft when it needs scapegoats. For many years, this was the fundamental historical explanation of the Salem witchcraft episode that staggered Massachusetts in 1692. In the last ten years, historians have reexamined Salem witchcraft and have developed a number of other explanations. One writer has suggested that witchcraft was actually practiced in Salem, and that the victims who felt tormented by witches were suffering from hysteria, rather than deliberately misleading the community by false accusations. Another writer has suggested that a peculiar fungus in the rye grain in one part of the town, which some of the citizens used in baking, caused them to experience hallucinations similar to an LSD trip. Others have argued that the witchcraft affair was a religious and socioeconomic conflict between two different parts of the town.

The Salem episode has fascinated novelists and dramatists from Nathaniel Hawthorne to Arthur Miller. Like the historians, they have seen very different things in the outbreak of witchcraft. Miller, writing his play *The Crucible* in the 1950s when Senator Joseph McCarthy was conducting a Communist witch-hunt, saw parallels between the events of his own day and those of 1692. In the conclusion of a French film about the affair, a crowd storms the gallows area in a scene reminiscent of events at the Bastille in 1789. Other writers have viewed Salem witchcraft as little more than the logical outcome of a narrow-minded religious outlook, whether in Catholic Europe where thousands perished or in Puritan Massachusetts where twenty men and women died.

The following selection by John C. Miller represents an eclectic, and perhaps a somewhat old-fashioned, point of view in the sea of new interpretations. Miller suggests that socioeconomic conflict, the troubles that the colony had recently experienced, and a lack of enlightenment all contributed to the hysteria. He is a bit harsher on the Mathers than some recent writers, but on the whole, his essay gives a concise and balanced summary of the whole episode. His comments on witchcraft in Europe suggest that some restraint is in order before we label seventeenth-century Salem as an especially dark and bloody chapter of our past.

During the period 1670–1690, among the evidences of backsliding noted by the New England clergy was a growing disposition on the part of the people to take witchcraft lightly. The Reverend Increase Mather observed with alarm that even some church members were beginning to say that people possessed by demons mentioned in the Bible were simply epileptics or lunatics. Taking what he regarded as an extraordinarily tolerant attitude toward these skeptics, Mather said that he would not "suspect all those as guilty of witchcraft, nor yet of heresie, who call the received opinion about witches into question." But neither did he admit that they had a right to advance such heretical opinions.

To alert these skeptical citizens to their danger, Mather included in his *Essay for the Recording of Illustrious Providences* (1684) a long discourse upon witchcraft. The elder Mather prided himself upon taking a dispassionate, scientific view of witchcraft and of other natural phenomena. He admitted, for example, that many accounts of possession by demons were mere fables, and he denied that it was possible for spirits to generate bodies or beget children or that witches could transform themselves or others into another species of creature such as horse, wolf, cat, and mouse. "It is beyond the power of all the devils in hell to cause such a transformation," he asserted. "They can no more do it than they can be the authors of a true miracle." Moreover, he disapproved of many of the "superstitious and magical ways" of detecting witches — "whereby," he said, "much innocent blood hath been shed." Only by exhaustive cross-examination and scientific appraisal of the evidence, said Mather, could the guilt of witches be proved beyond all doubt.

The "Invisible World" was also very real to Cotton Mather — more real, it sometimes seemed, than the little world of churchgoers over which he presided. He invested commonplace events with supernatural, portentous meaning. For example, when he suffered from toothaches "he considered whether or not he had sinned with his teeth. How? By sinful and excessive eating; and by evil speeches." Thus even a simple case of caries was endowed with theological significance.

In sounding the alarm against witchcraft, Cotton Mather acted under what he supposed was a special mandate from Heaven. In 1686, God appeared to him in a vision and told him that his mission was to fight witchcraft. Accordingly, after protracted fasting and prayer, Mather took up his pen — specially consecrated, he believed, by the Almighty to expose "the whole Plot of the Devil against New England in every branch of it" — to write against witches. The result of his revelation was the publication in 1689 of *Memorable Providences Relating to Witchcraft and Other Possessions*.

Both Increase and Cotton Mather were impressed by the inability of science to explain the phenomena they studied. To them, science left the ultimate mysteries untouched. Lacking a scientific explanation for many baffling events in human affairs, they were driven to the conviction that demons were constantly at work among men and that the Devil, for God's own purposes, had been permitted to act through the medium of witches — always, however, within definite restrictions laid down by the Almighty.

The Mathers tried to buttress the case for witchcraft with pseudoscientific "evidence" derived from their observation of people under seizure. What they recorded were cases of abnormal psychology, but they presented them as irrefutable "proof" of the existence of demons. By their books and sermons they succeeded in inculcating the idea that witchcraft was increasing by leaps and bounds in New England and that God's own plantation might fall before the wiles and stratagems of Satan. "Tis *our* Worldiness, *our* Formality, *our* Sensuality, and *our* Iniquity," said Cotton Mather, that had provided Satan with an entering wedge into God's own plantation.

In the jeremiads, the clergy portrayed the crusade against sin and worldiness within their favorite frame of reference — the struggle between God and the Devil. All history, as they saw it, consisted of variations on this cosmic theme. Although the last thing the clergy wanted to see was a plague of witches descend upon New England — by their reckoning no greater disaster could befall a country — yet by their books and sermons they inadvertently prepared the way for Salem witchcraft. People who fear witches and who talk about them constantly are likely to be assailed by them sooner or later.

Salem witchcraft was merely an episode — hardly more than a footnote — in the history of an ancient superstition, for evidences of belief in the malefic power of certain individuals has been found in the most primitive societies. But it was not until the late Middle Ages, when witchcraft was identified with heresy and therefore came within the purview of the Holy Inquisition, that a witchcraft mania really began. The Reformation intensified the zeal of the witch-hunters. While Roman Catholics and Protestants disagreed upon many points, they agreed in holding witches in abhorrence and in putting an end to their existence as summarily as possible. In the sixteenth and seventeenth centuries — the age of the Renaissance and the New Science — over 100,000 people charged with having leagued themselves with the Devil were put to death.

Witchcraft was believed to originate in a bargain between a man or a woman and the Devil by which he or she agreed to sell his or her soul to Satan. This transaction, of course, was a great victory for Satan: he had turned against God one of God's own creatures and ensured the damnation of a human being. It was supposed that the Devil insisted that his victims sign a book agreeing to renounce the Christian religion, pay homage to the Prince of Darkness, and join in celebrating the Black Mass. Not until it was all down in writing did Satan feel that the bargain was truly consummated. Everything was neat, orderly and legal, the Devil having served his apprenticeship in Heaven where making contractual obligations — or so the Puritans believed — was the approved procedure. After the signatories signed the "contract," they were permitted to have carnal intercourse with devils, join in the witches' sabbat, revel with the Devil himself, and enjoy the power to subvert God's order on earth. Women who put their signatures to this horrid affidavit became witches; men who joined the Devil's legion were known as wizards.

Witchcraft was therefore treated as a legal crime — an offense against God

— which merited the death penalty. Every country in Christendom enacted laws against witchcraft and hauled suspects into civil or ecclesiastical courts to stand trial. . . . The act need not be malefic or destructive: if it were proved to have been performed through "conference with the Devil," it became a capital offense.

Witches were held responsible for storms, droughts, the death of cattle, sexual impotence, epidemics — and all the evils, in short, that the Devil chose to inflict upon mankind. But, clearly, malice, spite, and unreasoning fear played an important part in determining who were the Devil's agents. Unpopular eccentrics and "far-out" people were always candidates for suspicion. Old women were particularly vulnerable: being accused of practicing witchcraft was one of the hazards of being old, ugly, and unwanted.

The Devil was no respecter of persons. James I, who regarded himself as God's own anointed, also believed that he was the victim of a witches' conspiracy. He was firmly persuaded that they had almost succeeded in drowning him by brewing up a storm while he was at sea. As was his custom when he was particularly exercised by anything from tobacco to theology, James wrote a book against it. *Demonologie,* a dialogue upon witchcraft, appeared in 1597.

As a rule, outbreaks of witch-hunting occurred especially in countries distinguished by clerical power, popular ignorance, the breakdown of government, and the use of torture. Germany, where all these conditions existed, was the site of the most sanguinary efforts to suppress witchcraft. At the height of the mania, no one was safe from the suspicion of being in league with the Devil. The estates of wealthy people made them particularly vulnerable, and a lenient judge was liable to incur the charge of being an accomplice of the accused. Even the expression of disbelief in witchcraft was apt to be construed as circumstantial evidence of guilt. As James I said in *Demonologie,* the author of a book casting doubt on the existence of witches betrayed himself to be "one of that profession."

In whipping the people into a frenzy of fear of witches, intellectuals played a vital role. The belief in witches and the determination to stamp them out was in part a by-product of the scholarship of the age: the more learned and religious the individual, the more zealous and remorseless was his attitude toward witches likely to be. In the great witch-hunts of the sixteenth and seventeenth centuries, the prime instigators were men of learning who instilled their fear of the prevalence of witchcraft into the minds of the common people.

Vast ingenuity was expended by scholars upon the problem of determining how a witch could be detected. While such signs as moles or warts, an insensitive spot which did not bleed when pricked, a capacity to float in water, and an inability to recite the Lord's Prayer constituted only circumstantial evidence, they gave witch-hunters a clear lead in tracking down the Devil's agents.

On the European continent, torture was used to extract confessions from those accused of witchcraft. The rack, red-hot pincers, thumbscrews, scourges, leg-crushing machines — the familiar appurtenances of torture — together with a novel instrument, the witches' chair (a seat under which a fire was kindled), were the ultimate resorts of judges and inquisitors confronted with people who obstinately protested their innocence. By express orders of the Pope, issued in 1468, there were no limits upon the amount or degree of torture that could be applied. But the inquisitors were not content with a confession procured under torture: the accused had to be tortured until he or she confessed voluntarily.

In England, although those accused of witchcraft were not tortured, they were subjected to intensive interrogation, sometimes lasting for weeks or even months without benefit of habeas corpus. Those convicted in England were hung rather than burned at the stake — a distinction which, however finely drawn, was important to those who suffered the penalty. Moreover, James I and other authorities on witchcraft enjoined judges and juries strictly to observe the rules of evidence. Even so, about 30,000 people were convicted of witchcraft in the British Isles.

During the centuries when witchcraft was in flower, the professional witch-hunter and informer flourished in Europe. Judges welcomed the services of these itinerants who ferreted witches out of their deepest lairs. One of the most successful witch-hunters on record was Matthew Hopkins, who, during the 1640s, was personally responsible for the death of over 200 English witches. But Hopkins enjoyed an unfair advantage over his rival witch-hunters: he was said to have secured the Devil's own list of witches commissioned to operate in England.

As a result of the bloodletting of the period 1600–1660, when the mania reached its height, a reaction against witch-hunting set in. On the Continent, torture had been carried to such lengths that the confessions which had brought thousands of men and women to their deaths seemed worthless. During this period, thousands of people saw one or more of their relatives suffer death under one of the most terrible charges that could be made against a human being — selling his or her soul to the Devil and contracting to aid the Devil against God.

Being the most militant of English Protestants in the struggle against the Roman Catholic Counter-Reformation, the Puritans were peculiarly prone to believe in witchcraft and the ubiquitous power of Satan. Literal believers in the Bible, they took the injunction "Thou shalt not suffer a witch to live" to mean that they were under a religious duty to exterminate witches. As Calvin said, "The Bible teaches that there are witches and that they must be slain. . . . God expressly commands that all witches and enchantresses shall be put to death; and this law of God is an universal law." In Geneva, Calvin suited the action to the word. Before he came to that city, little had been heard of witchcraft, but in the 60 years that followed, over

150 witches were burned. It is not therefore merely coincidental that the most destructive witch craze in English history occurred during the period of Puritan ascendancy.

By the last quarter of the seventeenth century, the maniacal phase of witchcraft was clearly on the wane. Fewer and fewer of the "Accursed tribe" were sent to the stake or the gallows. As Montaigne said, "After all, it is rating one's conjectures at a very high price to roast a man alive on the strength of them." In the late seventeenth century, Holland abolished witch-craft trials altogether. In Geneva, the final witch burning occurred in 1652, and the last mass holocaust took place in Germany in 1679 when the Arch-bishop of Salzburg consigned 97 witches to the flames. In 1672, Louis XIV of France ordered that all prisoners recently condemned to death for witch-craft by the Parlement of Rouen should have their sentences commuted to banishment.

But the belief in witchcraft could not yet be dismissed as a mere peasant superstition. What had really changed was not the belief in witchcraft but confidence in the effectiveness of the methods used to detect it. While few doubted that many of those who perished at the stake were genuine witches who richly deserved their fate, it began to dawn upon the sober-minded, par-ticularly after the mania had spent itself, that many had fallen victim to biased evidence, rumor, hearsay, envy, and malice.

What is truly remarkable about Salem witchcraft is that it occurred so late in the history of an ancient superstition. Far from playing a leading part in the mania, the Puritans did not enter upon the stage until the final act. That, in part, is why they became so conspicuous: most of the other actors, having already played out their terrible parts, had left the scene.

In Puritan New England, the outbreak of witchcraft occurred in a social context characterized by instability, clerical power, tension, and fear. The decade 1680–1690 had seen the loss of the Massachusetts charter, the estab-lishment of the despotic Dominion of New England, the revolution of 1688–1689, and an abortive expedition against Quebec. The "great fear" abroad in the land was the fear of crypto–Roman Catholics in high places who were believed to be plotting the overthrow of the Protestant religion. It is sig-nificant that the witch-hunt was preceded by a hunt for Roman Catholics. To a marked degree, Salem witchcraft was a continuation of the anti–Roman Catholic agitation. Puritans would have been hard pressed to tell which of the two — Roman Catholics or witches — was more malefic. In any event, at the very time that the threat of Roman Catholicism was approaching its climax, the country was infested with swarms of witches.

In Salem Village — now Danvers, Massachusetts — the anxiety and appre-hension felt by all the people of the colony were aggravated by dissension between the pastor and his congregation (just before the outbreak of witch-craft, two ministers had successively taken their parishioners to court to collect their salaries, and both had won judgments); by educational backwardness; by petty squabbles among the villagers over land, animals, and crops; and by the presence of Tituba, a slave woman of mixed black and Indian ancestry whose mind was filled with the primitive lore of her people. Tituba was a slave in the household of the Reverend Samuel Parris, who had come to Salem Village in 1689 and who, like his predecessors, had quarreled with his parishioners over his salary. The Reverend Mr. Parris's family consisted of his wife, his daughter, and his niece. Tituba regaled these highly impressionable adolescents with tales of the occult: Salem witchcraft was the product of the conjunction of the pagan superstition of Africa with the Christian superstition of Western Europe.

The Reverend Mr. Parris was a firm believer in witchcraft, and his young daughter and niece had probably learned at his knee all about black magic and the Invisible World. It certainly seemed very real to them; at the age of twelve they were experts on demonology. Growing up in the narrow world of a country parsonage in an intellectual atmosphere that came straight from the Middle Ages, with overtones of voodooism, and living in a backward, tension-ridden, credulous, quarrelsome community, these girls were in a strategic position to start a witch-hunt. Not surprisingly, they were seized with fits and convulsions, pinched and choked by unseen hands, pricked with invisible pins and needles, and visited by specters who tried to entice them into selling their souls to the Devil.

In 1691, few people doubted that the long-heralded assault on New England by the Invisible World had begun. . . . The most dismal predictions of the jeremiads seemed mild in comparison with the horrible reality. Cotton Mather declared that "prodigious Witch-Meetings" were being held all over the country at which "a fearful knot of proud, ignorant, envious and malicious creatures" volunteered for the Devil's service. But Mather was not surprised by this untoward event: "Where," he asked rhetorically, "will the Devil show most Malice, but where he is hated, and hateth most?" Mather rejoiced at the prospect of a decisive encounter with his old enemy who, he was persuaded, had sent the witches "as a particular Defiance unto *my* poor *Endeavours* to bring the Souls of men unto Heaven." . . . But at least the enemy was identifiable. From reports he had heard, Mather pieced together a picture of the Devil: "a short and a Black Man . . . no taller than an ordinary Walking-Staff," wearing "a High-Crowned Hat, with strait Hair, and had one Cloven-Foot."

In May 1692, at the advice of the clergy, Governor Phips appointed a special court of oyer and terminer in which those accused of witchcraft could be tried. This court was composed of merchants, public officials, and doctors. Most of the members were college graduates. There was not a lawyer among them, but this circumstance was not accounted important: college graduates were deemed sufficiently learned in the law to qualify as judges, and in any event, the problem of ridding the country of witches was thought to transcend the skill and erudition of any mere lawyer. Only the most pious, God-fearing men could cope with this assault.

In Salem witch trials, despite the strong sense of urgency and crisis, no precipitate action was taken. There was a three-month delay between the first accusations and the first trial. During this interval, the bodies of the accused were carefully examined for such telltale evidence of guilt as insensitive spots, supernumerary teats, warts, or moles. The physical checkup over, the accused were asked to recite the Lord's Prayer. If they stammered, stuttered, or missed a word, it was all up with them, for it was a well-known fact that the Devil could not get through the Lord's Prayer without stumbling. Inability to shed tears was likewise accounted an incriminating sign, since the Devil was incapable of feeling remorse for any of his misdeeds. Those who failed to clear themselves of suspicion were indicted and bound over for trial. Without legal counsel, they conducted their own defense — no easy task in view of the fact that the judges and jurors, who were all church members, were strongly inclined to regard them as guilty until proved innocent.

Among the accused was a backwoods preacher, the Reverend George Burroughs. Burroughs was alleged to be the "black man" who sounded the trumpet that summoned the witches to their rendezvous, and he was also accused of having successively murdered his two wives by incantation. The first witness against Burroughs was his own granddaughter! During his examination and trial, spectators cried out that he was biting them — and, wonderful to relate, marks made by his teeth were found on their arms even though he had not stirred from the dock. Evidence was presented that Burroughs had performed feats of running and weightlifting clearly beyond the powers of mortal man unless aided by the Devil.

For Cotton Mather, the clinching evidence against Burroughs was supplied by five witches from Andover who testified that he was their ringleader and that in that capacity he had presided over their infernal get-togethers. Thenceforth, Mather took a personal interest in seeing Burroughs brought to the gallows, unusual as it was for one clergyman to display such zeal for putting a halter around the neck of another wearer of the cloth.

Burroughs was duly convicted and sentenced to death. But as he was being prepared for the noose, he made a moving plea of innocence and recited the Lord's Prayer without making a single mistake, and the spectators were almost persuaded that Burroughs was not a wizard after all. At this point, Cotton Mather, mounted on a horse, proved that he was as effective an orator in the saddle as in the pulpit. He turned the crowd against Burroughs by pointing out that the condemned man was not really an ordained minister and that all the persons hitherto executed had died by a righteous sentence. Burroughs was strung up, and Cotton Mather rode home satisfied with having done a good day's work for the Lord.

A convicted witch could save herself by confessing; indeed, the object of the prosecution was not to kill witches but to extract confessions from them. Some of the accused took this easy way out, implicating others in their accounts of their dealings with the Devil. These confessions brought an ever-widening circle of people under suspicion. As in England, torture was not used to procure confessions, but wizard or witch could go to the gallows protesting his or her innocence or stubbornly refusing to speak.

Confession, while it usually saved a person's life, led to forfeiture of property. Giles Cory, who would have been found guilty in an ordinary court of law of nothing more serious than eccentricity, refused to answer his accusers when charged with entering into a compact with the Devil — in the hope thereby of preserving his estate for his heirs. By English law (not repealed until 1772), *peine forte et dure* — pressing by weights until a confession, or death, was forthcoming — was prescribed for those who stood mute. The weights were placed upon Cory, and after several days of torture, he died without opening his lips. At that incredible cost, he made it possible for his heirs to inherit his property.

Salem witchcraft was not merely the result of a welling up of ignorance, superstition, and fear from the depths of society. The clergy, the magistrates (including Governor Phips himself), and educated people in general shared the conviction of the most ignorant and deluded people that they were witnessing an outbreak of "horrible Enchantments and Possessions" instigated by Satan.

As long as the accusations were made against friendless old women and people of low degree, the clergy hallooed on the witch-hunters and sanctified the good work by quoting the injunction of the Book of Exodus: "Thou shalt not suffer a witch to live." In the trials, every kind of "evidence" — hearsay, gossip, old wives' tales — was admitted provided that it indicated the guilt of the accused. Some of this so-called evidence went back many years and obviously originated in personal spite. None of the defendants had counsel to raise objections to the admission of this kind of evidence or, indeed, to question the legality of the procedure or the jurisdiction of the court. As a result, there was no one to contest the legality of "spectral evidence."

In their confessions, or in giving evidence on the witness stand, many people alleged that they had been approached by people who passed as respectable members of society yet who now appeared in the guise of the Devil's agents urging their victims to sign the Devil's book and to commit other enormities. This was "spectral evidence," and if it were indiscriminately admitted to be valid, there was obviously no limit to the number of people who might be accused of witchcraft. The weighty question raised by spectral evidence was whether or not the Devil could assume the shape of an innocent person or whether or not every person who appeared to the afflicted actually served the Devil's purposes.

When their opinion was asked, the Mathers recommended that the judges observe "a very critical and exquisite caution" lest they be taken in by the Devil's legerdemain. Caution was especially important, they warned, in cases of "persons formerly of an unblemished reputation." "It was better for a guilty witch to live," said Increase Mather, "than for an innocent person to die." Cotton Mather admitted that the Devil might, by God's permission, appear in the shape of an innocent person, but he thought that this permission was rarely given.

In essence, Cotton Mather took the position that spectral evidence merely offered grounds for suspicion and, at most, a presumption of guilt but that corroborative evidence was required before a verdict could be rendered. The immediate danger, as he saw it, was that evil spirits would confuse the judges by appearing in the guise of innocent people, thereby permitting bona fide witches to escape scot-free. Chief Justice Stoughton, much as he revered the Mathers, did not accept their views on the admissibility of spectral evidence. In his opinion, the fact that the Devil assumed the form of a respectable individual, even though he was a pillar of the community, must mean that that individual had sold his soul, for, he declared, the Devil could not impersonate an innocent man or woman. He therefore instructed the jury that "as the Devil had appeared in the form of many of the accused, according to the eye-witnesses there, the defendants must be guilty." This instruction resulted in the conviction of several of the accused.

Nor did the people follow the Mathers in drawing these fine distinctions regarding the admissibility of spectral evidence. To them, any person who took the form of a specter must be an agent of Satan. In consequence, Massachusetts was gripped by a reign of terror. Ties of friendship and of blood ceased to matter. It was a case of every man for himself and the Devil take the hindmost. Wives testified against their husbands; children charged their parents with practicing witchcraft; a wife and daughter gave evidence against their husband and father in order to save themselves; and a seven-year-old girl helped send her mother to the gallows. When two young men would not confess, they were tied together by the neck until they accused their own mother. The roll of specters began to read like a *Who's Who* of New England. Captain John Alden, the eldest son of John and Priscilla Alden, was accused of being a wizard on the strength of spectral evidence, but the resourceful captain escaped from jail. Dudley Bradstreet, the son of a former governor, fled the colony before he could be brought to trial. The wife of the Reverend John Hale, secretary of the colony of Connecticut, was denounced as a witch, and one woman who was hung at Salem was a church member. Cotton Mather himself was not safe: in October 1693, a young woman swore that Mather's image threatened and molested her. "I cried unto the Lord," Mather wrote in his Diary, "for the Deliverance of my *Name*, from the Malice of Hell." Thus the work of casting out devils seemed likely to lead to the depopulation of Massachusetts. Who would be alive to hang the last witch?

Clearly, events were escaping from the control of the clergy and magistrates. Witch-hunting had reached the height of mass hysteria: the people clamored for more victims, and no one was safe from their zeal and fear.

To add to the danger, although Salem Village continued to be "the Chief Seat of these Diabolical Vexations," witches began to expand their operations until all Massachusetts reeled under "the horrible Assaults made by the Invisible World." The citizens of Gloucester, expecting to be attacked by an army of witches, took refuge in a stockade. In Andover, where an epidemic was blamed on witches, more than 50 people were accused of having had dealings with the Devil. One of the magistrates who dared to defy public opinion by refusing to institute proceedings against the suspects was himself accused of sorcery. But the mania was short-lived: one of the accused instituted action for defamation of character against his accusers. "This wonderfully quenched zeal," it was observed, "the accusers saw *his* spectre no more."

By September 22, 1692, the Salem judges had tried 27 suspects, one-third of them church members; all had denied being witches. All 27 had been sentenced to death, and of this number 19 had been hanged and 1 pressed to death. A man accused of bewitching a dog barely escaped with his life, but the dog, presumably possessed by devils, was killed. None of the 50 who confessed that they were witches had been executed; 100 persons accused of being witches were in jail awaiting trial; and an additional 200 had been accused but had not yet been imprisoned. Two judges had resigned from the court of oyer and terminer to protest the course the proceedings had taken. Among the suspects were Lady Phips, the wife of the Governor of the province, and the Reverend Samuel Willard of Boston, the president of Harvard College. Willard was under suspicion because he had questioned some of the evidence presented at the trials.

On September 22, 1692, at the advice of the clergy, now thoroughly alarmed by the use to which spectral evidence was being put, Governor Phips suspended the proceedings of the court of oyer and terminer. In December the accused were brought before the Superior Court for trial. Spectral evidence was sparingly admitted, with the result that of the 52 persons brought to trial, 49 were acquitted. Only three were found guilty and condemned, but Phips first reprieved them and then granted a general pardon to all under suspicion. In 1957, the Massachusetts Legislature adopted a resolution absolving all the Salem witches of wrongdoing.

Chief Justice Stoughton bitterly lamented the decision to call a halt to the trials: "We were in a way to have cleared the land of them," he said. "Who it is that obstructs the cause of justice I know not; the Lord be merciful to this country!"

It is ironical that Cotton Mather, who wished to be known above all as a man of God and a do-gooder, should be remembered chiefly for his part in the Salem witch trials and therefore held to be typical of all that was most narrow, bigoted, and repellent in Puritanism — the very epitome of the black-frocked, bluenosed zealot. He was by no means the most remorseless and bloodthirsty of the witch-hunters; indeed, his position on spectral evidence marks him as a moderate and a stickler for the observance of legal formalities. The people, and some of the clergy, demanded more witch trials and more executions, but Mather tried to calm the storm he had helped create. In his poem dealing with Salem witchcraft, Longfellow makes Mather say:

> Be careful. Carry the knife with such exactness, That on one side no innocent blood be shed By too excessive zeal, and, on the other, No shelter given to any work of darkness.

Yet Cotton Mather did not question the justice of the verdicts handed down at Salem, nor did he doubt that all who had been executed were guilty. Those who asked God to attest to their innocence were guilty, in his opinion, of "monstrous impudence." Lest it be supposed that innocent people had been condemned on the basis of inadequate evidence, Mather wrote a book entitled *Wonders of the Invisible World* (1692). Yet Mather was not as sure as he professed to be that justice had been done: in 1696, he recorded in his diary his fear that God was angry with him for "not appearing with Vigor enough to stop the proceedings of the Judges, when the Inextricable Storm from the Invisible World assaulted the Country."

The period of the Salem witchcraft marked the last occasion on which witches and wizards were executed in the colonies, but the belief in witchcraft did not end, nor did the indictment and trial of suspects stop. In Virginia in 1705, a woman was accused of practicing witchcraft. The court ordered that her body be examined for witch marks and that she be subjected to the trial by water. The incriminating marks were found, and she floated while bound — strong evidence of guilt. Nevertheless, she was not tried as a witch, nor, for that matter, was she given an opportunity to clear her reputation.

Nevertheless, even during the trials at Salem, doubts had been expressed by one of the judges and by some clergymen regarding the guilt of some of the condemned. Not, however, that they doubted the existence of the Devil and of witchcraft: their reservations extended only to the kinds of evidence held admissible by the court. Yet the feeling gained ground that New England lay under the heavy indictment of having shed innocent blood. For this reason, some of the jurors and witnesses publicly repented their part in the proceedings at Salem. In 1697, Judge Samuel Sewall stood before his congregation and acknowledged his "blame and shame . . . asking pardon of men, and especially desiring prayers that God, who has unlimited authority, would pardon that sin and all others his sins." On the other hand, Chief Justice Stoughton went to his death insisting that he had been in the right.

It was the educated laity rather than the clergy who took the lead in discrediting witchcraft. In 1700, Robert Calef, a Boston merchant, published *More Wonders of the Invisible World,* an attack upon Cotton Mather and witchcraft. Calef believed that a great deal of innocent blood had been shed at Salem, and he held Cotton Mather primarily responsible for it. The girls who had started the frenzy he called "a parcel of possessed, distracted, or lying Wenches, accusing their Innocent Neighbours." Cotton Mather denounced Calef's book as "a firebrand thrown by a madman," and Increase Mather, as president of Harvard College, ordered the book publicly burned in the College Yard.

The eighteenth-century Enlightenment completed the rout of witchcraft. Science shifted the attention of educated men from the supernatural to the natural world, thereby resuming a process which, having begun with the Renaissance, had been interrupted by the Reformation. Satan suffered the second of the two great disasters that befell him in his long and checkered career: having been cast out of Heaven, his power to control human events now began to be questioned. In short, Satan lost the thing upon which his power over men had always depended — his credibility. Witchcraft, after a long and bloody history, was relegated to the ignominious status of a mere superstition, and the thousands of men and women who had perished in the flames or on the scaffold were seen to have been the victims of a great delusion.

STUDY GUIDE

1. In the opening section of this essay, Miller suggests certain broad social conditions that are likely to exist in a country in which witch-hunting arises. What are these conditions, and to what extent did they exist in Massachusetts in the 1690s?

2. Miller says witch-hunting died out, not because people no longer believed in witchcraft, but because they doubted the tests used to discover witches. What were these tests? Which were used in the Salem trials and which were not?

3. The special court appointed in Salem had no lawyers on it, though witchcraft was a crime. On the other hand, clergymen played a prominent role in advising the court and in other respects. Can you think of ways in which the participation of trained attorneys might have affected the evidence, the examination of witnesses, or the outcome? Or would the lawyers, in that society, have acted much the way laymen did?

4. Summarize the role played by Cotton Mather in the affair.

5. Some modern cults embody elements of satanic worship and witchcraft; others do not, but some of the psychological motivation of the cultists may be similar to that exhibited at Salem. Considering such recent phenomena

as the Moonies and the mass suicide at Jonestown, how do you explain the
psychology of the modern cult member?

BIBLIOGRAPHY

The editors selected the preceding excerpt from John C. Miller's book because, in a relatively brief space, it presents a balanced view of the many
different facets of the witchcraft affair. There are, however, a number of more
specialized books that you might like to investigate. One of the best short
accounts of the affair ever written is by Marion L. Starkey, *The Devil in
Massachusetts: A Modern Inquiry into the Salem Witch Trials* * (New York,
1949). More recently, there have been a number of books and articles, each
with a distinctive point of view. Chadwick Hansen, in *Witchcraft at Salem* *
(New York, 1969), argues that the symptoms described by the bewitched suggest that they were suffering from hysteria. Making use of psychological
theory, John Demos suggested that the accusers — many of whom were ado-
lescent girls — exhibited an Electra complex against the older women accused
of witchcraft in "Underlying Themes in Witchcraft of Seventeenth-Century
New England," *American Historical Review* LXXV (1969–70). Still another
suggestion by Linnda R. Caporeal — which appeared both in *Science,* Vol.
192, April 2, 1976, and in *Horticulture Magazine* (Fall 1976) — was that some
of the rye grain in the community was contaminated by the fungus ergot. The
hallucinations and other symptoms of the bewitched, Caporeal argued, were
owing to a disease called convulsive ergotism.

While each of these explanations can be argued quite logically, it is difficult
to find evidence to prove hysteria, psychological anxiety, or ergotism. Historians have been more receptive to a recent study that suggests that the affair
arose because of religious and social-economic conflicts within the small
village. In *Salem Possessed: The Social Origins of Witchcraft* * (Cambridge,
Mass., and London, Eng., 1974), Paul Boyer and Stephen Nissenbaum examined disputes over land and other matters to argue this position. The same
two authors edited the first of the following two anthologies, which will give
you some flavor of the times: *Salem-Village Witchcraft: A Documentary
Record of Local Conflict in Colonial New England* (Belmont, Calif., 1972);
and David Levin, *What Happened in Salem?* * 2nd ed. (New York, 1960).
There are books on witchcraft in other colonies and Europe which are helpful
in affording a comparative view of the Salem outbreak.

Naturally, witchcraft should be understood within the broader context of
American religious and social life. A number of the books mentioned in the
bibliographies following the readings by Thomas J. Wertenbaker (Reading
No. 2) and Charles A. Johnson (Reading No. 9) may be helpful. Most significant, however, are studies that deal with the great Puritan movement of the
early seventeenth century and the revival movement known as the Great
Awakening that followed some decades after the witchcraft scare had abated.
Both of these movements have a very extensive literature, which cannot be
listed here. Any college library, however, is likely to have some of the key
studies by Perry Miller, Edmund Morgan, Larzer Ziff, David E. Stannard, and

others on Puritanism. Books by Edwin S. Gaustad, Wesley M. Gewehr, Clarence C. Goen, and Charles H. Maxson cover the Great Awakening in the New England, Middle, and Southern colonies. The bibliography of an American history textbook will list many of the titles of these works.

* Asterisk indicates book is available in a paperback edition.

"I Am Not Twenty" by Horace Doolittle, 1804. Doolittle was twelve when he made this etching.

5

EDMUND S. MORGAN

Colonial Women

As children, most of us take marriage and the family very much for granted, as a part of the natural order of things. Eventually, we may come to wonder just how natural matrimony is, whether or not people are naturally monogamous, and whether marriage exists because of love or social necessity. Several factors account for the heightened skepticism about marriage in recent years. One, of course, is the rising divorce rate. Furthermore, the romantic conception of love and traditional views of the biological and emotional differences between the sexes have been seriously questioned.

Anthropology, biology, psychology, and other disciplines are contributing to a better understanding of the relationships of men and women and to a clearer perspective of marriage as a social institution. History may also be useful, since it can assist us in perceiving the common elements — as well as the changes that have taken place — in courtship and marriage across the ages.

As was the case with most colonial institutions, marital attitudes and practices in British America were heavily influenced by English and continental European customs. But in this sphere — as in their language, their government, and their class attitudes — the colonists found that what they had brought across the Atlantic slowly and subtly changed. Comparing American patterns with those of Europe in either the eighteenth or the twentieth century might lead one to think that the similarities in marriage and family life are greater than the differences. But in both periods, one can also see the development in this country of some special patterns of courtship and marriage. Indeed, there were differences in attitude and practice between the colonial South and New England, as well as between different classes of people within a single region.

In the following selection, Edmund S. Morgan writes of courtship, marriage customs, and husband-wife relations in colonial Virginia. In the relative isolation of the rural society he describes, marriage and the family may have had a much greater importance in the lives of people than did schools, government, or even religion. In contrast to Calvinistic New England, Virginia's religious life was Anglican and lacking in vigor. This may have softened the character of male-female relationships in that region, or perhaps these relationships simply reflected the absence in the South of that concern for discipline and authority we find among many New England Puritans. Still another possibility is that Morgan's portrayal of marriage in the South is somewhat romanticized.

For most young people getting married was simple enough. The couple discovered one another in the usual ways, obtained the consent of their parents, had the banns published in the parish church, and were married by the local minister. They could forget their parents' consent — as far as the law was concerned — if the girl was over sixteen and the boy was twenty-one, but of course it was not good taste for children to proceed in these matters without their parents' advice. Custom in Virginia demanded what in some of the northern colonies the law required, that a man get the consent of a girl's parents before he presumed to propose marriage. Marriage was not entirely a private affair: it was family business, and the other members of a family had a right to say something about who should be admitted to their circle. However, the small farmers and artisans who made up the great majority of the population of Virginia gave their children a broad freedom in these matters. A poor man with a large family could not expect to leave much to his children when he died, nor could he afford to provide his daughter with a dowry or his son with a marriage portion. His children would have to make their way in the marriage mart as best they could; if they fell in love with other boys and girls who owned as little property as themselves, no one would be a loser by the match. It was a matter of courtesy and decency for them to consult their parents, but where no great fortunes were at stake on

From *Virginians at Home* by Edmund S. Morgan. Copyright 1952 by Colonial Williamsburg, Inc., Williamsburg, Virginia. Reprinted by permission of Holt, Rinehart and Winston, Inc.

either side there was little reason for parents to stand in the way of their children's wishes.

For the children of wealthier families, in Virginia as in every other part of the world, marriage was less simple. Boys and girls who could expect to come into an inheritance were not allowed to share their fortune with anyone who happened to please their fancy. They must take care to maintain and increase the portion allotted them. An eighteenth-century New Englander put the central problem of marriage eloquently if bluntly when he wrote that there was little to be said about marriage except this, that "if a man should be [so] unhapy [as] to dote upon a poore wench (tho' otherwise well enough) that would reduce him to necessity and visibly ruine his common comforts and reputation, and at the same time there should be recommended to him a goodly lass with aboundation of mony which would carry all before it, give him comfort, and inlarge his reputation and intrest, I would certainly, out of my sense of such advantage to my friend, advise him to leave the maid with a short hempen shirt, and take hold of that made of good bag holland." . . .

Since wisdom has never been the distinguishing mark of youth, the parents of families in the higher ranks of society frequently took an active part in planning their children's marriages. A man who had spent a lifetime in accumulating a fortune did not wish to see his son squander it on a maid with a short, hempen shirt, nor did he wish to see his daughter hand it over to a man who could not otherwise support her in a manner befitting her birth. Moreover, parents who had a position of dignity to maintain did not wish to be disgraced by connections with persons of ill fortune or ill repute. Sometimes parents arranged the whole business, with the children playing a comparatively passive role. More often, probably, a boy informed his father that some young lady had caught his fancy, whereupon the father, if he approved, would negotiate with the girl's parents. Thus Thomas Walker wrote to Colonel Bernard Moore:

Dear Sir: May 27th, 1764

My son, Mr. John Walker, having informed me of his intention to pay his addresses to your daughter, Elizabeth, if he should be agreeable to yourself, lady and daughter, it may not be amiss to inform you what I feel myself able to afford for their support, in case of an union. My affairs are in an uncertain state, but I will promise one thousand pounds, to be paid in 1766, and the further sum of two thousand pounds I promise to give him; but the uncertainty of my present affairs prevents my fixing on a time of payment. The above sums are all to be in money or lands and other effects, at the option of my son, John Walker.

I am Sir, your humble servant,

THOMAS WALKER

Colonel Moore replied the next day:

> Dear Sir: May 28, 1764
>
> Your son, Mr. John Walker, applied to me for leave to make his addresses
> to my daughter, Elizabeth. I gave him leave, and told him at the same time
> that my affairs were in such a state that it was not in my power to pay him
> all the money this year that I intended to to give my daughter, provided he
> succeeded; but would give him five hundred pounds more as soon after as I
> could raise or get the money, which sums you may depend I will most punctu-
> ally pay to him.
>
> I am, sir, your obedient servant,
>
> BERNARD MOORE

Probably not all negotiations were as smooth as these. Evidence from other colonies suggests that parents frequently bargained over the amounts to be given their children with all the enthusiasm they might have devoted to a horse trade. Samuel Sewall of Boston recorded in his laconic style an account of how he arranged his daughter's marriage with Joseph Gerrish: "Dine with Mr. Gerrish, son Gerrish, Mrs. Anne. Discourse with the Father about my Daughter Mary's Portion. I stood for making £550.doe: because now twas in six parts, the Land was not worth so much. He urg'd for £600. at last would split the £50. Finally Febr. 20. I agreed to charge the House-Rent, and Difference of Money, and make it up £600."

In Virginia as in New England there seems to have been a rule of thumb by which such bargaining was regulated: the girl's parents were expected to contribute about half of what the boy's parents did. Thus in 1705 Daniel Parke, a Virginian residing in London, wrote back to John Custis, whose son was courting Parke's daughter in Virginia:

> Sir: I received yours relating to your son's desire of marrying my daughter,
> and your consent if I thought well of it. You may easily inform yourself that
> my daughter Frances will be heiress of all the land my father left which is not
> a little nor the worst. My personal estate is not very small in that country,
> and I have but two daughters, and there is no likelihood of my having any
> more, as matters are, I being obliged to be on one side of the ocean and my
> wife on the other. I do not know your young gentleman, nor have you or he
> thought fit to send an account of his real and personal effects; however, if my
> daughter likes him, I will give her upon her marriage with him, half as much
> as he can make it appear he is worth. . . .

. . . If a boy or girl were under age, it was possible to prevent a marriage, but even then a couple might elope and persuade some gullible minister that they were of age. Occasionally the patrons of the *Virginia Gazette* read advertisements like the one inserted by Benjamin Bowles on August 27, 1756:

> Whereas *Sarah Holman,* a Niece of mine, under Age, and to whom I am
> Guardian, hath lately made an Elopement from me, and, as I believe, with
> an Intent to marry one *Snead* (alias *Crutchfield*) and as I think it will be

greatly to her Disadvantage, this is to give Notice to all County-Court Clerks not to grant them Marriage License, and to all Ministers not to marry them by Publication of Banns. I not knowing what Part of the Colony they may resort to, to accomplish their Design, am obliged to make Use of this Method to prevent them.

Doubtless most boys and girls who had been brought up in the elegant manner were content to abide by the rules of the game and seek their mates among those who were as genteel — and as wealthy — as themselves. There were plenty of opportunities for the children of the first families to meet each other at the balls and entertainments which formed part of the high life of colonial Virginia. Probably many a match began in the formal banter which passed between couples engaged in the steps of a minuet or a country dance. The gentleman would pour out a string of extravagant compliments while the lady blushed and protested. Soon perhaps the gentleman would come visiting the lady at her father's plantation, and if his character and financial qualifications were in order, might eventually ask for her hand. At this point both he and the lady were obliged to follow a ritual which required considerable dramatic skill. Though everyone agreed that marriage must be a union of properly proportioned worldly fortunes, nevertheless convention demanded that the actual proposal take place in an atmosphere of almost religious formality. The lady must be approached with fear and trembling as a kind of saint, the lover prostrating himself either literally or figuratively before her, while she betrayed great surprise and distress at the whole idea of marriage and agreed to consider the proposition only after much protestation. . . .

The ladies occasionally objected to the conventions which demanded that they act without regard to their inner feelings. The *Virginia Gazette* on October 22, 1736, carried a set of verses entitled "The Lady's Complaint," in which the author deplored the greater freedom which custom gave to men.

> They plainly can their Thoughts disclose,
>   Whilst ours must burn within:
> We have got Tongues, and Eyes, in Vain,
>   And Truth from us is Sin.
>
>   . . .
>
> Then Equal Laws let Custom find,
>   And neither Sex oppress;
> More Freedom give to Womankind,
>   Or give to Mankind less.

Perhaps it was the author of these verses who a week later inserted this advertisement in the paper:

WHEREAS *a Gentleman, who, towards the latter End of the Summer, usually wore a Blue Camlet Coat lin'd with Red, and trim'd with Silver, a Silver-lac'd Hat, and a Tupee Wig, has been often observ'd by* Miss Amoret, *to look very languishingly at her the said* Amoret, *and particularly one Night during the last Session of Assembly, at the Theatre, the said* Gentleman *ogled her in such a Manner, as shew'd him to be very far gone; the said* Miss Amoret *desires the* Gentleman *to take the first handsome Opportunity that offers, to explain himself on that Subject.*

N.B. She believes he has very pretty Teeth.

Such boldness was certainly bad taste, unless, as is quite likely, the advertisement was merely a printer's prank. In any case the ladies' complaints brought no change in custom. It was never leap year in colonial Virginia, and a self-respecting young woman of quality had to play out the role of aloof and unwilling goddess before she could gracefully take the part of a bride.

The wedding itself, when it finally occurred, was performed by the local minister according to the form prescribed in the Book of Common Prayer. It commonly took place at the home of the bride, usually in the afternoon. The friends of the bride prepared a handsome feast to follow the ceremony. There might also be a ball, and since balls frequently lasted for more than a single evening, the couple might have to put up with the wedding guests for several days.

The humbler people of Virginia, who had no time for the elaborate ritual of a genteel courtship, made as much of the wedding celebration as their wealthier neighbors did. In the frontier region known as the Valley, the German farmers who had come down from Pennsylvania used a wedding as the occasion for a frolic in which most of the community took part. In fact if neighbors or relations were not invited, they might take revenge by cropping the manes and tails of the horses of the wedding company while the festivities were in progress. Here, as in the Tidewater region, the wedding took place at the home of the bride. On the morning of the appointed day the friends of the groom, both male and female, assembled at the home of his father, in time to reach the home of the bride by noon. The whole party rode together with great hilarity until within a mile of their destination. Then at a given signal they raced to the bride's home at full gallop, the first to arrive winning "black Betty," a bottle of liquor.

The ceremonies took place at noon and were followed by a feast, during which the guests attempted to steal the bride's shoe. Four of the prettiest girls and four of the handsomest young men were appointed to defend her, each of them being presented with a beautifully embroidered white apron as a badge of office. Since these "waiters" had not only to defend the bride but also to serve the dinner, it was not impossible for a dexterous guest to succeed in stealing the shoe. If this happened the bride had to pay a forfeit of a bottle of wine and could not dance until she had done so.

The dancing, which began as soon as the dinner was over, lasted until morning. About nine or ten o'clock in the evening, when the music and dancing were in full swing, a party of young ladies quietly took the bride up a ladder to the loft and put her to bed. A delegation of young men then took the groom up. There followed a ceremony called throwing the stocking, in which the bridesmaids stood in turn at the foot of the bed, their backs toward it, and threw a rolled stocking over their shoulders at the bride. The groom's attendants did the same, aiming at the groom. The first to succeed in hitting the mark was supposed to be the next one married. Toward morning refreshments, including "black Betty," were sent up the ladder to the bridal pair. The festivities did not end with the morning but continued until the company were so exhausted that they needed as many days to recuperate as they had spent in reveling.

When the last of the guests had departed and the bride accompanied her husband to the home he had prepared for her, she had to face the hard work which marriage entailed. If her husband was a simple farmer, living remote from shops and stores and seeing very little money in the course of a year anyhow, her hands would have to make many of the things that another woman could purchase and do the things another woman could have done for her. She would have to spin cotton, flax, and wool, weave and knit them, sew, look after the hogs and poultry, milk the cows, make butter and cheese, bake bread, clean the house, and get the meals, besides bearing and rearing children. Sometimes she had to do part of her husband's work as well as her own. At hay and harvest time she would swing a scythe and help to gather in the grain, in the spring she might stand behind a plow, and in summer she would help to trim the weeds with a hoe. She and her family would have plenty to eat, but except for a wedding celebration or a house-raising or a harvesting bee, there would be little time for anything but work.

If she lived in the Valley, the wife of a hard-working German farmer, she would probably live to see the land prosper and in later life, after the Revolutionary troubles had passed, might at least enjoy security. If she lived on the southern frontier of Virginia, the region adjoining North Carolina, we may judge that her life was much harder. According to William Byrd, the women of this region got little help from their husbands in keeping the family alive. Byrd described the men as lazy and shiftless: "They make their Wives rise out of their Beds early in the Morning, at the same time that they lye and Snore, till the Sun has run one third of his course, and disperst all the unwholesome Damps. Then, after Stretching and Yawning for half an Hour, they light their Pipes, and, under the Protection of a cloud of Smoak, venture out into the open Air; tho' if it happens to be never so little cold, they quickly return Shivering into the Chimney corner. When the weather is mild, they stand leaning with both their arms upon the cornfield fence, and gravely consider whether they had best go and take a Small Heat at the Hough [Hoe]: but generally find reasons to put it off till another time. Thus they loiter away their Lives, like Solomon's Sluggard, with their Arms across, and at the winding up of the Year Scarcely have Bread to Eat." Byrd came across one family without even a roof on their house, so that whenever it rained, they had to take refuge in a haystack.

Life on a great plantation was never like this, but not even the greatest of Virginia matrons could boast the leisure of a woman comparably situated today. Though she might have all the servants she could ask for, most of them would be unwilling workers, indentured servants who looked forward only to the day when they would be free or slaves who had nothing to gain by their service. To manage a large mansion with such a crew was no small task in itself. It meant constant attention to see that the jobs assigned to every servant were completed. Getting a meal on the table was a major operation, for the housewife never knew how many mouths she must feed. Hospitality demanded that anyone who passed the plantation, whether friend or stranger, be invited to dine, and guests might stay for several days or even weeks. The Carter family at Nomini Hall consumed in one year 27,000 pounds of pork, 20 beeves, 550 bushels of wheat (to say nothing of corn, which was eaten exclusively by servants and slaves), 4 hogsheads of rum, and 150 gallons of brandy.

On special occasions, when the family gave a ball or entertainment for the neighboring planters, the preparations were on a grand scale, and the lady herself might work in the kitchen along with her helpers. Little Sally Fairfax recorded in her diary on December 26, 1771, that "mama made 6 mince pies, and 7 custards, 12 tarts, 1 chicking pye, and 4 pudings for the ball." There were doubtless many times when the mistress of a plantation felt that it was easier to do a job herself than entrust it to an irresponsible servant. [Philip] Fithian noted one evening after a visit to a neighboring plantation, that "When we returned about Candlelight, we found Mrs. Carter in the yard seeing to the Roosting of her Poultry." Mrs. Carter also managed the gardens which supplied her kitchen, and though there is no record in her particular case, it is known that on most plantations the lady of the house also took care of the sick, both white and colored.

Although her household duties required active hard work, the mistress of a plantation was obliged to maintain all the appearance of leisure. Fithian was much impressed with Mrs. Carter's grand manner. She was entirely accustomed, he said, to "the formality and Ceremony which we find commonly in high Life." Not only did she preside graciously over the dinner table, but she dressed with precise elegance. Fithian was perceptibly shocked one day, after he had been with the family for several months, by what he described as "a Phenomenon, Mrs. Carter without Stays!" Fashion demanded that ladies of Mrs. Carter's position be constantly enclosed in stays; not only that, but they must wear clothes which were clearly designed to hamper any sort of useful activity. This was the era of hoop petticoats, which made so simple a task as walking from one room to another a problem in navigation. At the time of Fithian's employment by the Carters, a memorable achievement of the clothes' designers was exhibited by an English governess who had just arrived on a neighboring plantation: Fithian describes with dismay the extent to which the latest fashion would cut the ladies off from the outside world: "Her *Stays* are suited to come up to the upper part of her shoulders, almost to her chin; and are swaithed round her as low as they can possibly be, allowing Her the liberty to walk at all: To be sure this is a vastly modest Dress!"

There were evidently compensations to being a farmer's wife. While Mrs. Carter sweltered in her stays in the Virginia summer, Molly, who worked beside her husband with a hoe, had at least the advantage of wearing only a linen shift and petticoat, with feet, hands, and arms bare.

The lady who graced the table of a Tidewater mansion and the housewife who cooked by the fire in a one-room cabin were equally subject to their husbands' authority. A single woman might own property, contract debts, sue and be sued in court, and run her own business, but a married woman, so far as the law was concerned, existed only in her husband. If he died before she did, she was entitled to a life interest in a third of his property, but during his lifetime he had the use of all her real property and absolute possession of all her personal property. He even owned the clothes on her back and might bequeath them in his will. Though he was not given power of life and death over her, he was entitled to beat her for any faults she exhibited. He had the right to order the lives of her children, even to the point of giving directions in his will for their management after his death. Her duty was submission to whatever he commanded. When William Byrd III, absent in the armed services, directed his wife to send her ailing baby to her mother-in-law at Westover, she replied submissively, "I am very sorry you have limited Poor, sweet Otway, so that he has but a short time to stay with me. . . . But Sir, your Orders must be obeyed whatever reluctance I find thereby." The force of convention was strong upon this point, so strong that it could even overcome religious prejudice. In 1708 Ann Walker, an Anglican married to a Quaker, objected in court to having her children educated as Quakers, but the Court, while acknowledging her own freedom to worship as she chose, instructed her not to interfere in any way with the instruction of her children, even forbidding her to expound any part of the scriptures to the children without her husband's consent. Such complete support for the husband's authority is all the more remarkable in view of the fact that the Anglican Church was the established church of Virginia, to which all the members of the court doubtless belonged.

In the face of all this testimony, it may be rash to suggest that eighteenth-century Virginia had as great a share of henpecked husbands as any other society. Yet one may venture a guess that women found ways to assert their power in spite of all the laws and conventions with which the men sought to protect themselves. One gets an inkling of this from the account by William Byrd II of a visit to one of his overseers on a remote plantation. Byrd found many things out of order and reprimanded the man for his neglect. "I also let him know," says Byrd, "that he was not only to Correct his own Errors, but likewise those of his Wife, since the power certainly belong'd to him, in

Vertue of his Conjugal Authority. He Scratcht his head at this last Admonition, from whence I inferred that the Gray Mare was the better Horse."

It is hard to know in how many families the gray mare was the better horse. In Byrd's own family it was often touch and go as to who should have the upper hand. On May 23, 1970, he wrote in his diary "I had a great quarrel with my wife, in which she was to blame altogether; however I made the first step to a reconciliation, to [which] she with much difficulty consented." Six weeks later he wrote, "In the afternoon my wife and I had a terrible quarrel about the things she had come in [that is, things she had had imported from London] but at length she submitted because she was in the wrong," and he added with insufferable smugness, "For my part I kept my temper very well." He did not say, however, whether Mrs. Byrd's purchases were sent back to England. On October 12, the same year, he noted that "After we were in bed my wife and I had a terrible quarrel about nothing, so that we both got out of bed and were above an hour before we could persuade one another to go to bed again." The next year on February 5, when the family was preparing to go to Williamsburg, there was another quarrel because Mrs. Byrd wished to pluck her eyebrows. "She threatened she would not go to Williamsburg if she might not pull them; I refused, however, and got the better of her, and maintained my authority." Byrd evidently regarded this as something of a triumph. In spite of all the restrictions which bound a woman to the will of her husband, it seems not unlikely that the colonial dame wielded as great a control over her husband as any modern wife does over hers.

There was, as a matter of fact, a good reason why women should have had something of an advantage over men in colonial Virginia: women were a scarce commodity. The first settlers of Virginia had been men, adventurers out to better their fortunes in the New World. Once the settlement was established women were sent over by the shipload in order to make wives for the colonists, and later immigrants included women as well as men. But in any colonization men are apt to predominate; they go first to prepare the way. By the eighteenth century most of the inhabitants of Virginia were of native birth, but there was always a stream of immigrants pouring into the land, and among these always a preponderance of men, so that throughout the colonial period there were never enough women to go around. Those men who had been left out in the marital game of musical chairs were constantly on the lookout for wives. A girl seldom had the opportunity to get beyond her teens before she married, and she might marry even earlier. William Byrd wrote to a friend in England that his daughter Evelyn, aged twenty, was "one of the most antick [antique] Virgins he knew of. And a widow, it would appear, scarcely had time to attend her husband's funeral before another suitor would be after her.

In view of this scarcity of women it would not be surprising if the Virginia wife managed to exert more authority in the household than custom and law allowed her. There are many examples in the records of wives who displayed an independence altogether out of keeping with what the etiquette books demanded. There was Sarah Harrison, who married Dr. James Blair, the founder of the College of William and Mary. At her wedding when the minister reached the part of the ceremony where she was supposed to promise obedience to her husband, she said "No obey," upon which, according to the only account of the wedding that has been preserved, the minister, a Mr. Smith, "refused to proceed and the second time she said No obey and then he refused again to proceed. The third time she said No Obey; yet the said Mr. Smith went on with the rest of the ceremony."

Another hot-tempered wife who refused to bow before her husband's su-periority was Mrs. John Custis. She and her husband lived a hectic life at Arlington on the Eastern Shore, where they sometimes went for weeks with-out speaking to one another. On one occasion when they were out driving the husband proceeded to drive the carriage into Chesapeake Bay. When his wife asked him where he was going, he answered "To Hell, Madam," "Drive on," answered Mrs. Custis, "any place is better than Arlington." When he had carried his whim so far that the horses began to lose their footing, Mr. Custis turned toward shore again, saying to his wife, "I believe you would as lief meet the Devil himself, if I should drive to hell." "Quite true, Sir," she replied, "I know you so well I would not be afraid to go anywhere you would go." John Custis was sixty-four years old when his wife died, and seven years later, when he himself died, he had inscribed on his tomb:

> Beneath this Marble Tomb lies the Body
> of the *Hon. John Custis, Esq.*
> · · ·
> Aged 71 Years, and yet lived but seven years,
> which was the space of time he kept
> a bachelor's home at Arlington
> on the Eastern Shore of Virginia.

A wife who found her husband unbearable could not hope to escape from him by a divorce, for there was no court in Virginia with authority to grant one. The courts did occasionally arrange legal separations, in which the hus-band was required to provide the wife with an independent maintenance, but the common remedy for an unbearable husband was to run away, either to another man or back to mother. The *Virginia Gazette* often carried ad-vertisements inserted by irate husbands warning all merchants to grant no further credit to their eloped wives. Most of these advertisements give no clues as to why the wife had eloped, but occasionally a wife answered the advertisement with another which indicated that the fault was none of hers. When Filmer Moore announced the elopement of his wife, she countered with a notice which read:

> As my Husband *Filmer Moore* has publickly said his Mother would sooner live in a hollow Tree than with me, and has removed me to my Father's House, with Promise to come and live with me until I could be better pro-

vided for (which I can prove by divers Witnesses) but since has falsified his Word, and has perfidiously absented, and kept himself from me these six Months, without any Provocation from me (*so that he has eloped from me, and not I from him*) I do here declare that I intend to remain in the Situation he has placed me until he does come and account for the undeserved scandalous Treatment which I have received at his Hands. And as he has forbid all Persons from crediting or entertaining me, I can prove this to be only Spite and ill Will; for I have not run him in Debt one Farthing, nor removed from my Station wherein I was placed by him.

Elizabeth Moore

In spite of such episodes there is no reason to suppose that colonial Virginia had more than its share of unhappy marriages, and it certainly had its share of happy ones. Among the letters from the eighteenth century which have been preserved are many which passed between husband and wife and which reveal as much warmth and tenderness as anyone could ask. Theodorick Bland, absent with the American armies in New Jersey in the winter of 1777, wrote back to his wife: "For God's sake, my dear, when you are writing, write of nothing but yourself, or at least exhaust that dear, ever dear subject, before you make a transition to another; tell me of your going to bed, of your rising, of the hour you breakfast, dine, sup, visit, tell me of anything, but leave me not in doubt about your health. . . . Fear not, my Patsy — yes, 'you will again feel your husband's lips flowing with love and affectionate warmth.' Heaven never means to separate two who love so well, so soon; & if it does, with what transport shall we meet in heaven?"

STUDY GUIDE

1. What differences were there between wealthy, upper-class women and lower-class women with respect to: the formalities of courtship and marriage; their lives after they were married?

2. What was the legal position of women in relation to their husbands? What factors — in actual daily relations — modified this legal position?

3. How might the position of a slave woman have differed from that of any white woman in such matters as her relationship with her husband, her control of children, her supervision of her household, her ability to preserve her self-respect?

4. How might the life of a woman in more settled areas, such as Boston or Philadelphia, have differed from that of a woman living in the rural, agricultural society depicted by Morgan?

5. In what ways has the position of women in American society changed substantially since the period described by Morgan, and in what ways has it remained basically the same?

BIBLIOGRAPHY

The other chapters of Professor Morgan's book, on childhood, servants and slaves, houses, and holidays, are as well written and informative as the selection on marriage. A fuller work, with a great deal of fascinating detail, is Julia C. Spruill, *Women's Life and Work in the Southern Colonies* * (Chapel Hill, N.C., 1935). Another work by a woman historian, also written in the 1930s but not restricted to the southern colonies, is Mary S. Benson, *Women in Eighteenth-Century America: A Study of Opinion and Social Usage* (New York, 1935). Morgan also wrote a work on family life in New England, presenting a somewhat different picture from his study of Virginia: *The Puritan Family: Religion and Domestic Relations in Seventeenth Century New England,* * rev. ed. (New York, 1966); his chapter on husbands and wives is especially interesting. John Demos, *A Little Commonwealth: Family Life in Plymouth Colony* * (New York, 1970) is a fascinating study of nearly all aspects of family life — husband wife and parent-child relationships, housing, furnishings, and the psychology of life in the seventeenth century.

The women's liberation movement of our time and the revived interest of historians in the history of minority groups have led to a virtual explosion in the study of women's history. Much of the writing thus far has concerned women in nineteenth-century America; these books are cited in the bibliography following the selection by Barbara J. Berg (Reading No. 10). Two recent general studies of women in American history are Page Smith, *Daughters of the Promised Land: Women in American History* * (Boston, 1970) and Mary P. Ryan, *Womanhood in America from Colonial Times to the Present* * (New York, 1975). Some of Nancy F. Cott's *The Bonds of Womanhood: "Woman's Sphere" in New England, 1780–1835* * (New Haven, Conn., and London, Eng., 1977) sheds light on the colonial period. Linda G. De-Pauw, *Founding Mothers: Women in America in the Revolutionary Era* (Boston, 1975) deals directly with the eighteenth century, and Chapter 3 is a good study of male-female relations and women's rights.

The history of childhood and of the condition of the aged are both of considerable interest in understanding the family in America. The books by Morgan and Demos mentioned above have chapters describing how children were viewed and reared in the colonial period. Later views are examined in Joseph F. Kett, *Rites of Passage: Adolescence in America, 1790 to the Present* (New York, 1977). Studies of educational history are helpful in understanding attitudes toward children. Among the most interesting of many volumes on this subject are Lawrence A. Cremin, *American Education: The Colonial Experience, 1607–1786* (New York, 1970); Robert Middlekauff, *Ancients and Axioms: Secondary Education in Eighteenth-Century New England* (New Haven, Conn., 1963); and James Axtell, *The School upon a Hill: Education and Society in Colonial New England* * (New Haven, Conn., 1974). Axtell considers the social aspects of childbirth and the effects of the postnatal environment on the colonial child. Much less has been written about the aged in American society, but David H. Fischer has attempted a broad survey of social attitudes in his *Growing Old in America* * (New York, 1977).

* Asterisk indicates book is available in a paperback edition.

*"The Bostonians Paying the Excise-Man" by Philip Dawe, 1774,
shows the punishment of John Malcolm.*

6

WALLACE BROWN

Social War

One of the most elusive goals of the historian, and of the human mind in general, is objectivity. In our time, most historians recognize that, try as they may to avoid it, some prejudice and personal values are bound to creep into their thought and into the history they write. One illustration of this is in the difference in treatment that history accords to the winners and losers in any revolution. Rebels who fail don't get a very good press from historians, since their society is likely to denounce the revolutionary leaders as traitors or madmen. If the revolution succeeds, the same men may be celebrated as patriots and statesmen, while the ruling group that is overthrown is castigated as oppressive or corrupt.

Between 1765 and 1775, British colonial society developed some serious internal divisions and antagonisms. Upon the outbreak of war, provinces, towns, and families were split, and brother fought brother with all the hatred that civil war can engender. By 1783, as many as 80,000 people had been driven out of the colonies; farms and businesses of Loyalists were confiscated, and thousands of these British adherents were intimidated and mistreated. Many of them had been distinguished contributors to colonial society — governors, judges, ministers, farmers, craftsmen, and laborers. Had the British won the war, the names of Thomas Hutchinson, Joseph Galloway, William Franklin, and Jonathan Boucher would today be as celebrated as are John Adams, Thomas Jefferson, Patrick Henry, and John Hancock.

One question worth pondering is what American society may have lost by the exile of the Loyalists and the victory of the Patriot cause. A substantial reservoir of political talent and experience certainly evaporated, but among the many who cast their lot for independence was an extraordinary number of men of talent to take the Loyalists' places. More difficult to judge is the loss to American thought and culture. A number of Loyalists were able or distinguished scientists, artists, writers, and religious leaders who made their contributions in Canada or Europe rather than here. More important than such individuals was the effect of the break upon American political and constitutional thought, which — it has been argued — suffered the loss of a valid conservative tradition with the exile of the Loyalists.

Another question that has interested historians since the Revolution began is just what a Tory or Loyalist was. The simplest definition is that he was one who remained loyal to England. This raises the question of why they were loyal, whereas immediate neighbors of similar background and position became revolutionary leaders. Many answers to this question have been offered — that it was one's religion that made the difference, or one's wealth, age, occupation, national origins, or temperament. Yet for all the Loyalists who were influenced by such factors, there were at least as many men of the same class who chose the Patriot side.

Wallace Brown, a contemporary student of these questions, has made use of statistical techniques to try to determine the percentage of Loyalists of different occupations, religions, and so forth. Since the statistical parts of his studies are based on fragmentary records, they have been criticized by some historians. However, his book *The Good Americans,* from which the following selection is taken, is a general study of Loyalism that is less dependent upon statistics than his earlier work. Chapter 5 of *The Good Americans* presents a vivid account of the suffering that Loyalists endured during the American War for Independence. If few groups have since been subjected to such direct violence, the persecution of the Loyalists nonetheless reminds one of the fate of many another unpopular minority in later American history. And it should make us cautious about accepting only a "winner's" view of historical losers.

In November, 1777, the Continental Congress recommended the confiscation of Loyalist estates, a suggestion already made by Thomas Paine, and in some places already acted upon. All states finally amerced, taxed, or confiscated

Abridged by permission of William Morrow & Company, Inc., from *The Good Americans* by Wallace Brown. Copyright © 1969 by Wallace Brown.

much Loyalist property, and in addition New York and South Carolina taxed Loyalist property in order to compensate robbery victims. Some towns simply raffled off Tory property. Patriot officers requisitioned horses and supplies from Loyalists rather than Whigs, and, of course, there was much old-fashioned looting, particularly of the property of exiles. Like Henry VIII's dissolution of the monasteries, the disbursement of Loyalist property created a vested interest in revolution. Also, the device of trying partially to finance the war with traitors' wealth was naturally very popular, if of limited success.

Although the majority of active Loyalists suffered much loss of property, some attempted by various subterfuges to preserve their estates quite apart from having a wife or third party act as purchaser. One scheme was to make over one's property, or make a sham sale, to a sympathetic, moderate friend who had escaped suspicion.

Much commoner was the device used by exiles of leaving their wives or relatives behind in order to keep a foot in both camps. For example, Benjamin Pickman fled from Salem, Massachusetts, in 1775, but left his wife behind to look after their property, to which he returned ten years later. Some brothers may even have chosen opposite sides for such a reason. As the British claims commissioners commented on one split family, "it is possible that this may be a shabby family Compact . . . to preserve the property whether Great Britain or America prevailed."

The overall severity of the various laws against the Loyalists has been estimated as follows:

"Harshest" — New York, South Carolina.
"Harsh" — Massachusetts, New Jersey, Pennsylvania.
"Light" — Rhode Island, Connecticut, Virginia, North Carolina.
"Lightest" — New Hampshire, Delaware, Maryland, Georgia.

With some exceptions, notably Georgia, laws were harshest in states where Loyalists were most powerful, and as the war progressed, the purpose of the laws changed from conversion to "revenge and hate." Similarly, enforcement varied and was usually severest where danger was greatest and civil war bitterest.

A prominent Southern Tory reported that in Virginia, where the Loyalists were weak and little problem, the property of those who joined the British army went to their wives and children "on the Spot . . . as if the Father was dead," and he noted that his own wife "had never been molested but on the contrary treated with the utmost Kindness and Respect." Other Loyalists described being turned off their property with only the clothes on their backs.

But perhaps more typical was the fate of the Chandler family of Worcester, Massachusetts. Colonel John Chandler, a very prominent citizen of distinguished Massachusetts pedigree, dubbed "Tory John" and later in England the "Honest Refugee," fled from Boston with the British army to become a permanent, proscribed exile. For over two years his wife and family continued to enjoy their property undisturbed, until the Worcester Committee of Correspondence began a process that resulted in the confiscation of all but a third of their real and personal property, which third was reserved for Mrs. Chandler's use as long as she remained in the United States. Her husband did not return (he was forbidden to by an act of October, 1778), and on her death special legislation was needed to secure her property for her children.

A myriad of particularities could play a part in determining the extent of persecution. A well-liked or respected Tory (and there were a few such) might well escape, as might someone whose skills were especially valued, for example, a doctor. Influential but quiet Loyalists were more apt to avoid penalties than those of lower social standing or those more vociferous in their beliefs.

The zeal of the patriots could be extremely capricious and, as always with witch-hunts, frequently ridiculous and heavy-handed. One citizen was accosted for naming his dog "Tory," the implication being that a Tory was forced to lead a dog's life. In 1776 at Stratford, Connecticut, an Episcopal minister was brought before the local committee because he had officiated at a baptism where the child was named Thomas Gage. The committee viewed the action as a "designed insult" and censured the cleric. In the same state Zephaniah Beardslee reported that he was "very much abused" for naming his daughter Charlotte, after the queen. It may be noted that Beardslee, apparently a very serious Loyalist, had also been found drinking the king's health. The frequent persecution of Tories for this activity, however, is not as picayune as it seems, because toasts presuppose groups in taverns and the chance of Loyalist plots and associations. Thus, Abraham Cuyler held a gathering in Albany, New York, in June, 1776, that featured drinking and the singing of "God Save the King." At last the enraged Whig citizens crashed the party and carried the royal merrymakers off to jail. . . .

The results of Loyalism might simply be social ostracism — being sent to Coventry — as, for instance, happened to James Allen, who noted in his diary for February 17, 1777: "I never knew how painful it is to be secluded from the free conversation of one's friends"; and to George Watson, a mandamus councillor, when he entered a church at Plymouth, Massachusetts, and "a great number of the principal inhabitants left." Or it might mean serious loss of services, as when the blacksmiths of Worcester County, Massachusetts, refused to work for any Loyalists, their employees, or their dependents; or an economic boycott, as in Connecticut, where the local committee forbade "all Persons whatever viz. Merchants Mechanicks Millers and Butchers and Co. from supplying . . . John Sayre or Family with any manner of Thing whatever." Lawyers, teachers, doctors, apothecaries, and others often lost their customers and hence their livelihoods. Mathew Robinson, a Newport trader, from the first branded as "a Rank Torey," suffered several indignities, including the pulling down of his fences by a "multitude . . . under colour of laying out a Highway" and climaxing in 1781 when, after "*a New England Saint*" charged that Robinson "drank the King's Health, and damn'd the Congress and call'd them damn'd Rebels and Presbyterians," he was imprisoned by the rebels without examination, this being even "against their own Bill of Rights."

In many areas — for example, New York — the Loyalists were allowed to sell their property before departing, but such hurried, desperate sales were unlikely to net a fair price, and the result amounted to confiscation.

All wars and revolutions cause great mental strain and suffering, most of which goes unmeasured. The history of the Revolutionary era is liberally punctuated with stories of Loyalists who succumbed to melancholia, became mad, died, or committed suicide.

Alexander Harvey, a Charleston lawyer, wound up in a private English madhouse, having been "driven to Distraction" by his experiences as a Loyalist; George Miller, a North Carolina merchant whose fright had conquered his Loyalist principles, was thrown "into Convulsions" by the strain of serving in the American militia; Peter Harrison's death came after the shock of Lexington, and with it America lost its greatest colonial architect; several Loyalists, including the wife of William Franklin, simply died of "a Broken Heart"; the widow of Dr. Robert Gibbs of South Carolina recounted that the prospect of the loss of his property "so preyed upon his Spirits" that he died. Andrew Miller, of Halifax, North Carolina, was estranged from all his friends by his Loyalism, which literally killed him; others chose suicide — Millington Lockwood of Connecticut was wounded in the head, lost his reason, and drowned himself, while some years later, in London, after years of fruitless waiting for compensation, an unnamed, ruined Loyalist shot himself in despair, blaming an ungrateful country.

Although Americans at the time of the Revolution would clearly have found it odd, today one of the sharpest historical debates is over the question of how far the American Revolution was a *real* revolution. Even those historians who, noting the social dislocation, argue that the American Revolution was rather like the French Revolution stress the absence of the Terror. Mass executions there were not, a guillotine there was not, yet atrocities and terror there most certainly were. It is fitting that in the beginning the rebels "hoisted the Red Flag or Flag of Defence."

Leaving aside civil-war aspects such as the execution and maltreatment of prisoners and the burning of towns (by both sides: for example, the Americans fired Norfolk and Portsmouth; the British, Falmouth and Fairfield), we can cite a great range of fates that awaited the

Loyalists; they were catalogued by "Papinian" as tarring and feathering, rail riding,

> . . . chaining men together by the dozens, and driving them, like herds of cattle, into distant provinces, flinging them into loathsome jails, confiscating their estates, shooting them in swamps and woods as suspected Tories, hanging them after a mock trial; and all this because they would not abjure their rightful Sovereign, and bear arms against him.

Tarring and feathering (pine tar and goose feathers) became the classic Whig treatment of the Tories, and the British Government believed there was "no better proof of Loyalty" than suffering this punishment. A famous instance of it occurred in Boston on January 25, 1774, and is worth recounting in some detail.

At about eight o'clock in the evening a club-wielding mob milled along Cross Street. Their objective was John Malcolm, a distinguished but hot-tempered veteran of the French and Indian War, a native Bostonian, an ex-overseas merchant turned royal customs official, and a highly unpopular man for many reasons connected with both his personality (he was inordinately quarrelsome) and his job.

His recent arrival in Boston had been preceded by the unpopular news that in 1771 he had helped the governor of North Carolina against those reputedly Whiggish rebels known as the Regulators and that in October, 1773, he had officiously seized a brigantine at Falmouth (now Portland), Maine. Malcolm waited, ready and armed, behind barred doors. Undeterred, the mob raised ladders, broke an upstairs window, captured their prey, dragged him onto a sled, and pulled him along King Street to the Customs House, or Butcher's House, as it was popularly known, where the spectators gave three mighty cheers.

Although it was "one of the severest cold nights" of the winter, so cold that both Boston Harbor and even the very ink as it touched paper had frozen hard, the wretched man was put in a cart, stripped "to buff and breeches," and dealt the punishment of tarring and feathering, which American patriots were soon to convert into a major spectator sport. Malcolm, self-styled "Single Knight of the Tarr," as opposed to English Knights of the Garter, had already suffered the same indignity the year before for his conduct at Falmouth. He later claimed to be the first in America tarred for loyalty.

A contemporary description gives a good idea of how Malcolm and many others were treated:

> The following is the Recipe for an effectual Operation. "First strip a Person naked, then heat the Tar until it is thin, and pour it upon the naked Flesh, or rub it over with a Tar Brush, *quantum sufficit*. After which, sprinkle decently upon the Tar, whilst it is yet warm, as many Feathers as will stick to it. Then hold a lighted Candle to the Feathers, and try to set it all on Fire; if it

will burn so much the better. But as the Experiment is often made in cold Weather; it will not then succeed — take also an Halter and put it round the Person's Neck, and then cart him the Rounds."

Malcolm, flogged and otherwise molested at intervals, was paraded around various crowded streets with his neck in a halter and was finally taken to the Liberty Tree, where he refused to resign his royal office or to curse Thomas Hutchinson, the hated governor of Massachusetts.

The crowd then set off for the gallows on Boston Neck. On the way Malcolm gasped an affirmative when one of his tormentors asked if he was thirsty and was given a bowl of strong tea and ordered to drink the king's health. Malcolm was next told to drink the queen's health; then two more quarts of tea were produced with the command to drink to the health of the Prince of Wales.

"Make haste, you have nine more healths to drink," shouted one of the mob.

"For God's sake, Gentlemen, be merciful, I'm ready to burst; if I drink a drop more, I shall die," Malcolm implored.

"Suppose you do, you die in a good cause, and it is as well to be drowned as hanged," was the reply.

The nine healths, beginning with the "Bishop of Osnabrug," were forced down the victim's throat. Malcolm "turned pale, shook his Head, and instantly filled the Bowl which he had just emptied."

"What, are you sick of the royal family?"

"No, my stomach nauseates the tea; it rises at it like poison."

"And yet you rascal, your whole fraternity at the Custom House would drench us with this poison, and we are to have our throats cut if it will not stay upon our stomachs."

At the gallows the noose was placed in position around Malcolm's neck and he was threatened with hanging, but he still refused to submit, whereupon he was "basted" with a rope for a while, and finally, on pain of losing his ears, he gave in and cursed the governor. The stubborn, brave man was further carted around the town, made to repeat various humiliating oaths, and finally deposited back at his home just before midnight, half frozen, an arm dislocated, and, as he said, "in a most mizerable setuation Deprived of his senses." Five days later, bedridden and "terribly bruised," he dictated a complaint to Governor Hutchinson, which his injuries obliged him to sign with an X.

The frost and tar caused an infection that made his skin peel extensively. However, he was careful to preserve a piece of skin with the tar and feathers still adhering (the stuff was the very devil to get off), which he carried to England as proof of his sufferings when, somewhat recovered, he set sail on May 2, 1774, to try to gain compensation for his loyalty.

Another Tory punishment that became traditional was the gruesome riding on a rail that sometimes followed tarring and feathering, but was severe enough in itself. It consisted of jogging the victim roughly along on "a sharp rail" between his legs. The painful effect of these "grand Toory Rides," as a contemporary called them, can readily be imagined. Seth Seely, a Connecticut farmer, was brought before the local committee in 1776 and for signing a declaration to support the king's laws was "put on a Rail carried on mens Shoulders thro the Streets, then put into the Stocks and besmeared with Eggs and was robbed of money for the Entertainment of the Company."

Persecution of the Loyalists came in many forms. In 1778 prisoners in Vermont were made to tread a road through the snow in the Green Mountains. The wife of Edward Brinley was pregnant and waiting out her confinement at Roxbury, Massachusetts, accompanied by "a guard of Rebels always in her room, who treated her with great rudeness and indecency, exposing her to the view of their banditti, as a sight 'See a tory woman' and striped her and her Children of all their Linens and Cloths." Peter Guire, of Connecticut, was branded on the forehead with the letters *G. R.* (George Rex). Samuel Jarvis, also of Connecticut, related that the following treatment made his whole family very ill:

> That your Memorialist for his Attachment to constitutional Government was taken with his Wife and Famely, consisting of three Daughters and one little Son by a Mob of daring and unfeeling Rebels from his Dwelling House in the dead of Night Striped of everything, put on board Whale Boats and Landed on Long Island in the Month of August last about 2 oClock in the Morning Oblieging them to wade almost to their Middles in the Water.

Probably the best-known mobbing in Philadelphia was that of Dr. John Kearsley, whose widow finally submitted a claim to the commissioners. Kearsley, a leading physician, pill manufacturer, and horse dealer, was a pugnacious American with strong Loyalist views. He was seized by a mob in September, 1775, and had his hand bayoneted; then he was carried through the streets to the tune of "Rogue's March." Sabine reports that he took off his wig with his injured hand and, "swinging it around his head, huzzaed louder and longer than his persecutors." This display of spirit notwithstanding, he nearly died following this treatment, according to his widow. His house was later ransacked, he was arrested, and he finally died in jail.

Atrocious punishments of Loyalists were sometimes carried out by local authorities in semilegal fashion — it was noted that the tarring and feathering of a New York victim in 1775 "was conducted with that regularity and decorum that ought to be observed in all publick punishments." But just as often mobs, drumhead courts, and all the horrors of vigilante policing were found. Indeed it is possible that the term "lynch law" derives from Charles Lynch, a Bedford County, Virginia, justice of the peace who became renowned for his drastic, cruel action against neighboring Tories.

The number of Loyalists subjected to cruel, often extra-legal, punishments can only be estimated, and likewise the number of those murdered or executed "legally" will never be known, but no one familiar with the sources — Whig newspapers are full of accounts of executions — can doubt that it is substantial, although the statement by a New York Loyalist that the rebels "made a practice of hanging people up on a slight pretence" is no doubt an exaggeration. Probably only fear of reprisals kept numbers from being much larger than they were. The carrying out of the supreme penalty was usually reserved for some overt aid to the British such as spying, piloting ships, guiding troops to the attack, recruiting, counterfeiting.

One of the most notorious executions of a Loyalist was that of John Roberts, a native-born Pennsylvania Quaker, who had aided the British occupying forces in Philadelphia and rather foolhardily had not departed with them. His trial was in 1778, and even many Whigs petitioned the authorities for a pardon, but in vain. A contemporary described the situation thus:

> Roberts' wife, with ten children, went to Congress, threw themselves on their knees and supplicated mercy, but in vain. His behaviour at the gallows did honor to human nature. He told his audience that his conscience acquitted him of guilt; that he suffered for doing his duty to his Sovereign; that his blood would one day be demanded at their hands; and then turning to his children, charged and exhorted them to remember his principles, for which he died, and to adhere to them while they had breath. This is the substance of his speech; after which he suffered with the resolution of a Roman.

In 1792 the state of Pennsylvania restored Roberts' confiscated estate to his widow, Jane, a belated act of justice, for it seems Roberts had been a scapegoat, only one among so very many who had cooperated with the British. Roberts' behavior would doubtless have made him a remembered hero had he suffered for the other side. Similarly, in Connecticut, Moses Dunbar was tried and hanged for accepting a British commission and recruiting troops at about the same time that Nathan Hale suffered the same penalty. Connecticut honors Hale but forgets Dunbar. One of the more bizarre executions was reported by the *Boston Gazette* for November 3, 1777, under the date line Fishkill: "Last Thursday, one Taylor, a spy was hanged at Hurley, who was detected with a letter to Burgoyne, which he had swallowed in a silver ball, but by the assistance of a tartar emetic he discharged the same."

But perhaps more moving across the years than accounts of atrocities are the more pedestrian misfortunes of war. Women in particular are always the great sufferers, being separated from their husbands and sons, living in constant dread of bereavement. In 1780 Mary Donnelly petitioned the British authorities in New York for relief. Her husband had been serving on board a privateer when "about seven months ago as my youngest Child lay expireing in my Arms an account came of the Vessil being lost in a Storm." Mrs. Donnelly was now destitute, "frequently being affraid to open my Eyes on the Daylight least I should hear my infant cry for Bread and not have it in my power to relieve him. The first meal I had eat for three days at one time was a morsel of dry bread and a lump of ice."

On June 6, 1783, Phebe Ward, of East Chester, wrote to her husband Edmund, a native of the province of New York:

> Kind Husband
>
> I am sorry to acquant you that our farme is sold. . . .
> thay said if I did not quitt posesion that thay had aright to take any thing on the farme or in the house to pay the Cost of a law sute and imprisen me I have sufered most Every thing but death it self in your long absens pray Grant me spedy Releaf or God only knows what will be com of me and my frendsles Children
> thay say my posesion was nothing youre husband has forfeted his estate by Joining the British Enemy with a free and vollentary will and thereby was forfeted to the Stat and sold
> All at present from your cind and Loveing Wife
>
> > phebe Ward
> > pray send me spedeay anser.

One of the most pathetic stories of all concerns Filer Dibblee, a native-born lawyer, and his family. In August, 1776, they fled from Stamford to Long Island, but a few months later the rebels turned Dibblee's wife and five children "naked into the Streets," having stolen the very clothes from their backs as well has having plundered the house. The family fled to New York City, where Dibblee obtained sufficient credit to settle at Oyster Bay, Long Island, but in 1778 the rebels plundered the family a second time and carried Dibblee as prisoner to Connecticut, where he remained imprisoned six months until exchanged. With further credit the family established themselves at Westhills, Long Island, where they were "plundered and stripped" a third time; then came a move to Hempstead, Long Island, and in 1780 a fourth ravaging. Dibblee now, for the first time, applied for relief from the commander in chief and received about one hundred dollars. In 1783 the whole family moved to St. John, New Brunswick, where they managed to survive a rough winter in a log cabin, but Dibblee's "fortitude gave way" at the prospect of imprisonment for his considerable indebtedness and the fate his family would suffer as a consequence. The result was that he "grew Melancholy, which soon deprived him of his Reason, and for months could not be left by himself," and finally in March, 1784, "whilst the Famely were at Tea, Mr. Dibblee walked back and forth in the Room, seemingly much composed: but unobserved he took a Razor from the Closet, threw himself on the bed, drew the Curtains, and cut his own throat."

Shortly afterward the Dibblee house was accidentally burned to the ground, was then rebuilt by the heroic widow, only to be accidentally razed again the same year by an Indian servant girl.

It is not surprising that imprisonment and escape loom large in Loyalist annals. The most celebrated prison was in Connecticut at the Simsbury (now East Granby) copper mines, where the ruins still afford a dramatic prospect. The isolated and strongly Whig back country of Connecticut was considered a good spot to incarcerate important Loyalists from all over the Northern colonies, and the mines, converted into a prison in 1773, were ideal. The "Catacomb of Loyalty," to quote Thomas Anburey, or the "woeful mansion," to quote an inmate, contained cells forty yards below the surface, into which "the prisoners are let down by a windlass into the dismal cavern, through a hole, which answers the purpose of conveying their food and air, as to light, it scarcely reaches them." The mere threat of the "Mines" could make a Loyalist conform. One prisoner regarded being sent there as a "Shocking Sentence (Worse than Death)." The mines received such celebrated Loyalists as Mayor Mathews of New York and William Franklin, who wrote of his "long and horrible confinement" and was described on his release as "considerably reduced in Flesh."

In May, 1781, there was a mass breakout. The leaders of the escape, Ebenezer Hathaway and Thomas Smith, arrived in New York some weeks later, and their alleged experiences were reported by Rivington's newspaper. Hathaway and Smith recalled that they had originally been captured on a privateer, sentenced, and marched the seventy-four miles from Hartford to Simsbury. The entrance to the dungeon was a heavily barred trap door that had to be raised

> by means of a tackle, whilst the hinges grated as they turned upon their hooks, and opened the jaws and mouths of what they call Hell, into which they descended by means of a ladder about six feet more, which led to a large iron grate or hatchway, locked down over a shaft about three feet diameter, sunk through the solid rock. . . . They bid adieu to this world,

and went down thirty-eight feet more by ladder "when they came to what is called the landing; then marching shelf by shelf, till descending about thirty or forty feet more they came to a platform of boards laid under foot, with a few more put over head to carry off the water, which keeps continually dropping." There they lived for twenty nights with the other prisoners, using "pots of charcoal to dispel the foul air" through a ventilation hole bored from the surface until the opportunity to escape came when they were allowed up into the kitchen to prepare food and rushed and captured the guards.

Some colorful Connecticut escapes in other places are also recorded. Nathan Barnum avoided appearing for trial in 1780 by inoculating himself with smallpox, whereupon he was "sent to the Hospital, where he was chained to the Floor to prevent his Escape, he found Means to bribe one of the Nurses, who not only brought him a File to cut off his Irons, but amused the Centinal, placed over him while he effected it. . . ."

Samuel Jarvis and his brother got out of prison "by the assistance of Friends who had privately procured some Women's apparel which they Dressed themselves in, and by that means made their escape through the Rebel Army." James Robertson asserted that while he was in jail at Albany, the British attacked and set the building on fire, whereupon, unable to walk, he managed to crawl into a bed of cabbages "and chewing them to prevent being suffocated" was found three days later badly burnt.

There was even a series of Tory hiding places between New York and Canada, rather in the fashion of the "Underground Railroad" of the pre-Civil War days.

The treatment of imprisoned Loyalists ranged over the widest possible spectrum. Simsbury was notoriously the worst prison, almost the Andersonville of the time. Many Loyalists suffered close confinement in much pleasanter conditions; others merely underwent house arrest; others were only prevented from traveling; some were on parole and, if banished to some remote part of America, were boarded with reluctant Whigs. Some worked in the normal way by day and simply spent the night in jail. In 1776 Thomas Vernon, a fanatically early riser, was removed, with three other prominent Rhode Island Loyalists, from Newport to Glocester, in the northern part of the state, because he had refused the test oath. The foursome's journey and their few months' stay in Glocester were pleasant and gentlemanly, almost Pickwickian. The friends walked and admired the countryside, ate, drank, and conversed well in the local inn where they lived; they planted beans, killed snakes, trapped squirrels, fished, played Quadrille (a card game); they were very well treated by the ladies of the house and by neighboring females. Their chief complaints were the lack of books, some local abhorrence of Tories, particularly by the men (their landlord said "the town was very uneasy" at their being there), a few fleas, tedium from the lack of friends and family, and some stealing of their food by their far from genial host. . . .

The Whigs suffered as the Tories did — legal persecution, mob action, imprisonment (the British prison ships were particularly horrible and gave rise to effective propagandist literature), and all the excesses of civil war. Adrian C. Leiby, the historian of the Hackensack Valley, for example, reports that there was barely a Whig family there that had not lost someone to a Tory raiding party. There is at least one recorded tarring and feathering of a Whig by British troops — of one Thomas Ditson, Jr., in Boston in March, 1775. In June, 1779, the *Virginia Gazette* reported the murder of a Whig captain by a party of Tories whom he had discovered robbing his house. A sentinel wounded him with a gunshot; then, after taking all the horses from the stables, the Tories pursued the captain into the house, where he was lying on a bed, and

> immediately thrust their bayonets into his body several times, continuing the barbarity while they heard a groan; and lest life might still be remaining in him, they cut both his arms with a knife in the most inhuman manner. The villain who shot him, had been his neighbour and companion from his youth.

The victim lived another two days.

STUDY GUIDE

1. Be prepared to discuss the following quotation from Sir John Harington, who lived two centuries before the American Revolution:

   Treason doth never prosper; what's the reason?
   Why, if it prosper, none dare call it treason.

   Evaluate Harington's epigram with respect to Loyalists and Patriots in the War for Independence; and second, explain why the favorable historical reputation of the losing Civil War general Robert E. Lee is an exception to Harrington's view.

2. Summarize the various devices used to punish the Loyalists — both in their persons and in their property. What was the relation between official policy by state governments and actual treatment of Loyalists by neighbors and townsfolk?

3. Does the picture presented in this chapter modify your view of the American Patriots? If so, how?

4. Is there any evidence here that would support the view that the Revolution was a civil war between different groups of colonials, as well as a war for independence from England?

BIBLIOGRAPHY

As suggested in the introduction to this selection, the Loyalists have not received very sympathetic treatment from American historians. Even more important than this is that they have generally been ignored. It was not until 1974, for example, that an extended biography of the distinguished Massachusetts Loyalist Thomas Hutchinson was finally published. Aside from the works of a few early scholars such as Claude Van Tyne, the serious study of Loyalism is a very recent phenomenon. A growing number of historians in the last two decades have devoted their attention to these forgotten Americans, most notably William H. Nelson, in *The American Tory* * (Oxford, Eng., 1961); Wallace Brown, in *The King's Friends: The Composition and Motives of the American Loyalist Claimants* (Providence, R.I., 1966); Paul H. Smith, who describes the military involvement of the Loyalists in *Loyalists and Red-coats: A Study in British Revolutionary Policy* * (Chapel Hill, N.C., 1964); and Mary B. Norton, in *The British-Americans: The Loyalist Exiles in England, 1774–1789* * (Boston, 1972). An earlier work that attempts to identify the character of the Tory mind and psychology is Leonard W. Labaree, *Conservatism in Early American History* * (New York, 1948).

Anyone who is interested in the antagonisms in British colonial society can find a comprehensive survey in Elisha P. Douglass, *Rebels and Democrats: The Struggle for Equal Political Rights and Majority Rule during the American Revolution* * (Chapel Hill, N.C., 1955). Since 1950, however, many historians have argued that this was simply a war for independence, rather than an internal social revolution, and have suggested that eighteenth-century colonial society was characterized by broad consensus rather than conflict. This view has been argued in studies of individual colonies, in studies of revolutionary ideology, and in studies of the consequences of the Revolution. For some years the views of Edmund S. Morgan, Daniel Boorstin, Robert E. Brown, and other scholars were so widely accepted that a general consensus as to the conservative nature of the American Revolution seemed in the offing. More recently, this view has been challenged by a group of younger historians, frequently identified as the "New Left." In a series of articles, Jesse Lemisch and Staughton Lynd, among others, have argued that conflict did in fact exist in the revolutionary period, and that the laboring men of urban areas were as important as farmers in the uprising.

The views concerning the causes and character of the American Revolution are so varied and the important books so numerous that they cannot be mentioned here. The bibliographies of most textbooks will refer you to the more important studies, or you can find a good bibliography, with selections from various historical writings, in Robert F. Berkhofer, Jr., *The American Revolution: The Critical Issues* * (Boston, 1971).

* Asterisk indicates book is available in a paperback edition.

III THE NEW NATION

The quarter-century that followed the end of the War for Independence in 1783 is a remarkable period in American history. Seldom has there been a time in this country when the future seemed so promising and the problems so profound. Having broken from the mother country, Americans thought of themselves as in something of a state of nature, with a clean slate on which they could design new, republican institutions of government. By the end of the eighteenth century, every state except Connecticut and Rhode Island had written new constitutions. Together, the American people had adopted a federal constitution, established a government that was truly national in its operation, and enunciated political ideas that became so deeply embedded in the national consciousness that they are referred to as the American Credo.

Besides the enduring monuments of American political and constitutional practice that were raised, these twenty-five years also witnessed remarkable achievements in other areas. The break from England did much to accelerate the development of American democratic thought and more equalitarian social attitudes. It also encouraged a spirit of nationalism in literature, architecture, and other aspects of American cultural life. Basic directions in foreign policy were enunciated, and there were significant developments in American economic life.

The essays in this section reflect three of the central tendencies of the late eighteenth and early nineteenth centuries — the rise of nationalism, the beginnings of the Industrial Revolution, and the tendency toward equalitarianism. As the new century opened, the American people were beginning to feel like a nation, and a small but mature society had passed well beyond the stage of settlement and colony. The first reading paints a portrait of the American people in 1800. It suggests that the diverse groups, classes, and sections of the young country had enough in common to promise the development of a single American society. The second selection describes two key inventions of Eli Whitney, and it also gives us a feeling of the broader technological achievements of nineteenth-century America that were to make her preeminent in the Industrial Revolution. During the colonial period, religious organizations and many other social institutions, as well as government, had been marked by a degree of exclusiveness. The last reading describes the emergence of broad-based national denominations of American Protestantism. Growing out of the great religious revival that swept the country after 1800, these religious groups held forth a promise of salvation to all men that the closed sects of the seventeenth century had not.

Courtesy The Historical Society of Pennsylvania

"Fourth of July Celebration" by John Krimmel, 1818, shows the hearty good humor and patriotism of young America. (Detail)

7

HENRY ADAMS

America in 1800

In 1893 the Wisconsin historian Frederick Jackson Turner wrote a short paper on American history and culture that was to have an influence upon historical writing and social thought for the next half-century. Entitled "The Significance of the Frontier in American History," it argued that too much emphasis had been placed upon our European origins and their influence upon American civilization. Turner claimed that the European heritage of ideas and institutions that the colonists had brought here had, of necessity, been greatly modified in the New-World environment. Living in a new land, with different flora and fauna, different problems of transportation and housing, and facing an untamed wilderness, the European found that the old ways did not always work. Every aspect of his life — agriculture, politics, language, religion, and social life — changed as he encountered the American frontier. Turner suggested that the frontier was an important cause of our early wars and a crucial force in the development of social and political democracy in the New World.

A number of eighteenth- and early nineteenth-century observers of the American scene had noted some special characteristics of Americans well before Turner wrote. One French writer considered the American a "new man," who was a model for the European. Writers have described a vast range of characteristics as being typically American — idealism, pragmatism, hospitality, violence, inventiveness, poverty of spirit, generosity, loquacity, boorishness, to name only a few. There are many reasons why different observers have seen Americans in different ways. One is that the customs, politics, and even the character of a people may change, and later writers may be viewing a nation substantially different from the one seen by those who wrote a century before. Equally important is the personal perspective of the observer, which depends on such things as whether he had a generally conservative or progressive outlook, whether he was a foreign traveler here for a few months or a native American, and, if American, whether he was a Yankee or a Southerner.

Henry Adams was a New England descendant of two presidents, and he wrote a multivolume history of the United States during Thomas Jefferson's presidency. The first of his volumes is a classic description of America at the opening of the nineteenth century. In chapter 2, Adams describes the American character and social life of the time. The nation had been independent from England for only a quarter of a century in 1800, and English influences upon American life were to continue for many years. But there was evidence, even before the American Revolution, that a distinctively American culture and outlook was developing.

Though Americans in 1800 might continue to read English books and imitate English manners, substantial changes were becoming apparent, especially in the development of popular attitudes and the American character. The country, of course, was remarkably diverse, as indicated by such coexisting stereotypes as the shrewd New England Yankee, the hard-working and pietistic German farmer of Pennsylvania, and the leisured southern gentleman. In view of the differences, the question has been raised as to whether or not there really was a single "American" character, in the sense that one can discern a French, Italian, or Spanish character. Adams believed that there was, but he also wrote separate chapters on the regional differences of New England, the South, and the Middle Atlantic states. While his portrait of the American character describes people who lived at the opening of the nineteenth century, certain features of it are relevant to an understanding of Americans in the 1970s.

The growth of character, social and national — the formation of men's minds — more interesting than any territorial or industrial growth, defied the tests of censuses and surveys. No people could be expected, least of all when in infancy, to understand the intricacies of its own character, and

From *History of the United States of America during the First Administration of Thomas Jefferson*, Vol. I, by Henry Adams. Published by Charles Scribner's Sons.

rarely has a foreigner been gifted with insight to explain what natives did not comprehend. Only with diffidence could the best-informed Americans venture, in 1800, to generalize on the subject of their own national habits of life and thought. Of all American travellers President Dwight [Timothy Dwight, President of Yale] was the most experienced; yet his four volumes of travels were remarkable for no trait more uniform than their reticence in regard to the United States. Clear and emphatic wherever New England was in discussion, Dwight claimed no knowledge of other regions. Where so good a judge professed ignorance, other observers were likely to mislead; and Frenchmen like Liancourt, Englishmen like Weld, or Germans like Bülow, were almost equally worthless authorities on a subject which none understood. The newspapers of the time were little more trustworthy than the books of travel, and hardly so well written. The literature of a higher kind was chiefly limited to New England, New York, and Pennsylvania. From materials so poor no precision of result could be expected. A few customs, more or less local; a few prejudices, more or less popular; a few traits of thought, suggesting habits of mind — must form the entire material for a study more important than that of politics or economics.

The standard of comfort had much to do with the standard of character; and in the United States, except among the slaves, the laboring class enjoyed an ample supply of the necessaries of life. In this respect, as in some others, they claimed superiority over the laboring class in Europe, and the claim would have been still stronger had they shown more skill in using the abundance that surrounded them. The Duc de Liancourt, among foreigners the best and kindest observer, made this remark on the mode of life he saw in Pennsylvania:

> There is a contrast of cleanliness with its opposite which to a stranger is very remarkable. The people of the country are as astonished that one should object to sleeping two or three in the same bed and in dirty sheets, or to drink from the same dirty glass after half a score of others, as to see one neglect to wash one's hands and face of a morning. Whiskey diluted with water is the ordinary country drink. There is no settler, however poor, whose family does not take coffee or chocolate for breakfast, and always a little salt meat; at dinner, salt meat, or salt fish, and eggs; at supper again salt meat and coffee. This is also the common regime of the taverns.

An amusing, though quite untrustworthy Englishman named Ashe, who invented an American journey in 1806, described the fare of a Kentucky cabin:

> The dinner consisted of a large piece of salt bacon, a dish of hominy, and a tureen of squirrel broth. I dined entirely on the last dish, which I found incomparably good, and the meat equal to the most delicate chicken. The Kentuckian eats nothing but bacon, which indeed is the favorite diet of all the inhabitants of the State, and drank nothing but whiskey, which soon made him more than two-thirds drunk. In this last practice he is also supported by

the public habit. In a country, then, where bacon and spirits form the favorite summer repast, it cannot be just to attribute entirely the causes of infirmity to the climate. No people on earth live with less regard to regimen. They eat salt meat three times a day, seldom or never have any vegetables, and drink ardent spirits from morning till night. They have not only an aversion to fresh meat, but a vulgar prejudice that it is unwholesome. The truth is, their stomachs are depraved by burning liquors, and they have no appetite for anything but what is high-flavored and strongly impregnated by salt. . . .

One of the traits to which Liancourt alluded marked more distinctly the stage of social development. By day or by night, privacy was out of the question. Not only must all men travel in the same coach, dine at the same table, at the same time, on the same fare, but even their beds were in common, without distinction of persons. Innkeepers would not understand that a different arrangement was possible. When the English traveller Weld reached Elkton, on the main road from Philadelphia to Baltimore, he asked the landlord what accommodation he had. "Don't trouble yourself about that," was the reply; "I have no less than eleven beds in one room alone." This primitive habit extended over the whole country from Massachusetts to Georgia, and no American seemed to revolt against the tyranny of innkeepers.

"At New York I was lodged with two others, in a back room on the ground floor," wrote, in 1796, [a] Philadelphian. . . . "What can be the reason for that vulgar, hoggish custom, common in America, of squeezing three, six, or eight beds into one room?"

Nevertheless, the Americans were on the whole more neat than their critics allowed. "You have not seen the Americans," was [William] Cobbett's reply, in 1819, to such charges; "you have not seen the nice, clean, neat houses of the farmers of Long Island, in New England, in the Quaker counties of Pennsylvania; you have seen nothing but the smoke-dried ultra-montanians." Yet Cobbett drew a sharp contrast between the laborer's neat cottage familiar to him in Surrey and Hampshire, and the "shell of boards" which the American occupied, "all around him as barren as a sea-beach." He added, too, that "the example of neatness was wanting"; no one taught it by showing its charm. Felix de Beaujour, otherwise not an enthusiastic American, paid a warm compliment to the country in this single respect, although he seemed to have the cities chiefly in mind:

> American neatness must possess some very attractive quality, since it seduces every traveller; and there is no one of them who, in returning to his own country, does not wish to meet again there that air of ease and neatness which rejoiced his sight during his stay in the United States.

Almost every traveller discussed the question whether the Americans were a temperate people, or whether they drank more than the English. Temperate they certainly were not, when judged by a modern standard. Every one acknowledged that in the South and West drinking was occasionally excessive; but even in Pennsylvania and New England the universal taste for drams proved habits by no means strict. Every grown man took his noon toddy as a matter of course; and although few were seen publicly drunk, many were habitually affected by liquor. The earliest temperance movement, ten or twelve years later, was said to have had its source in the scandal caused by the occasional intoxication of ministers at their regular meetings. Cobbett thought drinking the national disease; at all hours of the day, he said, young men, "even little boys, at or under twelve years of age, go into stores and tip off their drams." The mere comparison with England proved that the evil was great, for the English and Scotch were among the largest consumers of beer and alcohol on the globe.

In other respects besides sobriety American manners and morals were subjects of much dispute, and if judged by the diatribes of travellers like Thomas Moore and H. W. Bülow, were below the level of Europe. Of all classes of statistics, moral statistics were least apt to be preserved. Even in England, social vices could be gauged only by the records of criminal and divorce courts; in America, police was wanting and a divorce suit almost, if not quite, unknown. Apart from some coarseness, society must have been pure; and the coarseness was mostly an English inheritance. Among New Englanders, Chief-Justice Parsons was the model of judicial, social, and religious propriety; yet Parsons, in 1808, presented to a lady a copy of "Tom Jones," with a letter calling attention to the adventures of Molly Seagrim and the usefulness of describing vice. Among the social sketches in the "Portfolio" were many allusions to the coarseness of Philadelphia society, and the manners common to tea-parties. "I heard from married ladies," said a writer in February, 1803, "whose station as mothers demanded from them a guarded conduct — from young ladies, whose age forbids the audience of such conversation, and who using it modesty must disclaim — indecent allusions, indelicate expressions, and even at times immoral innuendoes. A loud laugh or a coarse exclamation followed each of these, and the young ladies generally went through the form of raising their fans to their faces."

Yet public and private records might be searched long, before they revealed evidence of misconduct such as filled the press and formed one of the commonest topics of conversation in the society of England and France. Almost every American family, however respectable, could show some victim to intemperance among its men, but few were mortified by a public scandal due to its women.

If the absence of positive evidence did not prove American society to be as pure as its simple and primitive condition implied, the same conclusion would be reached by observing the earnestness with which critics collected every charge that could be brought against it and by noting the substance of the whole. Tried by this test, the society of 1800 was often coarse and sometimes brutal, but, except for intemperance, was moral. Indeed, its chief offence, in the eyes of Europeans, was dullness. The amusements of a people were commonly a fair sign of social development, and the Americans were only beginning to amuse themselves. The cities were small and few in number, and the diversions were such as cost little and required but elementary knowledge. In New England, although the theatre had gained a firm foothold in Boston, Puritan feelings still forbade the running of horses. [President Dwight wrote:]

> The principal amusements of the inhabitants . . . are visiting, dancing, music, conversation, walking, riding, sailing, shooting at a mark, draughts, chess, and unhappily, in some of the larger towns, cards and dramatic exhibitions. A considerable amusement is also furnished in many places by the examination and exhibitions of the superior schools; and a more considerable one by the public exhibitions of colleges. Our countrymen also fish and hunt. Journeys taken for pleasure are very numerous, and are a very favorite object. Boys and young men play at foot-ball, cricket, quoits, and at many other sports of an athletic cast, and in the winter are peculiarly fond of skating. Riding in a sleigh, or sledge, is also a favorite diversion in New England.

President Dwight was sincere in his belief that college commencements and sleigh-riding satisfied the wants of his people; he looked upon whist as an unhappy dissipation, and upon the theatre as immoral. He had no occasion to condemn horse-racing, for no race-course was to be found in New England. . . .

. . . The rough-and-tumble fight [described by many writers as the most shocking characteristic of Virginia society] differed from the ordinary prize-fight, or boxing-match, by the absence of rules. Neither kicking, tearing, biting, nor gouging was forbidden by the law of the ring. Brutal as the practice was, it was neither new nor exclusively Virginian. The English travellers who described it as American barbarism might have seen the same sight in Yorkshire at the same date. The rough-and-tumble fight was English in origin, and was brought to Virginia and the Carolinas in early days, whence it spread to the Ohio and Mississippi. The habit attracted general notice because of its brutality in a society that showed few brutal instincts. Friendly foreigners like Liancourt were honestly shocked by it; others showed somewhat too plainly their pleasure at finding a vicious habit which they could consider a natural product of democratic society. Perhaps the description written by Thomas Ashe showed best not only the ferocity of the fight but also the antipathies of the writer, for Ashe had something of the artist in his touch, and he felt no love for Americans. The scene was at Wheeling. A Kentuckian and a Virginian were the combatants.

> Bulk and bone were in favor of the Kentuckian; science and craft in that of the Virginian. The former promised himself victory from his power; the latter from his science. Very few rounds had taken place or fatal blows given, before the Virginian contracted his whole form, drew up his arms to his face, with his hands nearly closed in a concave by the fingers being bent to the full extension of the flexors, and summoning up all his energy for one act of despera-

tion, pitched himself into the bosom of his opponent. Before the effects of this could be ascertained, the sky was rent by the shouts of the multitude; and I could learn that the Virginian had expressed as much beauty and skill in his retraction and bound, as if he had been bred in a menagerie and practised action and attitude among panthers and wolves. The shock received by the Kentuckian, and the want of breath, brought him instantly to the ground. The Virginian never lost his hold. Like those bats of the South who never quit the subject on which they fasten till they taste blood, he kept his knees in his enemy's body; fixing his claws in his hair and his thumbs on his eyes, gave them an instantaneous start from their sockets. The sufferer roared aloud, but uttered no complaint. The citizens again shouted with joy. . . .

Border society was not refined, but among its vices, as its virtues, few were permanent, and little idea could be drawn of the character that would at last emerge. The Mississippi boatman and the squatter on Indian lands were perhaps the most distinctly American types then existing, as far removed from the Old World as though Europe were a dream. Their language and imagination showed contact with Indians. A traveller on the levee at Natchez, in 1808, overheard a quarrel in a flatboat near by:

"I am a man; I am a horse; I am a team," cried one voice; "I can whip any man in all Kentucky, by God!" "I am an alligator," cried the other; "half man, half horse; can whip any man on the Mississippi, by God!" "I am a man," shouted the first; "have the best horse, best dog, best gun, and handsomest wife in all Kentucky, by God!" "I am a Mississippi snapping-turtle," rejoined the second; "have bear's claws, alligator's teeth, and the devil's tail; can whip *any* man, by God!"

And on this usual formula of defiance the two fire-eaters began their fight, biting, gouging, and tearing. Foreigners were deeply impressed by barbarism such as this, and orderly emigrants from New England and Pennsylvania avoided contact with Southern drinkers and fighters; but even then they knew that with a new generation such traits must disappear, and that little could be judged of popular character from the habits of frontiersmen. Perhaps such vices deserved more attention when found in the older communities, but even there they were rather survivals of English low-life than products of a new soil, and they were given too much consequence in the tales of foreign travellers.

This was not the only instance where foreigners were struck by what they considered popular traits, which natives rarely noticed. Idle curiosity was commonly represented as universal, especially in the Southern settler who knew no other form of conversation. [Wrote Weld:]

Frequently have I been stopped by one of them, . . . and without further preface asked where I was from, if I was acquainted with any news, where bound to, and finally my name. "Stop, Mister! why, I guess now you be coming from the new State?" "No, sir." "Why, then, I guess as how you be coming from Kentuck?" "No, sir." "Oh, why, then, pray now where might you be coming from?" "From the low country." "Why, you must have heard all the news, then; pray now, Mister, what might the price of bacon be in those parts?" "Upon my word, my friend, I can't inform you." "Ay, ay; I see, Mister, you be'ent one of us. Pray now, Mister, what might your name be?"

Almost every writer spoke with annoyance of the inquisitorial habits of New England and the impertinence of American curiosity. Complaints so common could hardly have lacked foundation, yet the Americans as a people were never loquacious, but inclined to be somewhat reserved, and they could not recognize the accuracy of the description. President Dwight repeatedly expressed astonishment at the charge, and asserted that in his large experience it had no foundation. Forty years later, Charles Dickens found complaint with Americans for taciturnity. Equally strange to modern experience were the continual complaints in books of travel that loungers and loafers, idlers of every description, infested the taverns, and annoyed respectable travellers both native and foreign. Idling seemed to be considered a popular vice, and was commonly associated with tippling. So completely did the practice disappear in the course of another generation that it could scarcely be recalled as offensive; but in truth less work was done by the average man in 1800 than in aftertimes, for there was actually less work to do. "Good country this for lazy fellows," wrote Wilson from Kentucky; "they plant corn, turn their pigs into the woods, and in the autumn feed upon corn and pork. They lounge about the rest of the year." The roar of the steam-engine had never been heard in the land, and the carrier's wagon was three weeks between Philadelphia and Pittsburg. What need for haste when days counted for so little? Why not lounge about the tavern when life had no better amusement to offer? Why mind one's own business when one's business would take care of itself?

Yet however idle the American sometimes appeared, and however large the class of tavern loafers may have actually been, the true American was active and industrious. No immigrant came to America for ease or idleness. If an English farmer bought land near New York, Philadelphia, or Baltimore, and made the most of his small capital, he found that while he could earn more money than in Surrey or Devonshire, he worked harder and suffered greater discomforts. The climate was trying; fever was common; the crops ran new risks from strange insects, drought, and violent weather; the weeds were annoying; the flies and mosquitoes tormented him and his cattle; laborers were scarce and indifferent; the slow and magisterial ways of England, where everything was made easy, must be exchanged for quick and energetic action; the farmer's own eye must see to every detail, his own hand must hold the plough and the scythe. . . . New settlers suffered many of the ills that would have afflicted an army marching and fighting in a country of dense forest and swamp, with one sore misery besides — that whatever trials the men endured, the burden bore most heavily upon the women and children. The chances of being shot or scalped by Indians was hardly worth considering when compared with the certainty of malarial fever, or the strange disease called milk-sickness, or the still more depressing homesickness, or the misery of nervous prostration, which wore out generation after generation of women and children on the frontiers, and left a tragedy in every log cabin. Not for love of ease did men plunge into the wilderness. Few laborers of the Old World endured a harder lot, coarser fare, or anxieties and responsibilities greater than those of the Western emigrant. Not merely because he enjoyed the luxury of salt pork, whiskey, or even coffee three times a day did the American laborer claim superiority over the European. . . .

If any prediction could be risked, an observer might have been warranted in suspecting that the popular character was likely to be conservative, for as yet this trait was most marked, at least in the older societies of New England, Pennsylvania, and Virginia. Great as were the material obstacles in the path of the United States, the greatest obstacle of all was in the human mind. Down to the close of the eighteenth century no change had occurred in the world which warranted practical men in assuming that great changes were to come. Afterward, as time passed, and as science developed man's capacity to control nature's forces, old-fashioned conservatism vanished from society, reappearing occasionally, like the stripes on a mule, only to prove its former existence; but during the eighteenth century the progress of America, except in political paths, had been less rapid than ardent reformers wished, and the reaction which followed the French Revolution made it seem even slower than it was. . . .

This conservative habit of mind was more harmful in America than in other communities, because Americans needed more than older societies the activity which could alone partly compensate for the relative feebleness of their means compared with the magnitude of their task. Some instances of sluggishness, common to Europe and America, were hardly credible. For more than ten years in England the steam-engines of Watt had been working, in common and successful use, causing a revolution in industry that threatened to drain the world for England's advantage; yet Europe during a generation left England undisturbed to enjoy the monopoly of steam. France and Germany were England's rivals in commerce and manufactures, and required steam for self-defence; while the United States were commercial allies of England, and needed steam neither for mines nor manufactures, but their need was still extreme. Every American knew that if steam could be successfully applied to navigation, it must produce an immediate increase of wealth, besides an ultimate settlement of the most serious material and political difficulties of the Union. Had both the national and State Governments devoted millions of money to this object, and had the citizens wasted, if necessary, every dollar in their slowly filling pockets to attain it, they would have done no more than the occasion warranted, even had they failed; but failure was not to be feared, for they had with their own eyes seen the experiment tried, and they did not dispute its success. For America this question had been settled as early as 1789, when John Fitch— a mechanic, without education or wealth, but with the energy of genius—invented engine and paddles of his own, with so much success that during a whole summer Philadelphians watched his ferryboat plying daily against the river current. No one denied that his boat was rapidly, steadily, and regularly moved against wind and tide, with as much certainty and convenience as could be expected in a first experiment; yet Fitch's company failed. He could raise no more money; the public refused to use his boat or to help him build a better; they did not want it, would not believe in it, and broke his heart by their contempt. Fitch struggled against failure, and invented another boat moved by a screw. The Eastern public still proving indifferent, he wandered to Kentucky, to try his fortune on the Western waters. Disappointed there, as in Philadelphia and New York, he made a deliberate attempt to end his life by drink; but the process proving too slow, he saved twelve opium pills from the physician's prescription, and was found one morning dead.

Fitch's death took place in an obscure Kentucky inn, three years before Jefferson, the philosopher president, entered the White House. Had Fitch been the only inventor thus neglected, his peculiarities and the defects of his steamboat might account for his failure; but he did not stand alone. At the same moment Philadelphia contained another inventor, Oliver Evans, a man so ingenious as to be often called the American Watt. He, too, invented a locomotive steam-engine which he longed to bring into common use. The great services actually rendered by this extraordinary man were not a tithe of those he would gladly have performed, had he found support and encouragement; but his success was not even so great as that of Fitch, and he stood aside while Livingston and Fulton, by their greater resources and influence, forced the steamboat on a sceptical public.

While the inventors were thus ready, and while State legislatures were offering mischievous monopolies for this invention, which required only some few thousand dollars of ready money, the Philosophical Society of Rotterdam wrote to the American Philosophical Society at Philadelphia, requesting to know what improvements had been made in the United States in the construction of steam-engines. The subject was referred to Benjamin H. Latrobe, the most eminent engineer in America, and his Report, presented to the Society in May, 1803, published in the Transactions, and transmitted abroad, showed the reasoning on which conservatism rested:

> During the general lassitude of mechanical exertion which succeeded the American Revolution, . . . the utility of steam-engines appears to have been forgotten; but the subject afterward started into very general notice in a form

in which it could not possibly be attended with much success. A sort of mania began to prevail, which indeed has not yet entirely subsided, for impelling boats by steam-engines. . . . For a short time a passage-boat, rowed by a steam-engine, was established between Bordentown and Philadelphia, but it was soon laid aside. . . . There are indeed general objections to the use of the steam-engine for impelling boats, from which no particular mode of application can be free. These are, first, the weight of the engine and of the fuel; second, the large space it occupies; third, the tendency of its action to rack the vessel and render it leaky; fourth, the expense of maintenance; fifth, the irregularity of its motion and the motion of the water in the boiler and cistern, and of the fuel-vessel in rough water; sixth, the difficulty arising from the liability of the paddles or oars to break if light, and from the weight, if made strong. Nor have I ever heard of an instance, verified by other testimony than that of the inventor, of a speedy and agreeable voyage having been performed in a steamboat of any construction. I am well aware that there are still many very respectable and ingenious men who consider the application of the steam-engine to the purpose of navigation as highly important and as very prac-ticable, especially on the rapid waters of the Mississippi, and who would feel themselves almost offended at the expression of an opposite opinion. And perhaps some of the objections against it may be obviated. That founded on the expense and weight of the fuel may not for some years exist in the Missis-sippi, where there is a redundance of wood on the banks; but the cutting and loading will be almost as great an evil.

Within four years the steamboat was running, and Latrobe was its warmest friend. The dispute was a contest of temperaments, a divergence between minds, rather than a question of science; and a few visionaries such as those to whom Latrobe alluded — men like Chancellor Living-ston, Joel Barlow, John Stevens, Samuel L. Mitchill, and Robert Fulton — dragged society forward. What but scepticism could be expected among a people thus asked to adopt the steamboat, when as yet the ordinary atmospheric steam-engine, such as had been in use in Europe for a hundred years, was practically unknown to them, and the engines of Watt were a fable? Latrobe's Report further said that in the spring of 1803, when he wrote, five steam-engines were at work in the United States — one lately set up by the Manhattan Water Company in New York to supply the city with water; another in New York for sawing timber; two in Phil-adelphia, belonging to the city, for supplying water and running a roll-ing and slitting mill; and one at Boston employed in some manufacture. All but one of these were probably constructed after 1800, and Latrobe neglected to say whether they belonged to the old Newcomen type, or to Watt's manufacture, or to American invention; but he added that the chief American improvement on the steam-engine had been the con-struction of a wooden boiler, which developed sufficient power to work the Philadelphia pump at the rate of twelve strokes, of six feet, per minute. Twelve strokes a minute, or one stroke every five seconds, though not a surprising power, might have answered its purpose, had not the wooden boiler, as Latrobe admitted, quickly decomposed, and steam-leaks appeared at every bolt-hole.

If so eminent and so intelligent a man as Latrobe, who had but recently emigrated in the prime of life from England, knew little about Watt, and nothing about Oliver Evans, whose experience would have been well worth communicating to any philosophical society in Europe, the more ignorant and unscientific public could not feel faith in a force of which they knew nothing at all. For nearly two centuries the Americans had struggled on foot or horseback over roads not much better than trails, or had floated down rushing streams in open boats momentarily in danger of sinking or upsetting. They had at length, in the Eastern and Middle States, reached the point of constructing turnpikes and canals. Into these undertakings they put sums of money relatively large, for the investment seemed safe and the profits certain. Steam as a locomotive power was still a visionary idea, beyond their experience, contrary to European precedent, and exposed to a thousand risks. They regarded it as a delusion.

About three years after Latrobe wrote his Report on the steam-engine, Robert Fulton began to build the boat which settled forever the value of steam as a locomotive power. According to Fulton's well-known account of his own experience, he suffered almost as keenly as Fitch, twenty years before, under the want of popular sympathy. [He said, according to Judge Story's report:]

> When I was building my first steamboat at New York, . . . the project was viewed by the public either with indifference or with contempt as a visionary scheme. My friends indeed were civil, but they were shy. They listened with patience to my explanations, but with a settled cast of incredulity upon their countenances. I felt the full force of the lamentation of the poet —
>
>> "Truths would you teach, or save a sinking land,
>> All fear, none aid you, and few understand."
>
> As I had occasion to pass daily to and from the building-yard while my boat was in progress, I have often loitered unknown near the idle groups of strangers gathering in little circles, and heard various inquiries as to the object of this new vehicle. The language was uniformly that of scorn, or sneer, or ridicule. The loud laugh often rose at my expense; the dry jest; the wise calculation of losses and expenditures; the dull but endless repetition of the Fulton Folly. Never did a single encouraging remark, a bright hope, or a warm wish cross my path.

Possibly Fulton and Fitch, like other inventors, may have exaggerated the public apathy and contempt; but whatever was the precise force of the innovating spirit, conservatism possessed the world by right. Experience forced on men's minds the conviction that what had ever been must ever be. At the close of the eighteenth century nothing had occurred which warranted the belief that even the material difficulties of America could be removed. Radicals as extreme as Thomas Jefferson and Albert Gallatin were contented with avowing no higher aim than that America should reproduce the simpler forms of European republican society without European vices; and even this their opponents thought visionary. The United States had thus far made a single great step in advance of the Old World — they had agreed to try the experiment of embracing half a continent in one republican system; but so little were they disposed to feel confidence in their success, that Jefferson himself did not look on this American idea as vital; he would not stake the future on so new an invention. "Whether we remain in one confederacy," he wrote in 1804, "or form into Atlantic and Mississippi confederations, I believe not very important to the happiness of either part." Even over his liberal mind history cast a spell so strong, that he thought the solitary American experiment of political confederation "not very important" beyond the Alleghenies.

The task of overcoming popular inertia in a democratic society was new, and seemed to offer peculiar difficulties. Without a scientific class to lead the way, and without a wealthy class to provide the means of experiment, the people of the United States were still required, by the nature of their problems, to become a speculating and scientific nation. They could do little without changing their old habit of mind, and without learning to love novelty for novelty's sake. Hitherto their timidity in using money had been proportioned to the scantiness of their means. Henceforward they were under every inducement to risk great stakes and frequent losses in order to win occasionally a thousand fold. In the colonial state they had naturally accepted old processes as the best, and European experience as final authority. As an independent people, with half a continent to civilize, they could not afford to waste time in following European examples, but must devise new processes of their own. A world which assumed that what had been must be, could not be scientific; yet in order to make the Americans a successful people, they must be roused to feel the necessity of scientific training. Until they were satisfied that knowledge was money, they would not insist upon high education; nor until they saw with their own eyes stones turned into gold, and vapor into cattle and corn, would they learn the meaning of science.

STUDY GUIDE

1. Summarize Adams's view of each of the following American characteristics: attitude toward privacy; coarseness and brutality; idleness or industriousness.

2. What evidence does Adams give that Americans were basically conservative in this period? Considering politics, religion, and social customs, what evidence might be given that Americans were progressive and innovative?

3. Early in his essay, Adams suggests that "the standard of comfort had much to do with the standard of character." Explain how the relatively satisfactory standard of living of white Americans may have influenced their character.

4. Be prepared to discuss the abiding influence of regionalism in our country today, and the extent to which there is a single American character. What modern developments in American life have tended to make regional differences in language, customs, politics, and the like less pronounced than they were in the 1800s?

5. Describe the characteristics of contemporary Americans with respect to: violence; conservatism; attitudes toward hard work; attitudes toward privacy.

BIBLIOGRAPHY

The study of the "American character" has been a favorite preoccupation of Americans and foreign travelers alike. Since the classic, early-nineteenth-century portraits of the American by Harriet Martineau, Frances Trollope, Alexis de Tocqueville, and Charles Dickens — all of whom came from Europe to visit and travel here — there have been numerous writers on both sides of the Atlantic who have made an effort to fathom the patterns of thought and behavior of our people.

The emphasis on the frontier as the predominant force in shaping the institutions and values of the American people will be found in the writings of Frederick Jackson Turner: *The Frontier in American History* (New York, 1920); *The Significance of Sections in American History* (New York, 1932); and *The Early Writings of Frederick Jackson Turner,* comp. by Everett E. Edwards (Madison, Wis., 1938). In an essay on "American Democracy and the Frontier" in the *Yale Review,* Vol. XX (Dec. 1930), Benjamin F. Wright, Jr., challenges Turner's contention that the West was the source of the American democratic impulse. Henry Nash Smith, in *Virgin Land: The American West as Symbol and Myth* * (Cambridge, Mass., 1950), suggests that Turner romanticized and exaggerated the significance of a frontier that was rapidly disappearing.

A number of volumes on the American character tend to concentrate on particular traits we exhibit as a nation — and in some instances at a particular point in our history. In *People of Plenty: Economic Abundance and the American Character* * (Chicago, 1954), David M. Potter describes the culture and the values of our nation as products of abundance; while the Englishman Geoffrey Gorer, in *The American People: A Study in National Character* * (New York, 1948), portrays us as rebels against authority. On the other hand,

David Riesman, with Reuel Denney and Nathan Glazer, in *The Lonely Crowd: A Study of the Changing American Character* * (New Haven, Conn., 1951), describes Americans as a nation of conformists; and Daniel J. Boorstin in three separate books — *The Americans: The Colonial Experience* * (New York, 1958), *The Americans: The National Experience* * (New York, 1965), and *The Genius of American Politics* * (Chicago, 1953) — depicts the American people as singularly pragmatic and innovative. A survey of virtually all the literature on the subject will be found in Michael McGiffert, *The Character of Americans: A Book of Readings* * (Homewood, Ill., 1970).

* Asterisk indicates book is available in a paperback edition.

The genius of Eli Whitney and other early inventors culminated in an extraordinary display of American technology at the Philadelphia Exposition of 1876.

8

JOSEPH AND FRANCES GIES

Beginnings of Industrialism

When it was first used, the term "Industrial Revolution" had a very limited meaning. An English writer, Arnold Toynbee, used it to describe the development of steam power and its application to coal mining and transportation, new inventions in the textile industry, the factory system of production, and the formation of new capital. He found the origins of this revolution in England between the mid-eighteenth century and 1830. Eventually historians realized that those developments were only limited facets of much broader changes that are still taking place and that have spread to much of the world. The rudimentary development of the factory system and mass production that took place before 1830 has now progressed to completely automated production lines that produce, among other things, McDonald's hamburgers with scarcely any human intervention. Today, the Industrial Revolution is seen as including new ways of organizing business and capital; new inventions and technology in office machinery as well as on the production line; new sources of power and raw materials, including man-made synthetics; a vastly expanded labor force; and new patterns of transportation and distribution. Many historians, in fact, consider the entire Industrial Revolution as only a part of a broad social, political, and economic development that they refer to as "modernization."

By any standard, the Industrial Revolution must rank with the invention of the wheel and the opening of the Western Hemisphere as one of the most influential changes in world history. Throughout most of history, only a very small elite had more than a bare subsistence level of living, while most of mankind was doomed to hereditary poverty. Before the Industrial Revolution, the wealth did not exist to provide a reasonable standard of living for most people in a society. It is the wealth of modern industrialism that has enabled society, for the first time, to consider educating most people, providing a nourishing diet, good medical care, and adequate housing. Virtually every aspect of modern existence, from skyscrapers to jet planes, reflects the influence of industrialization. Before the invention of steel, reinforced concrete, and the elevator, few residential or commercial buildings in the world were higher than six or seven stories. Transportation was such that most of mankind never saw any part of the world other than the isolated valley or village in which they were born, lived their lives, and died. Consider the impossibility of running General Motors by using only quill pens, without even the typewriter, much less the computer, available. Imagine the limits upon human awareness and communication before the invention of the telephone and radio, and the limits upon mankind's twenty-four-hour day before the invention of the light bulb. Industrial changes of the past century have had so radical a social impact that the changes in that period might be greater than the accumulated changes of the previous nineteen centuries.

Toynbee was correct in identifying eighteenth-century England as the seedbed of industrialism, but since that time the American people have embraced the movement with unparalleled enthusiasm. From the dawn of the republic, Americans seem to have had a special knack for fiddling with machinery and for developing ingenious inventions to solve practical problems. Busy as they were with other activities, such revolutionary leaders as Franklin and Jefferson spent some of their time devising a chair that would swivel, a dumbwaiter, and a machine to reproduce several copies of a letter as they used a pen to write the master copy. In the early nineteenth century, a whole host of American tinkerers invented or contributed to the development of steamboats, vulcanized rubber, the telegraph, and new textile machinery. Eli Whitney was one such, and his invention of the cotton gin and his contribution to the principle of interchangeable parts for machines were to have a far-reaching impact upon American agriculture, manufacturing, and social life. The second of these contributions may have been even more important than the first. Before the development of precision tools, each spring for a clock or lock for a gun had to be individually crafted, and it was impossible to use a part from one clock to repair a different one. In the following essay, Joseph and Frances Gies indicate

the tremendous implications that machine precision and interchangeable parts were to have upon labor and mass production.
The selection opens with a description of the great Philadelphia
Centennial Exposition of 1876, where American and foreign
visitors were awed by the technological marvels that Eli Whitney and his successors had developed.

After speeches and more music, at noon the flags were raised on all the buildings, and a hundred-gun salute thundered. Then President Grant and the
emperor [Pedro II of Brazil] led the way down the length of the cavernous
Main Building, out the far end, and past one of the Exhibition's many
fountains, to another immense new building, Machinery Hall.

Here George H. Corliss, wealthy Providence industrialist and Centennial
Commissioner for Rhode Island, waited on another platform. Behind him
towered his personal gift to the Exhibition, the Corliss Double Walking-Beam
Steam Engine, whose 30-foot, 56-ton flywheel was designed to supply the
power for all the machinery exhibited in Machinery Hall. With deferential
pride, Corliss showed the president and the emperor how to turn a pair of
wheels and, when as much of the crowd as could squeeze in was in place,
gave a hand signal. The two heads of state obediently turned their wheels,
and overhead the twin walking beams began to rock, stirring the mighty
flywheel into silent motion. Throughout the vast hall belts began to move
and wheels to spin, and in a few moments hundreds of machines were humming and clacking. Spontaneously, the crowd burst into a long, delighted
round of applause.

The tableau was perfect. Those who had come to Philadelphia bemused
with images of Betsy Ross and the Liberty Bell were awakened at a stroke
to the reality of America's first century — the transformation of the country
from a scattering of seaboard towns and farms on the edge of a continental
wilderness to an industrial colossus, bestriding North America and rivaling,
or rather surpassing, the old European powers.

Machinery Hall was the true heart of the Exhibition. Understandably,
Great Britain and the continental European nations were limited in their
contributions by the expense of shipping, but it was not short of amazing
that three-fourths of the whole mighty display was American.

Lathes, presses, power looms, steam hammers, milling machines, pumps — the variety and profusion were impressive without the numerous superlatives attached to them. The steam-hydraulic cotton press of the Taylor Iron Works of South Carolina was "the most powerful in the world." The section of wire cable for John A. Roebling's famous Niagara suspension bridge was the largest in the world, and about to be surpassed by that for the new Brooklyn Bridge, whose 1,595-foot main span dwarfed all the bridges of Europe. As a sort of analogue to the Corliss engine, a 7,000-pound pendulum clock by Seth Thomas acted as electrical master to twenty-six slave clocks around the building.

The central aisle was crowded with the latest models of one of America's most valued inventions, the sewing machine, a portrait of whose chief inventor, Massachusetts's Elias Howe, gazed benevolently down on visitors to the exhibit. Several other makes of sewing machine were also represented, but the largest manufacturer, Isaac Singer, had so many new models that he had built his own pavilion elsewhere on the grounds.

An array of locomotives and equipment included George Westinghouse's revolutionary air brake, just introduced on the Pennsylvania Railroad. Christopher Sholes's new "type-writer," manufactured by the Remington Arms Company, astonished visitors by printing neat and legible characters at the touch of the operator's fingers. Massive rotary presses of the Bullock and Hoe companies demonstrated their prowess by turning out thousands of copies of the *New York Herald* and the *Philadelphia Times*. A group of machines exploiting the invention of the late Charles Goodyear fashioned "India rubber" boots and shoes for visitors.

To the connoisseur of technology, perhaps the most telling display in Machinery Hall was in the area containing the products of William Sellers & Company of Philadelphia and Pratt & Whitney of Hartford, Connecticut, America's foremost manufacturers of machine tools — the machines that make machines. Sober black iron monsters whose varying steel edges could cut, chip, stamp, mold, grind, and otherwise shape metal, they had made possible the world-famous "American System of Manufacture," meaning high-speed mass production with interchangeable parts. In the separate U.S. Government Building nearby, workers and machines from the Springfield Arsenal demonstrated the system itself by assembling rifles from identical parts machined to a thousandth of an inch tolerance.

Between the Sellers and Pratt & Whitney displays the Midvale Steel Works of Philadelphia showed off its largest axles, shafts, and chilled-steel bars, demonstrating a sophisticated American capability with this once-exotic metal whose quantity production had first been achieved by an American. Steel's birth as a structural material was the subject of another display, a model showing how the steel arches of Captain James Eads's mighty St. Louis Bridge had been formed and joined.

Baffling to the layman, but nonetheless impressive, was an 8-foot-long mechanism mounted on a pair of trestle legs and looking like the insides of a thousand-keyed piano. This was George B. Grant's "Calculating Machine," an American version of Charles Babbage's much-talked-about British calculator. Grant's creation was considered an improvement on Babbage's, though certainly less original, but it suffered from the same inherent defect, the unsuitability of mechanical components to perform the lightning-swift operations that only electronics would permit. No one guessed the future relationship of the perforated paper rolls that programmed the twelve-piece "Electro-Magnetic Orchestra" in Horticultural Hall with the Babbage-Grant machines. . . .

The country had come so far so fast it found itself a little taken aback. No nation had ever before undergone an experience like America's first hundred years, and the more one looked back at 1776, the more the question seemed in order: how did it all happen? [To answer that, one must examine the origins of American technology in the early inventions and primitive mills of men like Samuel Slater, Eli Whitney, and David Wilkinson, nearly a century before the Philadelphia Exposition.]

At the moment when Samuel Slater's mill machinery was suddenly enlarging the demand for raw cotton, the tobacco, rice, and indigo planters of the South were encountering marketing difficulties that made them eager to turn to cotton as a staple. Unfortunately, there was a problem. Of the two great cotton-plant varieties, long-staple and short-staple, the first resisted cultivation and the second resisted cleaning. Only at Sea Island, Georgia (which gave its name to the variety in the United States), and along the Georgia-Carolina coast as far as Charleston did the long-staple plant flourish. The short-staple grew in more or less any warm, moist climate, but its seeds stuck like glue to the lint, from which they had to be torn or cut by hand. It took one person a day to clean a pound of the stuff.

The smooth seeds of Sea Island cotton were removed mechanically. The lint was run through a pair of wooden rollers, grooved lengthwise, and turned by a hand crank in opposite directions, like a clothes wringer. The cleaning device was neither an American nor a European invention, but a product of India, where for hundreds of years it had been known as a churka. In 1790 Dr. Joseph Eve of the Bahamas and Augusta, Georgia, fitted up the churka with accessories that permitted it to be powered by a horse or waterwheel, but though Dr. Eve and others who tinkered with it claimed that their improvements made it effective with short-staple cotton, they vastly exaggerated. The obstinate short-staple seeds either passed through or clung and broke between the cylinders, scattering fragments throughout the cotton.

Yet the churka supplied a basic starting point, and Carolina planters felt with a sort of gambler's prescience that an improvement was due any moment. In 1793 many actually raised short-staple cotton in the hope that someone would invent an effective gin ("gin" in the sense of trap) in time for the crop.

Throughout the planting country, people were talking about such a machine. Consequently, it was not surprising that three planters gathered at Mulberry Grove, Georgia, in the winter of 1792–93 fell to discussing it. Retired army officers, Majors Bremen, Forsyth, and Pendleton, they were paying a call on Catherine Greene, widow of their old commanding officer, General Nathanael Greene. Nathanael and Catherine were originally Rhode Islanders, and had settled in the South as a direct result of Greene's famous Southern campaign against Cornwallis in 1780–81 that had led to Yorktown. Mulberry Grove, the property of a Tory lieutenant governor, was a gift of the state of Georgia to the general for his services.

Captivating Catherine Greene was one of the most prominent and popular ladies in the South, famed for her charm as a hostess and remembered for her courageous spirit at Valley Forge. Listening to her guests, she had a sudden inspiration. "Gentlemen," she said, "apply to my young friend Mr. Whitney — he can make anything." She displayed an embroidery frame that the mysterious Mr. Whitney had made for her needlework, and several toys he had made or repaired. The gentlemen expressed a desire to meet the young mechanic, and Whitney himself was produced. He proved to be a handsome young fellow with a Yankee beak, luminous dark eyes, a firm chin, and a well-proportioned figure.

Although fresh out of Yale College, Eli Whitney was twenty-seven years old. Like Samuel Slater and Oliver Evans, he was the son of a prosperous farmer. On his farm in Westborough, Massachusetts, the elder Whitney had a workshop equipped with a lathe and other tools to make and repair household furnishings and farm implements. As a boy, Eli showed the mechanical curiosity and aptitude of Slater, Evans, and John Fitch, once feigning illness and staying home from church to take apart and reassemble his father's watch. At twelve he fashioned a violin that made, he recalled, "tolerable good musick." The oldest of four children, he was a reliable performer of chores, watering sixty head of cattle every morning. According to his sister, he was "remarkable for thinking and acting for himself." At fourteen he installed a forge in his father's workshop to make nails, in demand because the war had shut off the British supply, while the American industry had been handicapped by the old Parliamentary restraints. So successful was his nailmaking that he hired an assistant, and when the war's end brought a flood of British nails on the market, he switched his production to hatpins and walking sticks.

In 1783, at the age of seventeen, when an American boy's schooling was normally over, he suddenly decided he wanted some higher education. Answering an advertisement for a schoolmaster in nearby Grafton, he got the appointment and, by studying nights to stay ahead of his pupils, earned enough salary — $7 a month, poor pay even for 1783 — to finance a summer term at Leicester Academy. For three years he taught winters and learned summers, until he had enough arithmetic, Latin, and Greek to qualify "to keep a Grammar School." It was also enough to win admittance to college, and Whitney had decided he wanted to go to Yale. Harvard was nearer, but the head of Leicester Academy was a Yale graduate, and may have told him about the scientific apparatus recently acquired by Yale's progressive president, Ezra Stiles, who read the French *Encyclopédie* volume by volume as it came out and corresponded with Franklin. At any rate Whitney bade farewell to his little red schoolhouse where he had been a popular master; closing-day ceremony was well attended by parents as well as pupils, and "not an Eye in the house but was moistened."

His academy pay hardly sufficed to finance Yale, but his father, impressed by his scholarship and determination, advanced him money, not without risk and sacrifice. Whitney, Sr., a large corpulent man who often held town office and served as justice of the peace, drove his son to Brookfield, whence he could get the stage to New Haven. He "payd all expense — left me the Dollars and bid me goodby," recorded Eli.

Yale consisted of a dormitory (Connecticut Hall), houses for President Stiles and the one other professor, a refectory, and the chapel, which doubled as repository for the library and the "philosophical apparatus," i.e., scientific equipment. To the college collection, consisting of a set of the basic machine components (lever, wheel and axle, cord and pulley, toothed gear wheels, plane, wedge, screw), a quadrant, a theodolite, an air pump, and a variety of natural curiosities such as mammoth tusks and snakeskins, Dr. Stiles had personally added a three-foot telescope, a micrometer, and an orrery — a model for demonstrating the motions of the planets. Stiles and Professor Josiah Meigs conducted all lectures, while three tutors drilled students in grammar and composition, history and geography, disputation and theology. Because the jail was next door in crowded College Square, recitations and prayers were often accompanied by the audible groans, curses, and screams of the jail's mixed population of debtors, felons, and lunatics.

The library boasted 3,000 books, most of them comprising a gift dating from 1733, but including a copy of Newton's *Principia* donated by Newton himself, a volume that may have enlightened Whitney about the failure of a perpetual-motion machine he had once invented. Despite the cost of college — nearly $400 a year including bed and bedding, board, candles, fuel, laundry, and books, of which his father apparently paid half or more — Yale was not only a great experience but promised to provide him with a substantial reward in the shape of a legal career. At the graduation exercises in September 1792, marked by a fireworks display to celebrate the state's forgiveness of the college's back taxes ($40,000), Eli appeared in new store-bought clothes — pants, coat, waistcoat, cotton shirt, slippers, and silk hose. Following commencement, he received a disappointment that proved one of destiny's silver-lined clouds — a teaching post Dr. Stiles had lined up for him in New York to provide for him while he studied law had evaporated. Something vaguer and much farther off, a tutoring job in South Carolina, had turned up to replace it. The intermediary for the tutoring job was a recent Yale alumnus named Phineas Miller, who though only a year older than Whitney was manager of the estate of the late General Nathanael Greene. At the moment Miller was in New Haven, and suggested that Witney accompany him, Mrs. Greene, and the children, who were summering at Newport, back to Mulberry Grove, across the Savannah River from the household that was seeking the tutor. . . .

Exactly when General Greene's ex-officers introduced Whitney to the cottonseed problem is not clear from his account, written almost a year later, except that it was shortly after his arrival at Mulberry Grove in November 1792. His response was a modest disclaimer to the effect that he had never seen either cotton or cottonseed in his life. But he promised to study the problem, and soon after went to Savannah, brought back a parcel of cotton, and talked the problem over with Phineas Miller, who strongly urged him to try. His tutorial post had meantime disappointed him by promising only fifty guineas instead of the hundred he had anticipated. He soon "struck out a plan of a machine," and communicated it to Miller, who enthusiastically offered funds and a room in the basement for a workshop. "In about ten days I made a little model, for which I was offered, if I would give up all right and title to it, a Hundred Guineas. . . ." Putting Miller off, he returned to work, surrounded by the inquisitive Greene children, and produced a full-scale machine that one man could operate to clean "ten times as much cotton as he can in any other way before known and also clean it much better than in the usual mode. This machine may be turned by water or with a horse . . . and one man and a horse will do more than fifty men with the old machines."

Essentially Whitney approached the problem of separating seeds from cotton from the reverse side, designing a machine that pulled the cotton from the seeds rather than the seeds from the cotton. The principal element in his gin was a horizontal cylinder set in a frame and (like the churka) turned by a crank, armed with iron spikes or teeth that matched the slots in an iron guard on the face of the lint box, positioned directly in front of the cylinder. The spikes speared the cotton and yanked it through the slots with such force that the lint was torn from the seeds, leaving the seeds in the box. No plate iron was available, so he made his teeth from a coil of iron wire that "one of the Miss Greenes had bought . . . to make a bird cage."

The full-size machine (its cylinder was 26 inches long and 6 inches in diameter) gave scope for a full-size trial, and a problem immediately developed. The fibers caught by the teeth rolled up around the cylinder, clogging it and preventing it from turning. A popular story, origins unknown but not confirmed by Whitney, had it that Catherine Greene suggested the solution by picking up a stiff-bristled hearth brush and asking him why he did not try that. What Whitney actually did was to add a small supplementary cylinder, set with bristles, attaching it to the crankshaft by means of a belt that caused it to turn in the opposite direction to the main cylinder. It worked — the bristles pulled the lint free of the teeth.

Catherine Greene invited the neighbors in to admire the new invention.

Their exclamations began to make clear the dimensions of its value and even the dangers. Though they urged Whitney to take advantage of the new United States patent law, their excitement was a warning of potential piracy. Shortly after, on May 27, 1793, Whitney and Phineas Miller signed an agreement to share profits on the cotton gin while Miller continued to pay for the work of development. Whitney then sailed for the North.

Their idea was to establish a factory in New Haven to manufacture cotton gins. The first gins would be set up in Mulberry Grove to gin the district's 1794 cotton crop, whose planting Miller would stimulate by appropriate advertising. After that, they would gradually extend their operation into the Carolinas. It seemed a reasonable plan, but they entirely underestimated the demand for the gin.

Landing in New York, Whitney proceeded first to Philadelphia by stage, filing a patent application with Secretary of State Jefferson. En route to New Haven he stopped off in New York to witness an examination of cotton ginned by his machine at Mulberry Grove; the cotton was declared of good quality and sold at auction at "the highest price." At New Haven he set to work with energy and ingenuity, building a wire-drawing block, a lathe, and special turning tools. After waiting vainly for the yellow fever epidemic that had driven the government from Philadelphia to subside, he sent his full patent description to Jefferson on October 15, 1793. The application was destroyed by the Patent Office fire of 1836, but a "True Copy" Whitney made a few months later survives to provide evidence of what the final version of the original cotton gin was like:

"The cotton is put into the Hopper, carried thro' the Breastwork, brushed off from the teeth by the Clearer and flies off from the Clearer with the assistance of the air, by its own centrifugal force. The machine is turned by water, horses, or in any other way as is most convenient.

"There are several modes of making the various parts of this machine, which together with their particular shape and formation, are pointed out and explained in a description with Drawings." Jefferson assured Whitney of his patent as soon as he sent in a model, and expressed great interest in the invention.

At New Haven that winter Whitney had to battle serious difficulties. Determined to make his new gins as large as possible, he repeatedly cracked the wooden cylinders with the hundreds of iron wire teeth driven into them. To solve the problem, he built another machine, one for cutting wire teeth uniformly. By February of 1794 he had completed six large gins to take to Georgia and a miniature for the Patent Office. On March 14 Edmund Randolph, the new Secretary of State, granted the patent.

Two weeks earlier Miller published his announcement in the Georgia *Gazette*, stating that he would gin any amount of green-seed cotton on the basis of one pound of cleaned cotton for every five pounds delivered. Since it normally took three pounds of raw cotton to produce one pound of clean,

Miller proposed to keep two-thirds of a pound for each five pounds cleaned, or two-fifths of the cleaned cotton. Such payment in kind was the time-honored arrangement for millers, fullers, sawyers, and other processers. Miller's proposition may have been a little too greedy, but the terms were not really the problem. Planters did bring their cotton, in large quantities. Whitney crated his disassembled gins in New Haven, two gins to three large boxes, and Miller set them up in pairs, each pair turnable by a horse or waterwheel. Miller was successfully expanding the business in Georgia and had established one operation in South Carolina when in the spring of 1795 a fire destroyed Whitney's New Haven shop, with tools, materials, and twenty unfinished gins. At the same time Miller, trying for a quick fortune in another direction, lost heavily in the Yazoo land speculation that exploded in a scandal over bribes to the Georgia legislature. Catherine Greene came to his rescue by putting her resources, consisting of several plantations, at Miller's disposal, an arrangement formalized by their marriage in 1796.

Fire and scandal were remediable disasters. A worse catastrophe building for the firm of Whitney, Miller, and Greene was not. Using Miller's high charges as an excuse, and the mechanical simplicity of the gin as a means, the planters of Georgia and Carolina industriously set to work copying it. One pirate, Edward Lyon, not only stole the design through espionage but fabricated and sold gins that he brazenly declared to be "improved models." Another, Hodgen Holmes, actually did improve the gin by using teeth cut from sheet iron, Whitney's original preference, and won a patent from the federal government, even though he had actually copied Whitney's device from drawings. Dr. Eve and others who had made the earlier churka-type gins "improved" their models by adding all Whitney's features. Injury was compounded by insult as the swarm of imitators launched an incredibly malicious propaganda campaign in England to persuade British manufacturers that Whitney's original gin damaged cotton fibers, and for a time Whitney and Miller were unable to sell cotton in England. Miller sued Georgia trespassers only to have the local jury impertinently sustain the planters, using a loophole provided by faulty wording of the Patent Act, which read, "If any person shall make, devise, *and* use . . ." where it should have read "*or* use." Even the South's slave code helped protect pirates. Slaves, barred from testifying in court, could operate a cotton gin in a loft, where no white witness ever saw it. Whitney later wrote Robert Fulton about an occasion on which the rattle of three nearby pirate gins could be heard on the steps of the Georgia courthouse in which Whitney was vainly trying to prove that the machine had been used in Georgia. By 1800 Whitney succeeded in getting the Patent Law reworded, and eventually Miller and Whitney won substantial awards from the legislatures of South and North Carolina. A licensing arrangement, suggested by a Yale classmate of Miller's, also brought in revenues. By that time Miller and Catherine Greene had had to sell Mulberry Grove, and Miller died shortly after, a victim of fever. The awards and licensing fees mostly disappeared in litigation costs, and Whitney bitterly concluded that "An invention can be so valuable as to be worthless to the inventor." As he described the situation to Fulton, "The use of this Machine being immensely profitable to almost every individual in the Country all were interested in trespassing & each justified & kept the other in countenance."

Whitney of course was right, but what he could scarcely be expected to see was the degree of justice on the planters' side. An invention that the whole community badly needed had to be made available to it, if possible on terms favorable to the inventor, otherwise on terms unfavorable to him. Watt's steam engine was pirated; Samuel Slater and others plagiarized Arkwright's textile machinery; Oliver Evans's automatic flour mill was freely copied; and many other nineteenth-century inventors suffered similarly. The fatal characteristic of Eli Whitney's cotton gin was that it was so wonderfully simple. Given a good look at it, or a good drawing, any carpenter or smith could make one, in any size, to suit the pirate's needs and purse.

If Whitney got little profit, he at least got much honor. Yale awarded him a Master of Arts degree in 1795, when the gin's national importance was already apparent. Ultimately the economic benefit conferred on the South, and on the United States, was beyond anyone's most optimistic calculation. The 2 to 3 million pounds of green-seed cotton that a few upland planters in South Carolina and Georgia had grown hopefully in 1793 spread by 1820 to a cotton belt far expanded west and north that produced 80 million pounds, nearly a third of an immensely increased world supply. By this time a large part of the crop was going to the factories lining the New England river valleys, where copies of Samuel Slater's machinery, driven by the splashing waterwheels and tended by ex-farm women and children, were turning out cotton thread. That same year the Missouri Compromise signaled one of the major effects of the gin — the formal, fatal division of the United States over slavery, a result produced, strangely enough, by the economic partnership created between North and South by Samuel Slater and Eli Whitney. . . .

Chance had led Whitney to his first invention; need drove him to his second, of an entirely different order, but of a significance fully comparable to that of the cotton gin. The John Adams administration's quarrel with revolutionary France in 1798 disclosed the national weakness in arms manufacture. The new Springfield (Massachusetts) Armory had turned out scarcely a thousand muskets in three years, and the newer Harpers Ferry (Virginia) none at all in two. The government turned frantically to private gunsmiths, appropriating the huge sum of $800,000. But the few skilled gunsmiths in the country, fabricating weapons one at a time, lock, stock, and barrel, would take years to equip an army.

In a letter to Oliver Wolcott, Secretary of the Treasury, written May 1, 1798, Whitney put forward a remarkable proposal: "I am persuaded that

Machinery moved by water adapted to this business would greatly diminish the labor and facilitate the manufacture of this article — machines for forging, rolling, floating, boreing, grinding, polishing, etc. may all be made of use to advantage.

"Cartridge or Cartouch Boxes is an article which I can manufacture. I have a machine for boreing wood of my Invention which is admirably adapted to this purpose. The making of swords, hangers, Pistols etc. I could perform."

Whitney proposed to make 10,000 "stand of arms" — musket, bayonet, ramrod, wiper, and screwdriver, the complete arms needed to equip a soldier — for $134,000 or $13.40 apiece, not a particularly low price since in 1795 the government had imported muskets for $9 apiece. But with the French Revolutionary War peaking in intensity, imports could no longer be had, and Congress jumped at Whitney's offer. A contract was signed in Philadelphia after just three weeks' negotiations, including correspondence with Whitney's lawyer in New Haven. The government would supply a model, the French Charleville 1763, of Saratoga-Yorktown fame, and would furnish black walnut gunstocks at 25 cents apiece. Four thousand muskets with bayonets and ramrods were to be delivered by September 30, 1799, the remaining 6,000 by the following September. A $5,000 advance permitted Whitney to pay off pressing debts.

Implicit in Whitney's proposal to use "Machines for forging, rolling" and other operations was the momentous idea of interchangeable parts. With his waterpowered machines — which remained to be created — Whitney meant to manufacture rapidly large numbers of each part of a musket, then assemble the muskets. For Whitney, the beauty of the plan lay less in the speed with which powered machinery could turn out the parts than in the elimination of scarce, expensive skilled labor.

As in the case of John Fitch and Oliver Evans, Whitney had European forerunners of whom he apparently knew nothing. As early as the 1720s, Christopher Polhem, a Swedish scientist and engineer, built a mechanized factory that employed the principle of interchangeable parts to produce clocks, padlocks, knives, forks, scissors, files, and nails. In 1722 a French gunsmith, name unknown, undertook to apply interchangeability to musket manufacture; the idea was taken up again by Honoré Blanc, superintendent of the Royal Manufactory of Arms at St. Etienne, who established a special factory to produce musket locks in 1778. In 1785 Blanc demonstrated his method to Thomas Jefferson, then American ambassador to France, who wrote, "I put several [musket locks] together myself, taking pieces at hazard, as they came to hand, and they fitted in the most perfect manner. . . . He effects [interchangeability] by tools of his own contrivance, which at the same time abridge the work, so that he thinks he shall be able to furnish the musket two livres cheaper than the common price." Jefferson vainly "attempted to remove this Artist to the United States."

Jefferson's acquaintance with Blanc's work was of benefit to Eli Whitney when unforeseen difficulties plagued his enterprise. He had trouble acquiring a good mill site, and when he found one, at Mill Rock, on Mill River near New Haven, early winter stopped construction, Philadelphia's yellow fever epidemic delayed delivery of his gunstocks, and Connecticut floods prevented his Canaan machine-part contractors from fulfilling their contract. Despite his $5,000 advance, he could not work out credit arrangements that would permit buying in quantity. Finally, he had problems with his labor, and had to ask for an extension of his own contract deadline. He wrote Oliver Wolcott on July 30, 1799, "I must . . . candidly acknowledge that much more time must necessarily be taken up in the first establishment of the business than I had at first any conception of . . . I must not only tell the workmen but must show them how every part is to be done."

Wolcott sent Captain Decius Wadsworth, the army's inspector of muskets, to Mill Rock to determine if Whitney's excuses were valid. Captain Wadsworth was a Yale classmate of Phineas Miller who knew Whitney's cotton gin well and brought a sympathetic understanding to Mill Rock. On his recommendation, Wolcott granted Whitney's request for a reprieve from the contract, writing sensibly, "I should consider a *real improvement* in machinery for manufacturing arms as a great acquisition to the United States." Wolcott enclosed a letter of credit on the Collector of the port of New Haven for $1,500 to ease Whitney's financial problems.

The first batch of muskets was not in fact delivered until September 1801, two years after the original contract date, and numbering only 500 instead of 4,000. Twenty-six other contractors had delivered only about a thousand muskets (so it was just as well that the French war threat had passed) but Whitney felt he should make an explanation in person, and as a result a memorable incident took place. Setting out for the new capital on the banks of the Potomac, where Jefferson had now assumed office as president, Whitney took along one complete musket and the parts for several locks. At either the White House, the War Department, or possibly at the incomplete Capitol building, he deposited the lock components on a large table, then choosing parts at random, assembled a lock. He invited the officials present (who included Jefferson and new Secretary of War Henry Dearborn) to do the same. They were all delighted with the result — the parts were so uniform that a musket lock could be assembled from any appropriate group.

The demonstration was decisive as far as the government was concerned, Whitney was given further extensions and more money, and Jefferson wrote James Monroe, the governor of Virginia:

"Mr. Whitney . . . has invented moulds and machines for making all the pieces of his locks so exactly equal, that take 100 locks to pieces and mingle their parts and the hundred locks may be put together as well by taking the first pieces which come to hand . . . Leblanc, in France, had invented a similar process in 1788 & had extended it to the barrel, mounting & stock. . . ."

The machinery by which Whitney achieved his delayed but impressive performance in production remains obscure because, perhaps out of exasperation with his cotton-gin experience, he took out no patents. All we know is a description written by ten-year-old nephew Philos Blake to Blake's sister: "There is a drilling machine and a bouring machine to bour berels [barrels] and a screw machine and too great large buildings, one nother shop to stocking guns in, a blacksmith shop and a trip hammer shop. . . ."

Whitney set down the theory of his machine organization in a letter to Wolcott:

"One of my primary objects is to form the tools so the tools themselves shall fashion the work and give to every part its just proportion — which when once accomplished will give expedition, uniformity and exactness to the whole. . . . In short, the tools which I contemplate are similar to an engraving on copper plate from which may be taken a great number of impressions exactly alike."

For all his enlightened enthusiasm, Jefferson did not really grasp the significance of interchangeable parts in manufacture. In his letter to Monroe, he laid stress on the value of interchangeability in musket repair — "out of ten locks, e.g. disabled for the want of different pieces, 9 good locks may be put together without employing a smith." That advantage seems modest. After a battle, the army left in possession of the field might perhaps do such repair work, but would be more likely to salvage whole muskets from the casualties. Whitney himself was inclined to stress the economy of dispensing with skilled labor, a point of great importance to any manufacturing operation and especially valuable in early America. Blanc in France actually grasped the advantages of interchangeability better than did Whitney. The true economic sense of mass production, the dramatic lowering of unit costs, was as yet difficult to perceive.

Even in his limited aim, Whitney gained only a qualified success. The handicraft technique survived and for a while was credited with better results in the sense of more reliable weapons. Wood and iron machines could not yet attain — or maintain — the precision necessary for a really satisfactory mass-production operation, and standard gauges did not yet exist. Whitney's impressive demonstration for Jefferson was probably partly rigged by a careful selection of parts. His normal procedure was apparently to do some hand-finishing on parts at the moment of assembly. Whether he ever achieved genuine interchangeability remains in doubt.

Yet Whitney had started something and he had started it in fertile soil. In France Honoré Blanc and his successors made many thousands of muskets by interchangeable-parts manufacture, but French industry, dedicated to old-fashioned handicraft production of fine goods, made no attempt to adapt the technique. In Britain a Frenche émigré engineer, Marc Brunel, manufactured pulley blocks for the British navy by a well-thought-out system of interchangeable parts production in which he made use of the gifted British machine-tool expert Henry Maudslay. But though the experiment was technically a brilliant success, the Brunel-Maudslay system was no more copied by British industry than was the Blanc system by French.

Only in America did the idea take hold. Whitney had an imitator almost at once (possibly even a coinventor) in Simeon North, a gunsmith of nearby Berlin, Connecticut, who made pistols under government contract. Of far more significance was the adoption of the technique by the New England clock industry, whose craftsmen had always followed the European tradition of hand-fabricating their wheels and gears with compasses, saws, and files. In 1806 Eli Terry of Plymouth, Connecticut, built a waterpowered factory, installed lathes and other machinery, and by 1807 was astounding his competitors by turning out 200 wooden-movement clocks a year, a figure that ultimately rose to thousands, with movements of brass as well as wood. Any debt owed by Terry to Whitney remains conjectural, despite an assertion by Terry's onetime partner and later rival Seth Thomas that the Plymouth factory's machinery "was hinted to him by Eli Whitney."

Whitney's system had an important implication for the development of another basic component of American industry: machine tools. To make machinery, metal-working machines were needed. Britain was at this moment in the midst of creating these basic tools, adapting some from the lathes, planes, bits, augers, awls, chisels, and gouges of woodworking, and inventing others. Henry Maudslay was the leader in the development. Maudslay has generally received credit for originating the important "slide-rest lathe," in which the cutting tool was carried on a sliding carriage, advanced by a long screw that ran parallel to the axis of the workpiece.

But Samuel Slater's young friend, brother-in-law, and mechanic, David Wilkinson, invented a lathe very similar to Maudslay's in 1796, at least a year earlier than Maudslay, and it was Wilkinson's lathe that diffused in America (and in many other places in the world). In 1786–87 Wilkinson's father had started making large iron drive screws for paper-manufacturing presses, sending young David to Hope Furnace, in Scituate, Massachusetts, to cast the screws in clay molds, David then finishing them by hand in Pawtucket. The Wilkinsons expanded to making drive screws for clothiers' presses and oil mills. "But they were imperfect," David wrote, "and I told my father I wanted to make a machine to cut screws on centers [in other words, on a lathe], which would make them more perfect."

The project took several years and was interrupted by David's other activities — helping Samuel Slater, building lock machinery for the Middlesex Canal, even an early steamboat. In 1794 Oziel Wilkinson built a rolling and slitting mill in Pawtucket, and here David put into operation his new machine "on the principle of the gauge or sliding lathe now in every workshop almost throughout the world. . . . I cut screws of all dimensions by this machine, and did them perfectly."

Wilkinson was especially proud of the rocklike stability of his device. In 1797, he journeyed to Philadelphia to apply for a patent, returning home to find that the well-known ironmaster Jacob Perkins had come to see his machine, and had been so delighted with it that he had "laughed out, and remarked that he could do his engraving on cast steel for Bank Note plates with that machine, — that he could make a hair stroke with [it], for it would never tremble. . . ." Another visitor, a master machinist from England, had quite a different reaction: He "advised me as a friend to abandon my new machine, for said he, 'you can *ner* do it, for we have tried it out and out at *ome*, and given it up; and don't you think we should have been doing it at *ome* if it could have been done?' "

Wilkinson made patterns for his lathe and had it cast, "and it worked to a charm." He sold the patterns for ten dollars to Richard and William Anthony, sons of the Daniel Anthony for whom he had helped build a model of the Arkwright spinning frame in 1789 — "And this is all I ever received for so valuable an invention." It was all he received up to the time of writing his memoir in 1846, but two years later, when he was almost seventy-eight years old, he was the recipient of a significant as well as gratifying award of $10,000 by resolution of Congress "for the benefits accruing to the public service [i.e., the arsenals] from the use of the principle of the gauge and sliding lathe of which he is the inventor."

As for Eli Whitney, through the early years of the new century his life continued to be full of hard work, anxiety, and frustration. He wrote a friend:

"You will find me a solitary Being, without a companion & almost without a friend . . . living on plain fare in a humble cottage. . . . If I had a house, a wife & a home —." He referred to himself as "Old Bachelor." The fact seems to be that he had fallen in love with the magnetic Catherine Greene, but never to have dared tell her so. Twice-widowed Catherine would have been receptive to an offer from Whitney. Her letters were transparent. "I wish to god my dear friend you were married," she wrote. ". . . I am prepared to love any woman who would make you happy." And again, "Never — Never shall I Cease Considering you My Son — and never never Cease lamenting that you were not born so," a gross exaggeration of their twelve-year age difference. And, "I wish also to whisper other secrets in your Ear — which I certainly should do if you were seting by me. . . . I comfort myself sometimes in looking at your picture and mentally conversing with it — and sometimes in the Lover stile give it a kiss." And, "You see how little I can do without you — and I can see how much I could do — if I had your advice and assistance for a month . . . Save my life in saving your own — for I find I can not comfortably be in this world if you are not of it." And, "Your picture ornaments my toilet table — It is every day looked at and some times kissed — that is to say when you are sick." But Whitney, diffident, obtuse, or distracted by a large government contract resulting from the outbreak of the War of 1812, let Catherine die in 1814 without ever seeing her again.

Two years later he married, at the age of fifty-two. His bride, Henrietta Edwards, whom he had known since she was a little girl, was twenty years younger, not renowned for her beauty, and on the verge of becoming a spinster. Yet they were evidently happy in their eight years of married life. Whitney's death in 1825 left three children (another had died), of whom Eli Whitney, Jr., grew up to take over his father's arms business.

Despite the cataclysmic effect of his cotton gin on the South, Whitney never took any interest in politics, and the word *slavery* is not even mentioned in his correspondence. The indifference was mutual. The gin-created cotton kingdom, driven to expand to escape exhausted soil, took slavery with it westward, and created fatal conflict with the wheat and corn farmers of the old Northwest over the trans-Mississippi territories. Press and pulpit of the whole country debated slavery and bandied secession, but the man whose invention had loosed the whirlwind was largely forgotten.

In 1832 a South Carolinian published an article about Whitney with the avowed aim of rescuing the South's benefactor from oblivion, but it was not till the end of the century that American schoolchildren learned that "Eli Whitney invented the cotton gin in 1793."

Even longer delayed was recognition of his role in the history of mass production, partly perhaps because of his casual failure to patent machinery, but mostly because the significance of mass production was so tardily appreciated.

STUDY GUIDE

1. Some inventions may be a single stroke of the imagination of one creative mind, but many seem to develop through the cumulative contributions of several people. To what extent were Whitney's cotton gin and interchangeable parts original with him?

2. Some American inventors were uneducated farm boys, others were college graduates, though none had the equivalent of a modern engineering education. Yet there may have been some similarities in their backgrounds or turn of mind that account for their imaginative solutions to practical problems. What do you see in Whitney's youth that foreshadows his later career?

3. Some of the inventions of the early Industrial Revolution had been developed in England and France, but not much used there as compared to their rapid and wide acceptance in the United States. What factors can you think of in those countries — such as labor, tradition, markets, and the like — that might explain a somewhat more conservative attitude toward new inventions?

4. Suppose the cotton gin had never been invented, and it had proved impossible to grow the long-staple, or Sea Island, cotton any place except along

the coast of South Carolina and Georgia. How would this have affected slavery, westward expansion, and American social and political life?

5. How do the life, the rewards, and the conditions of one's work differ for an inventor in today's corporate, industrialized world? What examples can you think of, in inventions or improvements of products, that are not used because they would affect a company's sales or profits? What problems does a single, independent inventor face today in developing such improvements?

BIBLIOGRAPHY

The Gieses' book, from which the preceding selection is taken, is a delightful series of sketches of American inventors from John Fitch and Robert Fulton to Charles Goodyear and Thomas Edison. But the Industrial Revolution cannot be understood only through the lives of inventors and great business leaders. A volume that does provide a survey of the many factors involved, including transportation and labor as well as technology and business leadership, is Thomas C. Cochran and William Miller, *The Age of Enterprise: A Social History of Industrial America* * (New York, 1942). Technology in early America is discussed in Brook Hindle, ed., *America's Wooden Age: Aspects of Its Early Technology* (Tarrytown, N.Y., 1975). Roger Burlingame has written several books on the history of technology; his *March of the Iron Men: A Social History of Union through Invention* (New York, 1938) emphasizes the social environment of inventions. If you like a biographical approach to history, you might enjoy reading a full biography of Samuel Slater, Samuel F. B. Morse, or some other American inventor. Two of the best studies concern Eli Whitney: Jeannette Mirsky and Allan Nevins, *The World of Eli Whitney* (New York, 1952), and Constance Green, *Eli Whitney and the Birth of American Technology* * (Boston, 1956).

The literature on American economic development is too vast to be listed here. There are scores of fine studies of manufacturing, agriculture, railroads and canals, labor, the factory system, and finance. Gilbert C. Fite and Jim E. Reese, *An Economic History of the United States,* 3rd ed. (Boston, 1973) has individual chapters on these subjects and an excellent bibliography. One classic work on the pre–Civil War period is George R. Taylor, *The Transportation Revolution, 1815–1860* * (New York, 1951).

As you might imagine, the people who actually confronted the Industrial Revolution experienced considerable conflict and anxiety. Carefully acquired skills were outdated by the new machines, women and children competed with men for jobs, new and distant markets developed, the place of employment was now outside of the home, and the industrial system seemed to be in conflict with some deeply held social and ethical beliefs. These sorts of concerns are studied in three volumes: Marvin Fisher, *Workshops in the Wilderness: The European Response to American Industrialization, 1830–1860* (New York, 1967); John F. Kasson, *Civilizing the Machine: Technology and Republican Values in America, 1776–1900* * (New York, 1976); and Leo

Marx, *The Machine in the Garden: Technology and the Pastoral Ideal in America* * (New York, 1964). Your library might also have some of the works of Lewis Mumford, whose sweeping studies range over industrialization and urbanization, the social and psychological changes brought about by invention, and the European scene as well as nineteenth-century America. Two other works that relate aesthetics to industrialization are Siegfried Giedion, *Mechanization Takes Command: A Contribution to Anonymous History* * (New York, 1948), and John A. Kouwenhoven, *Made in America: The Arts in Modern Civilization* * (Garden City, N.Y., 1962).

Finally, some scholars have attempted to understand the impact of industrialism by cameo studies of individual towns or factories. Three exemplary works of this type are Alan Dawley, *Class and Community: The Industrial Revolution in Lynn* (Cambridge, Mass., 1976); Stephan Thernstrom, *Poverty and Progress: Social Mobility in a Nineteenth Century City* * (Cambridge, Mass., 1964); and Anthony F. C. Wallace, *Rochdale: The Growth of an American Village in the Early Industrial Revolution* (New York, 1978).

* Asterisk indicates book is available in a paperback edition.

*"Sing-Sing Camp Meeting" by Joseph B. Smith, 1838. (Detail)
One of the faithful is "treeing the devil."*

9

CHARLES A. JOHNSON

Religious Democracy

Religious organizations, like most institutions, reflect the social forces of their particular society and time. Even such a world-wide organization as the Roman Catholic Church has differed in doctrine and rites of worship in different countries, and most churches that survive a century or more undergo subtle changes. American Protestantism has been substantially transformed since It was first brought to these shores, and few of the changes have been so profound as those that came about in the first half of the nineteenth century.

Both New England Calvinism and the pietistic religions of Pennsylvania were brought to the colonies by small, tightly-knit groups of devout believers. But the churches soon faced the question of whether or not to modify their doctrines and soften their requirements in order to retain the membership of later generations who held the beliefs less intensely and found the worship less satisfying. By the early 1700s, many people felt that the churches had compromised too much, and they responded enthusiastically to the first "Great Awakening," a religious revival movement that attracted many followers in the 1730s. The second major revival movement, which began about 1800, had its roots in a society that seemed to be increasingly secular and among a people who found a highly rational religion emotionally barren. Yet the remarkable religious awakening that swept across the country at the beginning of the nineteenth century was quite different from the earlier revival and had a much longer-range impact upon American Protestantism.

Theologically, one of the characteristics of the Second Great Awakening was the new emphasis upon Jesus, rather than upon

God the Father or the remote Creator of the Deists, an emphasis that has dominated Protestant thought and worship ever since. Preaching the salvation of all men, Protestant churches in the early nineteenth century outgrew the boundaries of a single colony or state and developed broad, national denominations. Between 1800 and 1850, Protestantism also assumed a new sense of mission and destiny, as did the American secular philosophy of the period. Bible, tract, and missionary societies were formed to carry the Word to the unsettled West, and each denomination established a multitude of colleges to provide a Christian education for the young.

Many of these developments took place after the most emotional revivalism had subsided. Yet the whole first half of the century witnessed a strong element of religious emotionalism and democratization, as evidenced in the founding of several new faiths. Spiritualism, Mormonism, and Adventism all had distinctive appeals, but like the revival itself, they succeeded because they found a people who were receptive to an emotional religious experience. Evidence of the revival was seen in the eastern states even before 1800, but the frenzy took its most distinctive form in the frontier communities farther west. Kentucky camp meetings were awesome in the crowds they drew and the religious exercises that characterized them. In the following selection, Charles A. Johnson gives a composite portrait of such meetings.

The setting of the early Kentucky camp meeting was "nature's temple" — the forest clearing. Just one step removed from the cabin meeting place, frontier encampments "offered nothing by way of worshipful environment save the natural beauty of a grove of trees on a sloping green." This very lack of artificiality gave the open-air revival its great religious power, a power that was never more explosively demonstrated than during the era of the Second Great Awakening (1800–1805).

The first encampments were cleared areas of the forest close to meetinghouses which in their turn served the several functions of worship centers, refuges for prostate mourners, and lodging places for visiting clergymen. Since frontier churches were frequently located near waterways, it was only natural that camp sites were chosen near springs or

From *The Frontier Camp Meeting* by Charles A. Johnson. Copyright 1955 by Southern Methodist University Press. Reprinted by permission of the publisher.

creeks and if possible on navigable rivers. Hence the distinctive names of the encampments of the Great Revival — "Muddy River," "Drake's Creek," "Red River," and "Cabin Creek." Aside from its aesthetic appeal, the chosen site had to provide drinking water, dry ground, shade, pasturage for the horses, and timber for tentpoles and firewood.

These desirable locations were not hard to find in the newly settled regions, and men with ax and sledge could quickly convert a two- to four-acre tract of forest land into an encampment. There was hectic activity as the prospective worshipers arrived at the spot, a week before or just prior to meeting time. Underbrush was cleared away, trees were felled, and preparations were made for a tent city.

Through the years encampments adhered to three general patterns: the rectangular, horseshoe, and circular forms. The last-named was by far the most popular. Regardless of shape, tents formed the outer shell which enclosed the core of the camp meeting, the open-air auditorium. After a few years' experience, sponsors in the West urged that a supervisor be appointed to inform incoming wagoners of the encampment plan, so that much of the milling about on the first meeting day could be avoided.

Circular rows or streets of tents were irregularly arranged following the contour of the land on the edge of the area of cleared ground, with walks between. Camp meeting veteran Jesse Lee described the living facilities utilized in 1809:

> The land is cleared . . . to hold as many tents as will be erected, we then have the front of the tents on a line on each side, and at each end. Back of the tents we have a place cleared for the carriages to stand . . . so that every tent may have a carriage belonging to it in a convenient position. Just back of the carriages we have the horses tied and fed. Before the tents we generally have the fires for cooking, and to help in giving light at night to see who are walking about (if more convenient), fires are placed behind the tents.

The number of temporary camp structures that rose as if by magic varied with the stage of settlement in the community involved. There might be twenty or as many as two hundred tents, of various materials and sizes. Some were made of sail or cotton cloth "hung upon poles in the shape of a roof of a house." Others were strictly homemade affairs, fashioned from two or three old quilts or coverlets sewn together. Even several sheets tacked together served the purpose; wealthier folk might make a home out of a bolt of muslin. "Bush arbors" erected beside covered wagons or carriages served some as temporary housing. A few even had wooden shelters with clapboard roofs. These were the "log tents," although cloth ones were more usual.

The backwoods camp meeting differed from its eastern imitator in size as well as in the number of tents. Encampments of the East, although very similar in design to those of the frontier, were established on a grander and more pretentious scale. While some eastern shelters housed but a single group, a great number were large enough for many families. Perhaps twenty to fifty and even a hundred individuals found shelter under a single canvas. Mammoth tents were typical here. Likewise the eastern campers' furnishings included many of the comforts of home. The pioneer, by contrast, was lucky to have any piece of rude furniture. His bed might be of straw, or a makeshift one of poles and blankets. Indeed, many at the Great Revival camp meetings slept on the ground, rolled up in blankets, when the homes of neighbors and the meetinghouse were full.

Preachers shared the same simple accommodations as the worshipers. Bishop William McKendree's quarters at the initial encampment in the Missouri Territory were "made by sewing the preacher's saddle blankets together and spreading them over a pole supported by forks in the ground like soldiers' tents." One end of the tent was closed with green boughs, while the other was left open, with a fire in front of it. Bedding arrangements were often as primitive. At one eastern campground six ministers slept in a huge bed made up of overlapping blankets, ingeniously arranged.

The main physical feature of any camp meeting landscape east or west was the pulpit. Once a site was cleared, this was set up at one or both ends of the natural amphitheater, facing the parallel rows of seats. These stands were supplemented by fallen logs or wagon beds, from which ministers spellbound groups of listeners. Some of the pulpits were merely upraised platforms on stilts; others were sturdy, two-level affairs, often roofed to keep out the elements. Possibly ten feet square, the platforms were commodious enough to hold not only the speaker but also the several exhorters and ministers who were awaiting their turns to speak. Many were large enough to accommodate a dozen people. By standing in an elevated position four to eight feet higher than the milling crowds, a preacher had a better chance of being seen and heard. Competing attractions gave the flighty a chance to wander from one orator to another, and the din and disorder gave even certain "sons of thunder" trouble.

If the minister proved to be a pulpit thumper, members of the audience who seated themselves directly below the scaffold occupied a hazardous position. The Reverend James B. Finley recalled that more than once a front seat occupant was "suddenly aroused by the fall of a pitcher of water, or the big Bible upon the cranium." Seats for the audience, where they existed, were merely felled logs cross-laid, or planks supported by tree stumps. The bark was dressed and the top adzed off to make them as comfortable as possible. This crude arrangement was not only the result of necessity; it was also consonant with John Wesley's rule concerning church seating: "Let there be no pews, and *no backs* to the seats." Also in accordance with the founder's wishes, the open-air auditorium was carefully divided, the women located on the right and the men on the left. On some campgrounds a rail fence or wooden partition emphasized this demarkation of the sexes.

In both slaveholding and nonslaveholding regions, the Negroes were allowed to set up their own camps behind the preacher's rostrum. Because of the close proximity, their services often merged with those of the whites, adding no little to the general confusion and emotional excitement. The Negro housing area, with its crazy-quilt tents after the fashion of Joseph's coat, was a picturesque affair. As the camp meeting matured, the Negro camp section was sometimes separated from that of the whites by a plank partition. This barrier was torn down on the final meeting day when the two peoples joined together in a song festival and "marching ceremony."

Illumination for the evening services presented no problem to the resourceful campers. At first, the lighting was provided by candles and pine knot torches affixed to preaching stands, trees, or other convenient places. Jesse Lee, writing of the first campgrounds, recalled seeing one hundred and twenty candles burning at the same time. When campfires were located in front of the tents, they also helped light up the worship area. Gradually, fire stands known as "fire altars" came into regular use. These stands were erected in the four corners of the auditorium and consisted of earthen-covered platforms on upraised tripods some six feet high. Bark, twigs, or "pine wood fires" burned on top of a layer of earth and sod. Later, oil lamps were utilized. At night the glare of the campfire, the flickering candles and torches, and the blazing fire altars all added an eerie touch to the colorful services.

The communion table set up at the initial woodland meeting in Missouri in 1809 was doubtless similar to those used during the Kentucky Revival. That sacramental table consisted of a "puncheon" split from a log, smoothed on the upper side, and laid on crossties supported by four forks placed in the ground. The whole was covered with a sheet, "for there were no table-cloths then."

Usually no provisions were made for inclement weather; at the first Kentucky meetings enthusiasts worshiped out of doors in the midst of violent rainstorms. A few people could huddle in cloth or log shelters, but the western camp meeting was not noted for its comforts. The worshipers at the Goshen, Illinois, encampment of 1807 must have been surprised to find a large arbor in the form of an L erected there, an arbor spacious enough to cover seven hundred people. In the East, by contrast, most campgrounds were dominated by huge tents that afforded privacy for prayer in good weather and shelter in bad weather. Kentucky accommodations in 1800 were crude but sufficient, and the pioneer settler did not complain. He had journeyed to the camp meeting expecting no great physical comforts; he had come to see for himself this religious marvel that was transforming men's lives.

The Second Great Awakening was the era of the gigantic camp meeting — the "General Camp Meeting" — where the unusual was the usual, where Presbyterian, Methodist, and Baptist ministers worked side by side, where the crowds were numbered in the hundreds and frequently the thousands, and where scores were swept into mass hysteria by the frenzied proceedings. These joint meetings were of two types, the "Sacramental" and the "Union" meeting, the former being so named because of the celebration of the Lord's Supper. When the time arrived for this ceremony Baptist leaders withdrew and the Methodists and Presbyterians conducted joint communion services. It was at the Union encampments, however, that the three denominations worshiped together most successfully. About these early meetings [James] McGready could write glowingly that "bigotry and prejudice have received a death wound. . . . Presbyterians and Methodists love one another."

Among the Methodists, William McKendree looms large in the story of the "General Camp Meeting." He was assisted by a host of other traveling preachers, including William Burke, John Sale, Benjamin Lakin, and Henry Smith. McKendree had become enthusiastic over the camp meeting while an itinerant and district supervisor in southern Kentucky. In 1801 he overcame his denominational prejudice to co-operate with certain Presbyterian leaders who were pioneering the innovation. Joint committees were set up, empowered to make camp regulations and appoint speakers for the outdoor sacraments. It was evident that enthusiasm for a new technique and the excitement of leading great numbers to the Lord were bringing about close co-operation among frontier preachers of differing denominations. The future of interdenominational harmony looked bright as the camp meeting enjoyed its first tumultuous surge.

During his union arrangement with the Presbyterians McKendree temporarily suspended the Methodist class meetings, the "love feasts," and the regular operations of the itinerant system. By 1802 the highly successful General Camp Meetings of Methodists and Presbyterians (and sometimes Baptists) were well known. Yet rumbles of discontent with the practice were heard late in the very first year, indicating that the spirit of partisanship was still strong.

William Burke, speaking for the Methodists, complained bitterly that Presbyterians "were pressing in their invitations" to the sacramental gatherings but refused to support his denomination's open-air quarterly meetings, because of other appointments they had to meet. While the rivals of Methodism remained away from encampments on Friday, Saturday, and Sunday, continued Burke,

> on Monday we generally saw some of their ministers in the congregation, but having our plans filled up for that day we consequently paid no attention to them; for we were fully satisfied that they only wanted the Methodists to shake the bush, and they would catch the birds. My advice to our official members

in quarterly meetings was, to quietly withdraw from their meetings, and mind our own business. They did so.

Actually, the co-operative arrangement did last several years longer, although the union grew weaker and weaker, terminating in the last year of the Great Revival, 1804.

Attracted by the forest revival's novelty, families of every Protestant faith mingled at these Great Revival encampments. Reports of the frenzied services had caused some to think the world was coming to an end; others anticipated a dreadful calamity about to befall the young country as a judgment of God on an impious people; still others saw meetings as "the work of the devil who had been unchained for a season . . . to deceive the ministers of religion and the very elect themselves." The byways were alive with settlers, and the numbers in attendance were almost unbelievable. It seemed as if the entire population were hitting the camp meeting trail. Writing in the 1840's, Presbyterian Robert Davidson reflected upon the revival's lure·

> The laborer quitted his task; Age snatched his crutch; Youth forgot his pastime; the plow was left in the furrow; the deer enjoyed a respite upon the mountains; business of all kinds was suspended; dwelling houses were deserted; whole neighborhoods were emptied; bold hunters and sober matrons, young women and maidens, and little children, flocked to the common center of attraction; every difficulty was surmounted, every risk ventured to be present at the camp-meeting.

Participants in the 1800 and 1801 Kentucky and Tennessee camp meetings have insisted that the crowds numbered from three to twenty thousand at various times, according to the density of population in the neighboring territory. Although seemingly fantastic, these figures are borne out by more than one account. "Many thousands" met at Desha's Creek in August, 1800, to fall "like corn before a storm of wind." At the Cabin Creek Union Meeting in May, 1801, twenty thousand worshipers congregated; Point Pleasant had four thousand in attendance; and Indian Creek had ten thousand.

Perhaps equally significant was the great number of frontier preachers who turned their siege guns on the campers. Peter Cartwright said the number of churchmen of different denominations who joined forces at any one of these woodland Bethels in Kentucky, Tennessee, and the Carolinas might reach "ten, twenty, and sometimes thirty." They preached, harangued, exhorted, and prayed "night and day, four or five days together," and often for a week or more.

The immensity of the throng impressed a newcomer to a Cumberland Revival camp meeting — a "scene of confusion that could scarce be put into human language." There were not enough ministers present to keep the crowds seated or attentive; spectators walked about talking, laughing, smoking, and gesticulating during the services. Free of the restraint of a formal meetinghouse, the people indulged in complete emotional freedom and frequently reverted to herd behavior. If a particular sermon or song excited them, they cried, shouted, groaned, or repeated the spoken phrases over and over again in increasing tempo.

> There would be an unusual outcry; some bursting forth into loud ejaculations of prayer, or thanksgiving, for the truth; . . . others flying to their careless friends, with tears of compassion; beseeching them to turn to the Lord; some struck with terror, and hastening through the crowd to make their escape, or pulling away their relations; others . . . fainting and swooning away.

Preachers often found it impossible to maintain order when they themselves were physically exhausted from straining their voices so that thousands could hear them. At communion services their labors were intensified. The Reverend John Lyle, a Presbyterian, thought he was going to faint or die from the exertion of delivering the "action" sermon to about eight thousand at a Paint Creek meeting in 1801, "yet notwithstanding spoke above an hour."

Competing with the preacher most of the day were the typical background noises — outbursts from the audience, sermons being delivered from other stands, and the offerings of praying and singing circles and groups. Largely unplanned, the service routine was most often spontaneous. At two separate stands, said one itinerant,

> we had preaching alternately through the day. . . . Each public service was followed by a prayer meeting which was not to be broken off to make way for preaching, but the trumpet was sounded at the other stand, whither all who wished to hear preaching were wont to repair.

The Reverend John Lyle reported that ten, twenty, and sometimes the majority of people under conviction offered up individual prayers simultaneously. Since this was a social as well as a religious occasion, whiskey had to be available to ease the parched throats of the participants. The "dissolute and irreligious were frequently more numerous than the serious minded," and to cater to their tastes, barrels of whiskey were hidden in the bushes to be retailed by the cupful later. Preacher Richard McNemar commented on the dregs of frontier society that took this opportunity to heckle and carouse. Even harsher judgment was expressed by Methodist historian Nathan Bangs:

> It is admitted that in such vast multitudes, assembled in the open air, under circumstances of such peculiar excitement, and many of them not well instructed in science or morals, there must have been some disorder, some mingling of human passions not sanctified by grace, and some words and gesticulations not in accordance with strict religious decorum. Every action, therefore, and everything which was said and done [at these camp meetings], I am by no means careful to defend or pledged to justify.

Immoral practices were frequent enough at these encampments to be commented upon by the camp leaders. Such immorality is not surprising when the mixed character of the pioneer audiences is taken into account. Certainly, the precedent-shattering size of the crowds and the emotional hysteria of the services did nothing to weaken such tendencies. Preacher Lyle, a sharp critic of the revival, stated that acts of immorality took place on the grounds under cover of darkness, or in the neighboring forest. He candidly told the facts of the situation concerning his own congregation. Some of the women who were the most persistent victims of the "falling exercise" were the ones prone to forget the edict of virtue. Thus "Becca Bell, who often fell, is now big with child to a wicked trifling school master of the name of Brown who says he'll be damned to hell if he ever marries her." Several other of Lyle's female parishioners "got careless," including "Polly Moffitt who was with child to Petty and died miserably in child bed." A preventive measure of indeterminate value was the "night watch" set up at the Sugar Ridge, Kentucky, camp meeting of August, 1802. This consisted of two men who patrolled the grounds and checked the meetinghouse to prevent any irregularities.

Often setting the pattern of emotionalism was the camp preacher, himself overcome by the excitement and by his own success as a soul-saver. William McGee "would sometimes exhort after the sermons, standing on the floor, or sitting, or lying in the dust, his eyes streaming, and his heart so full that he could only ejaculate 'Jesus, Jesus.'" A Methodist minister claimed that Presbyterian leaders, not being accustomed to such noise and shouting, were particularly susceptible when they yielded to their emotions and "went into great excess, and downright wildness." When preaching had ended, the service was frequently carried on by the audience — men, women, and even little children — who exhorted one another, prayed, wept, and even preached. One tale is told of a seven-year-old child who "sat on the shoulders of a man and preached til she sank exhausted on the bearer's head." There was scarcely a moment when activity was not going on, whether staged by the minister or by his congregation. "When the shout of the King was in the camp" evening worship frequently extended until dawn. Old men who knew they could not spend the night awake brought "great coats" to keep themselves warm and took short naps on the ground with the sleeping children under the shelter of the trees while the worship surged around them.

The doctrines advanced during the Great Revival consisted of the preaching of universal redemption, free and full salvation, justification by faith, regeneration by the Holy Ghost, and the joy of a living religion. Often, the method used to convey this message created bedlam. A settler of sin-soaked habits was overwhelmed by electrifying tirades. The celebrated Presbyterian revivalist, James McGready, deliberately used strong language in classifying the erring members present. Blasphemers would be dragged by the fiends of Hell into the "liquid, boiling waves" only to fall to the "deepest cavern in the flaming abyss." With the shrieks and yells encompassing him, the listener could well believe Judgment Day was upon him at that very moment, and that he himself, found lacking, was at the mouth of Hell. Such frightening preaching amidst eerie surroundings mowed the weary and overwrought sinners down in sheaves.

Less violent methods were also effectively used to bring about conversion. Songs such as "Hark My Friend That Solemn Toll" and "Pray Cast a Look Upon That Bier" reminded the sinners sadly of the universal end of man. The refrain of one song by John A. Granade, a contemporary camp meeting song writer, was aimed directly at the wavering:

> Think on what the Saviour bore,
>   In the gloomy garden,
> Sweating blood at every pore
>   To procure thy pardon;
> See him stretch'd upon the wood,
>   Bleeding, grieving, crying,
> Suff'ring all the wrath of God,
>   Groaning, gasping, dying!
>
> 'Tis done! the dreadful debt is paid,
>   The great atonement now is made;
> Sinners on me your guilt is laid,
>   For you I spilt my blood.

The first response of the crowds to the novel encampment conditions and the high-tension services was improvised and diverse. Later, these first responses tended to become stereotyped and to be repeated in every meeting. Most of the disorder and at least a part of the physical excitement came under leader control as the camp meeting developed. These first camp meetings were tumultuous almost beyond comprehension, and the effect upon the participants was in proportion. It was almost impossible for the worshipers not to feel that something great and extraordinary — that is, the active participation of the Lord — was going on.

The record of "acrobatic Christianity" at the Kentucky and Tennessee revivals is the more understandable when viewed against the backdrop of the awe-inspiring evening worship, where candlelight and campfires lit the shadowy scene, and where impassioned exhortations, prayers, and spirituals contributed to the extreme excitement of the "awakened sinners." From this high-voltage atmosphere burst forth many strange things. Five hundred or more would shout aloud "the high praises of God at once," and the "cries of the distressed . . . the rejoicing of those that were delivered from their sins of bondage" would rend the air. Women, particularly, would be affected. Some in the "transport of their feelings" hugged and kissed everyone in their vicinity. As Methodist leader John McGee described the "Ridge" meeting of August, 1800:

> The nights were truly awful; the camp ground was well illuminated; the people were differently exercised all over the ground, some exhorting, some shouting, some praying, and some crying for mercy, while others lay as dead men on the ground.

Terror, distress, and despair seemed to overcome some congregations. Saints and sinners, young and old, white and Negro would, "with a piercing scream, fall like a log on the floor, earth, or mud, and appear as dead."

Along with the shouting, the "falling exercise" was the most common of all forms of bodily excitement. According to one participant, the "falling down of multitudes, and their crying out . . . happened under the singing of Watt's Psalms and Hymns, more frequently than under the preaching of the word." When six or more hymns were sung simultaneously by different groups at a Providence, Kentucky, revival in 1801, there were accompanying violent motions of the body. Women in their frantic agitations sometimes "unconsciously tore open their bosoms and assumed indelicate attitudes." Those falling would be affected in varying degrees:

> Sometimes, when unable to stand or sit, they have the use of their hands, and can converse with perfect composure. In other cases, they are unable to speak, the pulse becomes weak, and they draw a difficult breath about once a minute; in some instances their extremities become cold, and pulsation, breathing and all the signs of life, forsake them for nearly an hour. Persons who have been in this situation have uniformly avowed, that they felt no bodily pain; that they had the entire use of their reason and reflection, and when recovered, they could relate everything that had been said or done near them.

When the "fallers" had recovered, they often arose shouting, "Praise God!" Soon those saved broke forth in a volley of exhortation. Some had seen visions, heard unspeakable words, smelled fragrant odors, and had "a delightful singing in the breast." The Reverend George Baxter reported that the first persons who lost consciousness at the Cane Ridge revival were a source of amazement for some of the Presbyterians in the audience, but after a little time "the falling down became so familiar as to excite no disturbance." In the summer of 1801, a Fleming Creek encampment had one hundred fallers, a Point Pleasant camp meeting two hundred and fifty, and at Indian Creek eight hundred persons were reported struck down. When the falling reached such alarming proportions, to prevent those stricken from "being trodden under foot by the multitude, they were collected together and laid out in order, on two squares of the meeting house, til a considerable part of the floor was covered."

Some were struck down at the camp meeting after exhibiting symptoms of "deepest impressions" and the shedding of tears; others fell on their way home, or while working in the fields. The Reverend John Lyle was more concerned about the aftereffects of this manifestations. He feared they would become habitual: "The oftener they fall they will more easily fall again, and will become at length the sport of lesser passions." A case in point was Henry McDanal's wife, who had "swooned away" for two successive days at an 1801 encampment, "and since she came home has fallen again and again and still feels guilt and misery." Lyle's application of a "vial of hartshorn" to the fallen was without success in any case. The lancet was equally ineffective, although used to such an extent that according to one excited camper, the Gasper River meeting place "was crowded with bleeding bodies like a battlefield."

In many cases toughs and scoffers fell at the services "as suddenly as if struck by lightening," sometimes at the very moment when they were cursing the revival. One unbeliever tried to prove that the fallers were shamming, and so prodded them with a nail on a stick, but to no avail. He had boasted that he would not fall, and so got liquored up, thinking that would pacify his feelings. In a short time, however, he too was struck down, and when able to speak "acknowledged himself a great sinner, and hoped for pardon through Christ."

If the seizure was not so sudden, different manifestations might occur before exhaustion set in. Numerous leaders of the Kentucky Revival, including Stone, Baxter, Finley, McNemar, and Lyle, have described versions of nervous affection, in addition to falling — jerking, rolling, dancing, running, singing, laughing, and barking. The "jerking exercise" seemed to be the most common reaction to the stimulus offered at the Kentucky and Tennessee meetings, and the one that spread most rapidly through a congregation. Even preachers were not immune. The Reverend Samuel Doak insisted he was occasionally the subject of that bodily exercise for more than twenty years. The jerks varied in some degree from person to person:

> Sometimes the subject of the jerks would be affected in some one member of the body, and sometimes in the whole system. When the head alone was affected, it would be jerked backward and forward, or from side to side, so quickly that the features of the face could not be distinguished. When the whole system was affected, I have seen the person stand in one place, and jerk backward and forward in quick succession, their heads nearly touching the floor behind and after. . . . I have inquired of those thus affected. They could not account for it; but some have told me that those were among the happiest seasons of their lives. I have seen some wicked persons thus affected, and all the time cursing the jerks, while they were thrown to the earth with a violence. Though so awful to behold, I do not remember that any of the thousands I have seen ever sustained an injury in body. This was as strange as the exercise itself.

Peter Cartwright recollected that he had seen more than five hundred persons jerking at one time at Great Revival encampments. It would excite his "risibilities" to see the ornately dressed gentlemen's and young ladies' "fine bonnets, caps, and combs fly; and so sudden would be the jerking of the head that their long loose hair would crack almost as loud as a wagoner's whip." If one eccentric reporter is to be believed, some camp leaders in anticipation of this exercise cut saplings breast high to support the jerkers, who "kicked up the earth as a horse stamping flies."

Then there was the "rolling exercise." Starting with a violent jerk that threw the person down, it doubled him up and rolled him over and over like a wheel or ball. According to a Great Revival minister, "this was considered very debasing and mortifying, especially if the person was taken in this manner through the mud and sullied therewith from head to foot."

More socially acceptable was the "dancing exercise." This movement began with the jerking of the legs and feet and proceeded to assume the characteristics of a dance, as the person affected "continued to move forward and backward in the same track or alley til nature seemed exhausted." Spectators seemed to think this was "heavenly." Some insisted that "there was nothing in it like levity, nor calculated to excite levity in beholders."

The "running exercise" was merely an attempt to escape the nervous affections. If any person tried to resist, the jerks would become more severe. One rowdy, feeling the jerks coming on, tried to escape to the bordering woods and fortify himself with some liquor, but the bottle was knocked from his hands and broken on a seedling. At this he became so enraged that he cursed and raved, but "at length he fetched a very violent jerk, snapped his neck, and soon expired, with his mouth full of cursing and bitterness." This fatality is the only one on record attributed to the jerks.

To preacher Stone the most unaccountable phenomenon was the "singing exercise." The subject, with a happy countenance, "would sing most melodiously, not from the mouth or nose, but entirely in the breast, the sounds issuing thence. . . . It was most heavenly. None could ever be tired of hearing it." Equally indescribable to Stone was the "laughing exercise." He stated that it happened frequently but only to the devout worshipers. Paradoxically, this loud hearty laughter indulged in by a few individuals was not infectious, but produced solemnity in saints and sinners. Other chroniclers called it the "holy laugh," but referred to it as a form of hysteria that gripped audiences most frequently after 1803.

The "barking exercise" was intimately related to jerking. It seemed that the disorder passed from the nerves and muscles to the mind. Men fancied themselves dogs, "went down on all fours and barked til they grew hoarse. It was reportedly no uncommon sight to behold numbers of them gathered about a tree, barking, yelping, 'treeing the devil.'" Preacher Stone discounted this dog delusion, preferring to believe that the grunts or barks resulted from the suddenness of the jerks. The name of the exercise apparently originated when an old Presbyterian clergyman in eastern Tennessee got the jerks and grasped a tree for support. Some punster who found him in that position reported he had found the minister barking up a tree.

The most fabulous of all Great Revival camp meetings, the one which seemed to incorporate and enlarge upon every excess of the previous revivals, was Cane Ridge. A "General Camp Meeting," the Cane Ridge sacramental services were staged some seven miles from Paris in Bourbon County, Kentucky. This camp meeting began on August 6, 1801, and continued for six long days. From Friday to Wednesday the frenzied worship continued night and day without intermission "either in public or private exercise of devotion." Even heavy showers failed to scatter the audience. Although it was held under joint sponsorship, Cane Ridge seems to have been largely the work of the Presbyterian Reverend Barton W. Stone, a farmer-preacher. Another churchman of the same faith reported that he attended along with "eighteen Presbyterian ministers, and Baptist and Methodist preachers," although he could not recall the exact number of the latter two groups.

Cane Ridge is important not only as a turning point in the history of the camp meeting but as a phenomenon of the Second Great Awakening. In many ways atypical, it has been the model many critics have used to create their lurid pictures of the outdoor revival. Cane Ridge was, in all probability, the most disorderly, the most hysterical, and the largest revival ever held in early-day America.

Attendance estimates of Cane Ridge range from ten to twenty-five thousand, with most authorities placing the number somewhere between the two figures. Eager participants had boasted that "many had come from Ohio"— probably from the Miami River Valley. While every shade of religious opinion was represented, there were many visitors whose religious convictions were nebulous. Tumult and disorder were inevitable when a heterogeneous group of such large proportions assembled, especially since the occasions for social companionship were so rare on the frontier.

If there is no agreement among participants as to the exact number that attended Cane Ridge, neither is there unity of opinion as to its place in history. Peter Cartwright insisted that Cane Ridge marked "the first camp-meeting ever held in the United States, and here our camp-meetings took their rise." The "Kentucky Boy" was not alone in this opinion. Confusing the issue was William Burke, Methodist participant at Cane Ridge. He insisted that this sacramental occasion was no camp meeting at all. While it was true that there were carriages and wagons on the grounds, "not a single tent was to be found, neither was any such thing as a camp meeting, heard of at that time." Burke himself had the only true tent, one he made on the spot out of poles and papaw bushes.

The Cane Ridge services, if they can be dignified by that name, almost defy description. A visitor to the Sunday sessions reported four different groups meeting simultaneously at various crude speaker's stands about a hundred yards apart. One of the rostrums contained a colored exhorter addressing his race. Another contemporary described the continuous preaching and exhorting. The attractions that caught his eye were the many "small [prayer] circles of ten or twelve," close together where "all engaged in singing Watts's and Hart's hymns." At the same time a minister would step upon a stump or a log and would attract as many as could collect around him. William Burke's technique is a case in point. He mounted a log and

> commenced reading a hymn with an audible voice, and by the time we concluded singing and praying we had around us, standing on their feet, by fair calculation ten thousand people. I gave out my text in the following words: "For we must all stand before the judgment seat of Christ," and before I concluded my voice was not to be heard for the groans of the distressed and the shouts of triumph. . . . Here I remained Sunday night, and Monday and Monday night; and during that time there was not a single moment's cessation, but the work went on.

Peter Cartwright said that at times there were more than a thousand shouting at once, creating such a volume of noise that the sound carried for miles. The overwhelming impact of this deafening uproar and contagious bodily excitement has been depicted by James B. Finley, who was then, according to his own appraisal, somewhat of a free thinker in religious matters.

> The noise was like the roar of Niagara. The vast sea of human beings seemed to be agitated as if by a storm. I counted seven ministers, all preaching at one time, some on stumps, others in wagons, and one . . . was standing on a tree which had, in falling, lodged against . . . another. Some of the people were singing, others praying, some crying for mercy in the most piteous accents, while others were shouting most vociferously. While witnessing these scenes, a peculiarly-strange sensation, such as I had never felt before, came over me. My heart beat tumultuously, my knees trembled, my lip quivered, and I felt as though I must fall to the ground. A strange supernatural power seemed to pervade the entire mass of mind there collected. . . . Soon after I left and went into the woods, and there I strove to rally and man up my courage.
>
> After some time I returned to the scene of excitement, the waves of which, if possible, had risen still higher. The same awfulness of feeling came over me. I stepped up on to a log, where I could have a better view of the surging sea of humanity. The scene that then presented itself to my mind was indescribable. At one time I saw at least five hundred swept down in a moment, as if a battery of a thousand guns had been opened upon them, and then immediately followed shrieks and shouts that rent the very heavens. . . . I fled for the woods a second time, and wished I had staid at home.

Probably the most intense excitement at Cane Ridge was experienced when the Sunday sacrament was served to some eight hundred to eleven hundred Presbyterian communicants and an indeterminate number of Methodists. Then the delivery of the impassioned sermons and exhortations prior to the sacrament resulted in some breath-taking spectacles. One preacher commented on the "one hundred persons of all classes, the learned and the unlearned, at once on the ground crying for mercy of all ages from eight to sixty years"; another reported that "undue excitement of animal feeling" resulted in at least one thousand persons' being swept into the falling exercise. The old campaigner, James Crawford, perhaps the "most reliable" of the Presbyterian frontier preachers, conscientiously counted the fallers and gave the higher figure of three thousand. A regular system of caring for the afflicted was in force. When a person was struck down he was carried out of the congregation, and then some minister or exhorter prayed with him against the background of a hymn "suitable to the occasion."

At this largest of all encampments the greatest number of sexual irregularities occurred. After the Saturday evening worship, for instance, six men were found lying under a preaching stand with a woman of easy virtue. The following evening a couple were caught in the act of adultery. James B. Finley, present at Cane Ridge, observed that while the religious services were going on, "all manner of wickedness was going on without." "Men," he continued, "furious with the effects of the maddening bowl would outrage all decency by their conduct." Camp sponsors declared that such carnal actions of "unclean persons" were deliberately aimed at bringing the religious revival into disrepute. Thus they discussed plans for supervision — having the stands watched and placing elders in the meetinghouse to make certain of the separation of the sexes in the sleeping arrangements.

There is no means of weighing the seriousness of the impression that Cane Ridge made upon the hearts and nervous systems of its thousands of participants. Certainly thousands were deeply moved. The number of those who professed conversion was estimated somewhere between one thousand and two thousand. The healing touch of revivalism was apparent on every hand. Among the happy converts were many men destined to be vigorous champions of the Christian life. James B. Finley, the celebrated circuit rider, dated his conversion from his troubled state of mind while a Cane Ridge visitor.

But what of the Kentucky Revival as a whole? Whether the majority of the conversions were lasting is problematical. Yet one contemporary historian, evaluating the movement in 1809, wrote:

> The effects of these camp meetings were of a mixed nature. They were doubtless attended for improper purposes by a few licentious persons and by others with a view of obtaining a handle to ridicule all religion. . . . The free intercourse of all ages and sexes under cover of night and the woods was not without its temptations. It is also to be feared that they gave rise to false notions of religion by laying too much stress on bodily exercises, and substituting them in the place of moral virtues or inward piety. These are too often considered as evidences of a change of heart and affections, though they neither proved or disproved anything of the kind. After each deduction is

made of these several accounts, it must be acknowledged that the good resulting from the camp meeting greatly preponderated over the evil. They roused that indifference to the future destiny of man which is too common, and gave rise to much serious thoughtfullness on subjects confessedly of the most interesting nature.

Visible proof of the effectiveness of Great Revival camp meetings is offered also by the tremendous growth in church membership of those churches which used them. In Kentucky alone, between 1800 and 1803, the Baptists gained ten thousand members, and the Methodists about an equal number. The Presbyterians also added large numbers to their congregations during these years, although later evangelical schisms were responsible for the Presbyterian church's losing ground in the West. During the period in question the Methodists enjoyed an average increase of two thousand members a year, which necessitated a rapid division and redivision in church territories, districts, and circuits.

The 1801 Bourbon County meeting at Cane Ridge not only helped multiply church membership but also gave a powerful impetus to the revival itself. Richard McNemar declared that "the work breaking out in North Carolina resulted from people who had been to Cane Ridge." As the movement continued, the charting of its progress became increasingly difficult, as it spread out in ever-widening circles. A concurrent revival in the East, although mainly restricted to indoor "protracted meetings," made it appear that the "heavenly fire" from Kentucky had spread in almost every direction.

By the year 1803 the religious excitement had caught on in the Western Reserve District of Ohio, had spread back into western Georgia, North Carolina, and thence to South Carolina, and was strong in other parts of the East. An ardent advocate of the camp meeting, the Reverend Henry Smith, staged one in Virginia while serving on the Winchester Circuit in 1803 — this at a time when his constituents insisted: "It may do in the West, but it won't do here." From Virginia the outdoor revival spread through neighboring Maryland, Delaware, Pennsylvania, and New York, and fanned out into Massachusetts, Connecticut, Vermont, and New Hampshire. The camp meeting even caught on in certain sections of Canada. When settlers moved forward into the Mississippi Territory the open-air revival soon followed. In a short while evangelical Christianity blanketed the entire nation and found in the camp meeting its favorite method.

STUDY GUIDE

1. What might have led ministers living in such sparsely settled states as Ohio and Kentucky to cooperate with preachers of different faiths in "Union" camp meetings? What factors led to the breakdown of cooperation?

2. Considering the lives of the people in these areas, what might have contributed to their massive participation in camp meetings and to the exaggerated responses they displayed? What evidence does Johnson provide that the occasion might have been as much social as religious?

3. Different observers have given different explanations of religious exercises such as falling and barking. What arguments can you develop to support each of the following explanations: (a) the exercises represent a strong religious response by people who could not attend worship regularly; (b) the exercises provide people who have lived in social isolation for an extended period with a means of "letting off steam"; (c) the exercises are a result of poor diet, poor health, and exhaustion produced by the camp meeting environment?

4. Consider the reform movements of the 1830s, such as abolitionism and women's rights, and then think about the words of the Civil War song "Battle Hymn of the Republic." Is it legitimate to suggest that the sense of mission and the emotional urgency of Protestantism in this period shaped these other aspects of American life? Or was the character of American religious life simply a reflection of a broader sense of missionary zeal and destiny among all of the American people in that period?

BIBLIOGRAPHY

There are a number of works on religion in the West and the great religious revival of the nineteenth century. One of the most prolific writers on American religious history was William W. Sweet, who wrote *Revivalism in America: Its Origin, Growth and Decline* (New York, 1944) and also edited four volumes of writings entitled *Religion on the American Frontier* (New York and Chicago, 1931–1946). Ranking with Johnson's work as one of the most interesting books on the revival is Bernard A. Weisberger, *They Gathered at the River: The Story of the Great Revivalists and Their Impact upon Religion in America* * (Boston, 1958). William G. McLoughlin, Jr., *Modern Revivalism: Charles Grandison Finney to Billy Graham* (New York, 1959) is a delightful series of sketches of revivalists from the early nineteenth to the mid-twentieth century. Among special studies on certain regions or aspects of revivalism, two of the best are Timothy L. Smith, *Revivalism and Social Reform in Mid-Nineteenth Century America* (New York, 1957) and Whitney R. Cross, *The Burned-Over District* (Ithaca, N.Y., 1950), which concerns the revival spirit in New York State.

Besides the studies of individual denominations, there are several general books on American Protestantism. Winthrop S. Hudson, *American Protestantism* * (Chicago, 1961) is a general survey which provides an excellent introduction to the subject. Another book by Hudson, *Religion in America* (New York, 1965), is also worth reading, as are the works of two distinguished scholars — H. Richard Niebuhr, *The Kingdom of God in America* * (Chicago, 1937) and Sidney E. Mead, *The Lively Experiment: The Shaping of Christianity in America* (New York, 1963).

There are two basic introductions to Catholicism and Judaism in the United States, the bibliographies of which contain references to many other works: John T. Ellis, *American Catholicism,* 2nd ed. * (Chicago, 1969) and Nathan Glazer, *American Judaism* * (Chicago, 1957). Alice Felt Tyler's *Freedom's Ferment: Phases of American Social History to 1860* * (Minneapolis, Minn., 1944) describes some of the many smaller sects and new religions that arose in the early nineteenth century. Many of the special works on those subjects lack objectivity, but two good works on the Mormons are Thomas F. O'Dea, *The Mormons* * (Chicago, 1957) and Fawn M. Brodie, *No Man Knows My History: The Life of Joseph Smith, the Mormon Prophet* (New York, 1945).

The most comprehensive book on the religious history of American blacks was published more than fifty years ago: Carter G. Woodson, *The History of the Negro Church* (Washington, D.C., 1921). Shorter studies include E. Franklin Frazier, *The Negro Church in America* * (New York, 1963) and chapter 42 of the newest general survey of American religious history, Sydney E. Ahlstrom, *A Religious History of the American People* * (New Haven, Conn., and London, 1972).

IV THE AGE OF JACKSON

One of the questions frequently asked of historians is how closely their reconstruction of the past approximates the past as it really was. We seldom think of ourselves as being part of an "age," and we are scarcely aware of the "patterns of development" that later historians may detect. Fifty years from now, historians may look back on our time as a revolutionary period, an age of reform, a period of cultural decay, or a turning point in the disintegration of American society. Any such characterization of a period is somewhat artificial. It ignores many contradictory developments of the time and applies simple labels that are not always helpful in understanding the period.

The last decade of the eighteenth century and the first quarter of the nineteenth century are generally regarded as a period of centralization and nationalism. Following the adoption of the Constitution in 1788, the Federalist period of Washington, Hamilton, and Adams was characterized by the strengthening of the national government in both domestic and foreign affairs and the development of national interests quite distinct from those of European powers. This nationalistic thrust was continued under the Virginian presidents from Jefferson to Monroe, though support for a domestic program along these lines was stronger in Congress than in the executive mansion.

The second quarter of the nineteenth century has proved to be more difficult to characterize. Though some historians emphasize the democratic features of the "Age of Jackson," others have suggested that it was basically an age of business entrepreneurs and social inequality. There is little doubt that the years from 1830 to 1850 were a time of great social ferment and gave rise to the first great reform movement in American history. As the first reading indicates, there were ambivalent attitudes toward the position of women in American society during these decades, but the first women's rights movement originated then. A host of other concerns, including pacifism, help for the handicapped, abolitionism, and the temperance crusade grew into national movements during this period. The second reading, however, traces the callous and sometimes brutal treatment accorded the American Indian in the nineteenth century. The third reading describes one pattern of reform — the establishment of an institution for orphans and juvenile delinquents by a private, philanthropic organization. The last reading describes the very different approach of the Shakers to the reform of society and the creation of a perfect world.

Like many American women trying to live up to romantic ideals of womanhood, Harriet Beecher Stowe suffered serious psychological and physical illness.

10

BARBARA J. BERG

The Status of Women

The reform crusade of the 1830s, to aid the handicapped and unfortunate, was undertaken largely by committed individuals and private humanitarian societies, rather than by the national government. In this and succeeding decades, women were especially active in the various reform organizations. Dorothea Dix traveled thousands of miles investigating the care of the insane and petitioning legislatures for improved facilities. Angelina Grimké filled a Boston theater as she preached against slavery, while Harriet Beecher Stowe wrote her emotionally appealing *Uncle Tom's Cabin* and actively assisted runaway slaves.

Some of the women of the period extended their concerns to areas such as the antislavery crusade after they had become aroused by the discrimination they experienced as women. Many others first began working in abolition and humanitarian reform movements and turned their attention to the women's rights crusade only after discovering that their "meddling" in these areas evoked taunts, threats, and disparagement of women in public affairs. Their reforms ranged from dress styles that afforded more freedom to equality in marriage, law, and employment. Women entered industry, journalism, medicine, teaching, and other areas. Both women's colleges and coeducational institutions were founded before the Civil War to afford educational opportunities to women, and some changes were made in state laws on property holding, marital rights, and the like.

Yet, throughout the nineteenth century, the majority of American women continued to see their roles as that of wives and mothers. The "cult of true womanhood" created separate

165

spheres for men and women, with females being expected to devote all of their time and strength to providing a cultured retreat in the home for husbands and children. Womanly virtues included sexual innocence, healing the sick, teaching morality, and elevating the rougher nature of man. To write or lecture or engage in political causes was unfeminine. Though some women built up strong systems of support with other women, most languished at home, and the lack of meaning in their lives had devastating psychological and medical effects. Despite the reforms of the Jacksonian period, there is little evidence of substantial changes in either male or female attitudes toward women. They did not achieve the right to vote until after World War I, and women's liberationists of our time have contended that such legal changes are largely meaningless because of the continuation of discriminatory social attitudes toward the roles of men and women.

In the following selection, Barbara J. Berg describes the position of women in the early nineteenth century. Much of the selection describes the artificial ideal that women were expected to personify, but she also discusses the reality of daily life and the demands for change that were beginning to be voiced.

The greatest trial . . . is that I have nothing to do. Here I am with abundant leisure, and capable, I believe, of accomplishing some good, and yet with no object on which to expend my energies. . . . I cannot be happy without being employed. Alone as I am, my mind seems to prey upon itself until I am weary of life.

With these words, one female expressed the sense of stagnation and misery that scarred the lives of many nineteenth-century American women. The decrees of genuine womanhood, tyrannically governing feminine existence, thwarted efforts at self-realization. Women could neither control their own destinies nor help to free one another from society's bonds as long as the myths of the woman-belle ideal remained embedded in the nation's consciousness.

The contradictory mandates generated severe tension. Intense inner turmoil sought an outlet and impelled women to ameliorate their intolerable

Excerpted from *The Remembered Gate: Origins of American Feminism, The Woman and the City, 1800–1860* by Barbara J. Berg. Copyright © 1978 by Oxford University Press, Inc. Reprinted by permission.

condition. This search for personal fulfillment assumed different forms, sometimes even affording temporary abatement. But remaining individual and insular, it did nothing to improve the general plight of women until the interactions of the city brought a new understanding of woman's position.

Before the dynamics of urban growth would enable women to gain new insights and support from their shared experiences, nineteenth-century females suffered alone. Their numerous ailments became the observable symptoms of inner malaise. Visitors and residents alike expressed astonishment at the extent of ill health among American women. A British actress, Fanny Kemble, remarked that women in the United States "look old and faded" by the time they reach twenty-five years of age, while the "pallid and unhealthy complexions of the American ladies" struck her compatriot Richard Cobden with amazement. A journal reported that "foreigners who visit this country [comment] that American ladies have, almost without exception, a delicacy of complexion and appearance, amounting almost to sickness." Citizens concurred with these European observations.

Both James Fenimore Cooper and Nathaniel Hawthorne expressed dismay at the precarious health of American females. Other, less eminent writers voiced similar views. Joel Hawes described the "puny forms . . . feeble frames and sickly faces," as well as the "dismal train of ills," which characterized women of the "higher classes." Rev. Anson Smyth thought the "health of [the] American woman poor compared to what it used to be," and his colleague, Rev. Dr. Hawes of Hartford, bemoaned the fact "that the muscular vigor and strength of our . . . women have, for a long time past been undergoing a melancholy change. . . . But a small proportion of our adult females enjoy complete health." . . .

Doctors directed their attention to the womb, holding the reproductive system responsible for most female ills. Her uterus exercises a "paramount power" over her physical and moral system, and its grasp is "no less whimsical than potent," believed William P. Dewes, professor of midwifery at the University of Pennsylvania. Because doctors agreed that woman "is constantly liable to irregularities in her menstrua, and menaced severely by their consequences," they focused medical treatment on uterine and menstrual disorders. Female sexual organs bore the onus for headaches, nervous disorders, indigestion, insomnia, depression, and backaches.

The pages of the *Water-Cure Journal,* a contemporary periodical heralding the benefits of hydropathy, document the nineteenth-century obsession with "uterine-related diseases." Articles on such topics as "chlorsis or green sickness . . . the non-appearance of the menstrual discharge . . . [which] inevitably results in the serious derangement of the general health," "menstrual cramps" to which the "luxurious and idle are more subject," and "leucorrhoea and uterine catarrh" dominated the publication. The water-cure offered such novel therapy as "hip baths," "cold injections into the urethra," and "rubbing of the back, loins, and abdomen." Its remedies contrasted sharply with the practices of orthodox medicine, which often used "leeching" and "cauterization" to alleviate feminine discomfort.

Much female physical anguish did indeed relate to the reproductive system, particularly as the prevailing codes of delicacy prevented physically sick women from seeking help. Dr. Charles Meigs "rejoiced" at the difficulty of making a "local examination" as it gave "evidence of a high and worthy grade of moral feeling." Women, conforming to the dictates of modest behavior, suffered in silence rather than endure the "mortification" of a gynecological examination, as propriety combined with ignorance to make the womb a source of much distress.

The conventional wisdom of the era preached that "conception . . . is much more likely to happen from intercourse a few days before or after the menstrual period." Accordingly, women who wished to practice some form of birth control intentionally had sexual relations in the middle of the menstrual cycle. They no doubt found their repeated pregnancies not only surprising but physically difficult as well. The diverse ailments attending birth ranged from minor irritation, to severe infection, to prolapsus uteri, but doctors responded to all uterine disorders with the same antiquated and often harmful treatments. Even a normal, uncomplicated birth could prove debilitating. The traditional medical practices insisted upon complete inactivity for long periods of time following delivery. A Mrs. O. C. W. reported to the *Water-Cure Journal* that she was "kept confined to . . . bed nearly two months" with the birth of her first child, and "it was not until about the middle of the following summer that [she] attained [her] former health and strength."

Clearly, childbearing did have painful and dangerous aspects. Scholars seeking to understand the roots of feminine maladies have sympathetically suggested that women used the "pretext of being 'delicate' as a way of . . . closing the bedroom door," "an elaborate strateg[y] for limiting the occasions of sexual intercourse . . . and thus limiting their families." Undoubtedly some women fabricated illness to shield themselves from unwanted pregnancies. Others, obviously, were physically ill. Still others were merely dupes of subtle economic and social pressure to keep women nonproductive and dependent. But the prevalence of poor health among women of leisure, the comments of a few sensitive observers, and the strong psychological component of the various described afflictions, all combine to invite further investigation into the causes of feminine illness.

George Combe, the Scottish phrenologist, believed that "nervous disease of which females of the middle and upper classes were the most frequent victims" could be attributed to "inactivity of intellect and feeling." Dr. W. A. Alcott, the noted nutritional reformer, urged that ladies be given "some employment . . . to save them from ennui, and disgust, and misery — sometimes from speedy or more protracted suicide." Harriet Martineau blamed the "vacuity of mind . . . among women of station and education in the most enlightened parts of the country" for a host of problems.

Catharine Beecher, whose "extensive tours in all portions of the Free States" had "brought [her] into most intimate communion" with countless women, exclaimed "And oh! what heartaches were the result of these years of quiet observation of the experience of my sex in domestic life. How many hearts have revealed the fact that what they had been trained to imagine the highest earthly felicity, was but the beginning of care, disappointment, and sorrow, and often led to the extremity of mental and physical suffering." And, above all, Beecher wondered why she found so many women in comfortable circumstances "expressing the hope that their daughters would never marry."

Some thoughtful individuals, therefore, stated or implied that many women's ailments had a psychological rather than physical origin, and the personal experiences of nineteenth-century females seem to support this hypothesis. The private journals, letters, and case studies of diverse women . . . detail the symptoms of hysteria, severe anxiety, and constant depression. "I was quite ill, and my spirits depressed," wrote Sarah Connell Ayer often in her diary, revealing the perpetual mental anguish of this middle-class wife and mother. The phrase "my spirits were unusually depressed" covered the sheets of her journal. Ayer frequently confessed having to curtail activities because of her emotional state, "for which [she] could not account."

Having little understanding of the causes or nature of their afflictions, women described anger and anxiety. In 1841, Elizabeth Payson Prentiss, who later became an author of children's books, wrote of her constant nervousness, which often made life "insupportable." "I . . . think mother would not trust me to carry the dishes to the closet, if she knew how strong an effort I have to make to avoid dashing them all to pieces," she confided. "When I am at the head of the stairs I can hardly help throwing myself down. . . . Tonight, for instance, my head began to feel all at once as if it were enlarging till at last it seemed to fill the room. . . . Three days out of seven I am as sick as I . . . can be — the rest of the time, languid, feeble, and exhausted by frequent faint turns, so that I can't do the smallest thing in my family."

"My spirits are . . . depressed this forenoon," wrote Ann Warder countless times in her journal. Sarah Stearns suffered from "anxiety [and] vexation" and felt "quite unable to attend the concerns of [her] family." A brilliant student, Nancy Maria Hyde constantly complained that "[her] spirits have been unusually depressed, and [her] feelings have been those of languor and despondency." Susan Huntington's memoirs describe her perpetual battle with "distressing nervous depression," while Laura Clark's journal entries divulge a suffering so great that she states: "I sometimes . . . wonder that I am alive."

. . . Few women consciously expressed the wish to "flee" or escape from a life they found unbearable, but thousands of nineteenth-century females fell victim to a particular form of psychoneurosis. Manifesting itself in disabling symptoms, this illness gave women no choice but to retreat from their daily routines. The *Water-Cure Journal* disclosed the case histories of numerous females who had suddenly and inexplicably become totally incapacitated. Miss Elizabeth Pott was "an excellent scholar [who] had not been able to read or write for years," and Miss Isabella Thompson suddenly "could not do anything." These furnished but two examples of the thousands of women invalids who experimented with hydropathy. Among those who flocked to the flourishing water-cure centers was Harriet Beecher Stowe. Her case study provides an interesting illustration of the nature of much feminine malady.

The daughter of Lyman Beecher, a fiery minister who infused his children with a passionate desire to reform humanity, Harriet suffered from a tormenting apprehension that she could not fulfill her father's expectations. To her sister Catharine she confessed the fear that she might not be "fit for anything." Fortunately Catharine, ten years her senior, had plans to open a school for girls and very much needed Harriet's help. The two young women worked together until 1836, when Harriet married Calvin Stowe, a classics professor. Demanding, domineering, and irascible, Professor Stowe expected complete obedience from his wife. Within their first ten years of married life, Harriet bore three children and agreed to have Calvin's aged and complaining mother live with them. Then, suddenly, at the end of this decade, which Harriet described as filled with "pain, confusion, disappointment and suffering," when all she "proposed was met and crossed and in every way hedged up," her right side became totally paralyzed.

Harriet went to the famous water-cure sanitarium in Brattleboro, Vermont, for therapy. There, the "shattered broken invalid, just able to creep along by great care," began to reexamine her life. In the serene atmosphere, removed from the perpetual exactions of a domestic martinet, Harriet Beecher Stowe started her slow recovery. "Not for years have I enjoyed life as I have here," she wrote, ignoring her husband's repeated entreaties to return home. After a year away from her life of "constant discouragement," of "hasty and irritated censure," Harriet came to realize that she could not make her family "my chief good and portion."

During her stay in Brattleboro, Harriet gained the emotional strength to insist that her husband make certain concessions as a prerequisite for resuming cohabitation. He agreed to accept a teaching position at Bowdoin College in Maine and apparently pledged not to inhibit Harriet's fledgling career as an author. She began work on *Uncle Tom's Cabin* shortly after rejoining her family in Maine; her ailments, not surprisingly, disappeared. Until her death in 1896 at the age of eighty-five, she enjoyed vigorous health, free from all signs of her affliction.

Harriet Beecher Stowe's paralysis emanated from deep emotional distress.

Clinically called conversion hysteria, or conversion reaction, this crippling psychoneurosis is characterized by the tendency to represent inner psychological conflicts by means of symbolic somatic disturbances. Hysteria, then, as well as depression and anxiety, singularly or collectively, incapacitated Jacksonian women. Stowe benefited from a stable childhood, an indulgent, if somewhat awe-inspiring father, and an ambitious and supportive sister. Additionally, she had a comfortable economic situation that enabled her to remain in Brattleboro for over a year, a conciliatory husband, occupying interests, and a strong will. Harriet Beecher Stowe thus managed to overcome the more obvious, debilitating symptoms of illness brought on by the conflicts of her life. But most women did not share this good fortune and languished in their chambers alone and afraid.

Contemporaries could not understand why females, with every comfort and no responsibility, became so desperately ill. Yet an abundance of psychoneurotic symptoms plagued American women. These ailments afforded visible evidence of stifled anger, unassuaged guilt, and unfilled emotional and physical drives. Fear of punishment and loss of love from the realization of repressed drives and wishes, the overwhelming feeling of stagnation, and the lack of self-esteem became manifested in profound psychological and related physical distress. . . .

Female journals of this period reveal both woman's struggle to accept and comply with the era's concept of feminine nature and behavior and the harvest of unhappiness that her efforts inevitably reaped. The persistent vigil to conform to the precepts of the woman-belle ideal produced severe tension: "How soon one is wearied of the constant exertion to be agreeable, even when conscious of admiration!" complained one woman. Another believed that "it is the struggle to be patient and gentle and cheerful, when pressed down and worn upon and distracted that costs so much."

Taught from childhood that the true woman always sacrificed her self-interest for the happiness of others, women worried incessantly that they might not have these angelic virtues and blamed themselves for their apparent failings. "I think that to give happiness in married life a woman should possess oceans of self-sacrificing love and I, for one, haven't half of that self-forgetting spirit which I think essential," confided Elizabeth Prentiss to a friend in 1843. The introspection of one diarist exposed her "fear that this power of enjoying myself makes my pleasure too independent of others, and consequently renders me too little solicitous about them," while her contemporaries berated themselves for similar "shortcomings."

Another axiom of feminine nature — woman's innate desire to tend the sick — demanded compliance. Antebellum females constantly ministered to ill friends and family. Their diaries disclose irritation with these tasks and also the strain women experienced from the need to perform these duties with the cheerfulness required of them. Elizabeth Prentiss frequently confessed vexation at having "to drag one's self out of bed to take care of a sick baby," and Harriet Beecher Stowe complained that her choleric son acted like a "great fellow who thinks women [were] made for his especial convenience." The conflict between society's vision of the female happily and indefatigably caring for the sick and woman's resentment at these chores finds full eloquence in the diary of Hannah Backhouse. Feeling an overwhelming sense of repugnance at ministering to sick relatives, Hannah struggled to cultivate the "appropriate" feelings. When her brother became ill she had an opportunity to test her endurance. Her diary records a mixed success. "I often felt my aversion to trifles, and the want of employment and ideas made me feel it a great cross; this sometimes overcame me," she admitted.

Yet this young woman ardently hoped she would develop the requisite qualities: "Beginning to act from duty in such cases, one may end by acting from affection, and then it becomes necessary to one's satisfaction to do so. A woman who cannot suffer the confinement of a sick room, leaves unfulfilled one of her most marked duties and can never be fit for a wife. It is a difficult task when one is not spurred onward by the continual impulse of the heart, or in short, when self is a dearer object than the invalid. . . . I could often wish my heart were more susceptible of kindness and compassion than it is."

Secretly protesting the demands made upon them, women also writhed under the decrees of the era that fettered their activities. "How painfully sensitive am I to not being free to act as I like," asserted Hannah Backhouse. She admitted that as a child she most enjoyed "using the hammer and saw with dexterity, and [found] the greatest pleasure [in] being victorious in a game of trapball." When admonished against the unladylike nature of her amusements, she wrote: "I fell into a sulky mood in my own mind, growling over the misery of . . . restraint. I sometimes feel my want of freedom rather galling." . . .

Feminine thralldom assumed many forms, but economic deprivation emerged as one of the most visible signs of oppression. With opportunities for employment severely limited, impoverished women, as well as those whose families had recently suffered financial reversals, found themselves victimized by the prevailing legal and social codes. Nancy Maria Hyde, considered by her contemporaries to have been an exceptionally able student, endured great hardship after her father's death. Creditors pressed upon Nancy and her mother for the payment of debts, and "neither in the family of her father, her mother, or herself, was there a son or a brother, to stand up as their helper."

. . . Desperate for an income and unable to find work as a teacher, Nancy took a job painting artificial fruit. But as she explained to her journal: "Choice would never have instigated me to this employment." Other women, similarly situated, tried to support themselves by writing. Yet, like Hannah Adams, the gifted author whose scholarly works included *History of Reli-*

gions, they found that the "penalties and discouragements attending authors in general fall upon woman with double weight. To the curiosity of the idle, and the envy of the malicious, their sex affords a peculiar excitement."

The ethos of the woman-belle ideal prohibited women from most forms of financially remunerative endeavor. It also denied the value of independent feminine achievement and criticized females for developing pride in their accomplishments. The prevailing codes deemed few tasks ladylike. Embroidering, painting, playing musical instruments, and perhaps writing some trivial verses probably did not appeal to most women. Yet those who demonstrated talent and an eagerness to follow these limited, acceptable pursuits had still other restrictions. The perfect female never exhibited self-assurance nor even allowed herself to feel confident. "The love of painting has been uppermost in my mind for some weeks past," wrote Hannah Backhouse. After completing a canvas that gave her special satisfaction she admitted: "I did so well that I felt most uncomfortably elated with it. . . . How I disliked myself. . . . I strove much against my feelings." . . .

Women could expose neither mental ability nor knowledge, but the craving for intellectual stimulation forms a constant litany running through their private journals and letters. "Write me a long letter," Sarah Ayer begged her friend Maria. "Tell me everything . . . what books you have been reading, your opinion of them, and indeed everything that interests you." Before sealing the letter, Ayer enclosed a proposed reading list and asked Maria to comment on her selections. Hannah Backhouse records the "delightful hour" she spent "reading Locke," and Catharine Sedgwick's correspondence with her women friends contain frequent references to current authors.

Not surprisingly, most women could not satisfy intellectual needs within the narrow limits allowed them. And many anguished over insipid conversation resulting from women's lack of education and involvement. "I cannot bear talking about trifles," exclaimed Hannah Backhouse. Other women echoed these feelings. In a letter to her confidante, Sarah Ayer wrote: "I hate large parties, such as we have both frequently attended, where . . . improving conversation, and all intellectual enjoyments were banished, and trifling amusements fit only to please a child supplied their places." "How much more real pleasure and advantage is to be derived from solid and refined conversation," she continued, "than from that empty, unmeaning *chit-chat* which I am sorry to say so frequently forms the greater part of female conversation." . . .

Women who tried to "cultivate" their "mental powers" in a social milieu that mocked their attempts and undermined their efforts often experienced profound frustration and, ultimately, resignation. "My mind grows inactive and lethargic," complained Sarah Stearns, and Elizabeth Prentiss had the same grievance. "Don't ask me if I have read anything else," she wrote shortly after her marriage and subsequent relocation in New Bedford, Massachusetts. "My mind has become a complete mummy, and therefore, incapable of either receiving or originating a new idea." Wedlock had brought the end of her previous attempts to indulge intellectual curiosity. "Just what I expected would befall me has happened. I have got immersed in the whirlpool of petty cares and concerns which swallow up so many other and higher interests, and talk as anxiously about good 'help' and bad, as the rest of 'em do. . . . I sometimes feel really ashamed of myself to see . . . how my time seems to be wasted if I venture to take up a book. . . . [W]ives who have no love and enthusiasm for their husbands are more to be pitied than blamed if they settle down into mere . . . [household] managers."

Substantially barred from satisfying the requirements of her mind, the middle- and upper-class woman had to endure the agony of relentless boredom. "There is such a sameness in my life . . . that the particulars of it are hardly worth the pains of writing," recorded one young woman. And Ellen Parker of New Hampshire grieved that "another long day has passed into eternity. How slowly time passes to me." Mary Peacock's diary reflects her disgust at having to "sit idle," considering it as "the most tiresome thing a person can do." Hannah Backhouse, describing her friends who came to tea, exclaimed: "What dull worldly people they seem to be!" "Having done nothing all day, and being all assembled in the evening, vacancy pervaded the whole room to such a degree, that I wished I had been obliged to work for my bread, that my duty might not be in the listless inactivity of a parlour."

Forced leisure generated an oppressive sense of uselessness and caused the nineteenth-century woman to "[wonder] why [she] was made, and if anybody on earth [would] ever be a bit happier for it." Plagued by feelings of worthlessness, but immersed in the ethos of the woman-belle ideal, she could not appreciate the intricate origins of her anguish. She therefore accepted the wisdom of contemporary theorists and attributed all unhappiness to her individual failings. This self-blame ultimately intensified her conflicts and sense of isolation. Elizabeth Prentiss confessed to feeling "mentally and spiritually alone in the world," and Sarah Ayer, writing in Concord, Massachusetts, complained: "[I have] lived so much in solitude . . . that my mind has become somewhat enervated."

As women attempted to meet society's expectations, they resolved to become more self-sacrificing and patient and endeavored to enjoy their sickbed duties. They restrained themselves from exhibiting wit and intellect and tried to find meaning in a life of futility. And throughout this lonely search for fulfillment women entrusted their troubled emotions and thoughts to personal diaries. The myriad of confidential writings provided an outlet for stifled feelings but did little to enable women to challenge the womanhood myths. The persistent urge to find understanding could not be absorbed by scattered pages of private journals. And the need to communicate came streaming forth, eventually eroding the carefully constructed dam of male authorship. Feminine anguish flowed into countless novels and short stories; woman's creative literature emerged as a confluence of anger and sadness, hope and despair.

The astonishing outpouring of writing by females at once annoyed and amazed those accustomed to dominating the literary field. Predictably, resentment against women authors rose up to meet their hesitant efforts. Nathaniel Hawthorne damned the entire "mob of scribbling women." Articles warned women that they could not "be too cautious in assuming the privilege of presenting their thoughts to the world." And essays, cautioning those who "[devoted] themselves to studies and research" that they would soon "despise their duties and neglect them altogether," appeared frequently. . . .

The existence of voluminous printed material signed by women afforded evidence that middle- and upper-class females did not find domestic life engrossing or enriching. The theme of feminine tedium dotted the pages of woman's writings. "Oh, the weary years of unused life to which so large a portion of the human race is remorselessly consigned!" bemoaned the author of the novel *Three Sisters.* Written in the first person, this tale traces the maturation of three women. The author indicted the system that created and encouraged the useless lady: "I returned home . . . to find my elder sisters leading that living death to which it is the fashion to consign females of the wealthy middle-class . . . an aimless life."

Vesta, the courageous heroine of Charlotte Chesebro's *Children of Light,* sighed: "I'm tired of reading, and tired to death of embroidery; and one can not be forever praising the work of another." She asked her companions if they would "acknowledge that idle persons are, of all, most miserable?" Chesebro infused her character with a yearning for excitement and fulfillment. "If I were a man, I would very soon discover what there was for me to do. . . . I would be clear of dragging out my life in the kitchen, or of putting myself down to the mending of old clothes, or of finding my recreation in walking over the lawn and garden, for all the world like a stupid animal, . . . a well-trained dog! When I feel like rushing out — strong enough to fight all the battles of the world, and with some little disposition that way too." Yet, Vesta had to face the reality of her existence:

> But here I am, only a woman — a housekeeper, the mistress of an hospital as I might say, to be kept in my 'proper sphere' and 'place,' and never to stir an inch out of it in any direction, for fear that all creation would turn against me, and hunt me down, as they would a wild beast! Oh, these laws of propriety — these ridiculous customs.

. . . Women writers recognized the era's insistence upon matrimony as the only acceptable path to feminine fulfillment, but many attempted to invalidate this decree through their literature. Mary Howitt, author of "Single Sisters," printed in the 1845 edition of the *Keepsake,* objected to "fairy tales which portray 'old maids' as cruel and ugly." Indeed, Ada Lester, in a story bearing her name, did not marry and achieved much recognition. Leopoldine of Julia Delafaye-Brehier's "Two Sisters" claims that she does not regret being single, for "that condition, which appears to you so frightful, has its happiness. . . . I have called into my aid the arts and letters which it is so difficult for married females to cultivate with constancy." In another tale, the married Emily confesses to her spinster sister: "You have had years of happiness while I have never felt a single moment of unalloyed felicity." On her deathbed, Emily pleads: "My sister, teach my children the moral of our story."

Emily's small children might have required an explanation of their mother's dying words, but the countless stories of females forced into marriage by a deleterious dictate made the message clear to antebellum readers. The *Amulet* of 1846 relates the sad history of a sixteen-year-old girl "who abides her parents' wishes and marries a man she can't love." An autobiographical sketch appearing in the *Ladies' Wreath*, "A Life Without Love," tells of a woman who never loved her husband-to-be and whose wedding day, rather than bringing her joy, filled her with dread and a feeling of "strange repulsion." And Catharine Sedgwick expressed her opinion by writing that Grace "will soon be married, and then, like Eleanor, mere wife and mother to the end of her life." . . .

The narrator of *Three Sisters* longed to become a doctor and as a child performed operations on dolls. "Had I been a boy instead of a girl, these early indications would have been hailed with satisfaction as pointing unerringly to my future vocation. As it was, they procured me only reprimands and punishment for mischief; and as I could not play properly with my dolls, they were taken from me altogether." Eliza Woodson of Eliza Farnham's fictionalized autobiography had no books for her own. Desperate for reading material, she "devoured" congressional debates, political newspapers, and cabinet reports brought in by the men in her family. But her relatives, finding these pursuits "curious," ostracized Eliza and labeled her a "fool."

Fear of derision and exclusion forced women to hide their knowledge and skills. "Amelia's frosty reception in the best Philadelphia drawing rooms" led this character of the novel *Ferdinand and Elmira* "to warn her friends to display no learning or sentiment, for the moment it is discovered, your reputation is lost forever." Ruth Hall, the literary creation of the indefatigable Fanny Fern, aroused the curiosity of her friends. They "wonder[ed] . . . why she took so much pains to bother her head with those stupid books, when she was every day growing prettier" and would not be able to use or exhibit her imagination or learning.

"The Mysterious Picture," appearing in the 1832 edition of *Affection's Gift*, is a sensitive study of one young woman caught between her own needs and society's dictates. Josephine Vericour had "an ardent ambition to excel" in the painting of miniatures, but she "was the victim of a painful and unconquerable timidity, and entire want of confidence in herself." Josephine could not believe she was capable of producing anything of value. And, indeed, the work done under the scrutiny of her instructor was quite mediocre. Then one night a miraculous event happened. When Josephine awakened, she found the unfinished painting she had left on her easel transformed into a magnificent work of art. At first the startled young woman said and did nothing about this extraordinary occurrence. But she arose on several subsequent mornings to discover that more of her own undistinguished miniatures had been changed into truly beautiful paintings. Baffled, Josephine decided to stay awake and catch the artistic intruder who furtively worked in her bedroom each night.

When darkness gave way to dawn and no one appeared, the confused and tired Josephine confided these mysterious incidents to a friend and begged that her schoolmate keep vigil the next night. The friend agreed, and the scene she witnessed astonished her. In the dead of night Josephine, sleepwalking, approached an incomplete canvas and worked with a proficiency and talent never displayed in public. With the first rays of morning, the young artist finished her work. She crept back into bed and slept, having no awareness of her marvelous accomplishment. At first Josephine refused to believe her friend's story. Finally, however, when convinced of its authenticity, she "made vigorous efforts to conquer her timidity in the presence of her master. . . . [In] time she was able to paint as well under his inspection as she had done when alone and asleep in the gloom of midnight."

The story of Josephine Vericour seems to be no more than a charming tale of a gifted schoolgirl. But its author, Eliza Leslie, skillfully wove together many separate strands of the rope that bound her countrywomen. Josephine's master symbolized the antebellum male who watched, instructed, and inhibited the talents and needs of women. Josephine, the legitimate child of the woman-belle ideal, felt acute inferiority. Although wishing to excel in a loved activity, she could not perform well in her teacher's presence. She knew that a woman who displayed talent evoked scorn and contempt. Her artistic impulses, unable to be denied, manifested themselves in such a manner that they neither brought credit to Josephine nor enhanced her self-image. Yet Leslie implied that if woman could somehow be numbed or made impervious to the prohibitions against her abilities, the long-stifled talents would surely burst forth. Ironically then, somnambulism aroused Josephine's dormant skills. Confronted with the reality of her achievement, she was able to develop the self-assurance to shield her from society's disapproval. But most of Josephine Vericour's living counterparts did not share this good fortune and passed their lives unfulfilled and unhappy.

STUDY GUIDE

1. Today American women tend to be viewed as active and healthy, engaging in all sorts of sports, working at "men's" jobs, and perhaps less neurotic than in times past. Berg suggests that a lot of the physical ill health of women in the nineteenth century reflected an inner psychological anguish. What were the causes of the anger and depression that seemed so common?

2. How did nineteenth-century medical men view the causes of female sickness, and what cures were used?

3. Describe the behavior, education, and proper pursuits of a "true lady." What do these reveal about the nineteenth-century idea of a woman's mind and sensibilities? What changes in behavior and the like did these educated women advocate?

4. What changes do you see in the status of women and in male-female relations in the nineteenth century as compared to the earlier period described by Edmund Morgan in his essay on colonial Virginia (Reading No. 5)?

5. What differences do you see in the goals of the women Berg writes of and those of women's liberationists today, as represented by such organizations as NOW? Are the goals of either group relevant to the welfare of poorer, less well-educated women?

BIBLIOGRAPHY

Very few historical fields have developed so rapidly and resulted in the publication of as fine a body of scholarship as has women's history in the last ten years. Berg's book is on the woman and the city, but the selection you have read is a good summary of two of the central themes in women's history — the views that men and women had of women's proper role, and the relationship of women to American medical practices. Barbara Welter wrote influential essays on these and other topics which are collected in her book *Dimity Convictions: The American Woman in the Nineteenth Century* * (Athens, Ohio, 1976). One of the limitations of women's history is that it has tended to focus primarily on middle- and upper-class women, as exemplified in Barbara J. Harris, *Beyond Her Sphere: Women and the Professions in American History* (Westport, Conn., 1978), and Susan Conrad, *Perish the Thought: Intellectual Women in Romantic America, 1830–1860* * (New York, 1976). There are exceptions, such as a popular work by Barbara M. Wertheimer, *We Were There: The Story of Working Women in America* * (New York, 1977), and Walter O'Meara's *Daughters of the Country: The Women of Fur Traders and Mountain Men* (New York, 1968).

In the nineteenth century, male physicians took childbirth out of the hands of midwives, women were refused admission to medical schools, and a great deal of writing warned against the dangers of masturbation, prostitution, birth control, and the intemperate use of sex in marriage. A number of physicians recommended and performed an operation that removed the clitoris of women. Various aspects of these themes are covered in the following books: G. J. Barker-Benfield, *Horrors of the Half-Known Life: Male Attitudes Toward Women and Sexuality in Nineteenth-Century America* (New York, 1976); Jane B. Donegan, *Women and Men Midwives: Medicine, Morality, and Misogyny in Early America* (Westport, Conn., 1978); John S. and Robin M. Haller, *The Physician and Sexuality in Victorian America* (Urbana, Ill., 1974); James Reed, *From Private Vice to Public Virtue: The Birth Control Movement and American Society since 1830* (New York, 1978); Mary R. Walsh, *"Doctors Wanted: No Women Need Apply:" Sexual Barriers in the Medical Profession, 1835–1975* (New Haven, Conn. and London, Eng., 1977); and Ronald G. Walters, *Primers for Prudery: Sexual Advice to Victorian America* * (Englewood Cliffs, N.J., 1974).

There are several general works dealing with women's rights and the suffragist movement, including Eleanor Flexner, *Century of Struggle: The Woman's Rights Movement in the United States* * (Cambridge, Mass., 1959); Keith E. Melder, *Beginnings of Sisterhood: The American Woman's Rights Movement, 1800–1850* (New York, 1977); Robert E. Riegel, *American Feminists* (Lawrence, Kan., 1963); William L. O'Neill, *Everyone Was Brave: The Rise and Fall of Feminism in America* (Chicago, 1969); and Andrew Sinclair, *The Better Half: The Emancipation of the American Woman* * (New York, 1965). There are also specialized studies on other aspects of women's history. Anne F. Scott, *The Southern Lady: From Pedestal to Politics, 1830–1930* * (Chicago, 1970) is a recent work on the romanticized idea of southern womanhood. The history of black women has been given less attention than that of white women. Gerda Lerner discusses them in her short work *The Woman in American History* * (Reading, Mass., 1971), and has published a separate book of readings, *Black Women in White America: A Documentary History* * (New York, 1972).

On women's history, as with many subjects in this volume, some of the best writing has been in the form of articles in historical journals. There are three collections of such articles, the last of which is not confined to American history: Jean E. Friedman and William G. Shade, eds., *Our American Sisters: Women in American Life and Thought,* * 2nd ed. (Boston, 1976); Mary Hartman and Lois Banner, eds., *Clio's Consciousness Raised* * (New York, 1974); and Bernice Carroll, ed., *Liberating Women's History: Theoretical and Critical Essays* * (Urbana, Ill., 1976). If you read anything further on women's history, there is no better place to start than with some of the articles by Barbara Welter and Carroll Smith-Rosenberg that are reprinted in such anthologies.

---

* Asterisk indicates book is available in a paperback edition.

Robert Lindneux's "The Trail of Tears" vividly depicts the suffering of the Cherokees during their removal from their ancient homeland.

11

DALE VAN EVERY

Trail of Tears

In the Declaration of Independence, Jefferson had written that "all men are created equal" and are divinely endowed with the rights of life, liberty, and the pursuit of happiness. The members of the Continental Congress who signed their names to that proclamation were concerned with the rights of the colonists in relationship to the governing power of England. Few of them considered these ringing phrases as guaranteeing social or political rights to minorities within American society. Some few voices were raised to suggest that women, blacks, and Indians might have a greater cause to revolt than did the planters, lawyers, and merchants who led the revolution against the authority of King George III. Throughout much of American history, various national, racial, and religious groups were treated as less than equal and beyond the protection of the Bill of Rights.

The Age of Jackson exhibited some striking contrasts in American sentiment. In many respects, it is a most revealing period in judging both the achievements and the failures of the American people in living up to the philosophy expressed in the Declaration. The 1830s witnessed the first great period of American social reform, with scores of organizations founded to assist the handicapped and the unfortunate. But it is also a decade that, one might say, lives in historical infamy, because American Indian tribes were removed from their ancient homelands, as whites coveted and took over their lands.

In the selection that follows, Dale Van Every suggests that this is the ultimate catastrophe that can befall a people. Torn from the land of one's birth, losing most or all of one's belongings, forced to find a livelihood as best one can in an unfamiliar country, and losing one's very sense of identity are experiences we can hardly comprehend. The removal of the Civilized Tribes of the southeastern United States — the Creeks, Chickasaws, Choctaws, Seminoles, and Cherokees — to new territories beyond the Mississippi River, and the numerous casualties they suffered along the "Trail of Tears," is one of the most famous and tragic stories in American history. In the North, the same story was repeated with different characters on a somewhat smaller scale. Whatever the Declaration of Independence meant to white, male Americans in the early nineteenth century, it must have appeared to be a bitter mockery to the native Americans who were forced out of their homes by this cruel invasion.

History records the sufferings of innumerable peoples whose country was overrun and possessed by alien invaders. There have been relatively fewer recorded occasions, as in the instance of the Babylonian Captivity of the Jews, of an entire people being compelled to abandon their country. This has been universally regarded as the ultimate catastrophe that can befall a people inasmuch as it deprives them of the roots which sustain their identity. Upon the exiles has been pronounced a sentence that by its nature denies all hope of reprieve or relief. To Indians, with their inherited conception of the land of their birth as the repository of those spiritual links to their ancestors which were holy and therefore indissoluble, the prospect of expulsion was clothed with added dreads beyond human evaluation.

The threat was in all its aspects so monstrous that in the spring of 1838 the bewildered masses of the Cherokee people, homeless, hungry, destitute, still remained incredulous that so fearful a fate could actually impend. Outrageously as they had been harassed for the past ten years by Georgia and Alabama white men, they still clung to their trust that most white men wished them well. This was a confidence instilled in them by the reports of John Ross [a respected Cherokee chief] who had been made more conversant with the apparent truth by his wide travels across the immense white nation stretching beyond the Cherokee horizon. They had been further prepared to accept his judgment on the inherent goodness of the white race by their own experience with the many white men who had lived among them as teachers, missionaries and counselors, sharing their struggles and tribulations. Their more recent experience with [General

Adapted by permission of William Morrow & Company, Inc. from *Disinherited: The Lost Birthright of the American Indian* by Dale Van Every. Copyright © 1966 by Dale Van Every.

John] Wool and his officers and with [General R. G.] Dunlap and his Tennesseans had strengthened their impression that the white race could not be wholly committed to their destruction.

Ross was still in Washington engaged in a final frantic effort, with some dawning hope of success, to wring from the administration a temporary postponement of removal. His followers were continuing to obey his injunction that they persist in their nonviolent resistance. Most continued to refuse even to give their names or a list of their belongings to the agents commissioned to organize the details of the migration. May 23, two years from the date of the President's proclamation of the Senate's ratification of the treaty, was the day, as all had for months been warned, when their residence in the east would become illegal but they still could not believe that a development so frightful could be given reality by that day's sunrise. Even after five regiments of regulars and 4,000 militia and volunteers from adjacent states began pouring into their country they still could not believe.

Major General [Winfield] Scott arrived May 8 to take command of the military operation. His May 10, 1838 address to the Cherokee people proclaimed the terrible reality in terms no Cherokee could longer mistake:

> Cherokees — The President of the United States has sent me with a powerful army, to cause you, in obedience to the treaty of 1835, to join that part of your people who are already established in prosperity on the other side of the Mississippi. Unhappily, the two years which were allowed for the purpose, you have suffered to pass away without following, and without making preparations to follow, and now, or by the time this solemn *address* shall reach your distant settlements, the emigration must be commenced in haste, but, I hope, without disorder. I have no power, by granting a farther delay, to correct the error that you have committed. The full moon of May is already on the wane, and before another shall have passed away, every Cherokee man, woman, and child . . . must be in motion to join their brethren in the far West. . . . My troops already occupy many positions in the country that you are to abandon, and thousands and thousands are approaching from every quarter, to tender resistance and escape alike hopeless. . . . Chiefs, head men, and warriors — Will you then, by resistance, compel us to resort to arms? God forbid. Or will you, by flight, seek to hide yourself in mountains and forests, and thus oblige us to hunt you down? Remember that, in pursuit, it may be impossible to avoid conflicts. The blood of the white man, or the blood of the red man, may be spilt, and if spilt, however accidentally, it may be impossible for the discreet and humane among you, or among us, to prevent a general war and carnage. Think of this, my Cherokee brethern. I am an old warrior, and have been present at many a scene of slaughter; but spare me, I beseech you, the horror of witnessing the destruction of the Cherokees.

Scott sincerely hoped that the enforced removal could be accomplished not only without bloodshed but without undue hardship inflicted upon the unfortunate thousands being ejected at bayonet's point from their homes. He had been impressed by Ross during conferences with him in Washington and like most professional soldiers of his time had developed a genuine regard for Indians. In his May 17 general orders to his troops he sternly admonished them to practice restraint:

> Considering the number and temper of the mass to be removed together with the extent and fastnesses of the country occupied, it will readily occur that simple indiscretions, acts of harshness, and cruelty on the part of our troops, may lead, step by step, to delays, to impatience, and exasperation, and, in the end, to a general war and carnage; a result, in the case of these particular Indians, utterly abhorrent to the generous sympathies of the whole American people. Every possible kindness, compatible with the necessity of removal, must, therefore, be shown by the troops; and if, in the ranks, a despicable individual should be found capable of inflicting a wanton injury or insult on any Cherokee man, woman, or child, it is hereby made the special duty of the nearest good officer or man instantly to interpose, and to seize and consign the guilty wretch to the severest penalty of the laws. The major-general is fully persuaded that this injunction will not be neglected by the brave men under his command, who cannot be otherwise than jealous of their honor and that of their country.

Scott's intentions were humane but the larger portion of his army were state levies unaccustomed to discipline and without his professional susceptibilities. The nature of the operation required the army's dispersion in scattered detachments over a wide area. Most of the Cherokee to be removed were inhabitants of Georgia and their apprehension was conducted by Georgia militia who had long as a matter of policy been habituated to dealing harshly with Indians. Prison stockades had been erected at assembly and embarkation points in which the Cherokee were to be herded and confined while awaiting transportation west. There was little or no likelihood of attempted resistance. Most had been disarmed during Wool's regime and the irresistible military power that had been brought to bear was self-evident. The classic account of what next transpired is that recorded by James Mooney. His contribution to the Bureau of American Ethnology, eventually published in the 19th Annual Report in 1900 under the title *Myths of the Cherokee,* included a history of the Cherokee based upon years of field work. His narrative of the 1838 expulsion was drawn from personal interviews with survivors, white officers as well as Cherokee victims, and had therefore much of the vitality of an eyewitness report:

> The history of this Cherokee removal of 1838, as gleaned by the author from the lips of actors in the tragedy, may well exceed in weight of grief and pathos any other passage in American history. Even the much-sung exile of the Acadians falls far behind it in its sum of death and misery. Under Scott's order the troops were disposed at various points throughout the Cherokee country,

where stockade forts were erected for gathering in and holding the Indians preparatory to removal. From these, squads of troops were sent to search out with rifle and bayonet every small cabin hidden away in the coves or by the sides of mountain streams, to seize and bring in as prisoners all the occupants, however or wherever they might be found. Families at dinner were startled by the sudden gleam of bayonets in the doorway and rose up to be driven with blows and oaths along the weary miles of trail that led to the stockade. Men were seized in their fields or going along the road, women were taken from their wheels and children from their play. In many cases, on turning for one last look as they crossed the ridge, they saw their homes in flames, fired by the lawless rabble that followed on the heels of the soldiers to loot and pillage. So keen were these outlaws on the scent that in some instances they were driving off the cattle and other stock of the Indians almost before the soldiers had fairly started their owners in the other direction. Systematic hunts were made by the same men for Indian graves, to rob them of the silver pendants and other valuables deposited with the dead. A Georgia volunteer, afterward a colonel in the Confederate service, said: "I fought through the civil war and have seen men shot to pieces and slaughtered by thousands, but the Cherokee removal was the cruelest work I ever knew." To prevent escape the soldiers had been ordered to approach and surround each house, so far as possible, so as to come upon the occupants without warning. One old patriarch, when thus surprised, calmly called his children and grandchildren around him, and, kneeling down, bid them pray with him in their own language, while the astonished onlookers looked on in silence. Then rising he led the way into exile. A woman, on finding the house surrounded, went to the door and called up the chickens to be fed for the last time, after which, taking her infant on her back and her two other children by the hand, she followed her husband with the soldiers.

Within days nearly 17,000 Cherokee had been crowded into the stockades. Sanitation measures were inadequate in those makeshift concentration camps. Indian families, accustomed to a more spacious and isolated existence, were unable to adapt to the necessities of this mass imprisonment. Hundreds of the inmates sickened. The Indian was by his nature peculiarly susceptible to the depressions produced by confinement. Many lost any will to live and perceiving no glimmer of hope, resigned themselves to death. Those who had become converts found some comfort in the ministrations of their white and native pastors. In every stockade hymn singings and prayer meetings were almost continuous.

All physical preparations had been carefully planned in advance by the federal authorities in charge of the migration so that little time might be lost in getting the movement under way. In the first and second weeks of June two detachments of some 800 exiles were driven aboard the waiting fleets of steamboats, keelboats and flatboats for the descent of the Tennessee. They passed down the storied waterway by the same route taken by the first white settlers of middle Tennessee under John Donelson in 1780. In the shadow of Lookout Mountain they could survey the wilderness vastnesses from which for 20 years bands of their immediate forebears had sallied to devastate the white frontier, some of them commanded by war chiefs who had lived to be condemned to this exile. Then, at Muscle Shoals there came an ironic contrast between the past and the future as Indians being driven from their ancient homeland were committed to transportation by the white man's newest invention. They disembarked from their boats to clamber, momentarily diverted, aboard the cars drawn by the two puffing little locomotives of the railroad recently constructed to move freight and passengers around the rapids. Returning to other boats, they resumed their seemingly interminable journey in the dibilitating heat of an increasingly oppressive summer. The attendant army officers, however sympathetic, were helpless against the waves of illnesses. Scott, moving new contingents toward embarkation, was appalled by the reports he received of the mounting death rate among those who had already been dispatched.

The troops assembled for Cherokee expulsion had been by considered governmental design so numerous as to present a show of military power so overwhelming as to provide no faintest invitation to Indian resistance. By the army's first pounce more than nine tenths of the population had been rounded up and driven into the stockades. There remained only a handful of the wilder and more primitive residents of the higher mountains still at large. This handful, however, represented a problem causing Scott serious concern. Were they provoked to resist they might among their remote and cloud-wreathed peaks prove as difficult to apprehend as were the Seminole in their swamps. From this tactical threat sprang the one heroic action to gleam across the otherwise unrelieved despondency of the removal scene.

Tsali was an hitherto undistinguished mountain Cherokee who suddenly soared to an eminence in Cherokee annals comparable to the homage accorded an Attakullaculla, an Old Tassel, a Sequoyah or a John Ross. The stories of his inspired exploit, drawn from eyewitnesses, survivors and references in contemporary official records, vary in detail and have become encrusted by legend but coincide in most essentials. According to the more generally accepted version, a young Cherokee woman upon being assaulted by two soldiers killed both with a hatchet. Tsali hid the weapon under his shirt and assumed responsibility for his kinswoman's act. Scott could not permit the death of his soldiers to remain unpunished and served notice on the band of mountain Cherokee of which Tsali was a member that a scapegoat must be produced. The band felt that it had a reasonable chance to elude pursuit indefinitely but its councils were impressed by the advice of a white trader, William Thomas, a friend of his native customers in the notable tradition of Ludovic Grant, Alexander Cameron and John McDonald. Thomas pointed out the advantage that could be taken of Scott's demand. Tsali was prepared to offer his life for his people. His fellow tribesmen thereupon notified Scott that he would be turned over to American justice in return for American permission to remain unmolested in their mountains. Scott, eager to escape the uncertainties of a guerrilla campaign in so difficult a terrain, agreed to recommend this course to Washington. Tsali was brought in, the voluntary prisoner of his compatriots. His Cherokee custodians were required to serve as the firing squad by which he, his brother and his eldest son were executed. The story became one of the few Indian stories with a happy ending. Thomas continued for years to interest himself in the prolonged negotiations with the governments of the United States and North Carolina which eventually resulted in federal and state recognition of Cherokee title to their mountain holdings. Tsali's sacrifice had permitted this fraction of the nation to become the remnant of the East Cherokee [and] to cling to their homeland where they still are colorful inhabitants of the North Carolina mountains.

Aside from the Tsali episode the roundup of the Cherokee proceeded without interruption. By June 18 General Charles Floyd, commanding the Georgia militia engaged in it, was able to report to his governor that no Cherokee remained on the soil of Georgia except as a prisoner in a stockade. Scott was able to discharge his volunteers June 17 and two days later to dispatch three of his five regular regiments to sectors where military needs were more pressing, two to the Canadian border and one to Florida.

Meanwhile so many migrants were dying in the drought and heat to which the initial removal was subjected that Scott was constrained to lighten the inexorable pressures. The Cherokee Council, which though technically illegal still spoke for the Cherokee people, begged for a postponement to the more healthful weather of autumn. Scott agreed. In July Ross returned and in conferences with Scott worked out a further agreement under which the Cherokee would cease passive resistance and under his supervision undertake a voluntary migration as soon as weather permitted. Scott was glad to be relieved of further need to use military force. The administration was glad to be offered some defense against the storm of northern criticism. Even Georgia made no serious protest, inasmuch as the Cherokee had already been removed from their land to stockades and there remained no questioning of the state's sovereignty. The one remonstrance, aside from the complaints of contractors, was voiced by the aging [Andrew] Jackson from his retirement at The Hermitage in a letter of August 23, 1838 to Felix Grundy, Attorney General of the United States:

> . . . The contract with Ross must be arrested, or you may rely upon it, the expense and other evils will shake the popularity of the adminstration to its center. What madness and folly to have anything to do with Ross, when the agent was proceeding well with the removal. . . . The time and circumstances under which Gen'l Scott made this contract shows that he is no economist, or is, *sub rosa*, in league with [Henry] Clay & Co. to bring disgrace on the administration. The evil is done. It behooves Mr. [President Martin] Van Buren to act with energy to throw it off his shoulders. I enclose a letter to you under

cover, unsealed, which you may read, seal, and deliver to him, that you may aid him with your views in getting out of this real difficulty.

Your friend in haste,
Andrew Jackson

P.S. I am so feeble I can scarcely wield my pen, but friendship dictates it & the subject excites me. Why is it that the scamp Ross is not banished from the notice of the administration?

Ross, having at last recognized the inevitable, gave to his preparations for the voluntary removal the same driving energy and attention to detail he had until then devoted to resisting removal. All phases of the organization of the national effort were gathered into his hands. All financial arrangements were under his supervision, including the disbursement of the basic federal subsistence allowance of 16 cents a day for each person and 40 cents a day for each horse. For convenience in management en route the 13,000 Cherokee remaining in the stockades were divided into detachments of roughly a thousand to head each of which he appointed a Cherokee commander. At a final meeting of the Cherokee Council it was provided that the constitution and laws of the Nation should be considered equally valid in the west.

The first detachment set out October 1, 1838 on the dreaded journey over the route which in Cherokee memory became known as The Trail of Tears. The last started November 4. The improvement in weather awaited during the tedious summer months in the stockades did not materialize. The spring migration had been cursed by oppressive heat and drought. The fall migration encountered deluges of rain followed by excessive cold. To the hundreds of deaths from heat-induced diseases were now added new hundreds of deaths from prolonged exposure.

The most vivid general account of the 1838 migration is again that of James Mooney, assembled from the recollections of participants:

. . . in October, 1838, the long procession of exiles was set in motion. A very few went by the river route; the rest, nearly all of the 13,000, went overland. Crossing to the north side of the Hiwassee at a ferry above Gunstocker creek, they proceeded down along the river, the sick, the old people, and the smaller children, with the blankets, cooking pots, and other belongings in wagons, the rest on foot or on horses. The number of wagons was 645. It was like the march of an army, regiment after regiment, the wagons in the center, the officers along the line and the horsemen on the flanks and at the rear. Tennessee river was crossed at Tuckers (?) ferry, a short distance above Jollys island, at the mouth of the Hiwassee. Thence the route lay south of Pikeville, through McMinnville and on to Nashville, where the Cumberland was crossed. Then they went on to Hopkinsville, Kentucky, where the noted chief White-path, in charge of a detachment, sickened and died. His people buried him by the roadside, with a box over the grave and poles with streamers around it, that the others coming on behind might note the spot and remember him. Somewhere also along that march of death — for the exiles died by tens and twenties every day of the journey — the devoted wife of John Ross sank down, leaving him to go on with the bitter pain of bereavement added to heartbreak at the ruin of his nation. The Ohio was crossed at a ferry near the mouth of the Cumberland, and the army passed on through southern Illinois until the great Mississippi was reached opposite Cape Girardeau, Missouri. It was now the middle of winter, with the river running full of ice, so that several detachments were obliged to wait some time on the eastern bank for the channel to become clear. In talking with old men and women at Tahlequah the author found that the lapse of over half a century had not sufficed to wipe out the memory of the miseries of that halt beside the frozen river, with hundreds of sick and dying penned up in wagons or stretched upon the ground, with only a blanket overhead to keep out the January blast. The crossing was made at last in two divisions, at Cape Girardeau and at Green's Ferry, a short distance below, whence the march was made on through Missouri to Indian Territory, the later detachments making a northerly circuit by Springfield, because those who had gone before had killed off all the game along the direct route. At last their destination was reached. They had started in October, 1838, and it was now March, 1839, the journey having occupied barely six months of the hardest part of the year.

President Van Buren in his December 1838 message to Congress announced the administration's view of the event:

. . . It affords me sincere pleasure to apprise the Congress of the entire removal of the Cherokee Nation of Indians to their new homes west of the Mississippi. The measures authorized by Congress at its last session have had the happiest effects. By an agreement concluded with them by the commanding general in that country, their removal has been principally under the conduct of their own chiefs, and they have emigrated without any apparent reluctance.

A traveler who had encountered the Indians en route was moved by the President's words to write his own eyewitness report which was published in the January 26, 1839 *New York Observer* under the heading. "A Native of Maine, traveling in the Western Country":

. . . On Tuesday evening we fell in with a detachment of the poor Cherokee Indians . . . about eleven hundred Indians — sixty wagons — six hundred horses, and perhaps forty pairs of oxen. We found them in the forest camped for the night by the road side . . . under a severe fall of rain accompanied by heavy wind. With their canvas for a shield from the inclemency of the weather, and the cold wet ground for a resting place, after the fatigue of the day, they spent the night . . . many of the aged Indians were suffering extremely from the fatigue of the journey, and the ill health consequent upon it . . . several were then quite ill, and one aged man we were informed was then in the last struggles of death. . . . The last detachment which we passed on the 7th embraced rising two thousand Indians with horses and mules in proportion. The forward part of the train we found just pitching their tents for the night, and notwithstanding some thirty or forty wagons were already stationed, we found the road literally filled with the procession for about three miles in length. The sick and feeble were carried in wagons — about as comfortable for traveling as a New England ox cart with a covering over it — a great many ride on horseback and multitudes go on foot — even aged females, apparently nearly ready to drop into the grave, were traveling with heavy burdens attached to the back — on the sometimes frozen ground, and sometimes muddy streets, with no covering for the feet except what nature had given them. . . . We learned from the inhabitants on the road where the Indians passed, that they buried fourteen or fifteen at every stopping place, and they make a journey of ten miles per day only on an average. One fact which to my own mind seemed a lesson indeed to the American nation is, that they will not travel on the Sabbath. . . . The Indians as a whole carry on their countenances every thing but the appearance of happiness. Some carry a downcast dejected look bordering upon the appearance of despair others a wild frantic appearance as if about to burst the chains of nature and pounce like a tiger upon their enemies. . . . When I past the last detachment of those suffering exiles and thought that my native countrymen had thus expelled them from their native soil and their much-loved homes, and that too in this inclement season of the year in all their suffering, I turned from the sight with feelings which language cannot express. . . . I felt that I would not encounter the secret silent prayer of one of these sufferers armed with the energy that faith and hope would give it (if there be a God who avenges the wrongs of the injured) for all the lands of Georgia. . . . When I read in the President's Message that he was happy to inform the Senate that the Cherokees were peaceably and without reluctance removed — and remember that it was on the third day of December when not one of the detachments had reached their destination; and that a large majority had not made even half their journey when he made that declaration, I thought I wished the President could have been there that very day in Kentucky with myself, and have seen the comfort and the willingness with which the Cherokees were making their journey.

The first migrants reached their destination on the plains beyond the western border of Arkansas January 4, 1839. Other contingents continued to straggle in until late in March. Examination of all available records by Grant Foreman, outstanding authority on Indian removal, led him to conclude 4,000 Cherokee had died either during confinement in the stockades or on their 800-mile journey west.

While the Cherokee were traversing their Trail of Tears their fellow southern Indians were committed to afflictions as dismal. The processes of removal were grinding out the cumulative calamities that had been visited upon a race by governmental fiat.

The Chickasaw had at length embarked upon their self-governed migration. They were the aristocrats of the Indian world, long noted for the prowess of their warriors, the beauty of their women and the speed of their horses. They had bargained shrewdly until they had wrung every possible advantage from federal authorities, including uninterrupted control over their affairs and a good price for their lands in western Tennessee and northwestern Mississippi. When finally they started west it was a movement under their own leadership undertaken at a time of their own choosing after repeated inspections of their new territory and the route to it by their own representatives. They traveled in comfort, well supplied with equipment, food and money. It might have been expected that were removal ever to be conducted under acceptable conditions it might prove so in their case. But it did not. Their relative prosperity became one of the major causes of their undoing. Sensing unusual profits, contractors gathered stockpiles of supplies along the way in such quantities that the food spoiled before it could be eaten. The travelers were charged exorbitantly for transportation and their every other requirement. They picked up smallpox en route and the disease reached epidemic proportions after their arrival. Most had arrived too late to get in an 1838 crop and they were soon as hungry as their poorer fellow colonists. The move west had made plaintive beggars of the once proud and warlike Chickasaw.

Nearly 2,000 Seminole, rounded up by various devices, pseudo-agreements and military pressures, were also on the way west in 1838. Having suffered so much more than other migrants before their start, they continued to suffer more en route. Many had scarcely emerged from their swampland refuges before they were crowded, naked and undernourished, aboard ship. Others had already endured long periods of imprisonment by which they had been weakened. Most were detained for weeks and months en route in noisome concentration camps in Tampa, Mobile and New Orleans. In addition to all their other privations and afflictions they were continually harassed at every stop and in every new state jurisdiction by the claims of slave dealers to the ownership of Seminole prisoners who showed evidence of Negro blood. A considerable proportion of Seminole were Negroes who had for generations been considered members of the tribe and even though they were closely guarded prisoners each group of exiles fiercely resisted every attempt to single out any of their number for delivery into slavery. The problem of identification had been complicated by the flight to the Seminole of many actual slaves during the war. Some of the slave traders' claims were thus clothed with a species of legitimacy which made adjudication of every dispute more difficult. As one controversial example, among the Seminole prisoners of war taken by the Creek auxiliaries in 1837 had been 90 black Seminole whom they had sold to traders. In all these disputes federal and state authorities, except for the attendant army officers, in their anxiety to expedite the removal tended to support the traders' claims to an extent that provoked a congressional investigation. Meanwhile, in Florida the war went on, with American troops now under the command of Brigadier General Zachary Taylor, later President of the United States, continuing their attempts to run to earth the some 2,000 Seminole still in hiding.

The year 1838 also witnessed the initiation of a companion Indian removal in an adjoining country. Bowl's band of Cherokee, the first recorded migrants who had fled their homelands in 1794, had eventually settled on the Texas side of the Red River in what was then Mexican territory. Joined by other Cherokee and other Indians, the colony had increased to some 8,000. At the outbreak of the Texas revolution Sam Houston had negotiated a treaty of friendship with Bowl's Cherokee which saved the Americans in Texas from possible attack by Indians at the precarious moment they were being assaulted by Santa Anna in return for a Texan recognition of Cherokee title to the land on which they had settled. But in 1838 Mirabeau Lamar, upon succeeding Houston as President of Texas, immediately proclaimed his intention of expelling all Indians from the republic. In the ensuing 1839 campaign the aged Bowl was killed, still clutching the tin box containing the documents and deeds relating to the 1836 treaty of friendship with Texas. The Texas Cherokee were driven across the Red River to share the fortunes of the West and newly arrived East Cherokee on the upper Arkansas.

Indian removal had now been accomplished. Aside from a few scattered remnants, such as the Seminole fugitives in the Florida swamps, the few mountain Cherokee in North Carolina, the Choctaw residue in Mississippi and an occasional tiny enclave in the north, every Indian nation which had originally occupied the immense expanse of woodland extending across the eastern half of the United States had been compelled to seek new homes on the plains beyond that woodland's western margin. It had required a persisting effort over a period of 15 years, distinguished not only by the sufferings inflicted upon Indians but by the virulent disagreements excited among Americans, to give effect to the outwardly plausible policy announced by [James] Monroe and [John] Calhoun in 1825. Removal had been a contemporary success in the sense that the national government had proved able to impose its will and the states concerned had been rid of unwanted Indian inhabitants. But for the Indians and for the larger interests of the United States it had been a deplorable failure. The opportunity for Indians to become useful and valued members of American society, an achievement many had seemed on the verge of attaining in 1825, had been heedlessly postponed for more than a century.

Most informed Indians had long realized that such an assimilation represented the one lingering hope that Indians might ever regain comfort and security. The mass of Indians, less aware of the economic and political realities, had as long clung despairingly to the more appealing hope that they might yet contrive some escape from the white incubus. Removal dealt crushing blows to both hopes. In the west progressive Indians were compelled to begin again, under far greater handicaps, the painful climb toward citizenship and all Indians were subjected to white exactions more distracting than any they had known in the east. It was only after decades of miraculously patient struggle that Indians were finally to gain recognition of the principle that the rights of the conquered are even more precious than the prerogatives of their conquerors.

During the three centuries Indians had been retreating before the inexorable advance of alien invaders they had been bitterly conscious that they were suffering greater deprivations than the loss of their lands and lives. Their entire way of life, their whole world as they had known it, was in the course of obliteration. They understood, as could nobody else, by how wide a margin their post-invasion opportunities to pursue happiness failed to match the opportunities they had known before invasion. There was little enough comfort in the reflection that these opportunities were being denied them by a force physically too strong for them to resist.

In their despair Indians had sought consolation in resort to the supernatural. Native prophets, such as those who had inspired the followers of Pontiac and Tecumseh, had emerged again and again to preach the doctrine of original blessedness. They had exhorted Indians to eschew every compromise with white influence, especially by forswearing the use of white tools, weapons and alcohol, so that by a return to their ancient purity they might regain the strength to regain their former freedoms. These movements had been frustrated by their adherents' realization that obedience left Indians even more defenseless than before. By the time of the removal Indians were increasingly addicted to more extravagant religious phantasies. A favorite conceit, intermittently erupting for generation after generation until its final resurgence as the Ghost Dance excitement among the Plains Indians in the late 1880's, envisioned the evocation, by appropriate prayers, dances and rites, of the innumerable spirits of all Indian dead who would return to earth as a mighty host capable of expelling the white invaders and thus restoring the land of peace and plenty Indians had once enjoyed.

Even so superior an intellect as Sequoyah's was subject to wishful fancies. He had from his youth believed that the one Indian hope to retain their identity as a people was to withdraw from white contamination. He had himself moved west nearly 20 years before removal and all his life had sought by advice and example to persuade Indians to shun intercourse with whites. In his declining years he became obsessed with the possibility that the Lost Cherokee, reputed by tribal legend to have disappeared into the farthest west in the forgotten past, still lived in innocence, freedom and security in some distant land. In his frail old age, still in pursuit of this relic of the Indian golden age, he set out on a two-year journey in search of a remote Cherokee colony reported to have found sanctuary in the mountains of Mexico. His 1843 death in a Mexican desert, was giving ultimate poignancy to the discovery all Indians were being required to make. For them there was no way back. There was only the way ahead.

STUDY GUIDE

1. Describe where each of the Indian tribes discussed in this essay — the Cherokee, Seminole, and Chickasaw — lived before removal and how each of these nations reacted to the forced removal.
2. What problems did the Indians face with respect to weather, supplies, health, and transportation on the trail west?
3. How did the sentiment of General Scott, who was directly responsible for supervising the Indian removal, differ from that of Andrew Jackson? How does a knowledge of the politics of the period help in understanding the views expressed in Jackson's letter?
4. Discuss the deeper, psychological impact of removal upon the Indian tribes. Explain what factors in the nineteenth century made it difficult for the Indian to resist removal.
5. What differences can you think of between the removal of the Indians in this period and the forced removal of Japanese-Americans from their homes on the Pacific coast to concentration centers during World War II?

BIBLIOGRAPHY

A great deal has been written about the removal of the eastern Indian tribes to lands beyond the Mississippi. As Van Every's selection indicates, it is a gripping story. Unfortunately, some of the books that are most reliable are not very interesting, and some of the most interesting are not very reliable. Grant Foreman has probably written more on this subject than anyone. The first of his titles cited here is on the removal of the tribes north of the Ohio River, and the second is on the situation of the Indians in their new homelands following removal: *The Last Trek of the Indians* (Chicago, 1946); *The Five Civilized Tribes* * (Norman, Okla., 1934); and *Indian Removal: The Emigration of the Five Civilized Tribes of Indians* * (Norman, Okla., 1932). R. S. Cotterill, *The Southern Indians* * (Norman, Okla., 1954) is one of the best general works on the Civilized Tribes of the Southeast. Three other works dealing directly with those tribes are: Arthur H. De Rosier, Jr., *The Removal of the Choctaw Indians* * (Knoxville, Tenn., 1970); Angie Debo, *The Rise and Fall of the Choctaw Republic,* * 2nd ed. (Norman, Okla., 1967); and Gloria Jahoda, *The Trail of Tears* (New York, 1975). Alvin M. Josephy, Jr., *The Patriot Chiefs* * (New York, 1961) is a series of nicely written sketches of Indian leaders from Hiawatha to Chief Joseph.

Much of the recent writing in the field of Indian history has tried to "get inside" Indian life and culture. Valuable as such works are, it is also necessary to study white attitudes and government policy. Several works examine these subjects, both in earlier American history and in the 1830s, when the eastern Indians were removed. Two of the best works on the earlier period are Reginald Horsman, *Expansion and American Indian Policy, 1783–1812* (East Lansing, Mich., 1967), and Bernard Sheehan, *Seeds of Extinction: Jeffersonian Philanthropy and the American Indian* * (Chapel Hill, N.C., 1973). Two volumes on Indian policy during Jackson's administration are Ronald N. Satz, *American Indian Policy in the Jacksonian Era* (Lincoln, Neb., 1975), and Michael P. Rogin, *Fathers and Children: Andrew Jackson and the Subjugation of the American Indian* (New York, 1975). Politics and government policy, even in the nineteenth century, frequently reflect the values and attitudes of the American people, or a substantial majority of them. The popular beliefs that made Andrew Jackson such a hero with the American people are set forth in John W. Ward, *Andrew Jackson: Symbol for an Age* * (New York, 1962), a very readable volume that includes some suggestive passages on Jackson's personal attitude towards Indians. In recent years, legal suits by various Indian tribes in federal courts have raised the question of who actually owns parts of the United States. Wilcomb Washburn, *Red Man's Land, White Man's Law* (New York, 1971) is a study of land titles and Indian policy. Another work, not directly related to removal, but of considerable interest on Indian-white relations is Wilbur R. Jacobs, *Dispossessing the American Indian* * (New York, 1972).

The bibliography following the essay by Anthony F. C. Wallace, "Indian Life and Culture," lists several general works on Indian history. Two other readable works of this sort are William Brandon, *The American Heritage Book of Indians* * (New York, 1961), which includes many illustrations, and Angie Debo, *A History of the Indians of the United States* (Norman, Okla., 1970).

---

* Asterisk indicates book is available in a paperback edition.

Scores of new prisons, asylums, and reformatories, like the New York House of Refuge, were established in the pre–Civil War period.

12

JOSEPH M. HAWES

The Reform Impulse

Every society has to deal with social problems, which might range from controlling those who disobey its laws and mores to assisting the poor, aged, or orphaned who cannot care for themselves. In the Seneca culture described by Anthony Wallace (Reading No. 1), ridicule, as when Red Jacket was nicknamed Cow-killer, was often sufficient to enforce tribal mores. The British colonists used religion and law as tools of social control, but the family was the single most important social agency. In the absence of the many institutions that now exist, the colonial family served as a hospital for the care of the sick, an orphanage and retirement home, a house of correction and reform, a school and apprenticeship program. By the nineteenth century, various social changes including the rise of cities made it impossible for the family to handle all these services.

By 1800, the needs had become quite apparent, and a remarkable group of men and women undertook — in some cases, singlehandedly — to do something about the growing social problems. In every major city, societies sprang up to reform conditions in jails and almshouses, to help the handicapped, to combat alcoholic intemperance, to fight for women's rights, and to abolish slavery. Thomas Gallaudet established a school to help the deaf and mute, while Samuel Gridley Howe developed methods to assist the sightless. Dorothea Dix was scandalized by the treatment of the mentally ill, who were frequently jailed, sometimes in shackles, rather than treated in hospitals. It is estimated that she traveled 40,000 miles and investigated more than eight hundred jails and almshouses. Her petitions to legislatures led twenty states to adopt her recommendations, and thirty-two new hospitals were established. Thousands of lesser-known women and men worked in the antislavery crusade, the peace movement, and other reform organizations of the Jacksonian era.

Whether a society tries simply to punish its deviant members or to reform and care for them can help us in understanding the values and the view of human nature in that society. Through much of Western history, man has been viewed as having free will to do good or evil. The possible influence of social and psychological factors upon behavior was not recognized, so that criminals were entirely responsible for their crimes and punishments were often severe. The hand of a thief might be cut off, the tongue of a gossip pierced, or in a later period, an adultress be required to wear a scarlet *A*. Executions by flaying and impaling, disemboweling, and drawing and quartering were used for a long list of crimes. The holding of people in slavery, the shackling of the insane, and the use of execution and mutilation were not regarded by most people as either unusual or abhorrent.

Change began in the eighteenth century, on both sides of the Atlantic, with the development of a new feeling — a concern for other human beings that we call humanitarianism. A number of sensitive men such as John Howard, John Woolman, Anthony Benezet, and Phillippe Pinel questioned traditional ideas and provided a social philosophy directed toward a more humane world. The number of capital crimes was reduced, imprisonment rather than mutilation became more common, and institutions were developed that might reform offenders. Prisons at Philadelphia and at Auburn, New York, became models that attracted Alexis de Tocqueville and scores of other foreign travelers interested in reform. In the selection that follows, Joseph M. Hawes describes the institutions established in the 1820s and 1830s to care for homeless children and to separate juvenile offenders from hardened criminals. He discusses the nineteenth-century view of children and of why they became delinquent, as well as the daily routine and the system of discipline in these early reformatories. Newspaper headlines about juvenile delinquency, the criminal "repeater," and prison riots indicate that despite these noble efforts of the 1830s, the problems remain today.

In the fall of 1822 two men met in one of New York City's parks. They were James W. Gerard, a young lawyer, and Isaac Collins, a Quaker, and both were members of the Society for the Prevention of Pauperism. Every year

Excerpted from *Children in Urban Society* by Joseph M. Hawes. Copyright © 1971 by Oxford University Press, Inc. Reprinted by permission.

this Society presented a public report to suggest ways of carrying out its purposes. Usually, one man, with the assistance of two others "for form's sake," wrote this report. Gerard was talking to Collins about the street children of New York because he was going to write the report for 1822 on "the reformation of juvenile delinquents." Collins, whose father was a Philadelphia printer, became interested in the treatment of juvenile delinquents after reading the annual report of an English institution for young offenders. Gerard had become interested in juvenile crime as a result of the very first case he tried, that of a fourteen-year-old boy accused of stealing a bird. The young lawyer won acquittal for his client by arguing that prison would corrupt the boy. The case so interested Gerard that he began to investigate the facilities for detaining prisoners in New York. He also decided to join the Society for the Prevention of Pauperism.

Gerard presented his report at a public meeting held in the ballroom of the City Hotel in February, 1823. "Those who are in the habit of attending our criminal courts, as jurors or otherwise," Gerard said,

> must be convinced of the very great increase of juvenile delinquency within these few years past, and of the necessity of immediate measures to arrest so great an evil. . . . It is with pain we state that, in five or six years past, and until the last few months, the number of youth under fourteen years of age, charged with offenses against the law, has doubled; and that the same boys are again and again brought up for examination, some of whom are committed, and some tried; and that imprisonment by its frequency renders them hardened and fearless.

This was hardly surprising, Gerard said, if one knew the conditions of the prisons and the Bridewell. (A Bridewell then had about the same functions as a county jail in twentieth-century America.) At the Bridewell persons awaiting trial because they could not afford to pay bail were all packed into one large room, "the young and the old . . . promiscuously crowded together. . . . Boys who have been charged with picking pockets, stealing watches, and the like crimes," Gerard continued, "have declared before the police when [asked] how they came to such things, that they learned the art from the experienced offenders they met in [the] Bridewell."

Every year one to two hundred children between the ages of seven and fourteen appeared in the criminal courts of New York City. Some were homeless and most of them were "the children of poor and abandoned parents" whose "debased character and vicious habits" caused them to be "brought up in perfect ignorance and idleness, and what is worse in street begging and pilfering." Gerard concluded with a recommendation that a "house of refuge" for young convicts be established where juvenile delinquents might be reformed. "Unless the heart is corrupt indeed, and sunk deep in guilt," Gerard said, "the youth would undergo a change of feeling and character, and he would look on crime with greater abhorrence, because he himself had been a criminal." Gerard's report led to the creation of the first separate institution for juvenile delinquents in the United States, the New York House of Refuge. . . .

The act incorporating the Society for the Reformation of Juvenile Delinquents in the City of New York outlined the procedures for membership in the Society and made the Board of Managers responsible for the operation of the House of Refuge. Thus, America's first institution for juvenile delinquents was a "mixed" institution. That is, a private philanthropic group established and operated it, but the state had chartered it and provided for the conditions of its operation. The act of incorporation also contained the first statutory definition of juvenile delinquency in the United States. It authorized the Managers "to receive and take into the house of refuge to be established by them, all such children who shall be taken up or committed as vagrants, or convicted of criminal offenses" if a judge thought they were "proper objects." The Managers could also "place the said children committed to their care, during the minority of such children at such employments, and cause them to be instructed in such branches of useful knowledge, as shall be suitable to their years and capacities." The Managers had the power to bind out children (with their consent) as apprentices until they reached legal maturity. The children remained under the control of the Managers until the boys were twenty-one and the girls were eighteen, or until the officials at the House of Refuge decided that they were "reformed" and agreed to their discharge. Thus, the New York House of Refuge began the use of the indeterminate sentence long before penal reformers advocated it in the late nineteenth century as a necessary innovation in American penology.

The House of Refuge began its operations in the old arsenal building on January 1, 1825, with six boys and three girls. By the end of the first year, a total of seventy-three children had come to the Refuge, fifty-four boys and nineteen girls, and fifty-six remained in the institution. Of the seventeen children who left during the first year, nine had been indentured as apprentices or servants, four had been discharged, and four boys had "absconded."

Most of the children who came to the House of Refuge that first year and most of the ones who came later were "very ignorant." Even those few who had learned to read "had acquired no relish for intellectual improvement. Their habits, as it [sic] respects skill and useful industry, were still more deplorable." Particularly surprising was the fact that the girls could not perform any of the standard feminine tasks; they could not cook, sew, or iron. For the first year the boys spent most of their time cleaning up the grounds and helping to erect a new building and make the wall higher. When they were not busy with their newly learned domestic tasks, the girls planted grass. Once the maintenance tasks were finished, the boys began to learn shoemaking and tailoring, and the girls found themselves doing all of the mending and laundry for the institution.

The schedule, which the superintendent had worked out, allowed two hours a day, one in the morning and one in the evening, for formal instruction. The curriculum included spelling, reading, writing, and cyphering (arithmetic). To some extent the inmates taught themselves, since the Lancastrian or monitorial system was used. Apparently, the combination of labor and instruction and the system of discipline at the House of Refuge were effective. The *Annual Report* for the first year noted that "of the whole number in the house, the superintendent reports that [only] eleven are still restless and refractory." Four of the boys had run away, but the Managers and the superintendent were apparently satisfied with the other children, who had been in the House of Refuge at one time or another in 1825.

Methods of discipline varied; the superintendent sometimes put the "subjects" on a ball and chain. He also used handcuffs, leg-irons, and the "barrel." On January 28, 1825, Superintendent [Joseph] Curtis noted in his daily journal that six subjects, two of whom were girls, had been talking during a meal. He "took each of them to the barrel which supports them while the feet are tied on one side and the hands on the other. . . . With the pantaloons down [this device] gives a convenient surface for the operation of the 6 line cat." On that same day a boy wearing handcuffs made himself a key. The superintendent "put him in prison," locked his leg iron to the wall, and instructed the staff to feed him on bread and water. In spite of these restraints, however, the boy broke out of "prison," but the police soon recaptured him. Curtis refused to have this boy back at the House of Refuge, and so he went to the penitentiary. Corporal punishment was not confined to boys. On March 13, 1825, the superintendent put leg-irons on a girl who "does not obey the orders of coming when called, and neglects her work for playing in the yard." Curtis also gave one "sullen, ill-natured and disobedient" girl "a dose of salts" — apparently aloes, a purgative. She came to the House of Refuge in March, 1825, and was "very trying." She did not "transgress in things of importance" but she was "artful and sly" and told "many equivocating stories." Her conduct exasperated Superintendent Curtis and he "gave her a ball and chain and confined her to the house." She escaped twice; once the police recaptured her, and once she returned on her own. She went out as a servant, but voluntarily returned to the House of Refuge. Another indenture took the girl to her majority, but on December 26, 1829, the superintendent wrote that "she is said to be on the town."

The situation at the Refuge made some of these punishments necessary. The walls presented no real barrier, and the superintendent had to appoint some of the boys as guards. There were, consequently, a number of escapes. On October 4, 1825, Superintendent Curtis noted in the daily journal that "this evening has been spent in making confessions on the repeated attempts of escaping." As a result,

> great freedom of speach [*sic*] and frankness appeared to our entire satisfaction, all the movements and plans as well as the persons who have manifested

a desire to go has [*sic*] been fully exposed. . . . It tells us that the insecurity which we have daily felt on this subject has been well grounded; and that there is no security with our present encumbrances.

The fact that the magazine of the old arsenal still contained powder also added to the superintendent's worries. In addition many of the inmates in the House of Refuge were boys over sixteen, for legally any boy under twenty-one could be sent there. In September, 1826, the superintendent complained about the "large notorious & hardened villains" who came to the Refuge. "I fear," he said, "that our extended wish to do good will in consequence of introducing these ill bred hardened boys among the first and young offenders, will prove a curse rather than a blessing." Since the old arsenal building was clearly inadequate, the Acting Committee (which functioned as a board of trustees for the House of Refuge) decided to erect a new building which would provide "greater security." In April, 1825, the Committee resolved to add workshops and small utility buildings to their construction plans and decided that the new main building should contain "cells and accommodations for a number of delinq'nts not exceeding one hundred." In that same month the United States Army sent a man to remove the powder from the magazine, which somewhat reduced the "insecurity."

To pay for the new building the managers of the Society appealed to the public for more money. In May, 1825, they issued an *Address to Annual Subscribers* in which they claimed that "already the number of vagrant children who beg and steal in our streets is perceptibly diminished." There were thirty-five boys and eleven girls in the House of Refuge at that time "in a situation where there is no temptation to vice . . . and, where, instead of being left to prey on the public, they will be fitted to become valuable members of society." To continue this important work the managers felt compelled "to erect . . . an additional stone building with separate dormitories for each child, on a plan somewhat resembling the State Prison at Auburn. . . ." To be sure that their contributions were worthwhile "subscribers and the public" were invited "to call at the House of Refuge, and see that idleness has become changed to industry, filth and rags to cleanliness and comfortable appearance, [and] boisterous impudence to quiet submission."

The Acting Committee directed the superintendent to employ a foreman and four to six masons to erect the building with the assistance of the boys. The masons and the boys finished the new cell house in April, 1826. It was a two-story stone building with barred windows and heavy doors. Inside were small "dormitories" — three feet, three inches wide — for each boy. The new building did make it more difficult to escape and brought about the complete separation of the male and female departments. "We find ourselves in possession and enjoyment of all the long wished advantages of the new building," Superintendent Curtis wrote, "and we also find (as we may allways [*sic*] expect) that our anticipations are not realised." The boys now had to do their own cooking, and for a time they proved less adept than the girls.

From the first the House of Refuge attracted a stream of visitors, distinguished and otherwise. Soon after the Refuge opened, a father appeared and demanded the return of his son. Only after he had secured a writ of habeas corpus did the superintendent permit the man to take his boy. In May, 1826, Governor De Witt Clinton of New York, the Governor of Ohio, the Mayor of New York, "and various other dignitaries and their wives" came to the House of Refuge and left apparently well pleased. In July three men from Pennsylvania came to study the House of Refuge because they were planning to establish a similar institution in Philadelphia. "They left us highly gratified," the superintendent noted in the daily journal, "with a determined resolution to advance the same good cause they had witnessed." A week later, the sister of a former inmate came by to see some of her old friends. She was wanted by the police, however, and the superintendent arranged to have her detained. Such guests must have appeared frequently for on July 26, 1826, Superintendent N. C. Hart (Joseph Curtis had resigned on July 11, 1826) noted in the daily journal that "it is found that now and then improper persons get into our yard on visiting days. I have given direction to the gate keeper not to permit any to enter (even on visiting days) Unless they are very respectable looking persons." . . .

At the end of the second year, in the *Annual Report* the Managers explained the theories which guided the efforts to reform juvenile delinquents at the House of Refuge. "The young offender," they said, "should, if possible, be subdued by kindness. His heart should first be addressed, and the language of confidence, though undeserved, be used towards him." They added that the young inmate should be taught that "his keepers were his best friends and that the object of his confinement was his reform and ultimate good. If he is made to believe that he is still of some use and value, he will soon endeavor to act up to the character which is set upon him." This kind of discipline, the managers argued, "will be willing, cheerful and lasting." The remarkably gentle — and from the lights of modern psychology, appropriate — methods espoused by the Managers of the New York House of Refuge came from a nineteenth-century theory about children and the development of their personalities. As the Managers explained, men of the early nineteenth century believed that "the minds of children, naturally pliant, can, by early instruction, be formed and moulded to our wishes. An inclination can there be given to them, as readily to virtuous as to vicious pursuits." Not only can the plastic minds of children be turned to vice or virtue, but earlier inclinations can be altered if the child is not too old: "The seeds of vice, which bad advisers may have planted, if skill is exercised, can yet be extracted . . . and on the mind which appeared barren and unfruitful may yet be engrafted those principles of virtue which shall do much to retrieve the errors of the past, and afford a promise of goodness and usefulness for the future."

The Managers also reminded their readers that "these little vagrants, whose depredations provoke and call down upon them our indignation, are yet but children, who have gone astray for want of that very care and vigilance we exercise towards our own." They were, nonetheless, misbehaving children, whose actions had to be condemned. Furthermore, "a regard for our property and the good of society, requires that they should be stopped, reproved and punished. . . . But," the Managers continued, "they are not to be destroyed. The public must in some measure take the place of those who ought to have been their natural guardians and protectors." Here the Managers of the New York House of Refuge anticipated one of the key concepts of the Illinois Juvenile Court Act of 1899 — the idea that the public (in the Illinois law it was the state) has a collective responsibility to and for society's misbehaving children. Ironically, this provision of the Illinois law was hailed as a great innovation in the legal treatment of delinquent children.

In order to carry out their theories, the officials at the New York House of Refuge adopted rules which prescribed continuous activity for the inmates during their waking hours. They were to be employed "every day in the year, except Sundays, at such labor, business, or employment as from time to time [would] be designated by the Acting Committee." Other rules indicated that all the children wore "coarse but comfortable apparel of the cheapest and most durable kind," which was made on the premises. Inmates who refused to work or who used profane or indecent language, or who fought with their fellow delinquents, would be punished. Punishments included deprivation of play periods, being sent to bed without supper, and bread and water. In more serious cases, the officials might force the recalcitrant boy or girl to drink a bitter herb tea which caused them to sweat profusely, or they might put the offender in solitary confinement. In extreme cases, corporal punishment or iron fetters might be used. The rules provided that corporal punishment could only be inflicted in the presence of the superintendent (or the matron in the case of misbehaving girls). The rules also indicated that "the females shall eat their meals and lodge in a separate building from the males, with whom they shall have no intercourse or communication, except at family or public worship."

Scarcely a week passed without some sort of incident. On September 5, 1826, one of the worst troublemakers in the girls' department returned of her own accord after having escaped. She and the schoolteacher got into an argument, and he began whipping her. According to Superintendent Hart,

> She commenced swearing most bitterly, tore his shirt considerable & made battle with her fists — having a pen knife secreted about her, she succeeded

in opening it with her mouth, & made several attempts to stab him in his breast — to no purpose, but finally got it in the flesh of his arm and ripped a gash at least 1½ inches long and very deep.

The superintendent put the girl in irons. In December, 1826, two boys escaped through the attic of the male cell house, and an officer went to town to look for them. He found one of the boys "in a small rum hole in Anthony St. with girls and other company of ill fame." The boy drew out a knife, while one of the patrons of the establishment shouted "Stick him [!] Stick him [!]." The boy cut the officer severely on the arm and on the neck "near the jugular vein." When the police had returned this boy to the House of Refuge, the superintendent punished him "with a cowskin upon his bare back" and then put him in solitary confinement "without a book to divert his mind" on a bread-and-water diet. The boy remained in solitary for three days, after which the superintendent put him in a cell in the upper tier. The boy then attempted another escape:

> [He] tied three sheets & a cord together — broke through the plastered wall into the garret — again fastened the cord to the same place where he had been successful in making his escape but a few evenings since — but alas! no sooner than he had . . . [placed] his weight upon the cord thus fastened, it broke & he fell about 30 feet upon frozen ground & stones — broke his foot badly — pitched upon his face cut a hole over his eye to the skull bone & fractured it, broke his nose & drove the bones so deep as to endanger his life — cut his lip through nearly up to his nose. Thus he rolls in agony.

To prevent similar escape attempts the officers moved the older boys to the first tier and put the younger boys in their place.

The House of Refuge, following the penal theories of men like Thomas Eddy, also instituted a rudimentary classification system. When they entered, the officials placed the inmates in one of four grades, ranging from "those who are vicious, bad and wicked" in class four to "the best behaved and most orderly boys and girls; those that do not swear, lie, or use profane, obscene or indecent language or conversation," in class one. Every Sunday, the superintendent, his assistant, and the teacher reclassified the children according to their behavior. The upper classes enjoyed extra recreation, and the lower classes found themselves on a reduced diet and suffered from the loss of other privileges. The system of treatment at the New York House of Refuge, rudimentary as it was, is another example of an improvement in penal practice made in a juvenile institution which would later be hailed as an "innovation" in adult reformatories.

A typical day in the Refuge illustrates this system. A bell would ring at sunrise to arouse the sleeping children. They had fifteen minutes to dress, make their beds, and straighten up their cells; then they assembled in the corridors and marched off to the washrooms. After washing, the inmates lined up for a personal inspection. They were at best a motley group. Their clothing had been cut from "a coarse, cheap material" to six standard sizes. In 1848 Elijah Devoe, formerly an assistant superintendent, recalled that they had "collectively a slovenly and untidy appearance." From inspection the children went to morning prayers, after which they went to school for an hour and a half. Then they sat down to a breakfast which usually consisted of bread, molasses, and rye coffee. After breakfast, the inmates trooped off to their various workshops, where they worked until noon. Washing up again and the noon meal occupied the next hour, after which the children returned to work. During this afternoon work period the children could gain extra recreation time if they finished their assigned tasks early. The work period ended at five o'clock; then there was a half-hour for supper and another hour and a half of school. Following the evening school session, there were evening prayers; the inmates then marched back to their cells, turned in, and followed a rule of silence for the night.

The labor of the children in the House of Refuge was let out to contractors, who then paid the institution for the value of the work done by the children. While the contractors taught the children the skills necessary to perform their tasks, the officials of the House of Refuge maintained discipline. The girls worked mostly at sewing; and the boys made cane bottoms for chairs, various kinds of brushes, shoes, and boxes for soap and candles. The contractors represented an outside presence in the House of Refuge and an unending source of difficulty. On July 22, 1826, for example, two girls claimed that the shoemaker took them "into his dwelling & there perpetrated that heinous crime of seduction." An investigation quickly followed and on August 6, Superintendent Hart wrote that the shoemaker had "closed his business with us." On October 16, 1827, Hart noted in the daily journal that the parents of some of the boys in the House of Refuge had complained that their sons were not learning a trade since the shoemaker had set up an assembly line, assigning a separate task to each boy. "The remarks are in considerable degree true," Hart wrote, "& how the difficulty is to be obviated I cannot tell." It would take nearly half a century to eliminate the contract system.

When the officials at the New York House of Refuge concluded that a boy or girl had sufficiently reformed to be trusted outside the institution itself, they often bound them out as apprentices. Some of the boys signed on as sailors in whaling ships, a practice which the managers endorsed heartily in the *Fifth Annual Report* because such a boy would find himself under "wholesome restraint and discipline" and would have the examples of "moral, industrious, and religious companions." Most of the boys, however, were apprenticed to farmers, including some in the West — a practice which anticipated the placing out system of Charles Loring Brace and the Children's Aid Society. Generally, the girls became servants in families not too distant from the House of Refuge. Boys were indentured until they were twenty-one, girls until they reached eighteen. To explain the purposes and methods of the New York House of Refuge, the superintendent sent a form letter to the masters of the apprentices, which warned against the overuse of corporal punishment and reminded the masters that "it has not been concealed from you, that this child has been a delinquent." The superintendent also addressed a form letter to the apprentice. "We should not have consented to part with you at this time," it began, "had not your conduct given us reason to hope, that the religious and moral instruction you have received since you have been under our care, have disposed you to lead an honest, industrious, and sober life." The letter to the apprentice also cautioned him against bad company, especially his former associates. . . .

What distinguished the House of Reformation in Boston from the New York House of Refuge and the House of Refuge established in Philadelphia in 1828 was its system of discipline. As Tocqueville and Beaumont noted, "the Boston discipline belongs to a species of ideas much more elevated than that established in New York and Philadelphia"; but it was difficult to practice because it was "entirely of a moral character." The Boston House of Reformation used a classification system based on the conduct of the inmates, but unlike the New York House of Refuge it required each child to evaluate his own conduct, and a jury composed of children in the institution tried cases of serious misconduct. In the House of Reformation there were six grades of conduct — three good ones and three bad ones. Each of the good grades carried with it certain privileges; boys in the highest grade could go outside the bounds of the House of Reformation by themselves. Conversely, each of the bad grades carried a degree of privation; boys in the two lowest grades were not allowed to speak unless it was absolutely necessary. Before the boys could participate in this system of discipline, they went through a period of probation. A new arrival met with the superintendent, who interviewed him to determine his moral condition. Then, if the new inmate had been found guilty of a serious offense, he was placed in solitary confinement for two weeks so that he could reflect on his vices. Superintendent Wells then told him why he was in the Boston House of Reformation and explained the system of discipline. If the boy rebelled against the officials during his probationary period, they whipped him. Only at this first stage did the superintendent permit corporal punishment. At the end of the probationary period, the superintendent assigned the child one of the bad grades and encouraged him to move up. . . .

The public image of an institution, derived in part from the reports of well-publicized visitors and investigations and also from the institution's own annual reports, is rarely a complete picture of its daily life. In a book that amounted to a polemic against the New York House of Refuge, Elijah Devoe, a discharged assistant superintendent, contended that the New York institution had deliberately falsified its public face. He charged that officials had altered the records to give a higher rate of reformation and that the day-by-day practices in the institution were far more cruel than any outsider realized. The routine was "a stern, brutal, coercive government and discipline, entirely the opposite of that paternal establishment so amiable and ingeniously pictured in the 'annual reports.' " Devoe also indicated that the rule prohibiting corporal punishment unless in the presence of the superintendent was a dead letter: "Corporal punishments are usually inflicted with the cat or a ratan. The latter instrument is applied in a great variety of places, such as the palm and back of the hands, top and bottom of the feet, and lastly, but not rarely or sparingly, to the posteriors over the clothes, and also on the naked skin." Rattans were readily available and "liable to be used everywhere and at all times of the day." In addition, Devoe deplored the mixing of "hardened culprits over fifteen years" of age with "small, younger, and less corrupt children." The older boys were just as likely to corrupt the younger ones as hardened adult criminals were to corrupt juveniles in prison; it was therefore an injustice that "boys under a certain age, who become subject to the notice of our police, either as vagrants or houseless, should be thrust into the society of confirmed thieves, burglars, and robbers, and subjected to the same discipline and punishments."

Devoe's account, which was the work of an unhappy former employee, nonetheless provides an "inside view" of an early nineteenth-century juvenile institution. It seems probable that the annual reports of these institutions, which were made in response to state law and which represented to some extent arguments for state appropriations, presented only the most favorable aspects of houses of refuge and ignored the day-to-day activities which deviated from the high ideals set by the managers. In some respects, however, the view of juvenile institutions presented in their annual reports is more valuable than the "inside story," because the annual reports gave the public its only look at juvenile institutions. Thus, they are a rudimentary index to what nineteenth-century Americans knew about institutions for juvenile delinquents.

The creation of special institutions for juvenile offenders in the second decade of the nineteenth century indicated a growing awareness on the part of American city-dwellers of the problem of juvenile delinquency, and the new institutions also represented a modification in the application of criminal laws to young people. Under the common law as Blackstone explained it, children under seven were presumed to be unable to distinguish between right and wrong. Between the ages of seven and fourteen, "though an infant shall be *prima facie* adjudged to be *doli incapax* [not mentally competent]; yet if it appear to the court and jury that he was *doli capax,* and could discern between good and evil, he may be convicted and suffer death." That this understanding of the common law was generally adopted in the United States may be illustrated by a case involving a twelve-year-old Negro boy in New Jersey in 1828. The boy had been found guilty of the murder of a sixty-year-old woman by a lower court, and the case had been appealed to the New Jersey Supreme Court on the grounds that the boy was too young to be found guilty of such an offense. The Supreme Court upheld the verdict of the lower court, finding that the judge had correctly charged the jury with the relevant points of law in the case. The lower court judge had told the jury that "with respect to the ability of persons of his age, to commit crimes of this nature, the law is, that under the age of seven, they are deemed incapable of it. Between seven and fourteen, if there be no proof of capacity, arising out of this case, or by testimony of witnesses, the presumption is in their favor; a presumption, however, growing weaker and more easily overcome, the nearer they approach to fourteen." The judge went on to explain that a twelve-year-old boy in New Jersey at that time probably possessed "sufficient capacity" to commit murder. Finally, he told the jury: "You will call to mind the evidence on this subject; and if you are satisfied that he was able, in a good degree, to distinguish between right and wrong; to know the nature of the crime with which he is charged; and that it was *deserving* of *severe* punishment, his infancy will furnish no obstacle, on the score of incapacity, to his conviction."

None of the statutes which established the houses of refuge in New York, Boston, and Philadelphia changed the basic premises of the common law, but in effect they raised the age below which a child could expect to receive some kind of preferential treatment from the law. The sentiment behind the creation of the new institutions for juvenile delinquents recognized that children — even children over fourteen — required different treatment from adults. The new laws, although they did not mention any ages except those for the end of minority, created institutions which would provide that treatment. The laws also provided a legal definition of juvenile delinquency. A juvenile delinquent was a child who broke the law, or who was in danger of breaking the law, and the community hoped to keep him from becoming an adult criminal by providing reformatory treatment in a house of refuge. . . .

. . . The House of Refuge was a legal institution with certain well-defined powers. Primarily, it was an institution designed to reform youthful criminals, but it also functioned to prevent crime by accepting young vagrants who were potential juvenile criminals. Once a house of refuge received a child, the managers had a wide latitude of authority over him. In effect, they had the same powers over their charges that a natural parent had over his own children. Thus the state, by chartering a private or municipal association to take the place of inadequate or missing parents, had taken a bold step in the direction of providing for the welfare of its children. In addition, such a step appeared almost too attractive to resist. When houses of refuge first appeared, they seemed to have a good chance of preventing or drastically reducing the rate of adult crime. They not only gave the community something to do with juvenile offenders and vagrant children, they promised to cut future welfare and prison costs. When they insisted that the inmates of houses of refuge be taught a useful trade, the managers shrewdly responded to a community prejudice which not only condemned idleness as a sin but also linked it with serious crime. By teaching juvenile offenders how to work, then, houses of refuge were exorcising sin and providing for the future security of life and property. The creation of the New York House of Refuge and similar institutions in Boston and Philadelphia marked the beginning of nineteenth-century America's concern for wayward children. It also marked the beginning of the process of separating juvenile delinquents from adult criminals — a process that would not be complete until the creation of the juvenile court in 1899. But the house of refuge had one essential weakness as an institution — it was a charity, which, although chartered by the state, private citizens operated. The involvement of private citizens had been necessary to launch the first institutions for juvenile delinquents, but once their worth had been proved, many philanthropists felt that the reformation of juvenile offenders was a duty for which the state should take full responsibility.

STUDY GUIDE

1. A good many children and young people were placed in institutions not because of having committed a crime, but because of something in their character, circumstances, or behavior. Describe some of these factors.

2. What do you see as the views of the supporters and administrators of these institutions with respect to (a) the nature of children; (b) religion and an ethical code; and (c) the goals of institutionalizing children?

3. Certain of the practices in these institutions might be criticized today, but both the institutions and the theories by which they were operated were seen as great reforms. What practices do you see in that period that might be considered advances over the earlier period? What influences do you see from that period in our modern juvenile court system?

4. Many of the reforms of the Jacksonian period were undertaken by private societies with private funds. What factors in our time have caused most social welfare work to be carried out by government agencies with public funds? What private agencies still operate in such fields?

5. Cities like New York may have extremely high welfare costs because so many people migrate there from other states, which are thus relieved of such a burden. What would be the advantages and disadvantages of having all social problems handled by the federal government, since such problems cross state lines?

BIBLIOGRAPHY

The subject of the treatment of juvenile delinquents and orphans is but a part of such broader topics as the society's view of deviance, the development of state institutions in the modern world, and the spirit of reform in Jacksonian America. Three studies that deal very broadly with change in nineteenth-century America are Robert E. Riegel, *Young America, 1830–1840* (Norman, Okla., 1949); Alice F. Tyler, *Freedom's Ferment: Phases of American Social History to 1860* * (Minneapolis, Minn., 1944); and Glyndon G. Van Deusen, *The Jacksonian Era, 1828–1848* * (New York, 1959). The following three books on pre-Civil War reform are of special interest here: David B. Davis, ed., *Ante-Bellum Reform* * (New York, 1967); Clifford S. Griffin, *Their Brothers' Keeper: Moral Stewardship in the United States, 1800–1865* (New Brunswick, N.J., 1960); and Ronald G. Walters, *American Reformers, 1815–1860* * (New York, 1978).

The bibliography following the reading by Edmund S. Morgan (Reading No. 5), has a section concerning the history of childhood. Two works especially pertinent to the early nineteenth century are Bernard Wishy, *The Child and the Republic: The Dawn of Modern American Child Nurture* * (Philadelphia, 1968), and Robert M. Mennel, *Thorns and Thistles: Juvenile Delinquency in the U.S., 1825–1940* * (Hanover, N.H., 1973). Anyone interested either in social welfare as a profession or in American social values would do well to read some of the histories of American treatment of the criminal, the mentally ill, and the poor. Blake McKelvey, *American Prisons: A Study in Social History prior to 1915* * (Chicago, 1936) is an older study, while W. David Lewis, *From Newgate to Dannemora: The Rise of the Penitentiary in New York, 1796–1848* (Ithaca, N.Y., 1965) is more modern. Albert Deutsch, *The Mentally Ill in America: A History of Their Care and Treatment from Colonial Times*, 2nd ed. (New York and London, Eng., 1949) is a good survey, while two other books go into greater depth on mental institutions and views of insanity: Norman Dain, *Concepts of Insanity in the United States, 1789–1865* (New Brunswick, N.J., 1964); and Gerald N. Grob, *Mental Institutions in America: Social Policy to 1875* (New York, 1973). David J. Rothman, *The Discovery of the Asylum: Social Order and Disorder in the New Republic* (Boston, 1971) deals with nearly all of the social institutions, including orphanages and houses of refuge, in the period studied by Hawes. Raymond A. Mohl, *Poverty in New York, 1783–1825* (New York, 1971) and Paul S. Boyer, *Urban Masses and Moral Order in America, 1820–1920* (Cambridge, Mass., 1978) are other books for somewhat advanced students, while Robert H. Bremner, *American Philanthropy* * (Chicago, 1960) is a brief introduction of general interest.

* Asterisk indicates book is available in a paperback edition.

Shaker Village, Inc., Canterbury, N.H.

These New Hampshire women (c. 1914) reflect the continuity of nineteenth century Shaker values of simple dress and segregation of the sexes.

13

EDWARD D. ANDREWS

Utopian Communes

One of the most unusual developments of the counter-culture of the 1960s was the establishment of hundreds of communes across the United States. Ranging from a few people buying a farm they planned to work together to much larger groups with a distinctive philosophy of life, these experiments in living revealed a disenchantment with the larger, competitive society and emphasized the sharing and brotherhood of an "extended family."

This was by no means the first movement of this sort in American history. The first settlers of several of the colonies had been members of small, tightly-knit groups that stressed a strong sense of mutual responsibility among the members. The same spirit had sometimes characterized new communities on the frontier as Americans moved west. Such religious sects as the Mormons and Moravians had displayed a similar unity of spirit and purpose. The clearest parallel to the communes of the 1960s can be found in the many groups in the 1830s that established small settlements in the Northeast and Midwest in an attempt to create a perfect community as an example for society as a whole.

Some of the communities were formed by European immigrants, such as the Rappites of western Pennsylvania, and some were based on social philosophies of European origin. Others were natively American, such as the Brook Farm community in Massachusetts. Some were religiously oriented; others were socialistic. They embodied a wide range of beliefs including vegetarianism, free love, celibacy, and the abolition of money. So varied were they, that there was no such thing as a typical community that would give one an idea of life in any of the others.

Yet there were common impulses and common beliefs behind the founding of most of them. One, of course, was a dissatisfaction with the state of society. There was also a widespread belief that it was possible to establish a perfect social order among a small group of people. What constituted perfection differed from one group to another; some thought it was to be found in the common ownership of property, while others believed it would only be achieved by coming into a perfect kingdom ordained by Christ. Finally, most of these groups believed that if a perfect community could be created on a small scale, with thirty or one hundred people, it would serve as a model that could be extended to the entire society.

The Shakers, founded by Mother Ann Lee, were one of several religious groups that adhered to the rule of celibacy in their communities and thus died out for lack of new recruits. Like many of the religious minorities of the early nineteenth century, the Shakers were millennialists, who believed in the second coming of Christ as the answer to the world's problems. In their case, they felt that Mother Ann was the female embodiment of the second coming, and that the millenium was already here — in the small Shaker communities in which they lived. In his book *The People Called Shakers*, Edward D. Andrews explains the theology and worship of the Shakers and also describes the daily life and human relations in a celibate, religious community that hoped to create a perfect order for American society.

Chief among the factors affecting all Shaker life was the unique relationship existing between brethren and sisters. The application, under the same roof, of the seemingly irreconcilable theories of equality and separation set the movement apart from other communal-religious institutions and aroused, more than any other characteristic of the church, skeptical comment and barbed abuse. Every reliable source, however, indicates that the dividing line was held. One sex was always conscious of the presence and support of the other. But to pass that invisible boundary was to invite both bondage of soul and communal disfavor.

Convictions concerning a fundamental tenet of the order, of course, aided the adjustment: for the rule of celibacy was a selective agent, attracting not only those who believed in the principle on doctrinal grounds, but those

From *The People Called Shakers* by Edward Deming Andrews. Copyright 1953 by Oxford University Press, Inc. Reprinted by permission of Mrs. Faith Andrews.

others, chiefly women, who were drawn in because of their desire to escape from marital difficulties and broken homes. For persons oppressed by poverty and economic ills the Shaker community, like the cloister, offered the opportunity for a renewal of life in useful service, in which case the rule was accepted as a condition of security. Once the rule was accepted, the Shakers underwent a thorough course of instruction. The work of God, they were told, proceeded by a spiritual union and relation between male and female. If, in the course of the period of probation, the cross seemed repellent, they were free to withdraw or remain in an "out family." On the other hand, should they wish to travel on to the junior and senior order, they did so in full realization of what it entailed. If husband and wife entered together, they were usually assigned to separate families. . . .

. . . [Joseph] Meacham's basic law — that "no male or female shall support, or have a private union or correspondence together, neither shall they touch each other unnecessarily" — was also supported, in time, by detailed "separation acts" and ordinances for the "purity of the mind." It was "contrary to the gift," for instance, for a brother to pass a sister on the stairs, for a brother to go into a sister's room without knocking, for a sister to go to a brother's shop alone, for brethren to shake hands with the sisters and give them presents, and so on.

Surveillance was facilitated by the smallness of the family and the lack of privacy. From two to six individuals shared each sleeping or retiring room, the day's routine was organized, and most of the work was done in groups. In meeting, . . . the ministry could supervise proceedings through shuttered apertures; and at Pleasant Hill, two watchtowers on the roof of the dwelling served a similar purpose during the day. The Millennial Laws stated that if anyone knew of any transgression, he or she was morally obligated to reveal it to the elders, "otherwise they participate in the guilt." Under such conditions an atmosphere of mutual suspicion was almost inevitable; the feeling that one was being spied upon during every hour of the day and night was bound to deprive the individual of dignity and self-respect.

The most noteworthy device for regulating sex relations, however, was a constructive one. As the church was being organized, Meacham realized that "correspondence" was unavoidable, that brethren and sisters must consult on temporalities, that social solidarity could not rest on negative grounds. Since they "*would* have a union together," he testified, "if they had not a spiritual union, they would have a carnal." His corrective was the "union meeting," which for over seventy years, from 1793 on, played an important role in Shaker domestic life. These gatherings usually took place two evenings a week and twice on Sundays. A group of four to ten members of each sex met in a brethren's retiring room, where they sat facing each other in rows about five feet apart. (If girls and boys were present, they were placed beside their elders or by themselves in ranks in the rear.) Then, for a stated period, one hour on week nights and one or two on the Sabbath, each member of the group conversed freely and openly with the person opposite him on some familiar or suitable subject; or the occasion might be turned into a singing meeting. The pairs had been carefully matched, on the basis of age and "condition of travel," by the elders. No one was worthy to attend if he or she harbored any ill-feeling toward another.

The conversation — "simple, sometimes facetious, rarely profound" — was limited, for sacred, literary, and certain secular topics were all prohibited. Some visitors, like [A. J.] Macdonald, found the meetings dull. Nevertheless the time seemed to have been agreeably passed; the company had their own world to talk about, with zest and unrestraint if they wished; "gentle laughter and mild amusement" were not unknown; and in the early years smoking was customary. The union meetings, in fact, belied the common assumption that the Shakers were an austere folk, though discipline varied with the family or community and was likely to be more strict in the Church Order. Self-restraint and sobriety, however, never excluded simple joys. One observer comments on "the amenity of their intercourse [which was] much less restricted than is generally supposed." Another noticed that they were "disposed to be merry and enjoy a joke." Mary Dyer attended meetings at Enfield (N.H.) where there were pipes to smoke, cider to drink, and melons, apples, and nuts to eat; and where the participants sang such "merry love songs" as

> I love the brethren the brethren love me
> Oh! how happy, how happy I be,
> I love the sisters, the sisters love me,
> Oh! how happy, how happy I be.
> How pretty they look, how clever they feel,
> And this we will sing when we love a good deal.

A former member of a Niskeyuna family recalled that two aged brethren, one a Whig and the other a Democrat before they joined the order, used to argue their political principles in these meetings; and that a young sister, on one occasion, raised the issue whether members would not be better Shakers if they were allowed to study instrumental music, languages, and fine literature. The aristocratic Mrs. Hall found the Believers at this community "a very conversible set of people" — a verdict later shared by Howells, who felt that the renunciation of marriage was "the sum of Shaker asceticism."

These social gatherings were nevertheless misinterpreted by the world: as Isaac Youngs put it, "advantage was taken by some apostates and evil minded persons . . . to construe this sacred order of union, [especially the placing of certain brethren with certain sisters] into a particular union or connection, as savoring of husband and wife." Eunice Chapman, for one, testified to seeing "the spiritual husbands, each with their spiritual wife," withdraw after meeting to their different apartments — observing to one of the sisters that there must be "general courtship throughout the house." Furnishing further grounds for detraction was a custom connected with the meeting, namely, that of assigning to each sister general "oversight over the habits and temporal needs" of the brother sitting opposite her — taking care of his clothes, looking after his washing and mending, providing new garments when they were needed, and so forth — in return for which the brethren "did needful favors for the sisters." Visitors sometimes noticed the tender solicitude of a brother toward a certain sister, or vice versa. Though such attention was a violation of the letter of the Separation Acts, it seems to have been accepted, quite naturally, as a justifiable expression of spiritual union.

A combination of factors — the system of orders and surveillance, communal opinion, the rites of confession and atonement, the force of principle, the union meeting, the freedom to withdraw from the society — fostered and enforced a relationship between the two sexes which one enthusiast called "more harmonic than anyone seriously believes attainable for the human race." As to its effectiveness, we have the empirical judgment of the student Macdonald:

> I have always found that those who spoke ill of the Shakers on this subject, to be ignorant, and low minded persons, who probably judged others by themselves, and who founded their opinion upon mere supposition. Those who have been most among them, and consequently the best Judges, have been compelled to believe, that the Shakers are generally speaking, sincere, both in the Belief and practice of abstinence from sexual coition. I have heard Individuals who have lived with them, for periods varying from thirty years, to a few months, all declare, that there was no such immorality among the Shakers, as had been attributed to them. In the vicinity of Union Village, O. I heard suspicions and suppositions, in abundance, and have no doubt the same surmises may be heard in the vicinity of any of their settlements. But I have never met with one individual who was a Witness to or could prove a Case of immoral conduct between the Sexes in any of the Shaker Communities. . . .
>
> It is quite true that sometimes, young Shakers in whom the tender passion is not entirely subdued, fall in love with each other, but these generally contrive to leave the Sect, and go to the "World" to get married and reside.

The "order of the day" left little room, indeed, for vain or idle thoughts. At the sounding of the bell or "shell," the Shakers arose early in the morning, between four o'clock and five in summer, between five and five-thirty in the winter. After kneeling together for a moment of quiet prayer, the occupants of each retiring room stripped the sheets and blankets from their narrow cots, laying them neatly over two chairs at the foot, on which the pillows had previously been placed. Fifteen minutes after rising, the rooms had been vacated, the brethren had gone to their morning chores, and the sisters were entering to close the windows, make the beds, and put the room in order. At breakfast time, six, six-thirty, or seven, the chamber work was finished, fires had been started in the dwelling rooms and shops, the cattle fed, the cows milked, and arrangements for the day's industry were all complete.

Before all meals — the early breakfast, the noon dinner, the six o'clock supper — brethren and sisters would assemble, each group by themselves, in appointed rooms, where for a ten or fifteen minute pause which was a kind of "broad grace," they quietly awaited the bell. Then, in two columns led by the elders and eldresses, respectively, and in the order in which they were to be seated, they proceeded to the dining hall. Taking their places behind their chairs or benches, the sexes at separate tables, they knelt in prayer at a sign from the lead, and after a meal eaten in monastic silence, knelt again before departing directly to their labors. . . .

A series of table monitors, emphasizing economy and good manners at meals, testifies to the concern with standards of behavior. An early monitor (undated manuscript) illustrates how detailed was the instruction:

> First, All should sit upright at the table.
> 2d The Elder should begin first, after which all may take hold regularly.
> 3d When you take a piece of bread, take a whole piece (if not too large) and when you cut meat, cut it square & equal, fat & lean, & take an equal proportion of bones — take it on your plate together with the sauce, whether it be cabbage, herbs, potatoes or turnips; and not be cutting small pieces in the platter and putting directly into your mouth.
> 4th When you have tea or coffee, and any kind of minced victuals or meat cut into mouthfuls, it may be proper with a knife or fork to eat it directly from the platter. . . .
> 8th Eat what you need before you rise from table, and not be picking & eating afterwards.
> 9th When you have done eating, clean your plate, knife & fork — lay your bones in a snug heap by the side of your plate — scrape up your crumbs — cross your knife & fork on your plate with the edge towards you.
> 10th When you reach a mug or pitcher to a person give the handle; and when you take hold of bread, biscuit, pies, etc. to cut or break, take hold of that part which you intend to eat yourself, and cut it square & equal — then you will not leave the print of your fingers for others to eat. . . .
> 12th If you are obliged to sneeze or cough, don't bespatter the victuals, make use of your handkerchief.
> 13th Clean your knife on your bread before you cut butter, & after cutting butter before you put it into apple sauce, etc. but never clean it on the edge of the platter etc.
> 14th Scratching the head, picking the nose or ears, belching, snifing the nose, drinking with the mouth full of victuals, or picking the teeth, are accounted ill manners at a table & must be left off.
> 15th And lastly, when you drink, never extend your under lip so far down that one would think the cup was agoing to be swallowed whole. Always wipe your mouth before & after you drink your bear (beer) or water at the table.
> Note — Children under the age of 12 or 14 years must have their pie cut for

them & laid by their dishes — Also, when they have bread & butter, suitable pieces must be properly spread & laid by their dishes. . . .

After the evening chores were done, at seven-thirty in summer and eight o'clock in winter, all repaired to their apartments for half an hour, known as "retiring-time," when, on the evenings devoted to family worship, the Shakers disposed themselves in ranks, sitting erect with hands folded "to labor for a true sense of their privilege in the Zion of God." If perchance one should drowse, it was the order to rise and bow four times, or shake, and then resume one's seat. At the end of the period, announced by the ringing of a small bell, brethren and sisters formed separate columns in the corridors, marched two abreast to the meeting-room, and, after bowing as they entered, formed ranks for worship.

Assemblies varied with the time and place. In the early years of the order, and often during revivals, "labouring" meetings were held nightly, and sometimes during the day. As the society expanded, however, evenings not devoted to union meetings or the regular religious service were given over to the practice of songs and exercises. Thus, at New Lebanon in the 'seventies, singing meetings were held on Tuesday and Friday, union meetings on Sunday and Wednesday, and "labouring" meetings on Thursday and Saturday. On Mondays, during this more liberal period, there was a general assembly in the dining hall, where the elder read letters from other communities, selections from the news of the week, or some appropriate book. At the conclusion of such gatherings, to which strangers were admitted on occasion, the family retired quietly to rest. The occupants of each room, after kneeling again in silent prayer, went to bed at a uniform hour — nine o'clock in winter and ten in summer.

Anyone watching such temperate people in the intervals between work and worship would have been impressed, above all else, by the tranquillity of their movements and behavior, as though the daily round was itself a service. No sign of tension or aggressiveness was apparent; speech was subdued; doors were opened and closed with care; all "walked softly." The dwelling, whose orderly, neatly furnished rooms were seldom occupied during the day, was also, in a true sense, a sanctuary. Many a visitor, like Hester Pool, was sensitive to that "indescribable air of purity" which pervaded everything, feeling with her "that this purity is a portion of the mental and moral as well as the physical atmosphere of the Shakerian home." Though all comings and goings followed the pattern of plainness, in the simplicity of domestic life there was an element of freedom, grace, and the contentment, or perhaps resignation, of those who had made peace with themselves and with the world.

The Children's Order was also carefully regulated. Boys and girls lived apart from each other and the rest of the family under "caretakers" responsible to the elders or eldresses. In the indenture agreements the trustees bound the society to provide them with "comfortable food and clothing," the common branches of learning, and training in such manual occupation or branch of business as shall be found best adapted to the "minor's genius and capacity." In return, the parent or guardian relinquished all rights over the child's upbringing. At maturity the youth was free to leave or remain.

In education emphasis was placed on character building and the useful arts. Though the early Believers, "being chiefly of the laboring classes and generally in low circumstances of life," were not in a condition to pay much attention to letter learning, Mother Ann strongly recommended religious and "literary" studies. Meacham advocated the kind of learning that would lead to order, union, peace, and good work — "works that are truly virtuous and useful to man, in this life." The idea that instruction should concentrate on developing good habits and useful talents was subsequently expanded by Seth Wells, the superintendent of the Shaker schools. Self-government, Wells believed, was the prerequisite of both moral and literary education. "When a man is able to govern himself, and subdue his evil propensities . . . he is then in a fair way to be benefitted by moral and religious instructions. . . ."

Nor was innocent recreation considered superfluous. The girls at Canterbury had gymnastic exercises and a flower garden; the boys played ball and marbles, went fishing, and had a small farm of their own. Picnics, sleigh rides, and nutting and berrying parties lent diversion to the ordinary routine. Elkins' frank account of his boyhood at Enfield is the record of a not uncolorful life, with interesting companions, mild paternal control, and normal healthful experiences in a beautiful countryside. Elder Briggs recalls that wood-chopping and maple-sugaring were gala times, like picnics, and mentions the diversions of fishing, swimming, and playing ball, the half-holidays once a week during warm weather, the refreshments during haying, which consisted of sweet buttermilk; lemon, peppermint, checkerberry, raspberry, and currant shrub; cake, cheese, and smoked herring. One who had been a young Shakeress at Niskeyuna remembers many happy days in the Children's Order there:

> Hiding beneath an arcade of the bridge which spanned the dear old creek, we would pull off shoes and stockings, and wade knee-deep in the cool, bright water. Then, loading our long palm-leaf Shaker bonnets with dandelions, which, grown to seed, looked like little white-capped Shakeresses, we would float them down the stream in a race, the boat which won being decorated with buttercups and violets. What mud-pies we made and baked in the sun! What fun we had secreting golden kernels of corn in clam-shells, and peeping from our hiding-place to see the chickens find them and peck them up, firmly believing that they "gave thanks" when they turned their bills up to heaven after sipping water. . . . We had no world's toys, but were just as contented

with our corn-cob dolls, clam-shell plates, acorn-top cups, and chicken-coops for baby houses.

From sources such as the above we suspect that Shaker life was not always as austere as its principles would have had it be; that the Believers, in their effort to extinguish natural affections, tried to do the impossible — particularly where children were concerned. We read of candy-making parties, culinary favors tendered by the "kitchen-sisters," humorous tolerance when children behaved "contrary to order," the attachments for favorite children, close friendships within the Children's Order. Human nature was constantly breaking up the artificial restrictions designed to subdue "carnal desire." It seems that the lot of Shaker youth compared favorably with that of the sons and daughters of farmers in the rural America of the period. . . .

The belief in progress, or "travel," found expression in the field of medicine as in education. Ann Lee's bias against physicians was shared by Joseph Meacham, who assured a doubter that "they that have my spirit have no occasion to go to world's doctors." In the early years Shakers were healed by faith or the laying on of hands. The "gift" against professionals was still held in 1813, when Mother Lucy's attitude to that effect was recorded; but Father Job Bishop, speaking "beautifully" on the same subject, qualified his stand by asserting that a surgeon might be called "in case of a broken bone or any very bad wound." About this time greater reliance was placed on regimen and simple medicines, with resort to shocking, bleeding, sweating, poulticing, and blistering. With the development of the herb industry in the 1820's, the Thomsonian medical practice, which relied on steam baths and herbal remedies and required little academic knowledge, came into increasing favor. Another step was taken in 1840, when messages prohibiting the use of strong drink, swine's flesh, and tobacco ushered in a reform which was more than temporary. In mid-century, largely through the influence of Elder Frederick Evans of New Lebanon, Grahamism and vegetarianism won converts in certain families. Proper diet, supplemented by the water treatment, simple massage, and hot herbal drinks in case of sickness, was the prevalent prescription late in the century. Faith in the "healing gift," however, persisted all this time, with many a cure allegedly effected by spirit touch and mental control.

As interpreted by Elder Evans, the science of health had a theological basis. To provide better food, clothing, and housing, a better distribution of heat, improved lighting, ventilation, and sanitation was the proper field of science. In the "new earth" the human body should be "the central object of influence and attraction," whose "salvation" was no less important than the "health" of the soul. Evans suggested eight main principles of dietetics:

1. Supply the family with at least one kind of course grain flour. Avoid cathartics.
2. Have the "sickly and weakly" cease using animal food, especially fats.
3. Keep the skin clean by regular bathing, with the water at such a temperature as to cause a warm, glowing reaction.
4. Keep room at a temperature not exceeding 60°.
5. Clothing — "regulated on the same principles as water and fire" — should be light, "a little less than you could possibly bear." The young should dispense with underclothes. "Sleep under as little clothing as possible."
6. Breathe pure air. Every room of the home should be of equal temperature. Ventilation of bedrooms important.
7. Thorough ventilation of beds and bedding.
8. "Be comfortable in mind and body."

While these views were the opinion of one person, a natural reformer, they were not unrepresentative of Shaker practice. The vent pipes over the lamps, the slots placed between the two sashes of every window, and the holes in the baseboards in the halls and under the radiators in the gathering rooms were additional evidences of a concern for fresh air. Baths, sinks, and water closets were well ventilated. Pure spring water was ingeniously piped for refrigeration. Temperate outdoor labor, regular hours, wholesome food, good clothing, comfort of mind, and the utmost cleanliness everywhere combined to promote the health of all. On the latter characteristic in particular, often contrasting favorably with conditions elsewhere, strangers were wont to remark from the earliest times. "Great importance is attached to cleanliness," *Blackwood's* correspondent reported in 1823; "this luxury they appear to enjoy in a truly enviable degree." "Visit them upon any day in the week," the historian of the town of Shirley wrote, "at any hour of the day, and when they are engaged in almost any employment, and you will scarcely ever find them in dirty dishabille. The shirts and pants and frocks of the men are rarely soiled, and the plain linen caps and kerchiefs of the women never." "Everything is . . . kept so delicately clean," remarked an English visitor in 1884, "that an air of refinement, not to say luxury, seems to pervade [the] bedchambers, in spite of their absolute simplicity."

Testimonies on the health of the Shakers are nevertheless conflicting. . . . With allowances made for prejudice, it is a matter of wonder, from the phrases used about the sisters, whether they were in health or out. They were called "a wretched-looking lot of creatures" (Fountain); "their pale faces . . . and flabby condition indicated . . . a low state of health" (George Combe); "the females and sedentary people . . . were occasionally indisposed" (*Blackwood's* correspondent); "the females . . . look remarkably pale and sallow" (Silliman); the women were "pallid, thin and withered" (Martineau); the sisters, with few exceptions, were "old, wizened, ascetic — perfect specimens of old maids" (Colonel A. M. Maxwell). The difference in the physical appearance of males and females was due, according to one mid-century author, to the "unaspiring, earthly" quality of the former, and the effect on such natures of a comfortable life, outdoor work, plenty of food, and an absence of anxieties. "The Shaker woman, by contrast, has a more melancholy lot. Love — 'the first necessity of woman's nature' — is dwarfed, in her case, to most unnatural ugliness. She must renounce the natural affections." On the other hand, Finch was struck with "the cheerfulness and contented looks" of the people in all the communities; Dixon remarked on "the rosy flesh" of the people of New Lebanon — "a tint but rarely seen in the United States"; and the usually reliable Nordhoff spoke of the "fresh fine complexion [which] most of the Shaker men and women have — particularly the latter."

If the Shaker way of life was detrimental in any way to physical well-being, certainly life was not shortened. The longevity of members of the sect has often been reported. In 1875 Nordhoff, making the first fact-finding tour of the communities, was impressed by the low rate of mortality: at Harvard, where the average age at death for a number of years was 60 to 68; at Union Village, where a large proportion of the members were over 70, and many over 90; at North Union, where many were past 80; at Pleasant Hill, where a considerable number lived past 90; and at Enfield (N.H.), Watervliet (N.Y.), and South Union, where the brethren and sisters often lived well over 75 years.

To support an argument on the "Longevity of Virgin Celibates," Elder Giles Avery advanced facts [selected?] that in five families at New Lebanon, during the period 1848–50, the average age of 29 members at death was 70½ years; at Alfred, during an unspecified period, the average age of 200 members at death was 62¾ years (with 100 over 70, 37 between 80 and 90, and 13 between 90 and 97); at Watervliet (N.Y.), in the decade 1870–80, the average age of 39 members at death was 73 years; and at New Gloucester there were "at the present time" (*c.* 1880) 14 persons over 70 years of age, of whom seven were between 79 and 89 years old. Elder Evans estimated that life expectancy among the Believers was over a decade more than that of the world. . . .

When death occurred, complete simplicity marked the funeral. The coffin was pine, plainly lined, unpainted and unadorned. In the mind of the Believer, the life of the spirit was so real that death was but a way-mark in "travel," and the "trappings of grief" superfluous. Following the Quaker custom, the Shakers, led by the elders and eldresses of the family, devoted the main part of the service to personal tributes and memories. Songs were sung, and during one period of Shaker history, messages from the spirit were communicated by the instruments. The procession to the grave was not unlike the heavenly march of worship. Throughout the ritual the tone was one of reverence, strength, and inspiration.

Since followers of Mother Ann did not believe in physical resurrection, they thought of the living soul and not of the dead body. "He is not here," they testified at the burial service. Appropriate, therefore, were the simple slabs of stone, all alike and engraved only with initials, age, and date, which marked the resting place. Many advocated that even these be replaced by a mound of earth, or perhaps a shrub or tree, not as a memorial but rather as a contribution to earth's fertility and beauty.

Comparison of the living conditions of the early Shaker colonists with those prevailing a century or so later furnishes an index to the temporal progress of the society. In 1780 its possessions were limited to a few unpromising acres, a single cabin, the slim resources of John Hocknell. Eight years later the Believers at Niskeyuna were still poor. Money was scarce, and the community was not allowed to run into debt. According to the account of Jonathan Clark of Hancock:

> Our principle food was rice and milk, sometimes we went to the river to procure fish. . . . We had little, and sometimes no bread, butter or cheese, but upon this simple fare, we all subsisted during the Spring and Summer. . . . All our work was very laborious, and at the end, we looked more like skeletons, than working men. . . . Our breakfast consisted of a small bowl of porridge. Supper the same. Dinner, a small bit of cake about 2½ inches square which Aaron Wood cut up, and gave to us. One day Joseph Preston and another brother went to the River to catch Herring; and Joseph stated that he was so hungry, that he ate two *raw,* as soon as they came out of the water. . . . We had but little house room, and of course were obliged to lie upon the floor. . . . Fifteen of us lay upon the floor in one room; some had one blanket to cover them, while others had none. . . .

The "manner of dress and building" was in the same inferior state. "Those who first believed, in America," Youngs wrote, "adopted such dress as seemed the most suitable, of the common plain forms that prevailed among people at the time they lived in England"; and the form, fashion, and quality of garments were "extremely various." In form and manner of construction, buildings also were of poor quality and ill-adapted to the purpose for which they were needed.

In all departments, however, the Shakers, by the will to make everything uniform with the best, steadily raised their standard of living. During the nineteenth century the preparation of wholesome food was considered more and more important, and as a result the Shakers achieved a considerable reputation for their recipes and public meals. As for clothing, painstaking care came to be paid to the needs of age groups and occasions, to uniformity of color and material, to the marking and laundering of garments. Buildings, too, were constantly improved and their numbers increased to meet the expanding needs of the colony. In New Lebanon, for instance, from the few small farmhouses which the Shakers took over in the 1780's, the community grew until it had 125 buildings in 1839, and property, including 2,292 acres of land, valued at $68,225. Within the same period the original colony at Watervliet had grown to a community of over 2,500 acres, valued, with buildings, at $46,900. When Nordhoff made his survey in 1875, the home farms of the eighteen societies, taken by themselves, amounted to nearly 50,000 acres, to which figure must be added extensive outside holdings in mills, wood lots, and "outfarms" — one in Kentucky, owned by the Watervliet (N.Y.) society, as large as 30,000 acres — which were often operated by tenants.

Following the eight immigrants from England some seventeen thousand persons, at one time or another, were gathered into the society. To the Shakers this was a "great harvest" — the "blessed binders" had followed closely on the reapers, "severing all the worthless cockle till the work was done complete."

STUDY GUIDE

1. Explain the techniques the Shakers used in order to maintain celibacy. What explanation can you give for the skepticism about celibacy and the rumors of sexual excesses that often develop in the outside world with respect to convents, monasteries, and other celibate communities?

2. Describe the "order of the day" in a Shaker community and the religious life of the Shakers. Aside from separation of the sexes and the religious doctrines, what values and attitudes do you see among the Shakers that were not substantially different from those of many other rural, farm folks in the period?

3. Though some might consider the Shaker life as barren and harsh, Andrews suggests that most of the Shakers felt a sense of freedom, contentment, and peace. What evidence is there in the selection that Shakers really felt this way, and how can one explain such a disciplined, plain, celibate life bringing happiness? What parallels are there between the Shaker philosophy and other experiments in alternative life-styles that you know of (such as Henry Thoreau's experiment at Walden Pond)?

4. In terms of permanence and long-range influence upon American society, none of the other communitarian groups were any more successful than were the Shakers. What forces in American life and in the development of the American nation made it unlikely that these small-group experiments could successfully serve as a pattern for all of American society?

5. What do you see as the explanation for the development of so many communal groups in our own time? What evidence is there that such groups continue to have — on a reduced scale — the same problems that exist in the larger society?

BIBLIOGRAPHY

The historical literature on the Shakers and on other communitarian groups that flourished in the pre-Civil War years is both ample and interesting. A number of volumes can serve to introduce you to the entire range of communitarianism. You might begin with Arthur Bestor, Jr.'s prize-winning work, *Backwoods Utopias: The Sectarian and the Owenite Phases of Communitarian Socialism in America: 1663–1829* * (Philadelphia, 1950), or with the same author's essay on "Patent-Office Models of the Good Society: Some Relationships Between Social Reform and Westward Expansion," *American Historical Review*, Vol. LVIII (1953), pp. 505–526. Additional surveys of the topic will be found in the following: Alice Felt Tyler, *Freedom's Ferment: Phases of American Social History to 1860* * (Minneapolis, Minn., 1944) — a description of almost all of the reform movements, communitarian and otherwise, of the period; Charles Nordhoff's older but still valuable volume, *The Communistic Societies of the United States* * (New York, 1875; reprinted, 1960); Mark Holloway, *Heavens on Earth: Utopian Communities in America, 1680–1880* * (New York, 1951); and Everett Webber, *Escape to Utopia: The Communal Movement in America* (New York, 1959). More specific in focus is the volume from which the preceding selection was taken, Edward D. Andrews, *The People Called Shakers: A Search for the Perfect Society* * (New York, 1953). Andrews also wrote volumes on Shaker furniture and on their music and dance. Other works on the Shakers have been written by Marguerite Melcher, Francis D. Nichol, and Clara E. Sears.

There are biographies of Owen, Fourier, and many other communitarian leaders, and studies of most of the communities of the pre-Civil War period. Jane and William Pease describe communities founded to aid recently freed Negroes in their book *Black Utopia: Negro Communal Experiments in America* * (Madison, Wis., 1963). Other works of merit include: Herbert W. Schneider and George Lawton, *A Prophet and a Pilgrim* (New York, 1942); Maren L. Carden, *Oneida: Utopian Community to Modern Corporation* * (Baltimore, Md., 1969); and Lindsay Swift, *Brook Farm: Its Members, Scholars, and Visitors* * (New York, 1961). It is not possible here to list the many works dealing with the post-Civil War period of utopianism or the broader aspects of utopian thought in American life. Three works that are essential in understanding these subjects are: Donald Egbert and Stow Persons, eds., *Socialism and American Life*, 2 vols. (Princeton, N.J., 1952); H. Richard Niebuhr, *The Kingdom of God in America* * (Chicago, 1937); and Robert S. Fogarty, *American Utopianism* * (Itasca, Ill., 1972). The last of these is a collection of source material on utopian communities.

* Asterisk indicates book is available in a paperback edition.

V INDUSTRIAL NORTH AND PLANTER SOUTH

In our time, more than in any earlier period, the American people are a single people. They drive the same cars, use the same products, eat much the same food, and dress alike — whether they live in California or New England. With slight differences, their values and their popular culture — on the screen, on the airwaves, and in national magazines — are identical in Atlanta, Georgia, and Minneapolis, Minnesota. The homogeneity of modern American society tends to obscure the fact that differences among classes, nationalities, and sections played a prominent role in earlier American history.

The strong nationalistic sentiments of the first three decades of the nineteenth century faded rapidly after 1830. Always somewhat distinct in language, politics, and social life, North and South now saw their respective economic interests as being in conflict with each other. Both hoped for the support of what was rapidly emerging as a third distinct section, the trans-Appalachian West. Industrialization and urbanization were making the Northeast a region of constant change. In mining fields and factory towns, on canal and railroad projects, the strange tongues of several European nationalities could be heard. In contrast, the South was largely untouched by industrialism and the urban growth that would eventually characterize the entire country. Few immigrants went South, and slavery, with all its social as well as economic implications, swept westward from the South Atlantic states into Mississippi, Alabama, and other newly opened cotton lands.

The West was less clearly defined than the North or South; indeed, what was West was ever-changing as the line of settlement passed from western New York to Ohio, Iowa, and beyond. What we now call the Midwest was a region of non-slave-holding farmers, many of them Scandinavians and Germans who had come directly west from the port of entry. On the slavery issue, they were frequently in conflict with their border-state neighbors in Kentucky and Missouri, but on such questions as government support of internal improvements and banking, they found they had much in common.

The first reading in this section provides a graphic picture of slavery, the institution that was more important than any other in setting the South apart. The second tells the story of the massive migration of peoples from Europe to the United States in the nineteenth century, which contributed to the extraordinary population growth of the country. Though the vast majority of Americans lived in rural areas, many of the immigrants settled in eastern cities such as New York, which numbered 813,000 by 1860. The rapid urban growth, the development of violence and crime on a new scale, and the need for new city services are discussed in the third selection. The last reading is on labor conditions during the early years of the Industrial Revolution, especially among the new immigrants and women who entered the factory work force.

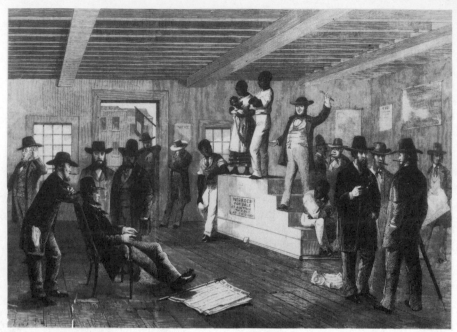

The opening of new cotton lands in the West made the slave auction a striking feature of southern life.

14

LESLIE H. OWENS

The Black Family

By 1800, slavery had been eliminated in the North, and in 1808 Congress banned the further importation of slaves from Africa. Some illegal importation continued, but it was other factors that accounted for the extraordinary elaboration and expansion of slavery in the nineteenth century. One was the invention of the cotton gin, described in the essay by Joseph and Frances Gies (Reading No. 8), which allowed the quick cleaning of as much cotton as slaves could pick. A second was the acquisition of vast new territories beyond the Mississippi River, which created a market for slaves and gave rise to the domestic slave trade within the United States. Between 1820 and 1860, the slave population of the state of Mississippi alone increased from fewer than 35,000 to more than 435,000. In short, southern planters found slavery to be economically profitable. There was also a high birth rate among American blacks, and by the eve of the Civil War nearly four million black people lived as permanent, hereditary slaves. Forming the chief labor force from the tobacco fields of Virginia to the cotton fields of Alabama, blacks were crucial to southern agriculture and to several other parts of the southern economy. As chattels, bought and sold like livestock, they were an easily marketable property that could bring ready cash to the slave-owner.

But slavery was more than a key feature of southern economic life. Its influence was all-pervasive, affecting law, education, social class, sexual mores, and other aspects of life. No one in the South entirely escaped the influence of slavery and racism, whether he was slave or slave-owner, free Negro or non-slave-holding white. Wilbur J. Cash has written, "Negro entered into white man as profoundly as white man entered into Negro —

231

subtly influencing every gesture, every word, every emotion and idea, every attitude."

Few things were influenced more radically than the black family. Today, much is made of the growing instability or breakdown of the American family. The daily press has become a record of divorce, juvenile delinquency, alcohol and drug abuse, wife-beating, and parent-child hostilities so extreme that murder is sometimes the outcome. Imagine, then, what might happen to a family under these conditions: a mother and her children might have to watch the father being whipped; a mother-wife might be forced to have sexual relations with a stranger who invades the family cabin; the children might be sold at the age of ten or twelve to a distant owner, never to see their parents again. Such were the possibilities for the black family under slavery, and some people have suggested that such experiences scarred the black family to the present day.

A full understanding of the black, or any other, family can be gained only by comparisons with families in other periods and societies. Recently, historians have devoted considerable energy to studying the family as a social institution in periods ranging from ancient China to medieval France to contemporary America. They have come to new conclusions as to the role of the Industrial Revolution in affecting the family, how pervasive single-parent households were in earlier periods, and whether or not the "nuclear" family — consisting of parents and children only, rather than broadly extended kin relationships — is a typically modern form. Leslie H. Owens's book *This Species of Property* is an excellent study of slave life and culture, and his chapter on the black family is especially poignant. Despite their enslavement and the breakup of families owing to the slave trade, blacks had a strong sense of family ties and family affection. Many slaves who attempted to escape seem to have been trying to get back to their families, and after the Civil War, thousands of ex-slaves solidified their informal alliances with marriage licenses and wedding ceremonies.

Few aspects of the slave's bondage have come in for as much speculative writing as the impact of slavery upon the slave family. Researchers in many

Excerpted from *This Species of Property* by Leslie H. Owens. Copyright © 1976 by Oxford University Press, Inc. Reprinted by permission.

disciplines have argued that bondage rent asunder this most basic of American institutions, injured black identity, and left scars to haunt black Americans down to our day. But all this needs further examination.

Planters usually evidenced concern and not a little ambivalence, as several historians have preferred to put it, when reaching the decision to split up a black household. The practice was in sharp contrast to what many felt to be right, though planters consistently overcame nagging doubts. An agent representing John McDonogh of Louisiana complained to him that a slave trader "refused to give me a little negro boy and girl belonging to the Mulattresses, claiming that he could not separate the families." He added bluntly, "It was a poor reason." It cannot be denied that the slave family took a tremendous beating; its members were sold to satisfy creditors and purchased to increase personal wealth. . . .

To avoid the public disapproval that increasingly attached to putting slaves on the auction block, some masters sold their bondsmen privately. For the slave, however, the impact remained the same, and scenes of mothers crying because they would never see their children again are more than products of historical imagination. George Tucker, a nineteenth-century Virginia novelist, offended many of his southern readers by writing, "One not accustomed to this spectacle [an auction] is extremely shocked to see beings, of the same species with himself, set up for sale to the highest bidder, like horses or cattle; and even to those who have become accustomed to it, it is disagreeable."

Historically, the auction block has both real and symbolic importance. The lyrics from a slave melody, "No more auction block! No more, no more," capture both meanings. For slaves it meant a parting — often final — from relatives and friends. Unable to face such doubtful futures some ran off or mutilated or killed themselves. To curb such occurrences planters sometimes gave only a day's or even just a few hours' notice to bondsmen selected for selling and then guarded them closely or locked them up. One master, no doubt guilty of understatement, conceded that his "Negroes will probably be somewhat distressed at being sold." He therefore advised his son, "You must say what you can to reconcile them."

Slave traders held auctions, advertised well in advance, several times during each year in local towns and cities. A great throng of slaveholders or potential slaveholders attended each session, accompanied sometimes by their wives, who might be clad in stylish dresses. It was, at the larger slave auctions, a time of gala social functions running through the day into late evening. The traders sponsored most of these events and invited planters up to their hotel rooms for pre-auction drinks and casual conversation. There was much imbibing and not a little carousing. Gangs of youths roamed the streets shouting names at free blacks, perhaps indicating a desire to see them returned to bondage. All had a good time except members of the black community — slave and free.

Of course the bondsman's participation in the auction began much earlier than these social functions. His psychological preparation started at the moment his master told him that he was to be put on the market. Parents gathered children too young to understand their fate around them and told stories of going on a long trip and not seeing one another for a great while. It could easily be the infants and adolescents who were being put up for sale, for nearly "all traders dealt in those from 10 or 12 years of age and many advertised for those from 6, 7, 8, and 9." A Virginia agent wrote to a prospective buyer in 1850, "Boys and Girls are selling *best*." For this reason Harriet Tubman, the underground railroad heroine, recalled that while she was in bondage, "every time I saw a white man I was afraid of being carried away." The domestic trade, few would deny, was a basic reason for some bondsmen having only faint memories of their parents and of children growing up under the adoptive care of childless slaves and other foster parents. Frederick Douglass's well-known confession is emblematic: "I never saw my mother to know her as such, more than four or five times in my life. . . . I received the tidings of her death with much the same emotions I should have probably felt at the death of a stranger." . . .

To soothe those slaves intended for auction planters sometimes explained their reasons for selling them, hoping to win their confidence. Dr. James Marion Sims of Alabama wrote to his wife about an impending sale: "Let them understand that it is impossible for us to keep them . . . already are there mortgages on some of them and there is no telling when they may be foreclosed. . . . Let them know too that it lacerates our hearts as much as it does theirs to be compelled to the course we suggest." Masters also promised not to allow reputedly cruel planters to purchase aggrieved bondsmen. Was this merely deception? In many cases it undoubtedly was. Yet there was not always cause to view a master's promises suspiciously, for some tried to keep their word. . . .

The time finally came for slaves to travel to the auction. In preparation, masters plucked out some of the older slaves' gray hairs or painted them over with a blacking brush. This was an illegal practice, but nonetheless widely engaged in, and traders delighted in outsmarting one another and uncovering the hucksters' deceptions. Masters also had some slaves grease their bodies to make their muscles or a smiling face shine, but also to cover up recent or old marks of abuse. At the larger slave markets such as Richmond, Natchez, New Orleans, and Wilmington, North Carolina, bondsmen were placed in slave pens to await the arrival of auction day. The abolitionist James Redpath visited the one in Wilmington in the 1850's and reported it filled with slaves of both sexes. . . .

The sale began as the auctioneer's voice boomed out over the crowd's noise: "Now gentlemen, who bids for Tom? . . . His only fault is that he has a great idea of his own reserved rights, to the neglect of those of his master." Several slaves were on the platform. The auctioneer commented on each one's relative value and merits, "and when the hammer at length falls, protests, in the usual phrase, that poor Sambo has been absolutely thrown away."

An historian has written that many slaves were apparently unaffected by the auction experience "and were proud of the high prices that they brought." This would seem to be an oversimplification of how slaves actually felt. Many, though colorfully dressed, wore somber expressions on their faces. At the Charleston market Captain Basil Hall noted a puzzling air of indifference in the slaves' manner. And another observer, on a different occasion, remarked that "the poor victims did not seem to think hard of this matter, but regarded it as a matter of course." In reality, some slaves had simply resigned themselves to being sold, and saw little need for a display of emotion that might later bring them punishment.

But it seems that many slaves determined ahead of time to take an active part in the direction of the bargaining. They looked over the buyers, as the buyers did them, and selected several preferable ones. Often their decision hinged upon a knowledge of the planter's wealth and the living conditions and work load he would subject them to. They learned the needed information by keeping alert, quizzing other slaves, and sometimes confronting purchasers directly with rather blunt questions. Some were deliberately offensive to small planters, believing that slaves owned by them lacked social status and also life's necessities. The slave John Parker explained: "I made up my mind I was going to select my owner so when any one came to inspect me I did not like, I answered all questions with a 'yes' and made myself disagreeable. So far as I was concerned the game was on, and I began to play it." William Hayden claimed that because of his "utter indifference and apparent independence" to the events around him when he was on sale at an auction in Natchez, Mississippi, many prospective "purchasers were at a loss to know if, in reality, I were a slave, and subject to the hammer." Slaves not as well attuned as Parker or Hayden to fine points of bargaining were less subtle. They might even kick or spit on buyers they did not like, and, according to the traveler E. S. Abdy, even shouted, "You may buy me . . . but I will never work for you." Such threats turned many buyers away, but others were willing to accept the risk, confident in their ability to handle any bondsman.

Another method employed by slaves was simply to complain of imaginary ailments to every buyer except the desired one. Prospective purchasers often believed these stories because of those real instances of doctored-up slaves whose masters sought to dupe the unsuspecting buyer. Female slaves acted the coquette, offending planters and the sensibilities of accompanying wives. They bickered and nagged at masters, convincing many that they would be a disruptive force in any work gang. They also made threats not to bear any children while owned by an undesirable master, and even to put infants that might be born to death. Only planters somewhat unfamiliar with slave management took these warnings lightly. For most, there was always a faint memory of a time on one's plantation or on a neighbor's when a slave had carried out an unheeded threat. . . .

But before a buyer sealed his purchase of a slave, he usually wanted to examine him physically. He looked at his teeth, limbs, and back, felt and poked muscles. Often buyers touched female slaves in most familiar ways, and the auctioneer and members of the crowd told obscene jokes. An English observer at Richmond noted, "I beheld with my own eyes a man . . . go and examine a poor African girl . . . grasping her arms and placing his course [*sic*] hand on her bosom!" Many domestic slaves were unprepared emotionally for such examinations, and when they occurred many broke into tears, almost as if for the first time the full weight of their bondage pressed down upon them.

For more intimate examinations, a small yard was set aside. Slaves carried back there, according to the ex-slave Solomon Northup, were "stripped and inspected more minutely." Buyers looked for scars or signs of syphilitic ailments, for example, and examined the pelvic areas of females for purposes of speculation on their future as childbearers. The ordeal was especially difficult for husbands who were powerless to assist weeping wives. Yet bondsmen submitted reluctantly to such examinations if they provided the chance of being purchased by a preferred owner. Prospective buyers also compelled slaves to jump and dance as further proof that their limbs were operative. . . .

Because of the frequency of auction block scenes, the composition and stability of the slave family has been the subject of much confusion. Was the family in a state of constant disruption? And if this was commonly so, what impact did such disruption have upon the development of its members' identities and general mode of being?

The primacy of one's family relationships in shaping one's character is axiomatic among today's social theorists. Family members gain personal strength from being loved and trusted by one another, and the family unit serves as a shield against outside attacks and the feeling of emptiness that often comes from being alone. The principles are easy to understand, but the elusive nature of the slave family makes them difficult to apply. Even the concept "family" as it applies to slaves needs reconsideration. With regard to them we might view it as several overlapping concepts. Slavery made it essential that the slave family be a great deal more inclusive than its white counterpart. Its ranks included not only blood relatives but also "adopted" relatives. Few slaves seemed lacking in aunts or uncles, real or otherwise.

The odds against survival of the slave family intact were formidable. To begin with, marriage was not legally binding between slaves in any of the southern states. As late as 1855 there was a petition before the North Carolina Legislature requesting "that the parental relation . . . be acknowledged and protected by law; and that the separation of parents from their young children, say of twelve years and under, be strictly forbidden, under heavy pains and penalties." Though such memorials were frequent, legislators never heeded them, for their implementation would merely have served to increase the moral questions that bothered many slaveholders, as well as greatly restrict the domestic slave trade. In the main, masters dictated the rules governing slave unions. What they were not able to dictate, however, was the seriousness with which bondsmen took their vows. These a sizable majority stood by steadfastly. . . .

Once married, separations were usually not a matter of impulse on the slave's part. The domestic trade annulled an inestimable number of unions, but in the instance of voluntary separations some planters wanted to know the causes for the disunion and, in the case of James Henry Hammond of South Carolina, believed in disciplining the offenders. Slaves, nevertheless, have gained a reputation for licentiousness and immorality that is out of proportion, considering the circumstances under which they lived. There were, of course, slaves who had several wives or husbands. But ulterior motives of both slave and master often spawned these arrangements. One planter thus discouraged his slave Peter from marrying a woman on another plantation because of "temptations to get into the rascality or meanness." He perhaps suspected that such a marriage would lead to eventual disobedience by Peter should their judgments differ on when Peter might visit his proposed wife. And he probably feared Peter's performing some unauthorized errands. Yet other slaveholders sometimes reasoned that preventing a slave from taking a wife of his choice could lead to serious managerial problems with him. At any rate, slaves whose spouses died often remarried as soon as they could. The practice was not uncommon among planters and overseers as well. It was "very common among slaves themselves to talk of" marriage, wrote ex-slave William Wells Brown. What bothered him was that after marriage, "some masters, when they have sold the husband from the wife, compel her to take another" almost immediately, ignoring her personal feelings. . . .

Many past and present researchers have assumed that the slave family was a very loosely organized group whose primary cohesion was provided by women. The black sociologist E. Franklin Frazier capsulized this interpretation in his 1939 study when he characterized the slave mother "as the mistress of the cabin and as the head of the family." Frazier also mentioned that the mother had a "more fundamental interest in her children" and was able to develop "a spirit of independence and a keen sense of her personal rights." His canonization of slave women catapulted them to the forefront of modern discussions about the slave family. Was he correct in his conclusion about the matriarchal structure of the family? His picture seems somehow too inflexible, for the slave family developed in ways which Frazier seems not to have imagined.

Under some conditions — when slave children were infants — southern laws provided that masters could not divide slave families. What these laws sought primarily to prevent was the separation of child from mother; the father might still be sold. Indeed, when planters spoke of slave families they often referred to husbandless women and their children. The logic rings familiar even today, in that when a husband and wife legally separate the wife normally obtains custody of the children. We seldom assume, however, that the husband has been a passive agent in the family. Why then should we assume this to be so in the case of the slave, when there is no significant precedent for such an assumption in the slave's African past or in many of his American associations? Of course, this is not to deny that a slave father was a great deal more helpless than a free father today.

A variety of circumstances determined the position of the slave mother as well as the father. If women were the heads of the households, they rarely gained that dominant status among slaves at large. Women worked side by side with men at nearly every task on the plantation, but there were certain duties considered women's work that men declined to do. Some male slaves refused to do washing for this reason. Cooking was usually the task of women, as was sewing and some forms of child care. Sometimes masters punished males by forcing them to work with women labor gangs in the fields or compelling them to wash the family's clothes and attend to housecleaning. So great was their shame before their fellows that many ran off and suffered the lash on their backs rather than submit to the discipline. Men clearly viewed certain chores as women's tasks, and female slaves largely respected the distinction. . . .

The often peculiar marriage and dating relations of bondsmen have caused many scholars to doubt their morality. Females have borne the brunt of unfavorable conjectures. Scores of mulatto children fathered by masters have been used to support arguments that bondswomen were indiscriminate in their selection of male sex partners. Added to this was the fact that in the "southern states the prostitutes of the communities are usually slaves, unless they are imported from the free states."

Motherhood in bondage provided extremely difficult tests of a slave's energies and identity. The slave had to play the role of wife and mother under circumstances that marred her effectiveness at each. Her plantation duties eroded the time she had to spend with husband and children. Distractions were infinite. This was akin to the condition that some planters' wives found themselves in, trapped in a continuous cycle of chores.

Slavery struck most directly at bonds of affection joining husband and wife. The slave trade occasionally separated slaves married only a few weeks. We may suppose that some slaves were reluctant to love anyone deeply under these circumstances. Yet most spent several years with one owner and one husband or wife, and came to know their fellow bondsmen well. Thus when slaves married it was often the consequence of courtship extending over some time. The resultant marriage was steeped in emotional attachment. "Our affection for each other was strong," wrote a slave of his marriage, "and this made us always apprehensive of a cruel parting." The slave Sam, like so many others, ran away from his Virginia master because he thought "it a hard case to be separated from his wife."

Planters understood such affections. "You have a woman hired in the neighborhood whose husband we own," began a letter to Colonel Barksdale of Virginia. His "name is Israel, he is our Blacksmith, and he seems to be so much attached to her we [would] like very much for her to be hired near him . . . would you sell the woman?" A sound marriage meant a better worker for the planter and often a sense of purpose for the slave.

But slavery compelled an uneven husband-wife relationship. A master could physically discipline either while the other stood by helpless, at least for the moment. Slaveowners worked both hard, and they often had little time left to enjoy each other's company in the evening. The relationship nonetheless had many interesting potentials. "A slave possessing nothing . . . except a wife and children, has all his affections concentrated upon them," wrote Francis Fedric. Occasionally, the marriage partners focused so much attention on each other that the slightest change in the routine of one tended to disrupt the other's habits. Sickness is a good example. Wives and husbands often insisted that they nurse each other back to health, fighting bitterly against efforts to force them into the fields when the possibility of a loved one dying existed. Slaveholders severely punished many and accused them of merely trying to escape duties — but discipline was seldom an effective deterrent. A planter could, of course, make arrangements for such times; expecting that wives and husbands might be off work briefly or difficult to manage during days when important personal matters came up. Sometimes a sick husband would prolong his sickness by refusing to take medicine from any but the hands of his wife, whom he could also trust to find out if someone had "hexed" him. . . .

The arrival of children served in large measure to solidify the slave marriage. Yet some parents feared that slaveholders would mistreat offspring or sell them away. A few adults also refused to assume parental responsibilities. They married and had children, but declined or allowed others to take care of them, and were occasionally abusive parents. Still, most assumed parental ties eagerly and were, according to a Mississippi mistress, "all so proud of showing their children." While discussing the possible sale of a slave to an Annapolis slaveholder, Charles Ridgely wrote that she "is married in the neighborhood and has a family of young children, and would I think now be extremely unwilling to be separated from them."

In Africa "tribal customs and taboos tended to fix the mother's attitude toward her child before it was born," making children greatly appreciated, and such tendencies were not absent in American slaves. Few women probably did not want children, though they were aware they might not be able to devote the attention to them that would be required. The emotional outbursts of mothers following the deaths of infants, and their resistance to being parted from offspring, indicate that female slave attitudes in this regard were not markedly distinct from those of mothers worldwide.

In fact, many disruptions of the workday stemmed from slave parents' requests to tend their children. Masters set aside a period during the day for the nursing of babies, but there was also frequent disciplining of bondswomen when they failed to return to their duties on schedule. Yet mothers repeatedly risked the lash in order to allow their body temperatures to cool down enough for effective milk nourishment. Still, Moses Grandy observed that overseers forced many to work in the field carrying full breasts of milk. "They therefore could not keep up with the other hands," and when this happened overseers whipped them "so that blood and milk flew mingled from their breasts." It does not appear that he was merely trying to achieve literary effect with this dramatic statement. But often mothers got their way, for it was difficult for a master to justify, either to his conscience or his hands, children found dead from want of care. The slave's human increase was also an owner's most valuable form of property. On many plantations masters periodically assigned one or two slaves to furnish the nursing needs of all infants. They also hired slaves to nurse their own offspring. . . .

In bondage, the varieties of adult family behavior served as the most significant models after which slave children patterned their own actions. We know that "where a variety of behavior or models is available, selection can be influenced either by affection and rewards, by punishment, or by awareness of what is appropriate." All these factors operated with peculiar force within and upon the slave family. J. W. C. Pennington, the fugitive blacksmith, experienced what he called a "want of parental care and attention." By way of explanation he added, "My parents were not able to give any attention to their children during the day." While this was not unusual, many parents did devote their evenings and weekends to family affairs — a first duty of which was to teach children the limits placed on their conduct. This was no simple task. . . .

For the young slave, family life was vastly important. His early years somehow slipped past with the idea probably seldom if ever occurring to him that he was but a piece of property. His main worries related to minor chores assigned to him at about age five or six by parents and master; and adult slaves at times bore much of the burden of these. Children also escaped much of the stigma of racial inferiority that whites attached to the personalities of their mothers and fathers. Concerning his childhood one slave reminisced, "let me say to you that my case were different from a great many of my colore so I never knew what the yoke of oppression was in the early part of my life." He was relatively carefree and innocent, he explained, until "the white boy . . . began to Raise his feathers and boast of the superiority which he had over me." . . .

It was not true that when black children learned to walk and then play with the master's children their "first lesson is to obey everything that has a white skin," as one bondsman claimed. Some masters' children learned this lesson the hard way when they tried to boss the little "niggers" about: "Every time they crossed me I jumped them," recalled one ex-slave about his white playmates.

Frequently the tendency among black and white children was towards a general equality. They played marbles together, and the slave children themselves spent many hours at this game: "My favorite game was marbles." They also played sheepmeat, a game of tag played with a ball of yarn that was thrown by one child at others running about the grounds. They enjoyed a great variety of childhood sports. Sir Charles Lyell, the English geologist, witnessed slave and white children playing, "evidently all associating on terms of equality." One slave narrator remembered too that he was very close to a son of his Virginia master: "I was his playmate and constant associate in childhood." He learned the alphabet and some of the elements of reading from him. "We were very fond of each other, and frequently slept together."

On large plantations communities of children were largely autonomous. Slave narratives relate that often one of the bondsman's earliest recollections of slavery was the sight of his mother or father being whipped or his brothers and sisters standing on the auction block. But this side of childhood can be overplayed. Fear did not perpetually pervade the environment. There are accounts of seeming childhood contentment which, though occasionally overdrawn by some interpreters, are to some measure accurate. The slaveholder did not constantly try to shape the character of slave children. There was little time for that. "The master, I think, does not often trouble himself with the government of these juvenile communities," observed a doctor from Kentucky. "He is not, therefore, an object of dread among them."

To a great extent, children learned to shape their behavior to the expectations of other slaves. A beginning lesson was to respect slave elders, particularly the aged. Tradition shaped this differential treatment. The child was, moreover, at the bottom of the hierarchy of both blacks and whites, while old slaves were in a manner the domestics of the slave quarters. Their functions were not unlike those of the slaves who ordered the master's children about and instructed them in etiquette. . . .

Some parents also saw initial work responsibilities, if properly performed, as an opportunity for their sons and daughters to escape the rigors of field labor. They encouraged their children to learn a trade if possible. A skill meant an opportunity to obtain preferred duties in later life. Masters wanted at least a few trained hands, chiefly as carpenters, for they increased the efficiency of the plantation as well as their own monetary value. John McDonogh of New Orleans hired a slave brickmason and later recommended him to a neighbor, suggesting that he might teach bricklaying to "two or three of your black boys" and "with two boys of 10 or 12 years of age to work with him in laying brick he will do all your buildings."

Occasionally, children's jobs required that they go through a prolonged or permanent separation from their families; but a determined parent was willing to accept this if it promised ultimately to provide an easier life for a son or daughter. The slave Julianna, age twelve, was the subject of a contract that engaged her services for six years. Her contractual master guaranteed "to teach her to sew, & bring her up to be a good seamstress, and a useful servant." The arrangement continued on a partially personal note: "In addition to the above I agree to allow the said girl Julianna to go to Shirley [Plantation] . . . once each year to see her relations, & remain with them one week each year."

Bondsman Henry Bibb was especially aware of the shortened childhood of the slave. "I was taken away from my mother," he wrote, "and hired out to labor for various persons, eight or ten years in succession." Other hired-out children were more fortunate than Bibb. Employed as families, as were "Great Jenny & her 3 youngest children," they partially escaped the emotional turmoil that accompanied separations. . . .

When the terms of bondage necessitated the division of families, parents often sought the aid of masters to reunite them. Lucinda, who served as a washwoman for a planter "nearly twelve years," asked him to hire her daughter Mary Jane from a nearby planter. "To oblige her," wrote her owner to Mary Jane's master, "I will become responsible for the amount, if you will let her have her daughter for the sum of Thirty dollars," which Lucinda was apparently willing to repay by her earnings during the remainder of the year. In another case, the slave George approached his master R. Carter about his daughter Betty — "7 years old, motherless, now at Colespoint-plantation —." In a letter to his overseer, Carter noted that "George wishes Betty live at Aires, with his Wife who lives there." As if not to appear overly accommodating to George's wishes, Carter continued, "If Betty is not useful where She now lives — I desire to indulge George . . . you will accordingly permit him to take his daughter." At other times, slaves acted on their own to reunite themselves with loved ones. One runaway was persistent in this way: "She has a husband, I think, at his [a neighbor's] house & tho' taken up by him the first time came straight back to his house."

When a master abused or humiliated one member of a family, the rebuff reverberated throughout the slave household and beyond. An example appears in the opening pages of the fugitive blacksmith's narrative. Following the whipping of his father, J. W. C. Pennington remembered, "an open rupture" developed in his family [against their master]. Each member felt deeply offended by the deed, for they had always believed their conduct and faithfulness was exemplary. They talked of their humiliation in the "nightly gatherings, and showed it in . . . daily melancholy aspect."

Planters' ill-handling of slaves was only one of many factors that brought out family consciousness. Bondsmen's misdeeds against other bondsmen sometimes marked families for harassment and shame. A serious offense, such as stealing another's hunting catches, might lead to brief periods of social isolation, with members of the offending family finding themselves excluded from slave gatherings or nightly ramblings. Bondsmen saw themselves as having their primary identification with a distinct family unit to which they had responsibility and which had responsibility to them.

However, the slave family was a unit with extensions. Quite frequently it seems to have consisted of more than just parents and their natural children. It could include a number of blood or adopted relations — uncles, aunts, and cousins — who lived on the same plantation or on nearby estates. Adults "claimed" parentless children, and the slave community seldom neglected old slaves. Local bondsmen usually absorbed new arrivals on a plantation into a family setting and expected them to make a full contribution immediately. But can such a group really be called a family? Slaves considered it as such and treated adopted relatives with real affection.

The extended slave family frequently arose to augment or replace the regular family unit split up by slavery's misfortunes. There were deaths resulting from disease, accidents, and natural causes that left wives husbandless and children without parents. Then there were the family breakups caused by the slave trade. In an important, though not typical, exception, however, Robert Carter of Virginia agreed to sell his slaves to the Baltimore Company only "if the Company will purchase men their wives & children [ten families]." . . .

In slave families wives seldom possessed greater financial stability than husbands, a circumstance that often gives rise to psychological problems in men of minority households in our day. Both worked at tasks that the slave culture did not stigmatize as menial, so there was no need for the male to feel a lack of importance in his family on that score. The power of masters to disrupt families at any time weakened male slaves' sense of responsibility and dignity, but they did not invariably see this as a slight to their manhood. Yet for the slave who experienced the breakup of his household there remained that indelible hurt, as perhaps exemplified by Charles Ball's father, who "never recovered from the effects of the shock" of losing a portion of his family and became "gloomy and morose." Whenever the slave family — natural or extended — was intact, however, and slave males were reliably performing their duties, they most likely did symbolize authority within the family structure.

Except for sales of its members, much of the time slaveholders left the

slave family to its own devices. And though the slave trade drove blood relatives apart, bondsmen's common persecution brought many of them back
together in extended family groupings which provided for many of the emotional needs whose satisfaction the regular family, had it remained untouched, might have rendered less vexatious. Under these conditions the
personalities of bondsmen were certain to gain much strength.

STUDY GUIDE

1. How would the following factors affect a slave's price on the auction block:
   age, sex, health, and attitude? What techniques were used by sellers to
   try to make a slave appear more valuable?

2. Summarize Owens's view of the role and attitudes of male and female
   parents in the black family under slavery. What kind of evidence does
   he use to argue that slaves made clear distinctions in the roles of men and
   women, though both did the same kind of field labor?

3. What generalizations can be made about the attitudes of masters toward
   selling slaves, toward slave marriages, and toward breaking up families?

4. Many European and American white families were "nuclear" — consisting
   only of parents and children without grandparents or uncles and aunts
   living in the same household. Owens suggests that the black family was
   more "extended," with considerable respect for age and the care of parentless children by others. Why would you expect such features to have developed in southern slavery?

5. What differences do you see today in families with different backgrounds
   and circumstances? Think, for example, of a southern rural and a northern
   urban black family; a second-generation Slavic family; a Chinese-American
   family; an Italian Catholic family. What factors in modern society have
   somewhat modified the differences that existed between such groups some
   decades ago?

BIBLIOGRAPHY

The book by Leslie H. Owens from which the preceding selection is taken is
a fine study of life and culture under slavery. While it reveals much about
slave conditions and the slaves' reactions to their enslavement, there are many
other studies of slavery in the period just before the American Civil War.
An older southern historian, who had a patronizing view of the Negro and a
rather rosy view of slavery, was Ulrich B. Phillips. Despite the limitations of
his work, he was one of the first scholars to study slavery as a total system,
rather than as only an economic or a racial system. The most important of his

works are *American Negro Slavery* * (New York, 1918) and *Life and Labor in the Old South* * (Boston, 1929). The most interesting works of a general nature written since Phillips are Kenneth Stampp, *The Peculiar Institution: Slavery in the Ante-Bellum South* * (New York, 1956) and John W. Blassingame, *The Slave Community: Plantation Life in the Ante-Bellum South* * (New York, 1972). Virtually every major conclusion of earlier historians on the social and economic aspects of American slavery has been challenged in the highly controversial study by Robert William Fogel and Stanley L. Engerman, *Time on the Cross,* * 2 vols. (Boston, 1974).

An issue of great interest is the influence of slavery upon the American black's personality and his reaction to slavery. In his work, *Slavery: A Problem in American Institutional and Intellectual Life,* * 3rd ed. (Chicago, 1976). Stanley M. Elkins compares the American slavery system with the Nazi concentration camp. Elkins believes that the slave identified with his oppressor, and he emphasizes the "Sambo" personality of the American black in studying the effects of slavery upon the black's psychology. Other scholars have argued that the Sambo role was merely a survival technique in a white world, and Mullin and Blassingame suggest that there were different personality types.

Equally interesting is the question of the influence of slavery upon the black family. A number of writers, including Daniel Patrick Moynihan in a very controversial book, have suggested that the black family was characterized by strong mothers, irresponsible fathers, sexual promiscuity, and a general lack of stability. In an important book entitled *The Black Family in Slavery and Freedom, 1750–1925* * (New York, 1975), Herbert Gutman disputed such conclusions, argued that there was a strong sense of family and kin among blacks, and provided the best study to date of the black family over an extended period. On this and other subjects, one can get the slave's own perspective from the collection of reminiscences of ex-slaves edited by Benjamin A. Botkin, *Lay My Burden Down: A Folk History of Slavery* * (Chicago, 1945). Eugene Genovese, who previously had written about southern slaveholders, used such reminiscences as well as other sources to get at the daily life of southern slaves in *Roll, Jordan, Roll: The World the Slaves Made* * (New York, 1974). Frank Owsley, *Plain Folk of the Old South* * (Baton Rouge, La., 1949), gives a fair picture of the life of poor whites, but the studies of slave life are generally better. Richard C. Wade, *Slavery in the Cities: The South, 1820–1860* * (New York, 1964) is a study of the sizable number of slaves who do not fit the plantation stereotype. John Hope Franklin, *From Slavery to Freedom: A History of American Negroes,* * 3rd ed. (New York, 1967) is a general history of black Americans.

---

* Asterisk indicates book is available in a paperback edition.

An immigrant transfer barge docked at Castle Garden offers transportation to the Erie Railroad, 1874.

15

CARL WITTKE

Nation of Immigrants

The extraordinary flow of people from Europe, Asia, and Africa to the New World for more than three centuries constitutes the largest migration of mankind ever experienced on this planet. All of us here are descendants of immigrants — of Indians who crossed the Bering land bridge from Asia, of early black and white migrants who settled the British colonies, of German, French, Italian, Russian, Hungarian, Chinese, or other immigrant ancestors who poured into the United States in the nineteenth century. By 1930, the tide had waned, but by then the country's history could not be understood without taking into account the impact upon American civilization of the many races and nationalities that had immigrated to the United States.

The most obvious question involved in the study of immigration history is why particular groups left their homelands to come to a strange country. As Carl Wittke indicates in the following selection, there were some factors common to most groups of Europeans, but in each country there were special influences that promoted emigration at a particular time. A second question is why certain nationalities settled in the areas they did and tended to enter particular trades and occupations. Some remained largely in eastern cities as unskilled manual laborers, while others went on to Minnesota or Wisconsin to enter farming. One of the striking characteristics of early nineteenth-century population movements was the extensive immigration to the North and the very small number of immigrants who were attracted to the southern states. This pattern was determined by a number of factors, including the greater industrialization taking place in the North, the slave labor system of the Old South, and the different social attitudes in the two regions.

Many immigrant groups, even in the colonial period, faced substantial hardship and considerable animosity in establishing their roots in this land. In many ways, the difficulties increased during the nineteenth century, and even English-speaking groups such as the Irish found that adapting to the new culture posed serious problems. Most nationalities developed one or another sort of agency to assist them in preserving their heritage while adjusting to their new society; churches, schools, recreational associations, and other institutions served such purposes. Wittke describes the special problems faced by one such group, the Irish, a group that one might expect to have had fewer difficulties than some others.

Attitudes of immigrants toward their heritage have varied, as have attitudes of older Americans toward immigration policy and assimilation of new nationalities. For many years, much of our thought was dominated by the "melting pot" metaphor, which implied that the distinctive characteristics of each group should disappear into a new American nationality. In our time, there has been a resurgent interest in preserving the cultural heritage of various nationalities, and a suggestion that the melting pot theory should be replaced by a cultural pluralism that recognizes the integrity and contribution of different ethnic groups.

In the nineteenth century, and with increasing volume after 1830, the tide of emigration set in again from Europe. Wave after wave rolled over the cities and prairies of the New America. The Irish, the Germans, and the Scandinavians, in more or less sharply defined but overlapping streams, poured into the United States; and these major groups, together with several minor ones, constitute the "old emigration" from western and northern Europe, in contradistinction to the newer groups that came in the last quarter of the century from the south and east. Each deserves detailed treatment. In each case, specific causes, . . . operated to start the emigrant tide on its way across the Atlantic and to keep it flowing steadily for decades. Aside from the universal desire for adventure and greater opportunity, there were certain causes for emigration common to all these groups; and it must be remembered that much of the European emigration was artificially stimulated and encouraged by interests in America desirous, for one reason or another, of bringing in a larger population.

First of all, . . . the earlier population movements were influenced by the "America letters," "the literature of the unlettered" written home by those who had ventured out first and whose accounts of the New Canaan were eagerly awaited and devoured by those who had remained behind. Christopher Saur's "America letters" praising "the goodness .I have heard and seen" were printed and reprinted many times in Germany during the latter half of the eighteenth century, in order to induce people to come to Pennsylvania. What the United States after 1776 symbolized to the liberty-loving, thwarted, and exploited Irishman can readily be imagined, especially when the glowing accounts that reached the Irish countryside assured the readers that "there is a great many ill conveniences here, but no empty bellies." In 1818, an enthusiastic reporter described the region around Wheeling in extravagant terms that must have been irresistible. He wrote:

> I believe I saw more peaches and apples rotting on the ground than would sink the British fleet. I was at many plantations in Ohio where they no more knew the number of their hogs than myself . . . . The poorest family has a cow or two and some sheep . . . good rye whiskey; apple and peach brandy, at 40 cents a gallon . . . . The poorest families adorn the table three times a day like a wedding dinner—tea, coffee, beef, fowls, pies, eggs, pickles, good bread; and their favorite beverage is whiskey or peach brandy. Say, is it so in England? . . .

. . . "There are no large estates," wrote one Swedish-American, "whose owners can take the last sheaf from their dependents and then turn them out to beg." Ministers and churches were said to be less worldly in America, and "there is ceaseless striving to spread the healing salvation of the Gospel." Hired men and maids ate at the same table with their employers and wore clothes of the same style. "Neither is my cap worn out," added another, "from lifting it in the presence of gentlemen." Small wonder that enthusiastic newcomers wrote: "We see things here that we could never describe, and you would never believe them if we did. I would not go back to Sweden if the whole country were presented to me." "It is no disgrace to work here," wrote a Swede in 1841. "Both the gentleman and the day laborer work. No epithets of degradation are applied to men of humble toil . . . . I do not agree . . . that in order to appreciate the blessings of monarchy, one must live in a democracy." . . .

Ship companies and organizations interested in land speculation did their part to keep the America fever burning at the proper temperature. Advertisements in American newspapers reveal a veritable flock of emigration agents; immigrant bankers dealing in remittances, steamship, and railroad tickets; and dealers in foreign exchange, each of whom had his special reasons for keeping the immigrant tide flowing in a steady, unbroken stream to the United States. Land agencies, with acreage for sale in Texas, Missouri, Wisconsin, and other parts of the West, advertised their bargains in newspapers published at the Eastern ports of arrival. . . .

In the middle of the last century, the Middle West needed population above everything else. To attract desirable immigrants was the overpowering ambition of practically every new state in this region. State after state began to enact legislation to encourage and stimulate migration to its borders. The attractions offered by favorable legislation and the persuasiveness of the agents of state immigration commissions were important factors in directing the immigrant tide into the Mississippi Valley.

By its constitution of 1850, Michigan gave the franchise to all newcomers who had declared their intention to become naturalized and who had resided in the state for two and a half years. Its immigration agency, established in 1848 and not abolished until 1885, issued attractive pamphlets in German, and its first immigration commissioner was instructed to spend half his time in New York and half in Stuttgart, Germany. Wisconsin had a special commissioner as early as 1851, and its board of immigration, created by legislative act in 1867, published pamphlets in seven different languages. From 1871 to 1875, 35,000 copies were printed for distribution in Europe. Other material was distributed in New York, in taverns and at the docks; and advertisements lauding Wisconsin's attractions were published in eight foreign newspapers, such as the London *Times,* the Tipperary *Free Press,* the *Baseler Zeitung,* and the *Leipziger Allgemeine Zeitung.* In 1880, Wisconsin issued 10,000 pocket maps of that state, with legends in English, Norwegian, and German. The Wisconsin Constitutional Convention of 1846 gave the franchise to immigrants after a declaration of their intention to become naturalized and one year's residence in the state. . . .

From 1860 to 1862, Iowa had a state commissioner of immigration, the German-born lieutenant governor, Nicholas J. Rusch, who maintained offices at 10 Battery Place, New York City. Later, an immigration board, similar to those in other states, was created. A handbook, *Iowa: The Home for Immigrants,* was prepared in English, German, Dutch, Danish, and Swedish; and agents were sent to Holland, England, and Germany to make propaganda for the state.

Steamship and railway companies [also] had a special interest in stimulating the immigrant traffic, for obvious reasons, but the latter had an additional objective in promoting the disposal of their railroad lands to actual settlers. In 1870, Jay Cooke, as the financial promoter of the Northern Pacific Railroad, employed Hans Mattson, who resigned his position as secretary of state of Minnesota to undertake the assignment, to go to Sweden to advertise the resources of the road and to draw up a plan for the disposal of its lands. J. J. Hill may have saved his road from financial disaster by promoting the settlement of Minnesota by Norwegian and

Swedish farmers, whose bumper crops quickly tripled the earnings of the railroad. Hill, in order to make the Red River Valley district more attractive to settlers, described it as an area "where the depth of the humus was equal to the height of a man." The Northern Pacific at St. Paul gave special passes to ministers of the Gospel, so that they might more frequently visit outlying immigrant settlements where no church had as yet been organized. When a trainload of Dunkards moved from Indiana to North Dakota, they went by special train, with streamers on the railroad cars advertising "the bread basket of America." The Atchison, Topeka, and Santa Fe Railroad, through its foreign immigration department, extended its activities to the Ural Mountains, bringing over 15,000 Russian-German Mennonites to Kansas. By 1883, they had settled along the route of the railroad in Kansas, with branch settlements in Oklahoma and Colorado. The Burlingame and Missouri Railroad also was active in attracting Mennonite settlers to the American West.

The sea voyage safely passed, the immigrant was likely to run afoul of the beasts of prey in human form who waited to pounce upon him on his arrival in New York, to exploit his ignorance of the English language, and his "greenness" about American conditions generally. New York was infested with "runners," who were paid by trucking firms, railroad ticket offices, and immigrant hotels and boarding houses for no other purpose than to compete with other runners and lead the unsuspecting immigrant into the clutches of the hotelkeeper or baggage agent. Runners were paid from $10 to $30 a week, or a certain percentage of the business they secured. Competition became extremely keen and, on many occasions, violent; for, in order to hold his job, a runner had to be a good "shoulder hitter" as well as a persuasive talker.

When a ship arrived, runners rushed to the gangplank and began fighting with other bullies over the immigrant's luggage, in order to get him to stop at a particular boarding house. These immigrant hotels and boarding houses were generally operated, not by native Americans, but by foreigners who congregated like vultures in the seaport towns to prey upon their own countrymen. In the worst of these houses, the immigrant was overcharged for everything, particularly for the storage of his baggage, which was then held as security until all bills had been paid. Occasionally, but not often, an immigrant runner's license was revoked for fraud. Usually, the law was indifferent to the plight of the stranger in a strange land. Occasionally, too, charges were lodged against runners and steamship, baggage, or railroad agents who had cheated unsuspecting immigrants out of hundreds of dollars or had collected sums of money as commissions for securing jobs that never materialized. The newspapers usually recorded that the culprit had "left for parts unknown," and that ended the case. An article in *The New York Times* for June 23, 1853, accurately described the arrival of an emigrant ship as follows:

Every one in the great City, who can make a living from the freshly arrived immigrants, is here. Runners, sharpers, pedlars, agents of boarding-houses, of forwarding offices, and worst of all, of the houses where many a simple emigrant girl, far from friends and home, comes to a sad end . . . .

Some immigrants hung around the German boarding houses in Greenwich Street, each day losing more of their savings. Others, Irish and Germans, settled down in the Eleventh Ward, to become peddlers and ragpickers and to succumb to the vice of intemperance. . . .

The ordinary prices by steamer and canal from New York to Albany and thence inland were reasonable enough, and the railroads tried to stop the selling of bogus tickets by swindlers in New York, but forwarding houses were hard to regulate and generally charged the immigrants higher rates, on one pretext or another, in order to divide the profits with their agents and runners. In the 1840's, the "official" table of prices was as follows:

New York to Albany	$ .75
New York to Buffalo	4.50
New York to Cleveland	7.00
New York to Detroit	8.00
New York to Milwaukee	14.50
New York to Chicago	14.50

Baggage up to 50 pounds was supposed to be transported free. Children under twelve paid half fare; those under two were carried free. A Norwegian immigrant, in 1847, was able to go from New York to Albany, up the Hudson, for $.50. To go by rail from Albany to Buffalo cost $12, but by way of the Erie Canal the rate was only $7.50, including meals, with a special price of $2 if immigrants brought their own food.

There apparently was little uniformity in the charges made. In 1844, a Norwegian immigrant went by steamer from New York to Albany, on a boat 290 feet long and with cabins on three decks, for $1.50. Nine hours were required to make the trip. The next year, a traveller who went by train from New York to Buffalo, in "wonderful closed wagons with windows," paid $3.50. The journey took several days, because in the dark nights "we stood still." To go from Albany to Buffalo in 1847 by canal boat required a day longer than by train, and the fare was $7.50, including meals. Some canal boats took longer to make the trip, furnished no food, and charged only two dollars.

Immigrant travel over this route, across New York and then into the West by way of the Great Lakes, was heavy. Immigrant trains were not distinguished for their accommodations and comforts. Often the cars marked "Immigrant Cars" were springless boxcars, with hard benches and no drinking water, and the immigrant passenger was expected to bring or buy his own food. Sometimes the coaches had absolutely no conveniences, not even seats, except for long boards running lengthwise along both sides of the cars, so that many had to sit or lie on the floor. Newspapers recorded the passage of long immigrant trains through Albany and Buffalo, trains with extra locomotives and long lines of cars, filled with Germans, Dutch, Swiss, or Scandinavians. In Chicago and other terminal points, runners for land companies, railroads, and state immigration commissioners met the incoming trains. In 1853, a resident of Chicago wrote: "One fourth of the persons you meet in Chicago cannot speak a word of English, and a good part of the remainder cannot speak it well. Germans, Irish and Norwegians seem to be as plenty as natives." The immigrants were so numerous in Milwaukee in 1842 that they were forced to lodge in the streets, while in Racine and Southport all tavern facilities were exhausted. In the 1850's, emigrant trains passed over the New York and Erie road at regular intervals, attracting much attention with their car windows trimmed with green vegetation and their passengers smoking long German pipes and singing German songs. . . .

The figures for the period of the Irish famine immigration mounted to startling totals: 92,484 in 1846, 196,224 in 1847, 173,744 in 1848, 204,771 in 1849, and 206,041 in 1850. The Census of 1850 reported 961,719 Irish in the United States; by 1860, the total had reached 1,611,304. These were to be found in greatest numbers in New York, Pennsylvania, Massachusetts, Illinois, Ohio, and New Jersey. The character of Irish immigration changed under the pressure of intolerable suffering and famine. The poor, small farmer, who had constituted the bulk of the migration up to 1835, who knew English, had sufficient energy to be proud of his independence, and was determined to rise, gave way to a new type — namely, the laborer, with little background aside from his potato patch, who was ignorant of the English language, and who was of a mercurial temperament, and likely to find life and progress in the United States very difficult.

Early in 1847, the roads to Irish ports were literally thronged with immigrant families. Sometimes strong men actually battled with each other at the ports of embarkation to secure passage on ships entirely inadequate to provide transportation for all who wished to go to America. The description of the ravages of the Irish famine tax the reader's imagination. Children and women were described as too weak to stand; the livestock had perished, people were eating carrion, and "the weekly returns of the dead were like the bulletin of a fierce campaign." Beggars crowded the roads and the city streets. People huddled half-naked in fireless and foodless hovels. Thousands crossed to Liverpool and demanded transportation to the United States on crowded and filthy emigrant ships whose resources were taxed to the utmost. . . .

The Irish temperament is noted for buoyancy, and hope sustained the voyagers across the Atlantic, but for many it vanished like the rainbow when the actual conditions of life in America had to be faced. Almost all Irish immigrants had to begin in the United States as unskilled laborers, and many got no farther. Year after year, the Irish Emigrant Society of New York advised immigrants to shun the cities of the Atlantic seaboard and to scatter throughout the United States, particularly into the West. "Thousands continually land entirely penniless and are at once in a state of destitution," the warning continued, "whereas such person should have at least five pounds on his arrival to enable him to prosecute his journey to the interior." The advice was sound, but thousands found it impossible to follow, for all their earthly possessions had been used up during the voyage. They arrived in the New Canaan with their pockets empty. The almshouses and hospitals were filled to overflowing, and beggars wandered aimlessly through the streets. Men and women accustomed to no other existence than eking out a living from the soil were suddenly left stranded in congested cities. They had no trade and no particular skills; some did not even know the language. They were destined to become the unskilled, marginal workers of the America of the middle nineteenth century, with all that that implies. Many lurid accounts of Irish "shanty towns" are available to the historian of the Irish immigration. Some are descriptions obviously colored by a deep hatred for the newcomer, but there is enough in the comments of friendly critics to indicate that conditions were deplorable, to say the least. Indeed, one who is familiar only with the Irish-Americans of the twentieth century may find it hard to credit the tales told about their ancestors of several generations ago.

The Irish, as a class, came to America with less means than many other immigrant groups. The majority were poverty-stricken. Having no money to proceed westward on their own account, they usually got out of the cities only when contractors for internal improvement projects recruited them in the labor markets of the East and transported them to the West and South. On their arrival in the port towns and larger cities, the Irish crowded the tenements, sometimes twenty or more families living in one house. These Irish tenements were hardly more than "human rookeries." What a difference it might have made, and what an excellent investment it might have turned out to be, had the government used its funds to transport the Irish into the West and helped them to become established as farmers on the public lands! There are many unnamed graves of Irishmen along the canal and railroad routes which they helped to build. In South Boston in 1850, the Irish slums were buildings from three to six stories high, with whole families living in one room, without light or ventilation, and even the cellars crowded with families. Saloons were the curse of the neighborhood, and police records abundantly reflected this unhealthy condition. The death rate among the children of the Irish poor was alarmingly high. Disease, particularly during cholera epidemics, always ravaged the immigrants living in hovels in the western and eastern sections of New York City worse than in other communities. Secret societies arose in the Irish shantytowns among Irish laborers with such names as "the Corkonians," "the Connaughtmen," and "the Far Downs," who engaged in bloody brawls and riots, which even the repeated denunciations of the Church authorities seemed powerless to stop. In some of the "better-class" tenement houses in New York, Negroes were preferred as tenants to the poor Irish and Germans. . . .

The Irish laborer in the middle nineteenth century frequently found himself in difficulties because of shameless exploitation and bad working conditions and because of the resentment harbored against him by native Americans who feared his competition, although apparently few Americans had any wish to do the heavy, dirty, unskilled labor that fell to the lot of the Irishman with his pick and shovel. Newspapers friendly to the Irish immigrant warned him to stay away from the canal and railroad construction projects, for "these railroads have been the ruin of thousands of our poor people" and their workers are treated "like slaves" by railroad contractors. Wages were low, usually $1 a day but often less; they were not clearly fixed and were paid partly in whiskey and "store pay," or merchandise, sold at high prices. Friends of the Irish urged them to form protective associations, with objectives somewhat like the trade unions, in order to stop competition, rivalries, and fights between warring gangs which drove wages down in their competition for the available jobs. Above all, the Irish were advised to go to the country to work on farms or squat upon government land in the West, to "do anything, in fact, in preference to railroading."

Irish longshoremen were employed at the docks in all the leading sea and lake ports. They bitterly resented the invasion of Negroes, who were often brought in expressly to depress the wage scale. Riots between Irish and Negro dock workers were not infrequent. It is this economic competition that helps to explain the strong hostility of the Irish toward the abolitionist movement and the New York draft riots during the Civil War. Workers on the Chesapeake Railroad and Ohio Canal were known as the Longfords and Corkonians. On some of the Ohio canals, Irish and German pick-and-shovel workers received only $.30 a day, with board, lodging, and a "jigger-full" of whiskey. Everywhere the Irish were doing the hard work, even in the South, where they were so badly treated at one time that Bishop England found it necessary to publish a warning in Irish newspapers advising Irish workers to avoid the South. Accidents, deaths, and injuries were numerous in road building and canal digging, and cave-ins occurred frequently in excavations for tunnels. Little tumble-down markers in tiny Catholic burying grounds along the route of these internal improvements still bear mute testimony to the hazards of pick-and-shovel work.

In the 1840's and 1850's, little "Dublins" sprang up in the factory towns of New England and in the Middle Atlantic states, for the Irish were invading the mill centers. The Irish population of Boston trebled in a decade. Often the mill population was the residue from the labor supply that had dug the canals or constructed the mill race. In Rhode Island, for example, the first Irish millworkers were recruited from those who had built the railroad between Providence and Boston, and the Woonsocket Irish Catholic settlement was due entirely to the construction of the Blackstone Canal. Irishmen went into the mill towns of Pawtucket and the "coal pits" between Fall River and Newport. At first, the competition of Irish labor was resented by other workers. Towns tried to restrict the sale of lots so as to keep out Catholic purchasers, and the sign "No Irish Need Apply" was posted in some of the factories. The children of the Irish were twitted and abused on the playground and in the school-yards much as some Irish children later joined in making life uncomfortable for "dagos," "wops," and "kikes." But the economic urge was irresistible; and the Irish captured the mill towns, only to be in turn dispossessed in a later generation by Poles, Italians, French-Canadians, and Greeks, the products of the "new" immigration.

Irish workers had a bad reputation for rioting and brawling, and the newspapers of the middle of the last century are full of graphic accounts of their bloody battles. In 1853, for example, the eviction of an Irishman from a circus performance at Somerset, Ohio, for smoking a pipe, started a battle in which Irish railroad workers fought all night and into the next day. A company of militia had to be called from Zanesville to restore order. Feuds between groups of Irishmen hailing from different counties in Ireland led to frequent riots. On one occasion, in Indiana, 400 militia had to be called out to stop an impending assault by several hundred belligerent Irishmen from County Cork. A riot that broke out along the line of a projected Pacific railroad, in 1853, over the election of a foreman of a labor gang, would have had serious consequences but for the timely intervention of a Roman Catholic priest, who served as peace-maker.

After reading the many accounts of brawling and fighting among Irish workingmen that appear in the American newspapers, one becomes aware of the fact that not all the trouble was due to the Irishman's belligerent temperament, his love of the bottle, or his belief that contentiousness is the spice of life. Much of this rioting was the result of intolerable labor conditions. The brawls were often efforts, however misguided and unwise, to achieve an improvement in labor standards at a time when the labor movement had hardly begun. There were strikes for higher wages on internal improvement projects, many of which led to a display of force, particularly when contractors refused later to respect the agreements they had been forced to accept. In 1840, a serious riot broke out when the wages of Irish laborers on an aqueduct in New York City were cut from $1 to $.75 a day. There were similar disturbances, caused by wage reductions, on the Illinois Central, the Buffalo and State Railroad, the Steubenville and Indiana, and other lines.

The reign of terror instituted by the "Molly Maguires" in the anthracite coal regions of Pennsylvania is well known to students of American history and is usually described as one of the worst examples of mob rule and blackmail in the whole history of labor relations, for which Irish coal miners are held primarily responsible. Viewed from a longer perspective, the incident is but another illustration of the battle for better working conditions in the coal-producing areas, although the movement fell under the control of criminals and ended in a number of executions. The anthracite coal regions of Pennsylvania had a mushroom growth in the 1830's, with immigrant labor, poor housing facilities, and all the evils of company towns and company stores as natural concomitants of this rapid expansion. The region suffered from the evils of overdevelopment and frequent business slumps, which weighed especially heavily upon the Irish coal miners. Working conditions in the mines were terrible, with no safety requirements, inspection, or proper ventilation. From 1839 to 1848, wages were $1 or $1.25 a day for miners and $.82 for ordinary laborers. In 1869, a peak of $18.20 a week was reached, but by 1877 the wage had declined again to $9.80. "Breaker boys," aged 7 to 16, worked like slaves in the mines under mine bosses whose character left much to be desired. An editorial in *The Boston Pilot* exposed conditions in the coal mines — the inadequate pay, the "murderous neglect" of ventilation, the "rancid provisions" available at high prices in company stores, the explosions in the firedamp caverns in which Irish and Welsh miners were blown to pieces, and the "scandalous ungenerosity" subsequently shown by the operators toward their mutilated workmen — and concluded by denouncing some of the owners as men with "the conscience neither of Christian nor of Pagan."

Irish benevolent societies were formed to deal with some of these problems. The Ancient Order of Hibernians, a semisecret organization, became the backbone of the miners' unions. In a very long story of real class war, the responsibility for violence in the Pennsylvania coal fields seems to be pretty well divided. By 1860, the Molly Maguires terrorized the whole anthracite region, elected sheriffs and constables, and resorted to arson, blackmail, and murder. The organization was not finally broken up until 1875, when, because of the detective work of James McParlan, 19 were hanged after trials held in an atmosphere of great excitement and prejudice. The incident for a long time blackened the record of Irish-Americans, and many refused to see the industrial conditions which had provoked such criminal action. . . .

The United States has been known and ridiculed as a nation of "joiners." One reason may be the large immigrant element, which has had its special incentives in a new land to form benevolent, patriotic, and social organizations to keep alive the memories of a common origin. The Irish were no exception, and Irish societies of many kinds — such as the Hibernians, athletic clubs, and sodalities — exist in large numbers, generally closely connected with the Church and the Catholic hierarchy. . . .

For many years, fire fighting in the United States was in the hands of volunteer companies. The opportunity to become a "fire laddy" was irresistible for many Irishmen. These companies performed superhuman feats of strength and heroism. Each firehouse, especially in large cities like New York, also attracted a group that ran along to every fire, so that "running with the machine" eventually degenerated into a sport which attracted the hoodlums and gangs of the Bowery districts. The volunteer firemen of the 1840's and later decades appeared in brilliant uniforms and ponderous equipment of the comic opera variety. Much feasting and drinking seemed to be part of the routine of these organizations, and until the temperance movement made its inroads upon the profession, companies frequently had a steward, whose business it was to ladle out liquor to exhausted firemen from a barrel hauled along with the engine to each fire. . . .

How the Irish established themselves on the police force of the larger American cities needs no discussion. A study of the New York force in 1933 revealed that, out of a total of approximately 20,000 policemen, 2,309 were themselves foreign-born and 11,014 were of foreign-born parentage, representing 42 countries in all. Ireland led the list of foreign-born policemen with 1,533, and also the list of those of foreign-born parentage with 5,671.

Nearly all that has been said hitherto has concerned the Irish immigrant as a city dweller. It has been shown that most Irishmen began as unskilled laborers, working in construction gangs on the docks, in livery stables, in the streets, or, with the rise of industrial towns like Lowell and Paterson, in the mills — wherever brawn and not skill was the chief requirement. Many ended their days as unskilled workers in the cities and towns. But although it is true that the Irish immigrant is primarily a phenomenon of urban civilization in the United States, some did go into agriculture. Students of immigration have speculated on the reasons why a predominantly rural people should have shunned the land in their new home. Poverty, of course, made it impossible for large numbers to leave the port towns in which the immigrant ships happened to land them. Ignorance of improved American methods of farming was another reason, along with memories of bitter experiences on the land in Ireland. Irish gregariousness and the incentive of cash wages in the city were other factors. In some cases, the demoralizing effects of the saloon and political clubs in the cities operated to keep Irishmen from moving West. . . .

The importance of the Irish in the history of the Roman Catholic Church in the United States and the role of the Church in the life of Irish-

Americans are so generally recognized that the statement that the Catholic Church in America became essentially an immigrant church in the 1840's, and continued for decades to receive its strongest additions from abroad, will hardly be challenged by anyone familiar with the facts. There were Roman Catholics in America at the time of the Revolution, but they were under special disabilities in a number of the American colonies. The first great accession of Roman Catholics came from the purchase of Louisiana, which brought into the American Church about 100,000 communicants. Others came in with the annexations following the Mexican War, but none of these additions can be remotely compared in importance with the great flood of Irish who came across the Atlantic in the 1840's and later decades.

To the poor Irish immigrant, his Church was a part of home. It had always brought him consolation in time of trouble. In a new land it gave him a measure of dignity at a time when he was often made to feel that he was of a lower breed of humanity. It became the role of the Catholic Church to make law-abiding citizens from the hordes of newcomers, to provide parochial schools for the nurture of their religion, to dispense charity in many forms and to provide the counsel of priests for the crises an immigrant had to face in a new and strange environment.

Lay and clerical leaders have testified to the special mission of the Irish to preserve and spread Roman Catholicism in the United States. "What Ireland has done for the American Church, every Bishop, every priest can tell," wrote Maguire in 1867, in his book on *The Irish in America*. "There is scarcely an ecclesiastical seminary for English-speaking students," he added, "in which the great majority of those now preparing for the service of the sanctuary do not belong, if not by birth, at least by blood, to that historic land to which the grateful Church of past ages accorded the proud title — Insula Sanctorum." . . .

It has been estimated that there were 30,000 adherents of the Roman Catholic faith in the United States in 1790. By 1830, the Church claimed 600,000 and, by 1860, 4,500,000 members. Both figures are probably too large. The Metropolitan Catholic Almanac of 1852 listed 1,980,000 Catholics in the United States. By that time, there were Catholic newspapers in nine of the leading cities and Catholic publishing houses in Baltimore, Philadelphia, New York, and Boston. . . .

Devout Irishmen, of course, followed their clerical leaders in matters of religion and religious education. In politics, they learned to follow the ward boss. The latter's affiliations generally were more intimate with the saloon than with the Church, and saloons and fire houses were the centers from which ward-heelers carried on their activities. To an Irishman, politics proved to be the salt and breath of life, and Irishmen in America found it hard to resist the temptation to plunge at once, and deeply, into the American political stream. They learned the tricks of the political game from native American leaders, and then rapidly improved on their instruction. From the first, Irish allegiance was to the Democrats. The name itself had its allure. "Federalist" and "Whig" were names that had little significance for an immigrant who had come to the United States to enjoy freedom and democracy. Moreover, both Federalists and Whigs were suspected, with much truth, of a nativism that frowned upon the newcomer, seeking to protect American institutions from the inundations from abroad and opposed to the easy and quick naturalization of foreigners. Irishmen had little in common with the "Anglomen and monocrats" who supported Federalists and Whigs. Posing as friends of the poor, the Democrats, in the tradition of Jefferson and Jackson, opened their hearts to the immigrants and sought to win and hold their support by admitting them at once to the inner sanctuary and to the minor spoils of the American political system. Irishmen generally had an ingrained hatred for aristocracy and long-standing reasons to be "agin the government." By the year 1820, Tammany Hall was Irish. Tammany celebrations toasted Ireland's sons and their patron saint, St. Patrick, and Tammany used its charities to win and to hold the immigrant vote.

A regiment of well-drilled Irish voters, once organized in any of the larger port towns, was able to enlist new arrivals among the immigrants as soon as they landed. The Irish usually were more interested in local political issues than in national questions, but thorough organization in the local communities led to party solidarity on any issue that might arise. Needless to add, immigrants favored universal manhood suffrage, and the Democratic leaders championed what their supporters wanted. A deliberately cultivated Anglophobia helped to preserve Irish unity. Irish wit and adaptibility, a gift for oratory, a certain vivacity, and a warm, human quality that made them the best of good fellows at all times — especially in election campaigns — enabled the Irish to rise rapidly from ward heelers to city bosses, and to municipal, state and federal officials of high distinction.

The Irish added turbulence and excitement to political campaigns. They also contributed a new picturesqueness and dramatic quality to the methods of political campaigning and canvassing the vote of large masses of people. By building up strong political machines in the cities, they became, along with the Solid South, the one stable element that kept the Democratic party — then a minority group — alive after the Civil War and gave it its occasional chance for victory. Reformers have often overlooked the fact that the same political boss who bought votes, stuffed ballot boxes, and brazenly perpetrated naturalization frauds was also the warmhearted leader who got the immigrant his pushcart license, "fixed" arrests for petty violations of the law, and sent the poor their Christmas turkeys and coal in winter, paid their rent when the landlord threatened eviction, and sent flowers to their funerals. Indeed, some political bosses contended that they were public benefactors, for they took money out of the public till to help bring about a fairer distribution of the world's pleasures among the underprivileged. . . .

The Americanization of the Irish proceeded so rapidly, in spite of the alarmists of the 1850's and 1860's, that no detailed discussion of this process is necessary here. The Irish have become so much a part of present-day Americanism that it seems curious indeed to review the characteristics they brought with them several generations ago and to describe the reception they received from their American contemporaries. The Irishman is now so thoroughly Americanized that he is not averse to joining in denunciations of later immigrants whose ideas he considers dangerous to American institutions, apparently completely forgetful of the treatment his ancestors received 100 years ago. . . .

STUDY GUIDE

1. In this selection, Wittke mentions only a few of the common factors that operated in most countries to lead people to emigrate. Which ones does he mention, and what other common factors can you think of?

2. The selection is concerned only with pre-Civil War migration, which was mostly from northern and western Europe. Based on your own knowledge, indicate in what areas each of the following settled and what occupations they tended to enter: Germans, Scandinavians, Hungarians, Jews, Poles, Italians.

3. What special factors operated in Ireland to promote emigration? How do you explain the poor economic and social condition of the Irish once they arrived here?

4. In the final paragraph, Wittke suggests that there is not necessarily a positive relation between attitudes of tolerance toward other groups and a history of having been persecuted or discriminated against oneself. How can you explain this irony, which we know to be characteristic of many minority groups?

5. What factors in modern American economic life and in new social attitudes might make a cultural pluralism, in which various nationalities and races live in mutual respect and appreciation of their differences, more feasible in the United States today than in the early nineteenth century?

BIBLIOGRAPHY

The study of immigration as a significant theme in the American experience is a relatively recent phenomenon. In addition to the volume from which the preceding selection is taken, two older studies by Marcus Lee Hansen are well worth reading: *The Immigrant in American History* * (edited with a foreword by Arthur Schlesinger, Sr., Cambridge, Mass., 1940) and *The Atlantic Migration 1607–1860* * (edited with a foreword by Arthur Schlesinger, Sr., Cambridge,

Mass., 1945). More recent publications on this theme include a number of volumes by Oscar Handlin: his Pulitzer Prize-winning book, *The Uprooted: The Epic Story of the Great Migrations That Made the American People* * (Boston 1951, revised 1973); *Race and Nationality in American Life* (Boston, 1957), a series of essays on immigration; and *Immigration as a Factor in American History* * (Englewood Cliffs, N.J., 1969), a collection of documents relating to immigration with an introduction by Handlin.

A good, short survey of immigration as an aspect of American life is Maldwyn Jones, *American Immigration* * (Chicago, 1960). Another general work by Jones is *Destination America* (New York, 1976), which has a great many illustrations of the immigrant experience. Several of the major immigrant groups have been the subject of studies; others have not yet been seriously studied by professional historians. Three very good studies of different groups that migrated to the United States are: Rowland T. Berthoff, *British Immigrants in Industrial America, 1790–1950* (Cambridge, Mass., 1953); Theodore Saloutos, *The Greeks in the United States* * (Cambridge, Mass., 1964); and Terry Coleman, *Passage to America: A History of Emigrants from Great Britain and Ireland to America in the Mid-Nineteenth Century* * (London, 1972). Other specialized works treat the adjustment of different nationalities in America and the role of such traditional institutions as the church in the lives of the immigrants. Three works of this sort are: Oscar Handlin, *Boston's Immigrants, 1790–1880: A Study in Acculturation* * (Cambridge, Mass., 1941, revised 1959); Louis Wirth, *The Ghetto,* * (Chicago, 1928), a classic study of Eastern European Jewish response to Chicago; and a more recent study by Jay P. Dolan, *The Immigrant Church: New York's Irish and German Catholics, 1815–1865* * (Baltimore, Md., and London, 1975). Ray A. Billington, *The Protestant Crusade, 1800–1860* * (New York, 1938) is a study of nativism. An article on religious prejudice and anti-immigrant feeling is David B. Davis, "Some Themes of Counter-Subversion: An Analysis of Anti-Masonic, Anti-Catholic, and Anti-Mormon Literature," *Mississippi Valley Historical Review*, Vol. XLVII (1960), 205–224.

* Asterisk indicates book is available in a paperback edition.

Philadelphia's 1844 anti-Catholic riot, which required calling in the state militia, suggests the crime and violence that plagued early nineteenth-century cities.

16

DAVID R. JOHNSON

Urban Problems

Today a vast majority of the United States population lives in sizeable towns and large cities. Along the Atlantic seaboard, farmlands near the great urban centers have been turned into housing developments at such a rate that the hundreds of miles between Washington, D. C., and Boston are becoming one great urban corridor. The American people have become so thoroughly an urban people that few are left who know the difference between timothy and alfalfa or who have any idea of what the farm machine known as a harrow does. In recent years, an increasing number of farm museums have developed, where city folks can go on a Sunday afternoon to look at weathered farm equipment and see live sheep and cattle. There is a considerable irony in all this, since during much of American history, the country was predominantly rural and the American dream was the acquisition of one or two hundred acres one could farm for oneself.

In the eighteenth century, most centers of settlement were nothing more than tiny farming villages. Boston, the largest city in 1730, had 13,000 people, while Philadelphia was second with 11,500 and New York third with 8,500. As late as 1790, the largest American city, Philadelphia, numbered only 30,000. By 1860, it had risen to an incredible 565,000 residents; New York was home to more than 800,000; and the relatively new, western metropolis of Cincinnati had 160,000 people. In the earlier period, a seaport town of ten or twenty thousand people could get all of the water it needed from private wells and one or two town pumps. Poverty seems not to have been widespread, but the eighteenth-century city was not entirely free from urban problems. Drunkenness, prostitution, robbery, personal assaults, and uncontrolable fires were characteristics of most port towns. But the extraordinary growth of cities in the nineteenth century brought new problems and required new policies and institutions for the solving of some of the older problems.

Epidemics of cholera and yellow fever swept American cities in the early nineteenth century, taking as many as 3,500 lives in a single year in New York. In the same city, hundreds of homeless poor, including orphaned children, roamed the streets begging, and tens of thousands of people lived in dark cellar holes and tenement buildings. Crime and gang violence became critical problems in the larger cities, as did the problem of supplying water, fire protection, and other services to these vast metropolitan areas. Singing the old refrain that the city is "a great place to visit, but I wouldn't want to live there," a visitor to New York in 1828 said that something about it made it "more a gratification to visit, than to abide."

Some of the urban problems were solved by private efforts, some by the development of professional government service departments to replace the earlier private fire-protection clubs. In 1860, for example, 79 private companies and 57 public works supplied water to the cities. The following essay by David R. Johnson on nineteenth-century Philadelphia indicates the seriousness of fire, crime, and violence in the city, and describes the attempts of the city to bring these problems under control.

Thomas Welsh, down on his luck, was about to stumble onto a fortune. A clerk in the offices of Jay Cooke and Company, at Third and Chestnut, had spilled the contents of a bag of gold coins he had been counting. While he and the other clerks scurried about on the floor retrieving the money, a shabbily dressed man walked in. Everyone assumed he had business in the rear of the office; but the stranger departed hastily and someone noticed another bag containing $5,000 had disappeared with him. When pursuit proved useless, the clerks notified the police. Headquarters sent officers to watch all the railroad depots and other exit points in the city, and began a fruitless search. Several hours later a prosperous looking fellow walked into a jewelry store only five blocks from the scene of the crime. He bought a ring, paying for it with a $20 gold piece. Another customer, having heard

From *The Peoples of Philadelphia: A History of Ethnic Groups and Lower-Class Life, 1790–1940*, Allen F. Davis and Mark H. Haller, editors. Copyright © 1973 by Temple University Press. Reprinted by permission of the editors and publisher.

of the robbery, became suspicious because of the mode of payment. He took
the liberty of hefting the gentleman's valise, and thinking it rather heavy,
called for the police. After his arrest, Welsh made no attempt to deny the
theft, "but said he thought that he needed the money as much as Cooke
& Co."

This robbery typified crime in Philadelphia during the years from 1840
to 1870. Opportunity and inclination proved time and again to be the
combination which resulted in thefts and assaults. This does not mean that
each criminal incident had no larger context. Some thieves, such as Welsh,
stole because they either needed or wanted money. For others larceny constituted part of a life style — a group of rowdies might deprive a passing
stranger of his cash in order to buy themselves liquor or amusement. Those
of a more deliberate turn of mind might plan and execute a burglary of a
store or home. Physical violence often derived from racial prejudice. Rival-
ries between various gangs also accounted for a large number of assault
cases. And deep hostilities among volunteer fire companies produced a long
series of riots and minor battles which enlivened urban life. Crime was
therefore both rational and random: rational because individuals had sufficient reasons (at least in their own minds) to commit these acts; and random
because opportunities to steal or to assault someone depended upon time
and circumstance. . . .

With the advent of the omnibus, the upper classes began to leave the
central city for the suburbs. Sidney George Fisher, a local Philadelphian,
noted in 1847 that "the taste for country life is increasing here very rapidly.
New & tasteful houses are built every year. The neighborhood of German-
town is most desirable." Led by the wealthier citizens, people began moving
in large numbers toward the northwest and across the Schuylkill [River]
into West Philadelphia. The main thrust of this migration was up Ridge
Avenue, though many residents also bought new houses within the city, west
of Broad. The slum district along South street remained the worst section
of the city and expanded slowly toward Broad Street. By 1870 these population movements had reversed the character of the suburbs and city. The
outlying districts now contained the best, not the worst, housing.

Philadelphia's downtown grew steadily as the well-to-do citizens moved
outward. Shopkeepers either took over abandoned houses or demolished
them to make room for imposing new commercial buildings. These conversions occurred most rapidly on Chestnut Street, but the other major east-
west avenues (Walnut, Market, and Arch) were not far behind. Some of the
north-south streets also developed major concentrations of businesses. Third,
from Walnut to Willow, and Eighth and Ninth from Walnut to Vine were
especially noteworthy for their fine stores. By the mid-1860s the area
bounded by Third, Eighth, Market, and Walnut had emerged as the center
of the downtown district. The merchants on these streets served the upper
and middle classes.

South Street became the major shopping thoroughfare for low-income families. A miscellaneous collection of stores, offering a vast assortment of cheap wares, lined this artery running through the heart of the slums. The division of the city's two business districts along socioeconomic lines also occurred in the types of entertainment located near each. While the streets adjacent to Walnut, Chestnut, and Market offered such diversions as theaters and museums, the avenues surrounding South (especially Bedford and Spafford) enticed the passerby with numerous houses of prostitution.

Philadephia's property crime patterns closely followed residential and business shifts. . . . Throughout the period under study the emerging downtown area from the Delaware to Broad, and from Vine to South (wards 5 and 6 after 1854) had a persistent concentration of this type of offense. Sneak thieves, till-tappers, and window smashers victimized merchants in that district. Shopowners sometimes aided the thieves by placing merchandise on the sidewalk fronting their stores during business hours. Daring sneak thieves simply walked off with whatever they could carry. In the days before cash registers, the merchant kept his money in a till (a drawer under the counter). A group of boys could send the smallest of their number around the counter to raid the till while they occupied the owner's attention. Or a customer might ask for something which he knew was in the back of the store, and, while the clerk searched for it, the thief reached over the counter and emptied the cash drawer. There were many variations of till-tapping which seems to have been a favorite endeavor among juveniles.

Thieves also took advantage of improvements in displaying goods. In the 1820s merchants began to replace their old, small shop windows with large bulk windows. A handy brick or stone and nimble hands combined to make window smashing a prevalent form of larceny by 1840, and the offense continued to plague store keepers throughout the period. Because of the noise involved in this particular crime, its practititoners soon turned to various glass cutting instruments to reduce the possibilities of attracting attention (and perhaps to reduce the chances of getting cut on jagged glass fragments).

As the residential pattern of Philadelphia spread, so did the incidence of thefts from houses. . . . The heaviest concentration of these property losses occurred in those areas where the upper- and middle-income groups settled, especially in the western and northwestern parts of the metropolis. The sneak, or entry-way thief, was very prevalent. His victims contributed to his success by habitually leaving coats, hats, umbrellas, boots, and similar wearing apparel hanging on a rack just inside the doorway of a home. The criminal had only to step inside briefly, grab whatever was within reach, and depart. Bolder sneak thieves, posing as service or repairmen, entered homes and stole any watches, jewelry, and clothing that was lying loose. Juveniles were especially persistent depredators. Among their favorite targets were new houses which had not yet been occupied. They broke into many such residences and stripped away the plumbing fixtures to secure the brass and lead. When elaborate door knobs and knockers became popular, youthful thieves developed the ability to quickly rip those objects from their fastenings without undue noise. Even the family wash disappeared frequently, as did any miscellaneous household items carelessly left in view. The cash loss in most of these thefts was low, but these incidents were extremely annoying to the victims.

And finally there was a special class of property crimes, highway robberies, which often shaded into violent attacks on persons. This form of theft occurred anywhere in the city or suburbs, though its perpetrators seem to have favored either side streets or the less densely settled areas. Juveniles and young men, especially those wandering about in small groups, committed many of these offenses. Two social customs aided the thieves. First, most victims usually had enough money in their possession to make the robbery worthwhile. In the days before checking accounts and credit systems, people normally carried their cash with them when conducting business or while engaged in shopping. In one variation on this practice, merchants employed messenger boys who conveyed large sums from their employers to the banks. This arrangement made robberies even easier, since a juvenile could offer only minimal resistance. Secondly, watches (a favorite target with thieves) were scarce before the Civil War because few people could afford them. Due to their relative rarity, it became customary to ask strangers for the time of day. Thieves used this habit to their advantage. When a pedestrian pulled out his watch in order to answer a query as to the time, the criminal grabbed it and ran. Or, if the watch happened to be attached to a chain, he pulled the victim off balance by jerking the watch toward him, at the same time quieting the owner with a blow on the head. Either method usually proved successful.

Philadelphia's thieves stole everything from washtubs to diamonds. They took anything which might have some cash value because a market existed for these goods. The city's numerous pawnbrokers and junk dealers purchased most of the pilfered items for a fraction of their value, and they asked few questions about ownership. Because those merchants were so willing to buy whatever was offered, the petty thieves (and even the more serious offenders such as burglars) always had a way to convert their day's work into ready cash. A part of the commercial structure of the city therefore provided the incentive for these particular offenses.

Crimes against property, then, tended to concentrate where the property was available: in the commercial district and in the rapidly expanding residential neighborhoods of the relatively well-to-do. Crimes of violence against persons, in contrast, tended to occur where the poor lived. Because the residential areas of the poor remained fairly stable, crimes against persons exhibited a rather stable pattern throughout the period. . . .

Customs of a different sort from those involving property crimes produced the opportunities for violence. The city's streets were centers of social life in the nineteenth century. Every evening, and especially on the weekends, the avenues teemed with people seeking relief from the day's tasks. The street corners performed a special function as the focal point for crowds of youths. Numerous citizens throughout the period complained about corner loungers, and the *Public Ledger's* frequent attacks on the practice led one such "lounger" to write a defense of that habit. He justified his companions behavior by claiming young men had nowhere else to go, and he asserted it was only natural for them to gather and talk among themselves. Furthermore, he argued that corner loungers had redeeming social values: they helped pull fire engines and were the first to volunteer in wartime. He suggested that, if the citizens of Philadelphia wanted to stop the practice of congregating on the corners, they should provide places for juveniles to go "where we could talk ourselves and not have an orator or preacher to do the talking."

This champion of the corner lounger had a point. Urban society provided few places for recreation, and proper society tended to feel that leisure time should be spent listening to informative lectures or in other educational pursuits. But the weight of the evidence favors the critics of the corner loungers. Unfortunately for many citizens, those youths did a great deal more than talk among themselves. Their amusements also included loud, obscene verbal abuse of other pedestrians. They pelted the passing citizenry with snowballs, rocks, or bricks, and anyone who objected to this treatment faced the prospect of a beating. The loungers' defender correctly noted their eagerness to pull fire engines. Men had to haul these primitive mechanisms to a fire. Long ropes attached to the engine enabled many people to join the regular crew and somewhat increased the speed with which the apparatus arrived at a fire. But the prospect of a good fight probably had much to do with the readiness to help. After a fire, and sometimes while getting to it, the followers of an engine often clashed in battles ranging from a brief fist fight to a full-scale riot.

The corner loungers also swelled the ranks of Philadelphia's gangs. Although no one knows how many of these bands existed, a survey of a single newspaper from 1836 to 1878 uncovered fifty-two gangs which were identified by name. Whatever the total might have been, the pre-Civil War era was one of the most gang-plagued periods in urban history. These associations concentrated their activities along South street and in Southwark and Moyamensing. Although a few were located in the northern working-class districts, newspaper coverage suggests these were neither as numerous nor as dangerous as their brethren on the south side of town.

The distribution of violent gangs was due in part to the age composition within the city's wards. In 1840, just before the height of juvenile gang activity, those ages which tended to form these associations (ten to fourteen and fifteen to nineteen) comprised 3.6 and 4.4 percent of the total city population. Cedar Ward (bounded by Seventh, Spruce, the Schuylkill River, and South street) had 12.9 and 9.6 percent, respectively, in those age categories. Among the ten- to fourteen-year-olds that was the highest density in the entire city. Other wards had percentages higher than the average, but none had so many violent gangs operating within its borders.

Newspaper accounts said little about the internal structure of these bands. The author of a fictional romance dealing with an actual gang, the Killers, left the only contemporary description of that group's composition:

> They were divided into three classes — beardless apprentice boys who after a hard day's work were turned loose upon the street at night, by their masters or bosses. Young men of nineteen and twenty, who fond of excitement, had assumed the name and joined the gang for the mere fun of the thing, and who would either fight for a man or knock him down, just to keep their hand in; and fellows with countenances that reminded of the brute and devil well intermingled. These were the smallest in number, but the most ferocious of the three.

The Killers, according to this account, used an abandoned building as their headquarters. Other gangs also had clubhouses, but most had only a street corner which they reserved for themselves. The vast majority of these groups had very short lives of three years or less. But a few persisted for much longer periods. The Schuylkill Rangers held the record (at least twenty-six years). Others, like the Buffers (ten years), the Forty Thieves (nine), and the Snakers (seven), provided additional exceptions to the general rule of a short, violent life.

Street warfare between rival gangs formed one of the basic themes of city life during the middle years of the nineteenth century. These clashes generally occurred in the evenings and lasted as long as the participants felt like fighting. Any law officer who appeared on the scene did so at his peril. The weaponry ranged from fists to pistols. Since the newspapers usually listed only fatalities, not more minor injuries, it is difficult to judge how deadly this behavior became. Battles erupted so frequently, however, that the fighting developed some semiformal aspects. By 1850 there was an area of ground known as the "Battlefield" where opposing bands met regularly for combat. The place even attracted spectators who watched the fun and offered encouragement to their favorites.

Gangs provided one type of organized violence. . . . The volunteer fire companies supplied a related, and in some ways more serious, form of disruption. The volunteer system had been a product of necessity in the eighteenth century when fire posed one of the greatest hazards to urban life. That danger persisted throughout the nineteenth century as well, but while the problem remained, the nature of the fire fighters changed. Initially composed of the "best citizens," the membership in many companies shifted by the 1830s to include some of the worst elements in society.

The conflicts between these rival associations became the major source of organized violence before the Civil War. Though fires were too frequent to suit most city residents, the volunteers' brawls had reached the point by the 1840s where many blazes were set deliberately to provoke a riot. As a company charged along a street in the direction of the fire, its opponent either collided with it, or lay in ambush. The engine was the supreme prize in these affairs, and several valuable pieces of equipment received severe damage or were totally destroyed in the battles. Any fire, incendiary or otherwise, became an excuse to fight. Whenever two companies met, the encounter usually ended in some form of combat. Most of these engagements were brief, but some went on for hours, covered several city blocks, and occasionally continued the next day or evening.

One source of this conflict derived from the circumstances surrounding fire fighting. In the early nineteenth century good-natured contests to be first to a blaze, and first to a hydrant, slowly altered into determined battles between claimants for those honors. Once this change occurred, partisans of one or another organization began attempting to prevent competitors from arriving at all. Fights developed on the route to a conflagration. As rowdies infiltrated some companies, the crowds which usually followed the engines also changed. Corner loungers and gangs attached themselves to several fire associations. When rivals, reinforced by their supporters, met in the streets, the excitement of the moment combined with an eagerness for combat to produce an outbreak of violence.

Deeply rooted social conditions also accounted for this warfare. Religious differences provided one excuse for conflict. The Irish Catholics of the Moyamensing Hose hated the Irish Protestants belonging to the Franklin Hose. Their fights were among the most savage contests which occurred. Community loyalties formed another basis for trouble. Many volunteers came from the same neighborhood. This gave cohesion to an outfit, but it also made the company competitive with others formed along similar lines. The internal structure of these organizations also contributed to a combative nature. Firehouses were built to include living quarters or a meeting place for members. What had been public associations became private clubs for the city's young men who had few other places to spend their time. This social aspect of fire fighting bred the same sort of pride as that connected with neighborhoods. The sense of belonging expressed itself in such rituals as elaborate parades and in battles with rivals.

Small groups of rowdies wandering through the streets constituted another form of violence. Unprovoked assaults occurred with distressing frequency on the city's south side and in the less densely settled areas to the north. The victim might be a rival gang member, a lonely stroller, a man (or woman) suddenly slashed by a knife as he brushed past a gathering of juveniles, or — especially along South Street — a Negro. Racial antagonism kept the ghetto area in turmoil for years. Philadelphia experienced five major anti-Negro riots between 1829 and 1849. In the intervals between major battles, white and black youths constantly attacked one another. Raids and reprisals became commonplace and kept tensions high until the mid 1850s. Though the antagonism behind these assaults seems to have declined somewhat by 1860, it flared occasionally after that date, as in 1871 when a minor race riot erupted.

Law officers were also frequent victims of assaults by bands of rowdies. Until the city and districts consolidated in 1854, the policing establishments in the metropolitan area suffered due to inadequate manpower and conflicting jurisdiction. A watchman pursuing an offender had to give up when the culprit crossed into another district. Roaming toughs took full advantage of this state of affairs. When a policeman interfered in an assault, they frequently turned upon him and beat him badly. Officers who attempted to disperse corner loungers also faced the prospect of an attack. If help arrived during these affairs, the rowdies simply headed for the nearest dividing line. In a refinement of this situation, some malefactors took to shooting at patrolmen of one district while standing in another. Under these circumstances, officers had great difficulty maintaining any semblance of public order.

At the same time that crime, and particularly violence, seemed to be gaining momentum, other factors were at work to impose a higher degree of discipline on urban society. Philadelphia's more orderly citizens did not remain passive bystanders while the rowdy elements indulged themselves in a miscellaneous assortment of riots, assaults, and thefts. A reorganization of the police, the abolition of the volunteer fire companies, and the emergence of political bosses all contributed to the decline (though not the elimination) of crime.

Philadelphians reduced the amount of criminal violence by creating a more effective police force in the 1850s. The multiplicity of jurisdictions within the metropolitan area complicated the struggle to achieve this particular reform. As a result, the movement to establish an efficient police became one of the themes in the consolidation crusade which culminated successfully in 1854. The Marshall's Police (1850–54) served as a transitional force between the old watch system and the more modern organization which emerged in 1855.

Though a temporary solution at best, the Marshall's Police did set a pattern regarding the recruitment of a particular type of man who did much to curtail crime in the nineteenth century. Since a law officer's life was not particularly pleasant, individuals in the middle and upper classes did not find the work very attractive. Policemen came, therefore, from the lower classes in urban society. They also came from the volunteer fire companies and other rowdy elements. These latter groups were among the best equipped to handle the people whom the respectable citizens regarded as threats to the stability of society. A precedent did exist for appointing some men to the police who belonged to the very organizations which needed regulation. In a particularly bitter riot caused by a Moyamensing gang in 1849, the authorities had imported a rival band to suppress the disorder. The example, which had succeeded, was not ignored when the time arrived to select officers for the Marshall's Police, and the practice continued after that organization dissolved. Samuel Ruggles, chief of police under Mayors Richard Vaux, Alexander Henry, and Morton McMichael (1856–69), belonged to the volunteer Columbia Hose Company. Ruggles was only the most prominent officer on the force who had connections with the violent fire-fighters.

Appointing such men to the police in effect legitimized hitherto illegal violence. Because patrolmen refused to wear distinctive uniforms throughout most of the 1850s, they did not change their outward appearance or habits with their altered status. Animosities which had been built up through the 1840s continued unabated, and a man's new position did not confer immunity from the hatreds held by rivals in opposing companies and gangs. The level of violence, though impossible to measure precisely, does not appear to have declined following the creation of the Marshall's Police, or after the emergence of the consolidated force in 1855. Although the number of physical assaults declined between 1850 and 1860, the decrease probably resulted from a shift to "legal" police violence (which the newspapers would not have considered criminal). There were some criticisms of the amount of force the police employed, but such complains did not reach a peak until after 1870. In the early years of creating discipline on the streets, "respectable" opinion generally supported the patrolmen's methods for suppressing disorder.

Not every officer had connections among those whom he had to control. Assaults on policemen, and the prevalence of force in making arrests, also derived from the newness of policing. Individual patrolmen had to learn their jobs. No academies existed to teach a man how to become a good officer. Consequently, the city's streets became his school. The problems arising from improvising arrest procedures in a hostile environment help account for some of the violence perpetrated by these men. Force came easily because it seemed to settle so many disputes, at least temporarily. The policemen's authority also represented something new on the urban scene. For volunteer firemen and gang members who had never respected anything but superior physical prowess, a certain amount of muscle was necessary to convince them that an officer meant business. The habit of obeying orders which came from a patrolman had to develop over time; many rowdies learned that lesson with the aid of "legitimate" violence.

Reorganizing the fire companies proved to be as difficult as the effort to consolidate the districts and city. This reform also took more time. Politics proved to be the most stubborn roadblock in the way of reformers. The volunteers wielded considerable voting power at elections, and they were very effective at carrying on the daily chores of running a campaign. Any politician who dared suggest that the existing fire-fighting system should be abolished risked defeat. In 1855 the city council improved conditions slightly by creating a single fire department run by a chief engineer. That official could not exercise much control over the various companies because he was elected by the membership of those organizations. As a consequence, although service became somewhat more efficient, the old habits of disorder returned by 1859.

Technology drove a wedge into the volunteers' ranks which reformers eventually exploited to establish a paid fire department. The steam-powered engine proved to be the instrument of destruction. The first of these machines arrived in Philadelphia in 1855 when some public-spirited citizens, impressed by the capabilities of these devices, purchased one for the city. It proved to be a financial disaster because it weighed 20,000 pounds and could not be moved without breaking down. But the idea began to catch on. In 1857 the Philadelphia Hose Company bought one of these engines; others followed their example until the old-style, hand-drawn pumpers became rarities by the 1860s. The adoption of these machines fundamentally altered the nature of fire-fighting. Because of their weight, horses replaced men as the means of locomotion. This reduced the number of men required to put the engine into operation. Secondly, these were delicate monsters which needed skilled mechanics to keep them in running condition. The volunteers, who knew more about fighting than machinery, thus lost part of their rationale for existence. Finally, the cost of maintaining these machines rose far beyond the means of any one company, and the city began to assume the greater part of the burden of keeping the engines in repair.

The cost of the new technology gave reformers the opportunity they had been looking for. The idea of economy in city government was as powerful a force politically as were the volunteers. The combination of increasing expenses and continuous street fighting between firemen at last convinced Philadelphia's politicians to vote for reform. After protracted debate, the city councils created a paid fire department which commenced operations in 1871. The volunteers maintained their old organizations as social clubs, but their excuse for rioting had disappeared.

Political developments also contributed to the decline in violent crimes. Following the uncertainties and shifting loyalties which characterized the 1840s, local leaders began to divide along ethnic lines during the 1850s. The latter decade also witnessed the emergence of the professional politician at the city and ward levels.

William McMullin became the boss of the Fourth Ward, the most violent section of Philadelphia. The Fourth's boundaries (The Delaware River, South Street, Broad Street, and Fitzwater Street) encompassed parts of the old districts of Southwark and Moyamensing, and it was in the latter that

McMullin first rose to fame and power. He was born in 1824, the son of a grocer at Seventh and Bainbridge. The future boss held a variety of jobs before he settled into politics. Apprenticed first to a printer and then a carpenter, he returned to work in his father's store for a time before joining the navy. After his enlistment expired, he came back to Philadelphia in the mid-1840s. At this point McMullin's later career began to take shape.

He became a member of a gang which used a market place in Moyamensing as its headquarters. In August 1845 this group assaulted several persons, and an officer arrested McMullin for his part in the affair. With his credentials as a rowdy established. McMullin enlisted in a local regiment and fought in the Mexican War. Afterwards he joined the Moyamensing Hose Company, one of the most notorious fire associations. The activities of the volunteers and the numerous gangs in the district made that area the most dangerous part of the metropolitan area. Their depredations, according to testimony before a grand jury in 1850, made ordinary citizens fear for their lives. One witness declared that the rowdies had formed political organizations, and had committed some of their violence under the pretext of campaigning for their favorite candidates.

In response to the deteriorating situation in Moyamensing, the grand jury indicted several persons who kept disorderly houses where rowdies congregated and handed the police a list of more than 100 other individuals whose reputations as dangerous characters made them liable to arrest. The results of the investigation remained secret while the police completed their preparations for a massive raid. One of their targets was a tavern at Fourth and Shippen where the Keystone Club, one of those political organizations which numbered rowdies among its members, had planned a meeting. The officers arrived at the saloon while the Club was in session in an upstairs room. At the door of the chamber "the officers were met by Wm. McMullin, who drawing a knife, made several blows" at the raiders. McMullin surrendered after a struggle and the patrolmen captured a few other Keystoners in a wild melee.

Politics, as well as a desire to suppress violence, probably played a role in the raid on the Keystone Club. The fall elections, held in October, were approaching and the Club was campaigning for the election of Horn R. Kneass, Democratic candidate for district attorney. Kneass won (a recount and investigation later nullified his victory) and the Keystoners were among the celebrants whom Kneass specifically commended for their zeal and exertions.

The Club and its followers were in a transition stage, moving from gang members to respected (if not respectable) citizens. Kneass represented the better element. A prominent Democrat in the 1840s, his conservative credentials earned him a place on the committee which successfully opposed the initial consolidation movement. By accepting the aid of the Keystone Club, Kneass and other politicians helped it become an eminent and powerful organization by the late 1850s. Rising from obscure origins and partially composed of disreputable types, the Club represented its party in trips outside Philadelphia and participated in important national political campaigns.

McMullin's power rose with that of the Keystoners. He became president of that group and opened a saloon in 1854 at Eighth and Emeline. After that date his power expanded considerably. He won election to the Board of Prison Inspectors and secured an appointment as Lieutenant on the Marshall's Police force. The Fourth Ward became a Democratic stronghold in the process. The ward's vote for Richard Vaux (Democratic candidate for mayor) in 1854 was one of the three largest in the city. When Vaux ran in 1856 and 1858 for the same office, McMullin's machine returned the greatest majorities of any ward for the mayoral aspirant.

McMullin's stranglehold on the Fourth Ward did not entirely eliminate violence there. He and his followers were too accustomed to the use of force for that to happen. Moreover, he could not control some assaults which occurred along South Street and elsewhere. Personal quarrels continued, and racial tensions, though considerably restrained, provided another source of trouble. But McMullin's political influence could channel some conflict into legitimate avenues, as when he secured the appointment of at least six volunteer firemen from the Moyamensing Hose to the police force. The presence of these men, and others like them, helps explain the paradoxical condemnation and praise of Mayor Vaux's policing policies. The *Public Ledger* complained that Vaux appointed disreputable men to the force; yet it complimented him for keeping "public order excellently preserved." The officers may have had reputations as rowdies, but they knew how to deal with disorder.

The emergence of a single man in charge of the politics of a ward also reduced violence by limiting the number of persons and groups who were allowed to commit illegal acts. Influence brought immunity from prosecution or punishment, but only if the offender belonged to the ruling clique. Hugh Mara, a one-time member of McMullin's organization, testified in 1872 that the Squire, as McMullin had been nicknamed, was responsible for concealing the murder of a policeman by one of his henchmen. McMullin had also given the order which resulted in an attempt to assassinate a federal revenue detective in 1869. When the plot failed, he secured defense attorneys for his men and tampered with the witnesses. After the jury convicted the assailants, McMullin used his power to obtain a pardon for the men.

In 1867 McMullin led his Moyamensing Hose followers in a riot involving the Hope Engine Company. The Common Council appointed a special committee to investigate because the Squire was an alderman. Although the testimony of several witnesses led the committee to conclude that McMullin was guilty of mob action, the city solicitor informed the Council that it had no power to impeach the alderman. A motion not to print the testimony passed, and McMullin escaped unscathed.

While the Squire obviously continued some of his previous violent activities throughout the 1860s, the general pattern of assaults showed a relative decline during the same period. McMullin's machine certainly did not monopolize that type of offense, but his rise to dominance in the ward had reduced the number of contestants who sought power. Rival organizations could not successfully compete against him. The violence associated with political agitation therefore declined. The machine, under McMullin's direction, brought its own peculiar form of social order to the neighborhood.

Other factors certainly influenced crime patterns from 1840 to 1870. The age distribution of the city's population had a great deal to do with the level of gang activity, for example. If the general birth rate declined in the years between 1800 and 1860, as one study asserts, then the relative drop in gang incidents by the latter year may be partially attributed to that fact. Business changes also altered the crime pattern. As South Street developed into a low-income shopping district, the dominant type of offense in that area shifted from assault to theft.

Crime did not disappear during these three decades. Rather, it continued while certain trends laid the foundation for the basic discipline of a modern urban society. The achievements of these years were structural in nature; they concentrated on reforms of the way the city was organized. The creation of publicly paid police and fire departments helped to control the excesses of rowdies and destroyed their social roots. The rise of the ward boss, though not a welcome change in other ways, made a contribution to the decline in the violence which had racked the city for so many years. None of these innovations solved the crime problem; but they were important stepping-stones for the future.

STUDY GUIDE

1. What were the factors in Philadelphia during this period that led to different kinds of crime: burglary, robbery, personal assault, and gang violence?
2. Property crimes and personal crimes, such as assault and prostitution, tended to take place in different districts of the city. Why?
3. What were the several factors involved in the fights between fire clubs? What role did technology play in suppressing these fights and creating a professional fire-fighting force?
4. Johnson suggests that, though the suppression of violence and crime was supported by upper-class leaders, the creation of order and discipline in Philadelphia also depended upon a new use of the gangs and ward politicians that had been involved in the violence. Explain the relationship of these earlier forces to the creation of a professional police force and the establishment of order.

5. How does a modern city of our time differ from the Philadelphia described by Johnson, with respect to the following: the organization of criminal activity, the causes of fire, the purpose of arson, and the bases of gang violence?
6. In general, Johnson deals with lower-class criminal activity. What is meant by "white-collar" crime? Why is it normally not the object of police activity, and what other agencies in society are supposed to regulate the various kinds of white-collar crime?

BIBLIOGRAPHY

Like many words in our language, the word "urban" is derived from Latin, a fact that suggests the long, influential role of cities in European civilization. Though the colonists were largely farmers, they came from countries where government, culture, and commerce were centered in such large cities as London and Paris. Through much of our history, Americans have had a kind of love-hate relationship with cities, with the pastoral life of the farmer being held up as the ideal while many farm children wanted to escape to the big city. The attitudes of intellectuals are traced in Morton and Lucia White, *The Intellectual Versus the City* * (New York, 1962). The sizeable towns of the colonial period were mostly seaports, the history of which is traced in two books by Carl Bridenbaugh: *Cities in the Wilderness* * (New York, 1938), and *Cities in Revolt* * (New York, 1955). The growth of cities has frequently been closely related to the development of transportation, commerce, and manufacturing. David T. Gilchrist, ed., *The Growth of the Seaport Cities, 1790–1825* (Charlottesville, Va., 1967) examines developments along the Atlantic seaboard in the first decades of the new republic.

The history of particular cities can serve as case studies that illustrate general patterns of urban development. A great many "biographies" of cities have been published; two illustrative works are Bayrd Still, *Milwaukee*, rev. ed. (Madison, Wis., 1965), and Bessie L. Pierce, *A History of Chicago*, 3 vols. (New York, 1937–1957). The essay by David Johnson is from Allen F. Davis and Mark H. Haller, *The Peoples of Philadelphia: A History of Ethnic Groups and Lower-Class Life, 1790–1940* (Philadelphia, 1973), which examines poverty, housing for the poor, violence, and several of the ethnic groups of Philadelphia. A more general study of that city is Sam Bass Warner, *The Private City: Philadelphia in Three Periods of Its Growth* * (Philadelphia, 1968). The study of particular urban problems is also interesting. Charles E. Rosenberg, *The Cholera Years* * (Chicago, 1962) is on the widespread epidemics that hit many nineteenth-century cities, and Nelson M. Blake, *Water for the Cities* (Syracuse, N.Y., 1956) is an interesting study of the problem of getting water for the large urban populations. Demography, the study of population trends, is used in much research in urban history; a fine example of this sort of study is Stephan Thernstrom, *Poverty and Progress: Social Mobility in a Nineteenth Century City* * (Cambridge, Mass., 1964).

Some broader works treat cities of a particular type or of one region, as

indicated in the following two titles: Robert R. Dykstra, *The Cattle Towns* *
(New York, 1968) and Richard C. Wade, *The Urban Frontier: The Rise of
Western Cities, 1790–1830* (Cambridge, Mass., 1959). Two general surveys of
urban history are Constance Green, *The Rise of Urban America* (New York,
1965), and Charles N. Glaab and Theodore Brown, *A History of Urban
America* * (New York, 1967). Glaab has edited a volume of documents entitled *The American City: A Documentary History* (Homewood, Ill., 1963).
Some excellent writing on urban history has been in the form of articles in
historical magazines; Alexander B. Callow Jr., *American Urban History*,*
2nd ed. (New York, 1973), is one of several collections of such articles.

* Asterisk indicates book is available in a paperback edition.

This magazine was one of the many projects of the "Improvement Circles" organized by women in the Lowell Mills.

17

NORMAN J. WARE

The Industrial Worker

There are few developments in all of human history as important as the Industrial Revolution. This great movement created wealth, material goods, and services on a scale unimaginable to the people of any earlier society. It created the resources to provide a reasonable standard of living for virtually the entire society, and standards of education, medical care, and nutrition unknown anywhere in the world before. The essay by Joseph and Frances Gies (Reading No. 8) describes the role of new inventions in the industrialization of America. Equally important was the contribution of the millions of men and women who made up the labor force in the new factory system.

Industrialization had some unfortunate social consequences as well as beneficial economic ones, and the history of labor was not necessarily characterized by steady improvement in either wages or conditions. A number of factors determined the condition of workers in a particular period. Among them were the available supply of labor, the skills necessary to a particular job, the type of industry in which one was employed, and the attitudes of courts and other governmental agencies toward labor and business. During much of our industrial history, the economic theory that considered labor a commodity whose value would fluctuate with supply and demand, just as the cost of raw materials or manufactured products might, dominated American thinking.

The first half of the nineteenth century is an especially interesting period in American labor history. During these years, industrialization — with substantial technological innovation and the introduction of the factory system of labor — proceeded quite rapidly. Yet there was a widespread ambivalence about the new machinery and the new spirit of industrial growth. There was also a well-established social philosophy as to the position of classes, the responsibilities of the employer, and the roles of men and women in the labor force and in the home. Such deep social beliefs are not easily discarded; only grudgingly were they modified to meet the demands of the new industrialism. However, one of the interesting facets of labor history during this period is the way in which some of the new capitalists attempted to reconcile the old social philosophy of the paternalistic employer and his responsibility for the worker with the factory system of labor and the introduction of women workers.

In his book *The Industrial Worker,* Norman Ware studies the period 1840 to 1860, when the controversy over the factory system and the issues of child and female labor were fully developed. He gives a graphic picture of the wages and conditions in the iron industry and the needle trades and describes the two different systems of factory labor that developed. As you read the selection, consider the difference of labor then and labor now with respect to standard of living, type of work, and union organization.

The problem of primary importance for the industrial worker of the forties and fifties is to be found in the changes in his status and standards of living. A rising money wage is no sign of improved standards. Increasing commodity wages constitute a better test, but if accompanied by losses in other respects of greater significance, conclusions drawn therefrom are of little value. Working conditions, hours, speed, or effort must all be taken into account before an approximation can be made to a true estimate of the worker's condition. But in the last analysis the status of the worker is not a physical but a mental one, and is affected as much by comparisons with past conditions and with the status of other groups in the community as by the facts in themselves. In other words, the problem of status is one of satisfactions, and satisfactions are relative.

The depressions of 1837–39 left one-third of the working population of New York City unemployed. [Horace] Greeley estimated that there were not less than ten thousand persons in the city "in utter and hopeless distress with no means of surviving the winter but those provided by charity." The same was true, in a somewhat less pronounced degree, throughout the industrial districts. The New England mills were either closed down or running only part-time and undermanned. Between 1839 and 1843 wages generally fell from thirty to fifty per cent, and the improved business conditions of the latter year were not reflected in the wages of the workers. In 1844 the same amount of labor that had once produced for the mechanic and his family a comfortable subsistence was inadequate to maintain his standards, and his only alternative was increased effort or the reduction of his wants.

Pauperism was increasing. "Thirty years ago," said Evans, "the number of paupers in the whole United States was estimated at 29,166, or one in three hundred. The pauperism of New York City now amounts to 51,600, or one in every seven of the population." In New York State the proportion of the poor was said to be increasing and the wages of labor to be steadily declining.

The labor papers that sprang up in these years constantly complained that the condition of the worker was growing worse; that he was becoming more and more dependent on capital; that his resources were being curtailed and a new uncertainty had entered his life as to wages and employment.

In the iron industry, the wage per ton of ore produced was being constantly reduced. The following are the "prices" for certain kinds of work in the Pittsburgh district from 1837 to 1858:

Year	Boilers	Puddlers	Hammermen
1837	$7.00	$4.25	$1.25
1838	7.00	4.25	1.25
1839	6.50	4.00	—
1840	6.00	3.75	—
1841	5.50	3.75	—
1842	5.00	3.50	1.00
1845	6.00	4.00	—
1850	4.50	3.50	—
1858	3.00 to $4.00	1.90 to $2.50	—

After a steady decline of wages in the iron industry from 1837, a strike of the boilers occurred in February, 1842, as a result of notification of a further cut to five dollars a ton. The strike lasted until July, when the boilers resumed work at the reduced price. This price was continued until May, 1845, when a second strike occurred for the recovery of the one dollar a ton they had lost between 1840 and 1842. This lasted until August and resulted in the advance being granted. The new price, identical with that of 1840, lasted until 1850 when reductions were again proposed:

Puddlers	from $4.00	to $3.50 per ton
Boilers	from $6.00	to $4.50 per ton
Refiners	from $1.00	to $0.80 per ton
Scrappers	from $3.75	to $2.50 per ton
Heaters	from $1.37½	to $1.00 per ton ...

The strike against these reductions had not been broken by February when some of the mills were started with imported labor. Riots broke out in which the puddlers took possession of one of the mills, in the face of the protest of some of their fellows and the pistol of the mayor. The wives of the workers were said to have been the most violent of the rioters. Some slight damage was done and arrests were made. But by the end of March the mills were fairly well filled with imported help working at the reduced rates. Many of the strikers left the city and those who remained returned to the mills in the summer. Of those who were arrested, three men were acquitted and two men and four women found guilty. The men were sentenced to pay fines of six and one-fourth cents and costs and imprisonment for eighteen months. The women were sentenced to pay fifty dollars each and costs and imprisonment for thirty days. On petition of the jury that convicted them and of a large number of citizens, they were pardoned and the fines remitted in August, 1850. . . .

No class of workers was better paid than those in the building trades. Where shoemakers, printers, hatters, cabinet-makers, and so on were getting $4, $5, and $6 a week, the carpenters, plasterers, and bricklayers were getting $10. But even this latter wage was inadequate to maintain the worker's family at anything like a decent comfort standard. In 1851 the carpenters of Philadelphia struck for an advance of twenty-five cents a day which would give them a wage of $10.50 a week. The [New York] *Tribune* published a week's budget for a family of five, as follows:

Budget for Family of Five for One Week

Barrel of flour, $5.00, will last eight weeks	$0.62½
Sugar, 4 lbs. at 8 cents a pound	.32
Butter, 2 lbs. at 31½ cents a pound	.62½ (*sic*)
Milk, two cents per day	.14
Butcher's meat, 2 lbs. beef per day at 10c per lb.	$1.40
Potatoes, ½ bushel	.50
Coffee and tea	.25
Candle light	.14
Fuel, 3 tons of coal per annum, $15.00; charcoal, chips, matches, etc., $5.00 per annum	.40
Salt, pepper, vinegar, starch, soap, soda, yeast, cheese, eggs	.40
Furniture and utensils, wear and tear	.25
Rent	3.00
Bed clothes	.20
Clothing	2.00
Newspapers	.12
Total	$10.37

"I ask," said Greeley, "have I made the working-man's comforts too high? Where is the money to pay for amusements, for ice-creams, his puddings, his trips on Sunday up or down the river in order to get some fresh air, to pay the doctor or apothecary, to pay for pew rent in the church, to purchase books, musical instruments?" . . .

There was not in [this] period, or probably in any other, a more helpless and degraded class of workers than the needlewomen of the cities. Their condition had earlier enlisted the efforts of Mathew Carey and others, without appreciable result. They were incapable of organizing themselves permanently because of the semi-industrial nature of their trade and the surplus of that sort of labor. What little organization was achieved among them depended rather on the spasmodic efforts of "humane persons" who interested themselves in their behalf.

From 1840 to 1860 a complete revolution occurred in the tailoring industry as a result of the introduction of ready-made clothing in common use. Until 1835 the only clothing kept for sale was "shop clothing" which was sold almost entirely to seamen. The wholesale manufacture of clothes began in New York in 1835, but went under in the panic of 1837. In 1840 the trade revived and offered employment, such as it was, to thousands of women. At first, much of this work was sent into the country to be made up, but it was gradually being brought into the "factories."

The sewing machine made its appearance in the clothing trade in the early fifties. At first the tailor was required to buy his own machine and, as those who had sufficient savings to do this were few, those who had not were compelled to pay the machine tailor for straight stitching. The machine tailor soon discovered that his investment was not a paying one. His earnings were no greater than before and his savings were gone. The profit of the machine went to the bosses; "they got their work quicker and it was done better." . . .

There were at this time four groups of needlewomen corresponding to the classes of work and the stages of advance toward the complete factory system of a later date. The journeymen dressmakers, who were employed by the week, often worked fourteen to sixteen hours a day, and were paid from $1.25 to $2.50 per week. The dressmakers who went into the homes of their customers were better paid, receiving 62½ cents, 75 cents, and $1 a day. Apprentices were usually paid nothing for the first six months and boarded themselves. They were frequently required to pay the employer $10 or $15 for the privilege of "learning," and, if they were unable to pay, they worked for a year without wages and boarded themselves. Instead of being taught the trade, the apprentices were usually kept at plain sewing, and at the end of the apprenticeship two-thirds or three-quarters of them were not trained dressmakers at all. The last group, and the lowest in the scale in every respect, were those who worked in their own homes, calling for their work and returning to the shop with it when finished. There were ten thousand of these women in New York City alone in 1854, and their wages, hours, and conditions of work were inconceivably bad. Widows in Cincinnati were supporting children by making shirts for ten cents each and pants for fifteen and seventeen cents. It was estimated that they could make nine shirts in a week, or ninety cents for a long week's work. In New York, in 1845, some of the needlewomen were being paid ten to eighteen cents a day for twelve to fourteen hours' work, while others, who were more proficient, were paid twenty-five cents a day. Work which had brought 97½ cents in 1844 was paid only 37½ cents in 1845. The average earnings of these women were $1.50 to $2 a week, though many of them could not earn more than $1.

> A great number of females are employed in making men's and boys' caps [said the *Tribune* reporter in 1845]. By constant labor, 15 to 18 hours a day, they can make from 14 to 25 cents. We are told by an old lady who has lived by this kind of work for a long time that when she begins at sunrise and works till midnight, she can earn 14 cents a day. . . .
>
> The manner in which these women live, the squalidness and unhealthy location and nature of their habitations, the impossibility of providing for any of the slightest recreations or moral or intellectual culture or of educating their children, can be easily imagined; but we assure the public that it would require an extremely active imagination to conceive the reality.

When the industrial worker and his friends protested that there was white slavery in the North as evil as the black slavery of the South, they were thinking of conditions of this sort. But the wages, hours, and homes of these women were not their only difficulties. It was a common occurrence for one of the seamstresses to carry back to her employer, after a week's work, a heavy bundle of clothing in her arms and find that it would not pass his examination. Many of the cheap "slop shops" required the women to pay a deposit of the full value of the material before it could be taken out. When work fell off and there was no more to be given out, this deposit was frequently retained by the employer. Needlewomen receiving only five cents for shirts, on which they were required to deposit the full value of the material, were said to have been paid at the rate of ninety-six cents on the dollar. In some cases only a part of the money due was paid, the woman being told to allow the remainder to stand over for later settlement. In this way many of the employers who professed to pay good wages reduced them to the level of the worst. Instances were known where fifty cents was paid on account and the remainder postponed week after week until the claimant became discouraged and gave up trying to collect. In the meantime she had to neglect her chances of getting other employment. One woman after seeking work for two days managed to get something that paid her sixty cents for the first week. When she returned the goods, she was given credit on the books to be settled when the amount was worth while. In another case, the girl delivering her work and asking for payment was kicked into the street and left without money to cross the ferry to her home. . . .

In New York, in 1853, prices were as low as they had been in 1845: summer vests were eighteen cents; pantaloons, twenty cents; light coats, eighteen cents. A twelve-hour day gave a return of about twenty-four cents, "provided [the goods] were not returned upon the hands of the worker." Shirts were made for four, five, seven, and eight cents apiece; three of them were a hard day's labor and brought the worker from twelve to twenty-four cents a day. "The average yearly income of these women at the best of the above prices, all doing full work the year round, amounts to ninety-one dollars!"

The beginnings of the "sweating system" are to be found here. The *Tribune's* reporter described it in 1853 as a "middle system." Near one of the streets running from the Bowery to the East River an old Irish woman was found with four girls working for her. Their pay consisted solely of their food for six days a week. Another woman had hired four "learners," two of whom received only board and lodging, while the other two were paid one dollar a week without their food.

The milliners of New York were [no?] better off than the sewing-women. As apprentices they received no pay or board for a year, and, in the better shops, had frequently to pay a bonus for the privilege of "learning." The hours were from ten to twelve, and at the end of the year they were turned out to find employment, and a new batch of apprentices was taken on. All through the period and in very many trades the apprenticeship system had become little more than a cheap method of getting the greater part of the work done. There was no attempt made to teach the full trade. One or two journeymen were sufficient as overseers to supply all the craft knowledge and skill required for the shop and the routine work was done by so-called "apprentices." The journeymen milliners working from sunrise to 9 P.M. could earn from $2.50 to $3 a week. Their board and washing cost at least $2. . . .

. . .

The new industrialism found its completest expression in the textile mills of New England, New York, and Pennsylvania. Here the New Power was most firmly established and the new discipline most intense. In the barracks-like mills by the swift rivers of the northern seaboard the Industrial Revolution reached completion, and the lesser status of the industrial worker was revealed. And there developed in the forties a remarkable controversy over the Factory System, originating, in part, in the political field and involving the tariff question, and, in part, in the feeling that the new industrialism was alien to and destructive of American ideals and standards.

The introduction of the cotton industry in Massachusetts at the beginning of the century was achieved under difficulties that arose, on the one hand, from the want of a labor force and, on the other, from the English control of the new machines and the technical knowledge required to set them in operation. A new labor force was available in the women and girls of New England, once their initial aversion to the factory discipline could be broken down. The degraded condition of the operatives of the English mill towns was notorious, and Americans, including the Boston capitalists intent on cotton manufacture, had no desire to reproduce those conditions here.

"The question . . . arose and was deeply considered," said Nathan Appleton, "whether this degradation was the result of the peculiar occupation or of other and distinct causes. . . ." The matter was decided in favor of the latter hypothesis, and the Boston capitalists who had interested themselves in cotton manufacture proceeded to make such arrangements as seemed good to them to attract the New England women into the mills and guard them from immoral influences as best they could.

This protection involved what is known as the "Waltham System" which was copied in the foundation of Lowell and came to be regarded as the perfection of what an industrial community should be. The basis of the Waltham system was the company boarding-house, where the girls were required to be in at 10 P.M. and generally to live under the somewhat fictitious supervision of the boarding-house keeper. Upon this basis was erected a puritanical paternalism originally intended for the welfare of the girls, but capable — in the hands of agents less high-principled than the early mill-owners — of being turned into a very effective and harmful despotism. In addition to the boarding-houses, the Waltham system involved the payment of wages in cash, the "moral police" or community censorship of morals, the requirement that the girls should attend church, discharge for immoral conduct, and a thorough understanding among the corporations as to wages, hours, and the "blacklist."

> I visited the corporate factory establishment of Waltham within a few miles of Boston [said Harriet Martineau in 1834]. The establishment is for spinning and weaving of cotton alone and the construction of the requisite machinery. Five hundred girls were employed at the time of my visit. The girls can earn two and sometimes three dollars a week besides their board. The little children earn one dollar a week. Most of the girls live in houses provided by the corporation. . . . When sisters come to the mill it is a common practice for them to bring their mother to keep house for them and some other companions, in a dwelling built by their own earnings. In this case they save enough out of their board to clothe themselves and have two or three dollars to spare. Some have thus cleared off mortgages from their fathers' farms; others have educated the hope of the family at college; and many are rapidly accumulating an independence. I saw a whole street of houses built with the earnings of the girls; some with piazzas and green venetian blinds, and all neat and sufficiently spacious.
>
> The factory people built the church which stands conspicuous on the green in the midst of the place. The minister's salary, eight hundred dollars last year, is raised by a tax on the pews. The corporation gave them a building for a Lyceum which they have furnished with a good library and where they have lectures every winter, the best that money can procure. The girls have, in many instances, private libraries of some value.
>
> The managers of the various factory establishments keep the wages as nearly equal as possible and then let the girls freely shift from one to another. . . . The people work about seventy hours a week on an average. . . . All look like well-dressed young ladies. The health is good, or rather it is no worse than elsewhere.

This picture is somewhat *couleur de rose* and naïve in its treatment of the compulsory tax for the upkeep of the church and the uniform wage and freedom of movement of the operatives. The only fault Miss Martineau found with the mills was the overcrowding of the boarding-houses where girls some-times slept three in a bed and six or more in a room. She must have been misinformed as to the hours of labor which were nearer seventy-five than seventy a week. . . .

In sharp contrast with the Waltham system there was found in the Middle States, and especially in Rhode Island, what can be called the English system of *laissez-faire*. This was the original method of cotton manufacture in New England, having been established by Samuel Slater at Pawtucket before the beginning of the century. The Rhode Island system, to be found also at Fall River, Massachusetts, was not a conscious method at all, but simply a growth along English lines with the material at hand. Instead of employing adults almost exclusively, as in Massachusetts, whole families were employed, and it is in this district that child labor was chiefly found. There was no attempt made by Slater and those who followed him to guard the morals of the operatives or to do anything for them within or without the mills. There were no company boarding-houses, the operatives being allowed to find what homes they could, and instead of cash wages being paid, factory stores were established and store orders issued. The first mill opened by Slater was op-erated by seven boys and two girls between the ages of seven and eleven, and some of the early mills recruited children from the almshouses and overseers of the poor.

The contrast of the two systems is interesting because the scarcity of fac-tory labor was probably as great in Rhode Island as in Massachusetts, which suggests that the Waltham system was the result of the Puritan traditions of the Boston capitalists, rather than the real necessities of the case, while the presence of the company store in Rhode Island reveals it as less a conven-ience for the operatives than a means of exploitation by the companies. For if the company store had been a real convenience to the operatives, as is often assumed, it would probably have been found in Lowell rather than Pawtucket, though the large percentage of single women at Lowell would have reduced its trade. . . .

But the essential difference between Lowell and Rhode Island or Fall River was the psychological one between paternalism and *laissez-faire*. Gen-eral Oliver, who had been an agent at Lowell, visited Fall River in 1855 and was greatly shocked by the attitude of the agents at the latter place.

> I inquired of the agent of a principal factory whether it was the custom of the manufacturers to do anything for the physical, intellectual, and moral wel-fare of their work-people. . . . "We never do," he said. "As for myself, I regard my work-people just as I regard my machinery. So long as they can do my work for what I choose to pay them, I keep them, getting out of them all I can. What they do or how they fare outside my walls I don't know, nor do I consider it my business to know. They must look out for themselves as I do for myself. When my machines get old and useless, I reject them and get new, and these people are part of my machinery."

A Holyoke manager found his hands "languorous" in the early morning because they had breakfasted. He tried working them without breakfast and got three thousand more yards of cloth a week made.

It would appear at first glance that there could be no comparison, from the standpoint of the operatives, between the two systems; that the puritanical paternalism of Lowell was infinitely superior to the callous indifference of Fall River. Nevertheless, two rather unexpected facts emerge to modify this opinion: the attack on the factory system by the intellectuals centered not on the evil conditions of Fall River, but on the relatively admirable conditions of Lowell; and the operatives' revolt began at the former rather than at the latter place. This would suggest, at least, that there were elements in the Lowell situation that were regarded as even more harmful than bad conditions, and that the Fall River system left the operatives greater initiative. It would be unwise to press these deductions too far because it is equally possible to say that the Fall River revolt was the result of exceptionally bad conditions and the attack on Lowell, the result of its proximity to Boston.

The Lowell factory system was being attacked in our period from two directions. The Battle of Books represented the opposition of the intellectuals and was directed chiefly against the alleged tendency to degrade the morals and health of the operative, while the attack of the operatives themselves was chiefly against the "tyranny" and "despotism" of the system, its increasing discipline and antirepublican nature.

> That the factory system contains in itself the elements of slavery, we think no sound reasoning can deny, and every day continues to add power to its incorporate sovereignty, while the sovereignty of the working people decreases in the same ratio.

Like other workers of the period, the factory operatives — men and women — felt that they were losing something of their dignity and independence, so that, from the point of view of the workers, much of the heated argument over factory conditions missed the point. The worker objected to his cage, whether it was gilded, as in Lowell, or rusty and unkempt, as in Fall River.

In the matter of discipline the Fall River system had advantages over that of Lowell. Once out of the Fall River mills, the worker was free, while in Lowell there was hardly an hour of the day or a relationship of any sort that was not covered by the regulations, written or understood, of the corporations. . . .

The factory controversy began with an editoral in the Boston *Daily Times* (Democrat) for Saturday, July 13, 1839, entitled "A Manufacturing Population." The interest of the *Times* in the matter was partly political. The Whigs had always contended that the factories gave easy, pleasurable, and remunerative employment to women and girls who would otherwise have been idle, and that the fears of the opponents of the system were unfounded. The *Times* undertook to show that the young girls are compelled to work in unhealthy confinement for too many hours every day; that their food is both unhealthy and scanty; that they are not allowed sufficient time to eat: . . . that they are crowded together in ill-ventilated apartments in the boarding-houses of the corporations, and that in consequence they become pale, feeble, and finally broken in constitution . . . and that hundreds of the vilest of the female sex throng to the manufactories with corruption in their manners and upon their tongues to breathe out the pestilence of the brothel in the boarding-places.

The *Times* objected to the fact that the girls were made to board at the company houses except when they had friends or relatives in Lowell; that they had to be in their rooms at ten o'clock; and that the price of their board was fixed by the corporations at $1.50 a week and deducted from their wages. It was claimed that the price of board was too low, that a decent table could not be maintained at the price when potatoes were selling for 75 cents to $1 a peck, flour was $9 to $12 a barrel, and beef 10 to 16 cents a pound. The girls were underfed and unhealthy-looking, except the newcomers from the country.

In the early days, the *Times* contended, conditions had been better. When the Merrimack Mill was started, besides the workmen employed from Europe the proprietors had to rely on such girls as they could obtain to attend the looms and spindles. These girls came in gradually from the surrounding country — daughters of farmers and mechanics, "generally poor, but of unblemished reputation." Provisions were cheap, the food sufficient, and the girls seemed happy and healthy. They dressed well and preferred the mills as their own mistresses to being servants. Many of them saved money and went home, but others squandered their earnings and found themselves tied to the mills. But the supply was still inadequate and the corporations had to send men out to scour the country through New Hampshire, Vermont, and Canada. Thus the permanent mill population increased and their dependence upon the corporations. The labor turnover was tremendous, one hundred girls arriving and leaving every day for several weeks in the spring and fall, but always some remained behind to swell the factory population, unfitted to be wives and mothers, in slavish dependence on the mills.

When the corporations began to realize, said the *Times,* that this permanent factory population was increasing, they reduced wages by agreement. On the first occasion the girls "turned out," but new hands were found, and "there has been created and there is now growing up in Lowell a manufacturing population whose tendency in the scale of civilization, health, morals, and intellectuality, is manifestly downwards."

As to the morals of the girls, the *Times* quoted a Lowell physician to the effect that

there used to be in Lowell an association of young men called "The Old Line" who had an understanding with a great many of the factory girls and who used to introduce young men of their acquaintance, visitors to the place, to the girls for immoral purposes. Balls were held at various places attended mostly by these young men and girls, with some others who did not know the object of the association, and after the dancing was over the girls were taken to infamous places of resort in Lowell and the vicinity and were not returned to their homes until daylight.

Another medical practitioner in Lowell stated that, in one week, he had more than seventy persons apply to him for remedies for venereal diseases, most of whom were girls. Occupants of brothels in New York and Boston who had become diseased were also said to have entered the mills. The late deputy sheriff of Lowell had stated that he had found three houses to which these professional prostitutes were in the habit of bringing factory girls.

Dr. Elisha Bartlett of Lowell replied to the *Times* articles in the Lowell *Courier,* and this was later published as a pamphlet under the title "A Vindication of the Character and Condition of the Females Employed in the Lowell Mills against the charges contained in the Boston Times and Boston Quarterly Review." The editor of the *Courier* also replied, as did Harriet Farley, editor of the *Lowell Offering.*

As is frequently the case in controversies of this sort, the opponents were not talking about the same thing and never really came to grips. Bartlett insisted that the morals and health of the factory operatives were good, while the *Times* claimed that their morals and health were getting bad. Bartlett was thinking of a condition, often of a past condition, and the *Times* of a tendency. Neither was concerned with the problem that bothered the worker, the problem of social status and freedom. The mill girls had been, and the majority perhaps still were, what Bartlett claimed, but at the same time they were becoming more or less what the *Times* insisted they were: "a permanent factory population" of a more degraded sort than the New England mill girls of the twenties and thirties.

Dr. Bartlett dealt chiefly with health, morals, chances of marriage and wages, and his argument was followed quite closely by Miles and Scoresby in 1845. He made a statistical comparison between Lowell and Portsmouth, New Hampshire, . . . and declared that "the manufacturing population of this city is the healthiest portion of the population." He defended the morals of the factory girls, claiming that the mill overseers, the "moral police" of the corporations, and the censorship of the girls themselves kept the tone of the community high. He insisted even that the morals of the girls improved on coming from the country where all was not as pure as it looked.

As to wages, the average, clear of board, amounted to about two dollars per week. The number of depositors in the Lowell Savings Institution was 1976 and the amount of deposits $305,796.75. Of these depositors, 978 were factory girls. The amount of their deposits is not given, but it is estimated at not less than $100,000, while it was a common thing for a girl to have $500 in the bank. Bartlett claimed that the girls' chances of marriage were good and the boarding-house keepers quite able to make a living and supply satisfactory food if they managed properly.

The controversy was continued by a reply to Dr. Bartlett which appeared in the *Vox Populi* of Lowell in 1841. This was written by "A Citizen of Lowell" and was later published under the title "Corporations and Operatives: Being an exposition of the condition of factory operatives and a review of the 'Vindication' by Elisha Bartlett, M.D." The reply was an able discussion that left nothing of Bartlett's mortality and marriage statistics, but began in a demogogic vein that tended to obscure the value of the later argument. The Lowell "Citizen" charged the defenders of the factories with being paid "servants of interested aristocracies," a "pensioned press" and "bought priesthood." The question of the hours of employment, that later supplanted all others, was here first emphasized. It was claimed that the operatives had only fifteen minutes in which to eat their meals when time was deducted for going to and from the boarding-houses. The price allowed for board had been $1.25 until 1836, when it had been raised to $1.37½ because the boarding-house keepers had been unable to live. There it remained until 1841, when it was again reduced to $1.25. The boarding-houses were overrun with vermin. The hours in the mills were nearly thirteen a day and not less than twelve and one-half of actual toil. But this was to reckon only the time actually in the mills, and even this was not correct because some corporations cheated the operatives by starting before the ringing of the bell. Reckoning the time stolen and the time occupied in preparing for meals, eating, and going to and fro, the operatives were engaged fifteen hours out of the twenty-four.

Not only were the hours long, but they were getting longer. The corporations were adding to them "year after year, week after week, minute by minute," until they ran fifteen minutes a day longer in 1841 than twelve years before. "I do not believe," said the "Citizen of Lowell," "that there is upon the face of the earth any large class of persons who labor incessantly for so many hours each day as do the factory operatives of New England." . . .

STUDY GUIDE

1. How did each of the following contribute to the debased condition of labor described by Ware: technological changes such as new, heavier machinery; machinery that required less skill to operate; a labor surplus; social attitudes toward labor?

2. In terms of potential labor force and the type of labor involved, why were the needle trades more susceptible to exploitative labor conditions than some other industries?

3. What were the differences between the Waltham and the Fall River or Rhode Island systems of factory labor? Which of them seems more exploitative and which more paternalistic? In what ways did the less paternalistic system have advantages from the worker's point of view?

4. In another country or another period, the expansion of the available labor force by the introduction of women, children, and immigrants might not have resulted in a general degradation of the position of all labor. What, in the position of labor in the early nineteenth century or in the general state of the Industrial Revolution at that time, might account for the fact that such degradation did happen in the United States?

5. What similarities and differences are there in the lot of the worker in the early nineteenth century and in the present with respect to: his ability to bargain to improve his position; the training necessary for his job; his mobility; his relationship to his employer; his security?

BIBLIOGRAPHY

While Ware's book is one of the best specialized works ever published on American factory labor, it is limited to the two decades before the Civil War. Also, there are many other aspects of the Industrial Revolution in the United States that merit attention, which were not within the scope of Ware's study. A number of books on technology and other subjects are listed in the bibliography following the selection by Joseph and Frances Gies (Reading No. 8). Carl Bridenbaugh, *The Colonial Craftsman* * (New York, 1950) is an interesting study of labor in the preindustrial period. Two of several works that elaborate on the topics of which Ware writes are Caroline F. Ware, *The Early New England Cotton Manufacture: A Study in Industrial Beginnings* (Boston and New York, 1931) and Hannah Josephson, *Golden Threads: New England's Mill Girls and Magnates* (New York, 1949). The writings of factory women themselves are published in Philip Foner, ed., *The Factory Girls* (Urbana, Ill., 1977), while Steve Dunwell, *The Run of the Mill* (Boston, 1978) is a marvelous collection of photographs of the factories, with an accompanying text. Indicating an extraordinary versatility, Anthony F. C. Wallace turned from studying the Seneca Indians to examining the social and economic life of small factory towns in his book *Rockdale: The Growth of an American Village in the Early Industrial Revolution* (New York, 1978).

There are a number of one-volume surveys of American labor history that carry the story beyond the Civil War. Henry Pelling, *American Labor* * (Chicago, 1960) is a very brief introduction. Foster R. Dulles, *Labor in America: A History* * (New York, 1949) and Joseph G. Rayback, *A History of American Labor* * (New York, 1959) are longer works. Barbara M. Wertheimer, *We Were There: The Story of Working Women in America* (New York, 1977) is a popular study of the subject.

---

* Asterisk indicates book is available in a paperback edition.

VI WESTERN EXPANSION AND CIVIL WAR

At the time of the Treaty of Paris of 1783, the boundaries of the United States had been set at the Mississippi River on the west and along the 31st parallel on the south. By 1853, the country had added the huge territory of the Louisiana Purchase, acquired Florida from Spain, and swept westward over Texas, California, and Oregon into every square mile of territory that was to make up the continental United States. This breathtaking acquisition of territory had involved American intrigue in Florida, revolution in Texas, a blustering threat of force in Oregon, and full-scale war against Mexico. Generally, however, the American people were in advance of their government. Land — to settle on or speculate in — rather than gold, was the chief lure that drew Americans westward into lands beyond the borders of their own country.

The acquisition of millions of acres of land beyond the Mississippi was one of the crucial factors in accentuating the sectional conflict that had begun in the 1830s. During the 1850s, the morality of slavery was the overriding issue in the minds of abolitionists. But for most people of both the North and the South a matter of more immediate concern was whether or not slavery would expand into the western territories. The slogan of the Free Soil party of the North embodied the several aspects of sectional conflict: "Free Soil, Free Speech, Free Labor, and Free Men." This party's concern that labor and soil in the West be free points up the economic division of North and South. But the other parts of the slogan — free speech and free men — suggest that the country was also divided by psychological and social differences.

By 1861, many national social institutions, including the major religious denominations, had broken apart along sectional lines. And by that time, many thousands of Southerners saw the triumph of the northern Republican party in the 1860 election as not simply a political defeat but a threat to all southern institutions and to the southern way of life.

The first reading in this section describes the travails of the pioneers, who, as they went westward with their few belongings in a wagon, discovered an incredibly rugged and beautiful land beyond the settled communities they left. As Americans moved across the country from the eastern seaboard to the Pacific, they modified the environment at virtually every step. The second reading describes the destruction of wildlife, such as the beaver and the buffalo, and the astoundingly rapid use of American forests and other resources. In terms of casualties, the conflict of North and South was the most costly war in American history. The last reading describes the feelings of the men who were turned into soldiers to fight those who had been their countrymen. American society had been torn asunder, and the reweaving of the disparate threads into a new social fabric was to prove a long and trying process.

Two extraordinarily courageous members of the Donner Party, James and Margaret Reed managed to survive near starvation, blizzards, and scorching deserts to reach California.

18

THOMAS FRONCEK

The Way West

Few movements in all of our history have captured the imagination as has the settlement of the great American West. The image of the sturdy pioneer, plodding beside his lumbering covered wagon, fighting off Indian attacks, fording swift streams, and finally looking out upon the blue Pacific has become enshrined in American folklore and on Hollywood celluloid. There is much in all of this that is sheer myth, but there is also much that is true.

The earliest opening of some American frontiers was accomplished by lone trappers and hunters who, because the game was there or because they weren't comfortable in more settled communities, turned their paths westward. Though such men served as guides and added to the scant geographical knowledge of nineteenth-century America, they were relatively unimportant in western settlement. Even in the case of the fur trade, the single hunter was rapidly supplanted by the business organization, and it was John Jacob Astor's Pacific Fur Company that led thousands of other Americans to dream of the Oregon country.

In fact, settlement of the West in large numbers required careful planning, substantial equipment and supplies, organization, and community effort. Whether seeking gold in California, land in Oregon, or a religious Eden in Utah, the pioneers usually went west in a group. Leaders were chosen, supplies carefully assembled, and laws of the trail set down. While pioneer life was that of an organized community, rather than that of the lone scout, this does not mean that the stories of struggle and hardship are entirely mythical.

Americans today are still a migratory people, and until very recently California was the chief lodestar. But as we speed on interstate highways alongside the Platte River or fly over the Rocky Mountains in jet comfort, we have little idea of life on the trail in 1848. For this we must turn to the diaries of the men and women who made the long trek, who gave birth to infants on the wooden beds of wagons and pushed on the next day, and who buried children and parents in unmarked graves to which they would never return.

Thorough as might be the preparations and organization of a wagon train party, discipline and control could easily break down. As the party became lost, as food got low, as delays led to impatience and short tempers, splits and sometimes violence might develop. In at least one case, that of the famous Donner Party, blizzard conditions and lack of any food at all led eventually to cannibalism. Such an occurrence seems foreign indeed to our comfortable existence, until a plane crash in an isolated region of our world creates a similar set of circumstances and an equally tragic outcome. The following selection by Thomas Froncek describes the high hopes, and the gruesome end, of the Donner Party on the California Trail.

To the brothers George and Jacob Donner the way to California seemed clear and simple. Both in their sixties, solid and well-to-do thanks to their own hard work, but beginning now to feel their age and the long Illinois winters in their bones, the two men sat in the glow of the hearth-fire that winter of 1845–46 and turned again the well-thumbed pages of *The Emigrants' Guide to Oregon and California*. With the snow piled outside and the Sangamon River lying frozen in its bed, the brothers read with wonder the book's description of a golden land. In California, winter was warmer than summer, said the author — one Lansford W. Hastings. Hollyhocks and sweet william bloomed at Christmastime. Clover stood five feet high and the cattle never had to be fed or housed. "Here perpetual summer is in the midst of unceasing winter; perennial spring and never failing autumn stand side by side, and towering snow clad mountains forever look down upon eternal verdure."

Oh, yes, Oregon had its virtues, Hastings admitted. It was more like the country most Americans knew: green and wooded. And it was claimed by the United States, not by Mexico. Also, the trail was shorter. But for much

From "Winterkill 1846" by Thomas Froncek. © 1976 American Heritage Publishing Company, Inc. Reprinted by permission from *American Heritage* (December 1976).

of the year Oregon was gray and misty; and the last stretch of the trail —
the part that took you through the Cascades — was dreadfully difficult. No,
it was better to try for California. Besides, said Hastings, it was possible to
shorten the trip.

All you had to do was follow the regular wagon route toward Fort Bridger
— the road used by emigrants ever since the first small band of American
settlers made its way overland in 1841. You started at the Missouri frontier
town of Independence, headed northwest across the grassy plains of what is
now Kansas and Nebraska, followed the North Fork of the Platte River to
Fort Laramie, and continued westward to South Pass, the broad, gently sloping plain that took you over the crest of the Continental Divide. From there
you headed southwest to Fort Bridger.

Then, instead of making the long, northward swing to Fort Hall and
down the Humboldt River, you took Hastings' shortcut: "bearing west
southwest, to the Salt Lake, and then continuing down to the Bay of St.
Francisco."

What could be more sensible? Anyone who glanced at a map could see
that the Fort Hall trail made sense for Oregon but not for California. Was
it not reasonable to suppose that there was a more direct route across the
still unmapped spaces that lay due west of Fort Bridger? Now here was this
man Hastings saying it was so. And in print. Between the polished leather
covers of a book!

So George and Jacob Donner made their decision: they would venture
the new route and get to California just that much sooner. It was a decision
that would have them remembering fondly, before another winter was out,
the comforts of their Illinois homesteads.

The trouble was that in 1845, when *The Emigrants' Guide* was published,
neither its author nor anyone else had yet broken the new route to California. So far, the so-called shortcut existed only in Hastings' imagination.
A restless young schemer from Ohio in whose head swirled dreams of empire, Hastings had written his book and created the cutoff as a means of
attracting enough American settlers to California to overthrow the Mexican
regime and declare an independent republic. Then, of course, the new government would need leaders and there he would be: Lansford Hastings himself, California's own Sam Houston.

Unfortunately the abstract logic of Hastings' new emigrant trail bore no
relation to the uncompromising facts of geography. The country that Hastings so blithely swept away with his pen was some of the worst for wagon
travel in the United States. Between Fort Bridger and the Great Salt Lake
lay the Wasatch Range — boulder-strewn, canyon-cut, and covered in many
places with miles of tangled scrub forest. And beyond the Salt Lake lay the
alkaline wastes of the Great Salt Lake Desert. It was a country that the
Rocky Mountain fur trappers had known and avoided for twenty years but
had failed to record except in their own heads. The fact was that in the

spring of 1846 the general public had plenty of legend but little hard information about the Far West. It was as though no white man had ever trod the Wasatch or the Salt Desert wilderness. No map showed what that terrible country was like. John Charles Frémont, whose widely read accounts were full of wonderful descriptions and adventure stories, inspired any number of restless young easterners to strike out for the far country — or to dream of doing so. But Frémont did not concern himself with opening new wagon routes, nor did he offer much information that would be useful to emigrants on the trail.

Hence the popularity of Hastings' *Emigrants' Guide*. Grossly inaccurate and not nearly so well written as Frémont's book, it nonetheless seemed to give the emigrants just what they needed — practical information about the Great Trek: how they could prepare for it, what they could expect along the way, and what they would find in the Promised Land. All up and down the Ohio and Mississippi valleys that winter Hastings' book was being read, talked over, and passed from hand to hand.

As to Hastings' proposed new route, vague as it was, there was about it that air of self-evident logic. Moreover, the theory of a more direct route seemed to be confirmed by Frémont's exploration of 1845. Arriving at Sutter's Fort (now Sacramento) at the end of that year, Frémont reported that he had crossed the Salt Desert and had pushed his way over the high Sierra just ahead of the snow. He was gaunt and worn from the ordeal, even though he had made the journey on horseback. Yet he declared grandly that the route he had just explored was "decidedly better" for wagons, being considerably shorter and "less mountainous, with good pasturage and well watered." Frémont, it seems, was cut from the same cloth as Hastings. Both were optimistic to the point of being irresponsible.

Encouraged by Frémont's report, Hastings started east from Sutter's Fort in mid-April, 1846, to scout the trail for himself finally and to persuade as many westward-bound emigrants as he could to follow him back to California. The party with which he traveled seems to have included a number of people who did not share his enthusiasm for the golden shore. As the saying went, they "had seen the elephant" and were going home. But Hastings was seldom perturbed by opposition; and at any rate, a man could not always choose his traveling companions. So the party moved east, over the Sierra and along the Humboldt River trail: a trickle of humanity against the westward tide.

In Illinois, meanwhile, George and Jacob Donner, together with their friend James Frazier Reed, a local furniture manufacturer, prepared to join the more than two thousand emigrants who were starting for Oregon and California that spring. Mustering in Springfield on April 15, they made a bustling and prosperous confusion: women in homespun, impatient to get started; white-topped wagons; dogs; children; high-booted teamsters; the unruly herd of cattle and horses.

They were probably among the best-off emigrants on the trail that year. The Donner brothers — with their wives, with twelve children between them, and with four young men hired to help with the animals — were setting off with three wagons apiece: one packed with goods to be used for setting up trade and housekeeping in California; one loaded with supplies for the journey; and one to live in. George Donner's wife Tamsen was taking water colors, oil paints, and "apparatus for preserving botanical specimens." She was bringing books and school supplies for the young ladies' seminary she planned to establish in California; and she was bringing a quilt into which she had sewn ten thousand dollars in bank notes.

Reed, who was forty-six years old, who had served in the Black Hawk War with a would-be politician named Abraham Lincoln, and who had later done well for himself in the furniture business, had loaded his three wagons with all the luxuries of a successful life, including cushions, bunks, a stove, and a store of gourmet wines and brandies. Heading west in hopes of improving his prosperity, he was traveling with his wife, his ailing mother-in-law, four children, and five employees, all in their twenties and all Sangamon County neighbors: Baylis Williams, his sister Eliza, and three young men working their way west.

This was the company that set out from Springfield on April 16, heading west at last along the muddy Illinois springtime roads. At different stages along the trail, the caravan was lengthened by the wagons of other travelers, the numbers fluctuating as emigrant parties grouped and regrouped. There was Patrick Breen, for one. He joined up at Independence, bringing with him his wife, six sons, a daughter, and a friend named Patrick Dolan. Breen, a transplanted Irishman, had enjoyed enough success at farming on the Iowa side of the Mississippi Valley to be traveling with three wagons and his own substantial herd of horses and cattle.

Then there was an Illinois carriage maker named William Eddy with his wife and two children; and the Fosters; the Pikes; the Graveses; the Kesebergs and Wolfingers (both from Germany); the McCutchens; a cutler named Hardcoop, who was in his sixties; and various unattached young men. Among these last were a few who seem to have come along simply for the adventure.

But there were a number, among both the single and the married, who neither shared the prosperity of the Donners and the Reeds nor were particularly adventuresome, but who hoped only to escape the hard times that had beaten down so many people in the Mississippi Valley during the depression of the late thirties and early forties. In the West, at least, a man might still be able to buy land cheaply and get a fair price for the fruits of his labor.

So they had headed for Independence. And having traveled first with one party then with another, as chance, convenience, and temperament seemed to dictate, they had fallen in at last with the Donners. One train, after all, was much like another. It was the people that made the difference. The numbers grew, and when the Donner Party was complete it contained a total of eighty-seven men, women, and children.

The trek was hard going right from the start. The emigrants were towns-people and farmers, not frontiersmen. They were used to having regular meals and a roof over their heads. For them, life on the trail took some getting used to. It was not just the strain of traveling for weeks at a time in an unknown country, but also of struggling with the cattle and of repairing broken wagons; of sleeping on the damp ground or on a hard wagon bed; of eating poorly; and of being soaked through by rain and blistered by the sun. Quarrels were frequent even in the first days of the journey. Illness, too, was commonplace: colds, bronchitis, agues, bouts of diarrhea. Reed's mother-in-law, Mrs. Sarah Keyes, aged and feeble, lasted only a few weeks. She was buried under an oak near the Big Blue River in May.

The Donners and their friends were faring neither better nor worse than most bands of emigrants on the trail that spring. Indeed, they were even managing to enjoy themselves a little. Having joined an enormous train of seventy-two wagons (itself a conglomerate of smaller trains), they found in that village on wheels as much congenial company as they wished — more even than they had known at home. There were sewing circles, glee clubs, debating societies, open-air church services on Sundays, the pleasant rituals of the campfire, and any number of playmates for the children. And they enjoyed as much as anyone the ample beauties of the springtime prairie — that luxurious rolling plain of grass and wildflowers, where diarists waxed eloquent at the thought of "prairie schooners" sailing gracefully upon an emerald sea.

But as they climbed the long slope toward the Rockies, a subtle change occurred. The heat of summer was coming on and enthusiasm was giving way to boredom and a gnawing anxiety. The country, too, was different now. Instead of the broad, smooth prairie highway, the wagons had to be pulled through a hard, dry land that was cut up by ravines and dusty alkaline hills. Water and grass had grown scarce, and now there were Indians to worry about. This was Pawnee country, and a man had to be constantly on his guard to prevent his cattle from being driven off or himself from falling be-hind and becoming a victim of a Pawnee raiding party. Tempers flared and quarrels turned into fistfights. The big parties began splitting up.

Then came new frustrations. Just east of Fort Laramie the now frag-mented party to which the Donners were attached met up with a grubby old wanderer named James Clyman, who told them that Hastings' route was a mistake. Clyman, it turned out, was an old friend of James Reed: a moun-tain man who had first crossed the Missouri in 1823, had later settled in Illinois and Wisconsin, and had been in the same company as Reed (and Lincoln) during the Black Hawk War. Restlessness had turned his needle for California in 1844. But this spring of 1846, satisfied that there was little promise in the Promised Land, he had started for home, traveling east with Lansford Hastings over the very trail the emigrants were planning to take.

That trail, Clyman had found, was appallingly difficult even on horseback. Hastings was waiting at Fort Bridger to tell the emigrants otherwise. But Clyman, nominating himself a one-man safety committee, was riding ahead to warn everyone he met against taking the supposed shortcut. Now, on this night of June 27, 1846, he found himself sitting beside an emigrant campfire, telling his friend Reed and a number of other wagon captains (including, probably, George and Jacob Donner) about the terrible country they would encounter if they took Hastings' route. Clyman's advice (as he later recalled in his journal) was for the emigrants to stick to the regular wagon route. "It is barely possible to get through if you follow it," he told them, "and may be impossible if you don't."

No one welcomed the news. It was too disheartening to think of stretching their tedious journey still further by making the long swing north to Fort Hall. Besides, they were already beginning to feel the pressure of time. By their constant quarreling and reorganizing, by taking time out for fishing and sight-seeing and fistfights, they had fallen behind schedule. After two months of travel they were barely a third of the way to California. At this rate, they would not get to the Sierra until the end of October, when they would be running low on provisions and when the mountain passes were likely to be blocked by snow. Fear of such a prospect had already prompted one of those at the campfire, a Louisville newspaperman named Edwin Bryant, to trade his wagon and oxen for mules and packsaddles. Several of his companions had done likewise.

Bryant put Clyman down for a liar, suspecting ulterior motives, though he had no idea what they might be. Another wagon captain, an old Santa Fe trader and former governor of Missouri named Lilliburn Boggs, took just the opposite view. Impressed by Clyman's report, he decided to take his party to Oregon by way of Fort Hall. But Reed held out. Did Hastings' book count for nothing? And all those months of planning? Tense and irritable, Reed spoke up: "There is a nigher route," he insisted, "and it is of no use to take so much of a roundabout course."

So in the end it came down to the word of one man against another: the word of Clyman, who had no more to his name than a pack and a horse and a timber claim in Wisconsin (and that probably worthless), against the word of a man who had written a book! No, Reed would go the way he had planned and the Donners would go with him. They were respectable men. They listened to respectable voices.

One chronicler, an Oregon-bound emigrant who took leave of the Donner Party a short time later, noted in his journal that "The Californians were generally much elated and in fine spirits, with the prospect of a better and nearer road to the country of their destination. Mrs. George Donner [Tamsen] was an exception. She was gloomy, sad, and dispirited, in view of the fact that her husband and others could think for a moment of leaving the old road and confide in the statement of a man of whom they knew nothing but who was probably some selfish adventurer."

Yet the soundness of their judgment seemed only to be confirmed when, having trekked across the Wyoming desert and up the long slope to South Pass, Reed and the Donner brothers came down on the westward side of the Great Divide and rolled up to Jim Bridger's ramshackle trading post. There they found that a large party of emigrants had already started westward over the new trail, with Hastings himself at its head. Bryant's party, too, had stuck to its plan despite his misgivings and was taking the new route. Even better, here was Jim Bridger himself, one of the greatest mountain men of all, telling them just what they wanted to hear: that the new trail was open and easy, and that Hastings would be marking the route for those who followed.

Perhaps it was Bridger's name, perhaps it was his manner, or perhaps it was their own anxieties and frustrations that prompted Reed and the Donner brothers to trust "Old Gabe" where they had failed to trust Clyman. In any case, their trust was misplaced. Bridger was lying. Why? Old Gabe had his reasons. Two years before, a new shortcut had been established between South Pass and Fort Hall — one that bypassed Fort Bridger and so threatened to put its proprietor out of business. If, by some fluke, Hastings and his followers did stumble on a new route out of Fort Bridger, why then Old Gabe stood to regain his share of the emigrant trade.

But the members of the Donner Party knew nothing of Bridger's motives. They took him at his word. The matter was settled. After stopping a few days to rest the oxen, the party left Fort Bridger on the last day of July and headed west toward the Wasatch Range.

Meanwhile, the parties that had gone ahead were finding the trail infinitely more difficult than Hastings had led them to believe. Even Bryant and his friends, mounted though they were on mules, were almost beaten by the rugged canyons of the Wasatch, and they were half dead with thirst before they got across the Salt Desert.

For the party of wagons led by Hastings the journey was hellish. Called the Harlan-Young Party, after two of its captains, it consisted of four fragmentary trains totaling about sixty wagons. Having been delayed on the trail, and having found Hastings himself awaiting them at Fort Bridger, the leaders of the party had been persuaded to risk the new route in hopes of saving time. Hastings, confident as ever, had agreed to guide them. At last he had found his following. After that, his only problem was deciding where to lead them.

Hoping to find an easier route over the Wasatch than the one he and Clyman had traveled on their eastward journey, Hastings led them straight into the narrow canyon of the Weber River, where the wagons at times had to be alternately driven and floated in the riverbed, and at other times, dragged up and over the sheer cliffs with a windlass. Once on the desert — eighty miles of glaring salt and sand instead of the forty that Hastings had promised — oxen died and wagons were abandoned. The sun wore down even the strongest men.

Eventually the party found its way to the Humboldt River. But instead of gaining time, the emigrants had lost nearly three weeks. Hastings' cutoff had proved to be not only more difficult but also 125 miles *longer* than the Fort Hall route. When the Harlan-Young Party crossed the Sierra in early October the snow was already beginning to fly. They were the last party on the trail that year — except for that of the Donner brothers.

The Donner Party, now numbering its full complement of twenty-three wagons and eighty-seven people, had been running into delays almost from the time it had left Fort Bridger. Thirteen-year-old Eddie Breen broke his leg in a fall from a horse and needed tending. That took time. Then, at the head of Weber canyon, the party found a forked stick with a note stuck on it, instructing any that followed to send a messenger forward to Hastings, who would come back and personally direct them to a better route. So the party went into camp and Reed and two others rode ahead to find Hastings. Five days the party waited, while supplies dwindled and the season grew shorter. When Reed returned he was alone. The other men's horses, he said, had broken down. Hastings had decided he must stay with the Harlan-Young Party, but from the top of a rise, he had pointed Reed a new path between the hazy peaks of the Wasatch.

Crossing the forty miles to the valley of the Great Salt Lake took the Donner Party fifteen days of almost unimaginable labor — of pushing aside boulders, hacking through trees and underbrush, bridging swamps and rivers, backtracking out of blind canyons, and dragging the wagons up one ridge after another. The road they cut was a good one — a godsend to the Mormons, who poured over it a year later. But, for their contribution, the men and women of the Donner Party paid dearly in time and energy. . . .

The party went ahead as best it could and reached the oasis east of the Salt Desert at the beginning of September. Another note from Hastings: they should load up with all the grass and water they could carry, for the desert, instead of taking only one day to cross, would take two days and two nights.

The crossing took them six days and most of six nights, and it strained still further the sorry fabric of their morale. A few drove their teams hard, hoping to shorten the journey. Others went slowly, hoping to spare the animals and so insure they got across. Reed and the Donners fell far behind, their progress slowed by their fine wagons, so grandly laden with the comforts of home. Eventually they left the wagons and set off on foot, Reed carrying his three-year-old Tommy on his shoulders.

Everyone made it to the spring at the foot of Pilot Peak. No one died. But they had lost precious days in the crossing, and now they spent more days recuperating, searching for lost and dying cattle, and bringing up their wagons. Few of them had come through without some loss. A number, finding their herds reduced, set about lightening their loads. Reed, who had lost most of his cattle, had to abandon two of his opulent wagons and divide his gourmet delicacies among his companions. Lewis Keseberg left a wagon behind, and so did Jacob Donner, who had exchanged his solid prairie home and his wealth of Illinois land for wagons and teams and cash in hand. But one team was gone now. He had no choice. No matter how painful the decision, a wagon simply had to be left behind.

When they moved on again, September was almost half gone and they were at least a month away from the Sierra. But they had to keep going. They were too far along to turn back (it would have meant the desert again). Ahead, if they were lucky, the mountain passes might still be open. Yet already the fall chill was in the air, and one day, as they pushed on toward the Humboldt, the people of the Donner Party encountered a little desert snowstorm.

Meanwhile, beginning to fear that their food supplies would run out before they even got to the mountains, they sent two men ahead on horseback to appeal to Captain Sutter for provisions. One was young Charles Stanton, a bachelor; the other, a family man, William McCutchen, who left behind a wife and child. The rest pressed on and reached the main Humboldt River trail on September 30. Hoping to make better use of the sparse grass, the company had split into two sections and spread out, traveling a mile or so apart. The Donners led one group, Reed the other.

Everyone was on edge now. The most trifling matters sent men flying into senseless rages. It was an experience common to all parties on this last stretch of the trail, when the novelty of the trip had long since worn off and everyone was travel weary. But the toll was seldom as grievous as it now became for the Donner Party. Shortly after striking the main trail, Reed jumped into a quarrel between two teamsters and ended by killing one of them with a knife. Banished from the company (some had wanted him hanged), Reed rode off toward the mountains, leaving his wife and children in the care of his friends. A short time later, the old cutler Hardcoop fell behind and never caught up, and the men with horses refused to wear out their mounts by going back to look for him. Then another man mysteriously disappeared: the German Wolfinger, who was thought to be carrying a lot of money. Having lost most of his team on a difficult stretch of Nevada desert, he had stayed behind to cache his belongings. Two single men — partners, also from Germany — stayed to help, and returned in a few days with a story about how the Indians had killed Wolfinger and burned his outfit. (But later, on his deathbed, one of them confessed to the murder.)

By the time it reached the meadows at the foot of the Sierra, the Donner Party was a party no more, but a straggling collection of individuals bound by family ties alone. There were only a dozen or so wagons left. The great crate of books that was to be the germ of Tamsen Donner's girls' academy had been cached in the Nevada desert. Loosely guarded, the cattle wandered away or were driven off by "Diggers" — impoverished bands of desert Indians, most of them Paiutes. A gun went off by accident and a man was killed. William Eddy, who had lost all his stock, could find no one to take his children into a wagon.

But then at last they had some encouragement: a pack train came loping down the trail out of the west. It was Stanton, returning from Sutter's Fort with seven pack mules loaded with food and with two of Sutter's Indian *vaqueros* to guide them. Here was hope for the first time in weeks: food, and word that Reed had gotten through (though he had nearly starved), and that McCutchen had given out on the crossing and was laid up at Sutter's. Word, too, that the mountain passes were still open. Yes, there had been snow. They could see it on the peaks above them when the clouds gave way. But at this time of year, Stanton had been told, it would be nearly a month before the pass was blocked.

So they still had time, they told themselves. They could even afford to rest a few days in this grassy meadow before starting the push for the summit. (How long it had been since they had seen grass so tall, so green!) And having rested, they started in three small groups up the rugged canyon of the Truckee River, and reached Truckee (now Donner) Lake at the end of October. Just ahead loomed the summit: a wall of granite rising two thousand feet above the lake.

It was the worst obstacle on the whole grueling journey, not least because it came at the end, when men and animals were so worn down. Even the parties that had gone before — in good time and in fair weather — had found the effort exhausting. As many as fifteen yoke of oxen had to be used to pull a single wagon up the steep trail that led to the summit at Emigrant Gap. Every man was needed to handle the ropes and crowbars and to block the wheels. More than one wagon had gone over the side. But the job could be done, and now the first group of the Donner Party began struggling up the slope.

They found the pass already blanketed with five feet of snow — too deep for the wagons. They went back to the lake, waited out a day of rain (snow higher up), and started again, this time with their belongings packed on the backs of oxen. Stanton and one of Sutter's Indians made it to the summit. They could have gone down the western slope, but they turned back to help the others. The others were spent. They could not go on. They camped. They would go over the summit in the morning. But that night a snowstorm blew in and they awoke to find themselves half buried, the cattle gone, the snow too deep for them to move ahead. So again they turned back. Later, when the snow stopped, they could try again. (The season was still early; the snow might still melt.) Meantime, the men set to work building huts of logs and brush and canvas from the wagon tops. The lead group set up near the lake, while the Donner brothers, their families, and their teamsters went into camp five or six miles down the trail, at Alder Creek.

It snowed almost continuously for eight days. Reed and McCutchen, leading a relief train of pack horses up the western slope, pushed through shoulder-deep snow until they could go no further and had to turn back. The Donner Party was on its own.

It numbered eighty-two people now, many of them children. And they knew the worst: winter had come early and they were trapped. They could still hope that a relief party would reach them from Sutter's, but in the meantime they would have to survive as best they could by eating their cattle and hunting. But who among them could have imagined that snow could get so deep? They were plains people, not mountaineers. They did not know what to expect of a winter in the Sierra. There, in the high passes, thirty feet of snow has been known to fall in a month. By February it can be packed sixty feet deep.

Day by day the weather grew colder and the snow grew deeper. The people killed most of the cattle, hoping that the snow and cold would preserve the meat. William Eddy, the party's one good shot, managed to bag a coyote with a borrowed rifle: also an owl, two ducks, a squirrel, and then a grizzly bear. But after that there was nothing. The deer and elk had descended below the snow line and the bears were staying in their dens.

Twice in November those who were most able tried to get over the divide in hopes of saving themselves and their children and of bringing relief to the others. The second time, they actually got over and started down the other side. They had been using Sutter's mules to break a trail, however, and when the animals gave out, Stanton refused to go on without them. The mules were Captain Sutter's property; they must be returned. The party went back, and soon afterward another storm broke. All the remaining cattle and horses were lost under the snow, and so were Sutter's mules. The huts, too, were buried, leaving only tunnels to the doorways and holes where the chimneys stood. The light was shut out.

Early in December, young Baylis Williams died — not from starvation, for some food was left, but from malnutrition. A few days later, old Jacob Donner (who had dreamed of warm California) died and was buried in snow. Stanton and Uncle Billy Graves, who knew New England winters, showed the others how to make snowshoes. Thus equipped, a few, perhaps, could get out and get help.

The snowshoers (the party later known as the Forlorn Hope) started for the pass in mid-December — fifteen men and women, including a boy of twelve, Stanton, Eddy, and Sutter's two Indians, who knew the trail. They took with them all the food that could be spared — two mouthfuls a day for six days — for a journey that was to last more than a month.

They were weak from hunger before they even began. The snowshoes slowed them down. They got over the divide, though, and started down the western slope. The first to give out was Stanton. He had been in California once and had come back. He had made the attempt twice in November. But he was finished now. One morning, when the others were preparing to set out, he sat quietly smoking his pipe. "Yes," he said, "I am coming soon." The others went ahead. Stanton never rejoined them.

By the day before Christmas they had been laboring through snow, at eight thousand feet, for more than a week, and had been without food for four days. Pat Breen's friend, Patrick Dolan, was the first to speak what they all were thinking: They should draw lots, Dolan said, to see who should be killed. Some agreed. Others objected. Eddy suggested that two of them, selected by lots, shoot it out with revolvers. Again objections. Then it occurred to them: someone would die soon anyway.

That night a blizzard engulfed them. Most of them were ready to die now. They would have died, except that Eddy remembered a mountain man's trick: he made them huddle together under the blankets, until the snow covered them up and they were warmed by the heat of their bodies. And there they stayed for two days. Delirium overtook many of them. They were raving and shrieking. When it was over, four were dead: Dolan, Uncle Billy, a Mexican herder named Antoine, and the boy Lemuel Murphy. The survivors, crawling out of their mound, managed to strike a fire against a dead pine tree. They cut strips from the legs and arms of Patrick Dolan and roasted them. Eddy and the Indians refused to eat, but after another day, they, too, gave in. The other bodies were butchered and the flesh dried at the fire for the journey ahead.

Back at the huts below the divide Christmas was nearly as grim. The refugees had not yet reached the final extreme. But five were dead, and many of the others were reduced to catching and eating the field mice that came burrowing into the huts. They had begun eating oxhides, which they first boiled into a thick glue, and some of them were easing the pains of hunger by chewing tree bark. At the lake camp, a little frozen meat was still left, and one woman had hoarded a few handfuls of flour, from which she made a kind of gruel for the infant in her care. But probably none felt themselves more fortunate that Christmas than the four children of Mrs. Reed. For nearly eight weeks their mother had kept hidden away the fixings for a holiday stew, which she now brought forth in all its meager glory: a mess of ox tripe, a cupful of white beans, a few dried apples, half a cup of rice, and a tiny square of bacon. "Children, eat slowly," she warned, "there is plenty for all."

Across the divide, the snowshoers stumbled on — ten of them now. The weather cleared and held, and the snow, in places, had finally crusted over enough for them to walk without their snowshoes. Eventually they started to see patches of bare ground. But by then the dried flesh was gone and they were eating the rawhide of their snowshoes. The Indians! Kill the Indians!

But Eddy warned them and they slipped away. It was the edge now. Even Eddy was failing. Spotting a deer, he hardly had the strength to lift the rifle to his shoulder. Uncle Billy's daughter, Mary Graves, stood by, weeping. But that night they ate venison and slept soundly.

Another man died. They cut out his heart. His wife saw it roasted on a stick.

Seven of them were left now, five women and two men, one of them mad: William Foster pleaded with Eddy to kill one of the women, pleaded until suddenly Eddy was at him with a knife, threatening to kill him if he said it again.

Days later, food gone, they came upon the two Indians, collapsed and dying. Eddy would not kill them, but left the gun for Foster. They ate again. Eddy ate only grass.

By the end they were crawling as much as they were walking. A small log in the path became a major obstacle. Their feet were bloody pulp. On January 12 they stumbled into a poor Indian camp, were given acorn meal, and were helped on their way. They managed to go five days more before the last bit of strength was used up and they lay down to die. Eddy alone, helped by two Indians, dragged himself the last six miles to Johnson's Ranch, the first settlement on the edge of the Sacramento Valley. His bloody footprints marked the trail for those who would go to rescue his companions.

It was two more weeks before the first relief party got under way. The American settlers in northern California had just fought their last campaign against the Mexicans and it took time to raise enough volunteers. Incredibly, William Eddy, who was determined to rescue his wife and children, was among those who started from Johnson's on February 4; and he got well up into the mountains before being sent back with the horses.

The seven who continued on foot found the climb hard going, even though they were healthy and well fed. Beset by violent rainstorms, fresh snow, and then a blizzard, they would have died if the storms had continued. But they came through it, and crossed over the divide on February 18. When they dropped down to the snowy silence of the lake, they saw nothing but a level plain of snow; no smoke, no sign of life. In the stillness, they wondered if anyone was still alive — until a shout brought a strange, half-human creature clawing its way up out of a hole. Then others appeared. Skinny and white they were, with staring eyes and tiny, lunatic voices. Still others were found under the snow, in their dark, reeking huts: the sick and the dying, who could not move from their beds. The bodies of those who had died since the last storm lay at the top of the ramps, the survivors having had strength to drag them up, but not to bury them.

What had occurred at the camp during the two months since the Forlorn Hope had started for the pass was recorded in the nightmare memories of those who survived and in the diary of Patrick Breen — a spare chronicle of weather and death, of courage, meanness, faith, insanity. The indomitable

Mrs. Reed, taking with her her daughter Virginia, Eliza Williams, and a teamster named Milt Elliot, had tried just after New Year's to get over the pass between storms and had to turn back. "I could get along very well while I thought we were going ahead," Virginia later recalled, "but as soon as we had to turn back I could hardly walk." Keseberg's child had died, and Eddy's daughter, and a man named Spitzer, and Eddy's wife, and Milt Elliot. Keseberg had stayed in bed, hoarding valuables that were not his. Eliza Williams' mind had dimmed; she was an infant now.

At Alder Creek, George Donner lay dying, and Tamsen would not leave his side to go with the relief party. She had come with her husband this far, had followed him despite his stubborn insistence on taking Hastings' word when all wisdom went against it. She would not abandon him now, nor would Jacob's wife Elizabeth leave her youngest children or the body of her husband. The rescuers chose the four strongest of the Donner children, and the women dressed them in the good heavy clothes that had been packed the previous spring on the Sangamon. The others would have to wait for the next relief party, which was expected in a few days.

Twenty-three started out with the First Relief, including all of the Reeds. But Tommy and his eight-year-old sister Patty had to be sent back. They were too weak, too slow; they were endangering the whole party. "Well, Mother," Patty said, "if you never see me again, do the best you can."

James Reed, leading the Second Relief up the western slopes, met his wife and two children coming down. On March 1 he arrived at the lake camp, where he found his Tommy and Patty still alive. But Reed had come too late to spare the survivors the final horror. Bones were scattered about, tufts of human hair, half-consumed limbs. Reed recognized the bearded head of his friend Jacob Donner lying in the snow, the skull opened. Inside the Donner hut, he found Jacob's remaining children devouring the half-roasted heart and liver of their father. Elizabeth was dying. She would not eat the food she had prepared for her children. Reed led her and the children and fourteen others back down the mountain.

Eddy and Foster, who had fought viciously in the snow two months before, led the Third Relief over the divide in March. They discovered that their sons had died, and heard the now deranged Keseberg tell them he had eaten the two boys. George Donner, they found, was somehow still alive. Tamsen wrapped her three remaining children in warm clothes and bade them goodbye. Her body had stood her well; she was still in good strength. She would stay to care for her husband and to close his eyes when he died. Foster's mother-in-law, aged and dying, would have to stay; she was too far gone to travel. So, it seemed, was Keseberg.

It was the end of April before the last survivor was brought down from the mountains. The final party of rescuers found only carnage at Donner Lake and Donner Creek (as the campsites were soon being called) — carnage and the demented Keseberg. He was lying down, one of the rescuers remembered, "amidst the human bones, and beside him a large pan full of fresh liver and lights." At the creek, the relief party had found a kettle full of pieces of the body of George Donner. Nearby, on a chair, were ox legs which had been perfectly preserved in the now melting snow but which had not been eaten. Why, they asked Keseberg, had he not used the meat of the bullock instead of human flesh? "Oh! it's too dry eating!" he'd answered.

And what of Tamsen, who had been in such good health just three weeks before? The party could find no trace of her body, but they believed that Keseberg had killed her. He denied it for the rest of his life. After George Donner died, Keseberg maintained, she had come to the lake in delirium. Keseberg said he had warmed her and put her to bed, and the next morning had found her dead. But he also told the rescuers that "he ate her body and found her flesh the best he had ever tasted. He further stated that he obtained from her body at least four pounds of fat."

When the Donner Party reached the Sierra, it had included eighty-two people, five having died on the way there. Thirty-five died in the mountains, along with the two Indians who had come to rescue them. As Bernard DeVoto points out in his classic *Year of Decision: 1846*, the party had shared the common chance of the emigrant trail and "the common chance turned against them." But chance alone is not enough to explain that disastrous combination of events, personalities, and interests that overwhelmed them. Chance was one factor, but so was the ambition of Lansford Hastings, the business enterprise of Jim Bridger, the cumbersome prosperity of the Donner wagons, the obstinate temper of Reed, the early winter, the tardiness of the relief parties . . . perhaps even so little a thing as James Clyman's grubby looks.

Among the forty-seven survivors there were not many who came through without being haunted for the rest of their lives by the memories of what they had had to endure. The sight of a rising moon forever reminded Mrs. Foster of that moonlit night in the mountains when her companions in the Forlorn Hope set to work on the body of Patrick Dolan, while her brother Lemuel Murphy lay dead in her arms. Eliza Donner never forgot how she had eaten the bark of trees to ease the pain in her stomach.

For the most part the survivors settled into blessedly ordinary lives. Fourteen-year-old Virginia Reed, for one, received a marriage proposal even before she reached Sutter's Fort. "Tell the girls that this is the greatest place for marrying they ever saw," she wrote home to Illinois. Keseberg, for a time, reveled in his notoriety, finding an audience for his ghoulish tales in the bars of Gold Rush San Francisco — until the town grew more respectable and he sometimes found himself taunted and stoned when he stepped outside his house.

And then there was Lansford Hastings, whom William Eddy set out one day to kill. But Eddy was dissuaded by a friend from carrying out his plan. The Ohio schemer lived on, forever optimistic, chasing one elusive dream after another. During the Civil War he went to Richmond with a plan for seizing Arizona and southern California for the Confederacy, but nothing came of it. Later, he tried to establish a colony in Brazil for ex-Confederate soldiers. To forward his scheme he even published an *Emigrants' Guide to South America*. But in 1870, before his plans were well under way, he died of a tropical disease. Not for him a cold winter death, starvation in the snow.

STUDY GUIDE

1. Consider the preparations for a journey to California or Oregon. What would be the essential food, clothing, shelter, transportation, medicine, and tools? What mistakes did the Donner Party make in what they did and did not take along?

2. Many of the parties began with considerable organization and high hopes. What conditions contributed to the individual quarrels and disintegration of parties along the trail? In this respect, consider the impact of the break from established laws in older states, the isolation the emigrants endured, and the particular problems encountered on the trail.

3. Would you say that the Donner Party was defeated by Nature or that the group defeated itself? What role did each of the following play in the tragedy: inadequate preparation; poor advice; poor leadership; breakdown of morale and unity; their background as midwestern farmers confronting totally new conditions?

4. Unlike the Donners, millions of people stayed home in the settled communities of the East, and many went to Texas or Oregon, rather than responding to the lure of gold in California. In social and psychological terms, rather than in terms of gold and land, how do you explain the motivation of the people who left their homes and went West?

5. In general, the date of admission of a state into the Union indicates that the area had become fairly well populated with a settled society. Explain why California (1850), Oregon (1859), Nevada (1864), and Colorado (1876) attracted people so that they were ready for admission years before the Dakotas, Montana, Washington, Idaho, and Wyoming, which were admitted in 1889–1890.

BIBLIOGRAPHY

If you are interested in a fuller account of the Donner Party, consult the book by George R. Stewart, *Ordeal by Hunger: The Story of the Donner Party,**

rev. ed. (Boston, 1960). One hardly needs to say that the experience of that emigrant train was not typical, and one must consult other works to get a balanced picture of the westward movement. In his many volumes on the frontier, Professor Everett Dick discusses virtually every aspect of life in the American West. Three of his books that are available in paperback editions and provide marvelous reading are *Vanguards of the Frontier* * (New York, 1941); *The Dixie Frontier* (New York, 1948); and *Tales of the Frontier: From Lewis and Clark to the Last Roundup* * (Lincoln, Neb., 1964). The first historian to call attention to the great significance of the frontier in American history was Frederick Jackson Turner, whose ideas are discussed in the bibliography following the selection by Henry Adams (Reading No. 7). Most college libraries will have at least some of his stimulating essays; see especially his book *The Frontier in American History* (New York, 1920). Various aspects of the "Turner thesis" have been elaborated or subjected to severe criticism over the decades since he wrote. A number of essays on the subject have been collected in Ray A. Billington, ed., *The Frontier Thesis: Valid Interpretation of American History?* * (New York, 1966).

Ray Allen Billington, a student of Turner, carried forward his teacher's work in a number of studies, especially *Westward Expansion: A History of the American Frontier,* 3rd ed. (New York, 1967). The deep symbolic and psychological significance of the West for Americans is set forth in Henry Nash Smith, *Virgin Land: The American West as Symbol and Myth* * (Cambridge, Mass., 1950). There are special studies of the mining frontier, the cattle frontier, and of particular groups such as the Mormons. The following books are especially interesting: Rodman W. Paul, *Mining Frontiers of the Far West, 1848–1880* * (New York, 1963); Wallace Stegner, *The Gathering of Zion: The Story of the Mormon Trail* * (New York, 1964); and Paul Horgan, *Great River* (New York, 1954). Daniel J. Boorstin, in his book *The Americans: The National Experience* * (New York, 1965), argues persuasively that community cooperation, rather than individual effort, was the key to western settlement.

---

* Asterisk indicates book is available in a paperback edition.

*The decimation of the huge buffalo herds for hides was but
one aspect of the assault on the natural life of the West.*

19

RICHARD A. BARTLETT

The Rape of the Land

Both the backpacking movement and the increased use of recreational vehicles in recent years indicate a desire on the part of people to get out of the urban congestion in which they earn their livings and vacation in a more natural environment. Though a very extensive system of national and state parks has been developed, many of those who are trying to escape the city are likely to be disappointed. They may wait hours in a traffic jam to enter a national park, be crowded in with hundreds of others at a camp site, be forced off a hiking trail by a minibike, and finally be driven out by the blare of radios in the woods. In our time, it has become impossible for most Americans to experience the sort of natural wilderness conditions, with the limitless variety of bird, animal, and plant life, which at one time all of North America had.

Even an environment untouched by man undergoes change. Erosion and forest fires swept away soil and burned over woods before man was in the Western Hemisphere. The Indian too changed the landscape of North America, but neither he nor the forces of nature made changes on the scale that resulted from the massive migrations of people from other parts of the world to this land. To the generations of men who lived here in the colonial and early national periods of our history, the resources of nature seemed inexhaustible. Nature was there to be tamed, and cutting down forests, damming rivers, and killing beaver represented progress.

Very early in its history the United States decided on the quick private use of its natural resources. Most of the hundreds of millions of acres of land that make up the country was once government owned. Rather than retaining it as a great public

321

resource, Congress passed a series of laws between 1785 and 1862 to dispose of it, much of it as a free gift to new farmers, railroads, land speculators, and timber barons. Purposely or un- consciously, nineteenth-century Americans reduced the millions of beaver, buffalo, and several other species to a point where extinction was imminent.

Most readers of this volume will remember the "Winter of '77," when energy shortages forced the closing of schools and factories. The first major task addressed by the administration of President Carter was the development of a long-range policy on energy conservation. The crucial question is the willingness of the American people to accept limitations upon the temperatures at which homes are kept, the freedom with which air condition- ing is utilized, and the consumption of automobile gasoline. In the following essay, from his book on the settlement and ex- ploitation of the American West, Richard A. Bartlett describes the thoughtless destruction of natural resources in the nineteenth century. From it, we may learn something about the need for a wiser use of nature in our own time.

The frontiersman's life-style involved only simple things; he lived at first almost entirely off the land. Civilization decreed that he have a shelter, and so he built a log cabin; that he have fields and raise grain, so he girdled the trees and burnt them when they dried. To the pioneer the sound of a good, clean lick of the axe in a two-hundred-year-old oak was but the pleasant staccato assurance of civilization's advance. Fields of waving grain, meadows in which cattle grazed, crossroads settlements — these were sure signs of the march of civilization. The existence somewhere of a virgin forest meant that man had not yet arrived.

Availability of wood in the new country meant that a civilization could be built. Wood is easily worked; much can be done with it using a minimum of tools. Coachmakers, cabinet makers, furniture makers, coopers, boat build- ers, coffin makers, gunsmiths, and housebuilding carpenters came to know the good and poor qualities of a dozen or more kinds of wood. They knew how to season it, how to cut it, how to use it. In the early days live oak, red cedar, and cypress were chosen for ships; black walnut made excellent furniture, supplied the framework for Singer's sewing machines, and pro-

From *The New Country: A Social History of the American Frontier, 1776–1890* by Richard A. Bartlett. Copyright © 1974 by Oxford University Press, Inc. Reprinted by permission.

vided the material for coffins fit to bury the affluent and the gunstocks for rifles. There were certain kinds of wood for blocks and pulleys, mallets and buggy whip handles, yokes for oxen, wagon and coach frames, felloes and hubs for wheels, for all but the springs of Connecticut-made wooden clocks, and for the floors of covered bridges whose sides and roofs were of a cheaper, softer, and less lasting variety.

The balloon frame house, an American innovation, housed much of the nation, and it was made entirely of wood. Sidewalks and corduroy and plank roads were constructed of wood. All river boats were of wood. Save for the running gear and the little pot-bellied stove, the railroad car was of wood, as were the water tanks, station buildings, platforms, and warehouses. Millions of ties were used to cushion and hold fast the rails that criss-crossed the nation. Wooden trestles reminiscent of some kind of gargantuan Chinese puzzle carried the trains across gorges. Wood fired the steamboats, each of which consumed about a cord of hardwood an hour — and a cord is a pile eight feet long, four feet high, and four feet wide. Locomotives continued to use wood long after the trend had turned towards coal burners. Both the Union Pacific's No. 119 and the Central Pacific's No. 60 (also called the Jupiter), which touched cowcatchers at Promontory Point on May 10, 1869, were wood burners. Here, then, is part of the explanation for the plunder of the forests. The nation could not exist without lumber. It wanted it in all kinds and in great quantities, it demanded steady, reliable supply, and it wanted it delivered to the door at a reasonable price.

Originally about 40 per cent of the contiguous forty-eight states were covered with forests, nearly all of which were in the public domain. Save for a minor exception or two, that forest cover was considered by the government to be like any other acreage. It was sold at a base price of $2 an acre, later reduced to $1.25, just like prairie lands, mountain lands, bottomlands, and even desert and swamp lands. At this point, in theory, the auction system was supposed to correct the obvious differences in value of lands. In theory prime timberland would command a much higher price than would scrub or farm land at auction time.

It did not work that way. In the "up for grabs" climate of opinion that prevailed during most of the nineteenth century, the government was a weak, far-off landlord, the new country was a vacuum, and the general attitude sanctified the right of possession and exploitation as a part of the scheme of things, as a part of natural law. The people were in a frenzy to build a civilization; and no one considered the terrible cost to the environment. That frenzy is only partially expalined by the profit system. It was that, and something more, something connected with the spirit of western man that demanded an end to the Garden of Eden.

Furthermore the plundering was done in illegal ways. Granted that government should have come up with a workable system, it is nonetheless true that fraud, deception, bribery, and other forms of chicanery were used to seize the forests which legally belonged to the government. The goal of the lumbermen was the acquisition as cheaply as possible (and often for nothing at all) of hundreds of thousands of acres of timber. There *did* exist a seemingly inexhaustible supply that was very weakly secured, and an insatiable demand for lumber; and thus opportunity for great profit. A corollary was the creation of a great and powerful industry employing thousands of people who became specialists — the lumberjacks; from it arose songs and stories, including the legendary figures of Paul Bunyan and his Great Blue Ox. Not just communities but entire regions flourished from the lumber business. Thus there existed a pressure group that possessed potentially great political power which it could guide in the direction of favorable timber policy. Political power in the nineteenth century, as in our own day, could accomplish much that was basically dishonest, immoral, and unethical. It is from this situation that the word *plunder* attains validity as a description of what happened to America's Great Forest. . . .

By the 1840's the forests of New England and New York had been sadly depleted, and the lumber trade began to shift to the Great Lakes states. An enormous timberland was opened at the same time that the prairie and plains states and the rapidly expanding railroads needed millions of feet of lumber. In 1842 some two million shingles were delivered in Galena, Illinois; in 1850 Wisconsin and Michigan alone produced about nine million feet of lumber. Long before 1860 Chicago had become the lumber center of the nation, replacing Bangor, Maine, and Albany, New York. The building of the Illinois Central contributed materially to this boom. Even the Pacific Coast enjoyed an early timber business, and in the 1850's was exporting lumber to the Orient.

Timber barons had by now emerged with prestige, political power, and great plans. They coveted the forest covering the public domain, but they did not desire to pay a minimum of $1.25 an acre for it or to compete for it with others at auction, nor even to wait until the federal government had surveyed it and formally opened it to purchasers; and they did not want it for settlements. One of their practices was the "round forty." By this subterfuge they actually did purchase forty acres of land, but it was often land poorly surveyed — very useful for legal defense if questions were asked. Upon this piece of private property they set up a saw mill, barracks, cook house, and field office. Then the owner cut to the horizon on the adjoining public domain, on land he described as being "captured."

They had also found ways of obtaining legal possession of lands by questionable means. The Preemption Act of 1841 permitted bona fide settlers to squat on public lands and then have first rights to the acreage at $1.25 an acre when the land was opened for sale. There was nothing to prevent the sale of such lands to timber barons as soon as the purchase had been made, and fraudulent preemption claims were widespread. Military bounty land script, issued to veterans of the War of 1812 and numerous Indian wars, was purchased in great quantities by lumbermen.

Perhaps the greatest windfall of all for the timber barons was the

Swamplands Act of 1850. This well-intentioned act was based on the grow-ing awareness that millions of acres along the new country rivers had not been purchased because of the danger of flooding. The idea was to give such lands to the states, which would use the revenue from their sale for reclamation projects. But soon the federal government was giving lands to the states without examining the plats to make sure the lands *were* swamp-lands. It was the greatest land grab in the country's history; some 63 million acres were transferred to the states which, easily manipulated by the timber barons, turned around and sold such prime land for as little as 25 cents an acre, less than the value of the lumber in a single harvestable tree. Or the states gave land grants to wagon road, railroad, or canal companies, which in turn certainly knew what to do with them. Florida did both: it sold 4 million acres for 25 cents an acre and disposed of 16 million acres of land grants to wagon road, canal, and railroad companies. Much of that state's total domination by special interests, nearly as powerful today as they were more than a hundred years ago, stems from these scamy beginnings. Louisi-ana sold prime cedar stands for 50 cents an acre. And what about all those funds for reclamation? Almost none of the revenue went for the avowed purpose. . . .

When the government reduced the size of Indian reservations, much of the freed land fell into the hands of timber barons, who received in this way some of the best timberlands in the Wisconsin and Minnesota north woods. Loopholes were found in the Homestead Act, and lumberjacks gladly took up homesteads and claimed settlement and improvements that were ludicrous as well as fraudulent (such as construction of a cabin eighteen by thirty *inches*). After fourteen months at most, the lands could be pur-chased for $1.25 an acre. Thousands of such fraudulent homestead entries were filed. . . .

[The timber barons] used sailors, hoboes, their own employees, and whole railroad carloads of people to stake out claims, even giving them the funds to buy. At all stages of the transaction the lumber company handled the formalities of publishing the proper notices, hiring men to swear to the validity of settlement, paying for the lands and receiving the receipts. Obvi-ously the local register and receiver had to be in collusion. In one case, over 14,000 acres in California went to one man under this [Timber and Stone] act; in a Washington case, a company gained control of 100,000 acres, at-tempted to bribe the investigating government agent for $5,000, and pre-vailed upon the government to have him dismissed. Local feeling, it should be added, was almost always in favor of the company; the government men were considered snooping pests. All told, some 13,500,000 acres were dis-posed of under the Timber and Stone Act; the record for the Timber Cut-ting Act is equally dismal.

Two Italian companies, one in Florida and one in Alabama, were charged with receiving, by way of fraudulent homestead entry, in the case of the former, 4,512,000 feet of timber from the public lands, and in the latter 17 million feet. Turpentine distillers brazenly hacked at the trunks of pines and took the sap; after a few years this killed the pines, but what matter? They were on the public domain. There was one case in which the turpentiners worked along the line of a southern railroad, destroying the trees of the public domain sections, but leaving the alternate sections belonging to the railroad strictly alone. Turpentiners, incidentally, were among the most vicious subscribers to the barbaric convict lease system which lasted well into the twentieth century in a few southern states.

The railroads quite understandably took a liberal view of the right granted them of using raw materials from the public domain "adjacent to the line of the road" for construction purposes. President Chester Arthur's secretary of the interior, Henry M. Teller (1881–85), interpreted this as meaning timber growing anywhere within fifty miles of the track. By the turn of the century some four-fifths of the timber in the United States had fallen into private hands. The Southern Pacific and the Northern Pacific railroads were the two largest owners, with the Weyerhauser lumber company third. At one time that timber baron purchased over 600,000 acres of prime forest land from the Northern Pacific. Most lumber men, however, were small operators who had control over relatively small acreages of forested lands.

Besides the lumbermen there was another forest destroyer that wreaked havoc in the new country: the forest fire. It is clear evidence of the absence of concern that terrible fires raged out of control and destroyed millions of acres in the nineteenth century with hardly a warning from officials. Timber thieves set fire to land . . . to destroy the evidence of their thievery. Settlers in piney woods areas of the South set the forest on fire to kill off snakes and insects. Fires raged out of control because hunters and campers never took such simple precautions as dousing their campfires when they left them; the big smokestacks of railroad locomotives shot sparks and cinders out into the dry fields and forests adjacent to the rails; and it was not at all unusual for entire regions to live in a late summer haze caused by the smoke of raging fires, with no attempt being made to control them.

In 1871, the same year as the famous Chicago fire, a blaze cut across the state of Michigan from Lake Michigan to Lake Huron; in that same year the terrible Peshtigo fire occurred, burning a million and a quarter acres and killing more than a thousand people. In 1881 a fire east of Saginaw, Michigan, killed 125 people and destroyed 1,800 square miles of forest. The fury of a forest fire is difficult to convey in words. The heat becomes so intense that whole trees burst into flame at once, and fire tops from one tree to another. The earth cover is destroyed, and six or eight inches of ashes may cover the ground where fertile humus once lay. . . .

Change, of course, is the very essence of life, and of nature. Long before the white man came, or the Indian roamed at will, nature itself was making alterations in the landscape. Forest and prairie fires, started by lightning, reduced millions of acres to ashes and desolation. Man had nothing to do with the climatic cycle that included long periods of drought, when prairie and forest became tinder dry, as ready to burst into fire as an open bucket of gasoline, and then wet periods resulting in prairies inundated with water, such as George Rogers Clark encountered on his winter expedition to Vincennes in 1778. Long before the white man there were swollen rivers that carried off everything in the way of their rushing waters. The mighty Missouri, by way of example, was always muddy — so much so that its waters permanently changed the appearance of the Mississippi into which it flowed. . . .

Basically man has done two things with the Missouri River country. In his haste to tear up the soil for farms and cut off the forest cover for lumber, he hurried the runoff from thousands of ditches, creeks, and rivers tributary to the Missouri, and so increased the big river's latent destructiveness. Then came those myopic twentieth-century beavers with bulldozers, the Army Engineers, who built dam after dam (and, if not restrained, will continue to do so). In a precarious and tenuous way, the mighty Missouri is today under control; it is less destructive than it was before the coming of the white man. But — let three or four heavy rains occur at just the right time and at just the right places — then, watch out! Moreover, the dams themselves upset the spawning of fish and the nesting of wildfowl where marshes once lay; and they inundate prime ranch and farm land.

Usually, man has made things worse. For example, in the 1840's and 50's there was much malaria in the Ohio and Mississippi valleys. Probably the disease was carried there initially by white men who had it in their systems and had then been bitten by New World mosquitoes. Settlers in the valleys made things worse by cutting timber, often leaving a wasteland full of pools in which stagnant water collected, providing breeding places for clouds of the humming pests. In Indiana reservoirs were constructed to hold and control the waters for canals; these too became breeding places for malarial mosquitoes. . . .

In the balance, man probably brought more flora and fauna that was detrimental than was beneficial to the new country. Sometime around the end of the nineteenth century someone imported some Chinese chestnut trees. They carried a fungus, *Endothia parasitica,* to which the Chinese chestnut was immune, but not the American chestnut. Today about nine million acres of chestnut trees have been killed by this fungus, which has defied all the scientific expertise of America's best parasitologists. The "spreading chestnut tree" is as rare in America today as the village smithy who once worked under it.

Or take birds: the house sparrow was imported into Brooklyn in 1850 and 1852 to feast on the pestiferous cankerworms that were attacking the shade trees there. Until about 1900 these blandly colored little chirpsters were seen mostly in the larger cities. Then a population explosion took place, and they spread throughout the land. They now number in the millions and have pushed out many prettier birds with pleasant songs. Or again, no one who has cringed as he walked away from some of the big public buildings, such as the National Archives, in Washington, D.C., has not cursed the presence of the ugly crow-like starlings there. These too were introduced — in New York in 1890 — and, being without natural enemies, have multiplied until they number in the millions. They too have displaced other more pleasurable birds but have given the new country very little in return.

Of more interest, but more tragic, is the story of what man did to the birds and animals that were already here. Perhaps nowhere in history is there a better example of man's destruction of entire species of bird and animal life. The bird life of the new country was rich almost beyond imagination in both numbers and varieties. Tanagers and swifts, owls and swallows, eagles and hawks, vultures and turkeys, parakeets and hummingbirds, ospreys and terns, swans and egrets, ducks and geese, flickers and chickadees, all flourished on the land and in the clear air above it. Hardly was there a pen-and-ink sketch or an etching made of scenes in nineteenth-century America that did not have little flocks of birds dappling the sky. Such flocks are no longer commonplace, and what was the normal scene then now strikes us as somewhat unusual. Men did not comprehend the human ability to destroy, just as a half century ago they could not comprehend automobiles so numerous as to cause smog; so there was no effort whatsoever made either to understand or to protect bird life. Not until 1918, with the passage of the Federal Migratory Bird Treaty Act signed by the United States and Canada, was spring shooting of game species forbidden, although the Lacey Act of 1909 and the McClean Law of 1913 (also known as the Migratory Bird Act) were the beginning steps in placing migratory birds under federal protection. Of what good was a protective law in one state when the birds flew next over a state without such legislation?

And so, as was inevitable, several species were destroyed. The great auk was already all but extinct by 1776, although the last one was not taken until July 3, 1844, off the coast of Iceland. These penguin-like birds, whose breeding place was Funk Island off the far northeastern side of Newfoundland, could be bopped on the head or otherwise killed easily. Their feathers were useful for mattresses and their meat edible and also good for fish bait. It is true that many species have become extinct due to natural selection, and that about 97 per cent of the birds that have become extinct in the past two hundred years have been island birds which were anomalies in the modern world. However, although it exhibited great stupidity and helplessness before man, the great auk was in no way endangered with extinction until man appeared.

Then there was that rather odd-looking bird, the Labrador duck, of which the last one ever seen was killed in New York in 1878. And there was the heath hen, resembling a small chicken or the still-flourishing great prairie chicken. Probably never abundant, the heath hen was known to have lived from New Hampshire to Chesapeake Bay. Active attempts were made to save this attractive bird: some 200 of them were coddled and protected at Martha's Vineyard, and their numbers grew to about 2,000 before fire, disease, an influx of their natural enemies the goshawks, and a poor sex ratio of about two females to ten males, reduced the heath hen to extinction by 1931.

A far more prevalent bird, and a beautiful species, therefore a more tragic loss, was the Carolina parakeet. Of some 500 species of parrots, this was the only one that lived and bred in the United States. Colored in beautiful yellows, oranges, and greens, a foot long overall, it lived in flocks and was found from the Atlantic coastal plain inland to the Mississippi and then south to the Gulf Coast. The factors in the bird's undoing were its taste for the farmer's fruits and seeds, its plumage, which was saleable, and its tendency to flock, so that large numbers were easily killed with a scattergun. It was a chattering species, and if caught was easily tamed. The last of these beautiful birds was taken in Florida in 1912.

But the greatest loss of bird life has yet to be mentioned. This was the destruction of the passenger pigeon. Sometimes new country farmers who lived along the Great Lakes or in Ohio or Pennsylvania, Kentucky or Tennessee, Missouri or Iowa, would pause in amazement at the sheer numbers of these birds. How many? A horde of them sometimes took twelve or fourteen hours to pass a given point, each flock at least a mile wide, one flock so close behind another as to be almost indistinguishable from the one ahead. And they were several layers deep. Anywhere from two to ten pigeons filled every square yard of space. This means that a single flyover of a day's duration involved hundreds of millions of pigeons — and the incredible part of it is that these statistics are almost certainly correct. Conservative estimates put the passenger pigeon population within the United States — essentially east of the Mississippi and northward to Canada — at three to five billion, 25 to 40 per cent of the total bird population of America at the time. Yet the last wild passenger pigeon was killed probably in 1899, the last one in captivity died in 1914.

It was an aristocratic, beautiful bird; it had a small head and neck, but red eyes so bright as to suggest flame, a proud, robust breast, a graceful body, and a long tail. Its wings were long and pointed. The male had a slate-blue head, a hindneck of a metallic iridescence of bronze, green, or purple (it changed with the light); its back was slate gray, and its lower back and rump grayish purple. The throat was a rich, wine-colored russet, changing gradually to white on the abdomen; the wings were grayish brown, grayish blue, or even purple. In length the male averaged over sixteen inches; the female was about an inch smaller and duller in color. From a short distance the birds seemed blue — and were so fast they were sometimes called "blue meteors."

From the earliest time of white habitation these pigeons were killed and sold commercially. The settlers soon learned how to preserve the flesh, even before ice was available. They roasted the birds, then packed them in casks and covered them with molten fat, which kept out the air; or they salted the meat down and stored it in barrels, as with fish; or they pickled the birds, especially the breasts; breast of pigeon pickled in spiced apple cider was a delicacy. Down in Virginia they put up the fat of the birds in tubs. It would last for months, and was described as being as sweet as butter. What seems worst of all, they even fed the carcasses to the hogs.

The precipitous decline in the passenger pigeon population began in 1871. Throughout the next three decades more pigeons were killed every year than were hatched. This decline was noted, but, save for a very few voices in the narrowing wilderness, little was suggested to stem it; instead the talk was all about bolstering the efforts to find and kill the diminishing supply of birds. No matter how small the nesting or the roosting, the pigeoners headed for it, sometimes two or three hundred strong, determined to kill every squab and adult with nets, stool pigeons, corn soaked in alcohol, axes, fire, and shotguns. The ice and the barrels were forthcoming in the freight cars arriving on the nearest tracks, and the buyers were there too, with instant cash. When the birds had become so rare that the commerce in pigeons had come to an end, "sportsmen" were always around, ready to pick up their shotguns and head for the rumored nesting or roosting on the double. If they discovered a score of lonesome passenger pigeons, they killed every one they could find. Could the pigeon have survived for just one or two more decades after the last wild pigeon was killed in 1899, the climate of opinion would have changed, and steps would have been taken which would probably have saved it; for one more decade would have placed the birds in the middle of the first great conservation movement in America. But this is a bitter afterthought: the pigeon is no more.

Thus far our concern has been primarily with the well-watered, heavily timbered lands east of the Mississippi. This is where settlement first occurred, and it is in this vast region that perceptive people first began to note the reduction in number of deer, bear, bison, wolves, bobcats, panthers, and other wild animals. The Southeast had abounded in deer, and as early as the beginning of the eighteenth century, long before our story opens in 1776, well over a hundred thousand deerskins a year were being shipped out of Charleston. Two hundred bearskins were shipped out of the Ohio Valley on an early steamboat. The last buffalo south of the Ohio was seen in 1810; north of that river but south of the Great Lakes in the same year; and east of the upper Mississippi country in 1830.

But the trans-Mississippi West still retained the fresh breath of nature, and while wildlife was becoming rare or extinct east of the Mississippi, it remained, for a little while longer, wild, unrestrained, and vigorous on the other side of the river. In the spring of 1805 Lewis and Clark observed hundreds of bloated buffalo carcasses bobbling downstream amongst the ice flows, the victims of the ice cover breaking up in the spring thaw. Below Great Falls [Montana] the explorers also found many dead bison, the victims of pressure from the back of the herd which pushed the leaders out into the river too far as the beasts came down to the banks to drink. Those in the lead lost their footing in the swift current and were carried over the falls to destruction. The explorers noted that the pesky prickly pear was rampant at one of the principal fords used by the bison to cross the Missouri on their annual migrations; the bison had destroyed the grass cover and the prickly pear had grown up in the breach. They noticed, too, that the Indians occasionally fired the prairie, and at least once Lewis and Clark did it themselves, to signal the Indians to come in for a conference.

Buffalo were so numerous in places that the explorers had to fire their guns to prevent the top-heavy-looking beasts from inundating their camp, and one time as the party floated downstream they were held up an hour while buffalo crossed the river. There were mule deer and elk, too, and that strange little beast of the western plains, the pronghorn, better known as the antelope. It is estimated that there may have been thirty million buffalo in pre-white man's North America, and there may have been just as many antelope.

Lewis and Clark were also intrigued by the prairie dogs, those little rodents that live in "towns," sometimes of ten or twenty square miles in size. (They are not dogs at all, and would be better known by the Indian name of "wishtonwish.") Today, although they are apparently not in danger of extinction, there are few left. They are considered destructive, and have been heavily poisoned in most places.

Wherever there were prairie dogs, jackrabbits (really hares), bison and deer, antelope and elk, the lobo — the prairie gray wolf — was sure to be seen skulking along the fringes of their habitat. This intelligent but deadly predator made short shrift of the sick, weak and diseased animals, and thus helped nature maintain a balance. Lobo and his sneaky cousin, the coyote, fared well until the coming of the cattlemen. For years rare was the cowboy who did not carry a pouch of strychnine in his pack. Whenever he came upon a cow dead by disease, freezing, locoweed, lightning, or attack by a predator, he planted strychnine on the carcass. It was not long before the wolf and the coyote — more especially the wolf population — as well as grizzlies, bobcats, mountain lions, vultures, bald eagles, and other devourers of carrion, began to diminish materially. Few are left.

Lewis and Clark also saw the beaver, their signs on the trees — or tree stumps — and the dams and ponds they had built. The beaver is a big rodent, weighing thirty to fifty pounds; he measures from two and a half to three feet from tip of nose to butt of tail, and that wide, flattish, useful muscular appendage adds another ten inches.

Beaver have always been good citizens in the animal world, minding their own business, killing no fish or animals, choosing one mate, and raising four to six kits a year. When the country was new, no one ever thought of those sixty to a hundred million beaver as water conservationists, but in constructing their dams they did — and do, where allowed — control the water level of streams.

Man soon discovered, however, that the beaver's pelt was soft and thick, with, closer to the skin, a velvety, downy buff that could be worked into attractive, stylish, long-lasting hats, coat collars, and even shoes. No other readily available animal had a pelt with such characteristics, and so the beaver was trapped nearly to extinction.

Centuries before the white man splashed ashore in North America the European beaver had been in demand, and by the sixteenth century it had become almost extinct. Peltry had been the prime reason for the demand, but something else produced by the rodents had also been used, as it was in the New World: the granular, yellowish substance taken from two large glands in front of the rectum of both sexes. Castoreum, as it was called, has a sweetish, musky, but not offensive odor. Indians sometimes sweetened their tobacco or kinnickinnik with it. In the Old World, even in classical times, this substance had been considered a nostrum, a cure-all for just about everything. In America it was used as a medicine, but primarily it was valued as a beaver bait. A stick dipped in castoreum was too tempting for the beaver to pass by. So he went to sniff the stick, stepped in the trap and, if an expert had set the instrument correctly, splashed around in water so deep that he soon drowned.

Peltry and castoreum had made him nearly extinct in Europe, but until the white man came, *Castor canadensis* held his own in America. The sparse Indian population trapped or otherwise killed him, used the castoreum for medicine, kept warm with the peltry, or ate the roasted flesh, sweetish and succulent, prepared over the fire while still unskinned; the tail was especially good. There were plenty of beaver for the Indians, but things changed with the coming of the white man. Understanding the quest for beaver does, in fact, reduce admiration for the trading or trapping frontiersman. He may have been curious about what lay on the other side of a mountain or a pass, but there was a mercenary purpose even more prominent in his mind. Were there beaver over there?

By the time of the American phase of the fur trade the beaver had been exterminated or so reduced in number from the Mississippi east that the companies and their men had to move west. The phase Americans know best began about 1800, with St. Louis the center. . . .

By the 1830's the mountain men ranged from New Mexico, Arizona, and California northward in a great sweep extending to British Columbia and Alberta.

These men softened up the Far West for the Oregonians, the Forty-niners, and the Fifty-niners who came later. They were also ravishers. They "worked out" beaver stream after stream, until only the change of fashion in Europe and the East saved that hard-working rodent from extinction. They exposed the Indians to smallpox, measles, and venereal diseases, corrupted them with alcohol, and made them dependent on firearms, ammunition, and even blankets. When beaver peltry became scarce they turned to the buffalo, the very basis of the plains Indians' way of life, and killed them by the hundreds of thousands for their hides and tongues — this prior to the terrible slaughter of the bison after the Civil War. . . .

For the white man, the hide and tongue of the bison were all that were worth taking; these constituted a marketable product that was so cheap to obtain that the selling price and the profit were very nearly identical. For food out on the range the hunters might also roast a hump rib. Mountain men occasionally wrapped the fatty lower intestines around a stick, roasted them and consumed them with gusto (today we still eat crunchy hog chitlings with cold beer).

The immensity of the hide and tongue trade, even prior to the Civil War and the coming of the railroads to the prairies, is startling. The first systematic hunt appears to have been out of the Red River settlements in Manitoba. The year was 1820; it is recorded that 540 squeaky, two-wheeled Red River carts carried the hides to the place of sale. This was just the beginning. By the 1840's the average number of hides per year arriving in St. Louis was 90,000, and in the 1850's and 1860's it went up to at least 100,000. By the mid-1840's buffalo tongues had become a gourmet delicacy. More tongues than robes appear to have been sent down the Missouri, meaning that more buffalo were slaughtered than the statistics in hides indicate. After the Civil War, the hide trade reached massive proportions. The ten million bison that existed in 1865 were reduced to approximately one thousand by 1890, all of which were captives in private hands. Although a few states had passed laws to protect the bison, these were virtually unenforceable. Not until the 1890's were voices raised against the slaughter, voices that were heeded because of the intelligence and position of such men as William T. Hornaday, a zoologist and first director of the New York Zoological Park, who made the public realize that the bison had become nearly extinct.

What did the new country men think of all this slaughter? It is unreasonable to expect that they should have thought as we do. For them, there was no question but that nature's system must be destroyed. Just as the hardwood forests of the East had been cut down or burned to make way for an agrarian society, so must the millions of bison, antelope, wolves and coyotes, jackrabbits, and prairie dogs be destroyed. When the buffalo were gone they would be replaced by kine. When antelope, deer, and elk were destroyed, the hay men cultivated in the stream bottoms and the wild grasses elsewhere could be used to feed cattle. And where prairie dogs and jackrabbits had lived, dry land farming could produce wheat and corn. Where there had been worn buffalo trails, two gleaming lines of rails could be laid, and a black, belching monster could whiz along faster than any buffalo. Where Indians had pitched tepees, sod houses and dugouts, then white frame houses, then water tanks, grain elevators, cattle pens, railroad sidings, a public school, and a white frame church could rise; ash and elms planted by the townspeople could provide a heavy shade on hot days when the prairie that surrounded the village like desert around an oasis shimmered in the blazing, silvery summer sun.

One rarely finds evidence that the new country man was concerned about what was being done to the Great Plains. The pioneer carried with him the vision of western man, and, as he surveyed the treeless sea of grass with bison grazing on it as far as the eye could see, he contemplated nothing but improvement resulting from the changes he proposed to make. Cattle were a step above the undomesticated and unbreakable bison; to remove the bison and replace those ugly, prehistoric beasts with manageable bovines was nothing but improvement. Once in a while a sensitive newspaper editor, a far-sighted member of a state legislature, or an eastern sportsman might lament the passing of the buffalo, but this was usually in the nature of a sigh and a shrug. The pioneer, far from regretting the extermination of the buffalo, helped in every way to hasten its demise.

STUDY GUIDE

1. Though the destruction of our natural resources is closely related to a lack of government regulation, an even more important factor may be the profit and convenience that groups within our society find in the rapid exploitation of such resources. What groups besides the timber barons and the fur trappers had an interest in the exploitation of the forests and beaver? What sorts of vested interests are involved today in the pollution of air and water and the depletion of energy resources?

2. Think of several examples from Bartlett's essay of how the introduction of new species upset the balance of the existing environment. What examples of this can you think of in the last decade or two?

3. How might government have developed policies to protect American timber reserves, and such animal resources as beaver and buffalo? What modifications in patterns of settlement and styles of living would have been necessary to set aside several hundred million acres of forest and wildlife preserves?

4. Scientists have warned about the depletion of natural resources, population experts about the world food supply, and futurists about the possibility of life on earth becoming impossible. Some scholars have sug-

gested that it will be necessary to regulate all aspects of human existence — placing limitations on the private ownership of land and housing, the amount of food we are allowed, how many children a family may have, and the way in which we travel and heat our homes. If such drastic steps were necessary to preserve human existence, how might it be done and how would it affect our individuality, independence, and other traditional values?

BIBLIOGRAPHY

Though man is first and foremost a biological species, historians have seldom treated him as such, nor has much attention been given to his relationship to the natural environment in which he lives. From the very beginning of man's migration from other parts of the world to the Western Hemisphere, he has had an enormous — and mostly unfortunate — impact upon the flora and fauna of the New World. The influence of European diseases, plants, and animals upon North and South America is traced in Alfred W. Crosby Jr., *The Columbian Exchange: Biological and Cultural Consequences of 1492* * (Westport, Conn., 1972). Two other works that touch on the impact of Europeans on the land and the Indians are Victor E. Shelford, *The Ecology of North America* * (Urbana, Ill., 1963), and William L. Thomas, ed., *Man's Role in Changing the Face of the Earth* * (Chicago, 1965).

In order to get some idea of what America was like before the massive ecological changes brought about by the great migration, one can turn to several works on the age of discovery and exploration: Carl O. Sauer, *The Sixteenth Century in North America* * (Berkeley, Cal., 1971); John Bakeless, *The Eyes of Discovery* * (New York, 1961); and Russell Cutright, *Lewis and Clark: Pioneering Naturalists* (Urbana, Ill., 1969). The idea of the conservation of natural resources had its origins in the late nineteenth century; especially influential was a work by George P. Marsh, *The Earth as Modified by Human Action* (1874). In different periods, Americans have had varied attitudes toward nature. If you are interested in these changing outlooks, see Roderick Nash's *Wilderness and the American Mind* * (New Haven, Conn., 1967, rev. ed. 1973), and Hans Huth's *Nature and the American* * (Berkeley, Cal., 1957). Nash has also edited a volume of readings in this field: *The American Environment: Readings in the History of Conservation* * (Reading, Mass., 1968).

There are books on individual aspects of the subjects treated in Bartlett's essay, such as the destruction of the buffalo and the waste of forests. One of the most striking is Mari Sandoz, *The Beaver Men: Spearheads of Empire* * (New York, 1964). Unfortunately, much of the writing on the destruction of individual species, the pollution of streams, and the poisoning of the whole environment appears in publications with a limited readership. The publications of the Audubon Society are worth looking at, as is the Sierra Club *Bulletin*. A graphic example of this type of report is Harold Perry, "Predator Control Notes from Arizona: The Torture of Coyotes and Our Poisoned

Land," *Defenders of Wildlife News,* Vol. XLV (1970–71), pp. 31–36, and 406–32. Wilbur R. Jacobs also has a chapter on the effect of European settlement on the environment in his *Dispossessing the American Indian* * (New York, 1972). The impact of poisonous insecticides upon other life was first brought to popular attention in Rachel Carson's haunting book *Silent Spring* (Boston, 1962). At about the same time, the Secretary of the Interior in the Kennedy administration, Stewart L. Udall, brought out *The Quiet Crisis* * (New York, 1963).

* Asterisk indicates book is available in a paperback edition.

*Top, a young Confederate soldier.
Bottom, his Union enemy.*

20

BELL I. WILEY

Life in Wartime

The selections in this volume have illustrated the exceptional variety of American life in different parts of the country from the founding of the British settlements to the American Civil War. The editors hope that you have received some impression of the actual working conditions in early American factories, of the life of Indians and slaves, of education, family life, and social reform. The selection from Wallace Brown on the American Loyalists in the revolutionary period touched upon certain aspects of one of our wars. The final selection, from Bell I. Wiley's *The Life of Johnny Reb*, describes the life of soldiers under fire and behind the lines during the American Civil War.

In the twentieth century, there is little about war that is glamorous or chivalric. Those who fought in World War II, the Korean War, or the long war in Southeast Asia know the full import of General William T. Sherman's phrase, "War is hell." Massive bombings of civilian areas, atomic weaponry, napalm, massacres, and pushbutton slaughter have made a grim mockery of wartime heroism. The American Civil War has been described as the first modern war — partly because of tactical and logistic innovations and partly because of the astounding casualties, the use of scorched earth policies, and a number of other grim forecasts of the future.

Yet, there are common elements in nearly all wars — elements that connect the Civil War and our modern warfare with the so-called gentlemanly wars of the seventeenth and eighteenth centuries. Death, cruelty, callousness, cowardice, and bravery are a part of the human condition in wartime, and they know no special period. Equally common are the hatreds engendered in time of war, the boredom of army life, the loneliness for home and family, and the compassion for the enemy that Wiley describes. Such emotions might be found in any war in any country, but the sectional split of the United States that led brother to fight brother gave life in wartime a very special poignancy.

It was a hot July day in 1862. A Confederate soldier of twenty-three years sat beneath a tree on a hill near Richmond guarding a group of Yankees captured during the recent Seven Days' fighting. Ordinarily this Reb — whose name must remain in the realm of the unknown because of the incompleteness of his records — was a buoyant, zestful character, but on this particular day he was morose and inconsolable. He had just read a list of the casualties of Mechanicsville, Gaines's Mill, Frayser's Farm, and Malvern Hill. Included among the dead were a number of boys with whom he had frolicked during days of peace. But now they were gone.

As he mused over the loss of his comrades this young soldier laid aside his gun, drew from his pocket the small leather-bound diary that his sweetheart had given him when he left for camp, and began to write:

> July 10, 1862 . . . May God avenge us of our infernal enemies — and if I ever forgive them it is more than I Expect. "Forgive your Enemies" is the Divine precept — a hard one to obey — How can one forgive such enemies as we are contending against? Despoiling us of our property, driving us from our homes & friends and slaying our best citizens on the field are hard crimes to forgive — At any rate let me have a chance to retaliate & *then* I can forgive with a better grace. I hope to see many such epithets as this:
>
> > The Yankee host with blood-stained hands
> > Came Southward to divide our lands
> > This narrow & contracted spot
> > Is all this Yankee scoundrel got
>
> So May it be.

Most soldiers in the Rebel Army had feelings toward the Yankees very much like those expressed by this unidentified Virginian. There were some who excelled him in the pungency with which they recorded their antipathy. "I hope that we may slay them like wheat before the sythe," wrote a North

"Blue Bellies and Beloved Enemies," from *The Life of Johnny Reb* by Bell Irvin Wiley. Copyright 1943 by The Bobbs-Merrill Company, Inc. Reprinted by permission of Doubleday & Company, Inc.

Carolinian to his homefolk; "I certainly love to live to hate the base usurping vandals, if it is a Sin to hate them, then I am guilty of the unpardonable one."

A Mississippi private who had heard that his homefolk were being despoiled by the invaders blurted out, "I intend to fight them as long as I live and after this war stops. . . . I intend to kill Every one that crosses my path."

Not a few Rebs got so worked up over Yankee meanness that they swore to perpetuate hatred of the foe in generations to come. Typical of this group was the Georgian who wrote his wife in the spring of 1862:

Teach my children to hate them with that bitter hatred that will never permit them to meet under any circumstances without seeking to destroy each other. I know the breach is now wide & deep between us & the Yankees let it widen & deepen until all Yankees or no Yankees are to live in the South.

Hatred of Southern soldiers for those of the North was due to a variety of reasons. In their letters and diaries very few of the rank and file mention violation of states' rights as a cause of their antipathy. While most of them had heard small-fry politicians denounce the Lincoln government on this score, it is doubtful whether many of them either understood or cared about the constitutional issues at stake. The threat to slavery was resented rather widely, not so much as an unwarranted deprivation of property rights, but as a wedge for "nigger equality."

Common soldiers hated the men in blue primarily because they thought them to be an unsavory sort of people who came from a low and vulgar background. It is amazing how many Rebs commented on the crudity and obscenity of letters found on the battlefields addressed to Union soldiers. One Confederate who read a number of letters found in the Atlanta area in 1864 wrote to his wife, "I would send you a sample of them, but I am ashamed they are so vulgar. . . . I do not believe God will ever suffer us to be subjugated by such a motly crew of infidels." . . .

The Federals were also thought to be a bunch of thieves, having little regard for the rights of private property, particularly if that property happened to belong to Southerners. The robbery and despoliation that accompanied Union invasion was, indeed, one of the greatest of all causes of hatred. A Mississippi soldier whose home had been visited by raiders wrote to his mother as his regiment headed Northward on the Gettysburg campaign:

I can fight so much Harder since I have got a gruge against them it is my Honest wish that my Rifle may Draw tears from many a Northern Mother and Sighs from Many a Father before this thing is over.

Rebs liked to point out the superior regard of their own army for civilian rights. Whenever they invaded the Northern or border country, they were amused at the fear of brigandage manifested by the inhabitants along the way. "Poor fools," remarked a soldier marching with Bragg through Kentucky in 1862, "the Yankees treated them so badly, they thought we would do the same. They soon found out that there is a great difference. The Yankee army is filled up with the scum of creation and ours with the best blood of the grand old Southland."

This Reb's observation gives a clue to an impression that was widely prevalent in the Southern ranks and accepted by them as a partial explanation of the low character of Union soldiery; namely, that the majority of the Federals were recruited from the lowbred immigrant class which swelled the population of the East and the Midwest. It was pointed out repeatedly in home letters that prisoners encountered by the correspondents could not speak the English language. There can be no doubt that a particularly strong prejudice against foreigners in the South increased hatred of the Yankee soldiery. The comment of a sergeant of Bragg's army is typical of a general attitude. "Quite a number of Northern bums, called U.S. soldiers passed our camps," he wrote; "most of them were imported from Germany." . . .

The concept of heartlessness or brutality swelled considerably the hatred springing up in the hearts of the soldiers of the South. Atrocity stories circulating through the camps told of the bayoneting and shooting of Rebels after they were captured; of helpless Confederate wounded having throats slashed and tongues cut out; of gray-clads shot in the act of ministering to suffering Federals lying between the lines; of Yankees using poisoned bullets; and of the denuding and abuse by Northerners of defenseless Southern women in areas of invasion.

Warriors of all ages have been quick to resent affronts to women. The South, with its chivalric traditions, was unusually touchy on this score. It was this oversensitiveness that caused the Northern general B. F. Butler to be so thoroughly despised. For his alleged thievery the General was derided as "Spoon" Butler, but it was his notorious Order No. 28, in which he threatened to regard as harlots some New Orleans ladies who were "acting up" under his rule, that gave him the sobriquet of "Beast." . . .

Hatred for Sherman, Sheridan and other generals was hardly less than that for Butler. Lincoln was likewise regarded as low and brutish, so much so in fact that even intelligent soldiers regarded his demise as a blessing, as witness the entry of April 19, 1865, in the diary of Private R. W. Waldrop: "Everything in mourning today for old Abe who ought to have been killed four years ago." The attitude of the man in the ranks toward those of the North, both high and low, was aptly if not accurately summed up by the Virginian who wrote his mother that "the Yankee horde have forgotten the laws of war & have not natural honour and chivalry enough to suggest them on the conduct they enforce. . . . They are like ferocious monkeys which I believe the Spanish proverb makes the most cruel, wicked, and capricious of tyrants."

Another factor which contributed to Johnny Reb's loathing of the Yankees was the conviction that the men in blue were lacking in courage. This belief had a powerful hold on Southerners before hostilities began; it gained wider currency after the battle of Bull Run, and continued to flourish till the end of the war. Occasionally a soldier's letter or an officer's report of a battle conceded gallantry to the foe. After Missionary Ridge, for instance, Lieutenant James Hall wrote to his father that the scaling of the heights by the Federals "was a sublime spectacle and I could not withhold my admiration."

In similar vein wrote Captain B. E. Stiles after an encounter on the Virginia front in 1862. "It is all stuff saying that the Yankees are cowards," he concluded. "They fought as boldly as men ever fought and they fight well every time I'v been in front of them," was the testimony of still another officer after Second Manassas. But complimentary expressions such as these are amazing for their rarity.

Derogatory sentiments on the other hand were often recorded. "I saw a house full of Yankee prisoners," wrote a Texan in 1861; "they were large hardy looking men, but as you know they lack the courage."

A short time later an Alabamian boasted to his brother, "We whip them everytime We meet, no matter how great their Numbers, or how few ours. The infernal Scoundrels cant stand the Bayonet — they Scamper like a herd of cattle." A year and a half later this Reb held his antagonists in the same low esteem. "I hope it won't be long," he wrote then, "untill fighting Jo Hooker will be able to advance . . . with his army of white livers and give us a chance to enrich some of the poor land of old Virginia with their corrupt Bodyes." But, on second thought he retracted the statement attributing fertilizing qualities to Federal remains, recalling that a farmer whose property included a portion of the Manassas battlefield had told him that "one Yankee body will kill an acre of land whereas a Southerner's bones will enrich it for all time to come." . . .

Antipathy toward ordinary Yankees was deep and pervasive, but it was mild in comparison with the hatred which most Rebs felt for Negroes who wore the blue. All in all some 200,000 Negroes were taken into Federal ranks during the war. These colored soldiers did not get to do their full share of fighting, but they did figure prominently in a few engagements, including Port Hudson, Fort Pillow, Brice's Cross Roads and the Crater. The mere thought of a Negro in uniform was enough to arouse the ire of the average Reb; he was wont to see in the arming of the blacks the fruition of oft-repeated Yankee efforts to incite slave insurrections and to establish racial equality. Anticipation of conflict with former slaves brought savage delight to his soul. And when white and black met on the field of battle the results were terrible.

Negroes were taken prisoners in several engagements, but if the wishes of the private soldiers who fought them had prevailed, no quarter would have been granted. Most of the Rebs felt as the Mississippian who wrote his mother: "I hope I may never see a Negro Soldier," he said, "or I cannot be . . . a Christian Soldier."

On more than one occasion Negro troops were slain after they were captured. Following the Crater affair a Reb wrote his homefolk that all the
colored prisoners "would have ben killed had it not been for gen Mahone
who beg our men to Spare them." One of his comrades killed several, he
continued; Mahone "told him for God's sake stop." The man replied, "Well
gen let me kill one more," whereupon, according to the correspondent, "he
deliberately took out his pocket knife and cut one's Throat."

But the War of Secession was not all hatred. Many Rebs whose anger
flashed to white heat in battle became indulgent and generous toward the
foe when fighting subsided. Others felt little or no hate for the men in blue,
even while they were pinning writhing bodies to the earth with their bayonets. To these latter, fighting Yankees was regarded more or less in the light
of a regular chore — disagreeable, indeed, but unavoidable.

The war of the sixties has been called a "polite war," and in a sense the
designation is apt. The conflict followed generally the pattern of a series of
battles. Men of the opposing armies when not actually engaged in a shooting
fray were wont to observe niceties that in twentieth-century warfare would
be regarded as absurd. And even during combat there were occasional exchanges of courtesy. The conduct of the war in its entirety had something
of the flavor of a medieval tournament.

The chivalric concept manifested itself at the very outset of the war. When
Beauregard's aides were conferring with Major Robert Anderson in April
1861 on the eve of Sumter's bombardment, one of the Union officers complained jokingly to A. R. Chisolm that the garrison's supply of cigars was
woefully short. The Rebel officers said nothing, but when they returned to
the Fort for further conference a short time later they brought to the Yankee
garrison not only a generous supply of cigars but several cases of claret as
well. Before the night was over, these same Rebs gave the order to the bat-
teries to open fire on the Fort — an order calculated to reduce the bastion
to utter ruin.

This Fort Sumter incident was but the precursor of thousands of acts of
mutual kindness. In many instances the motive was sympathy for an unfortunate antagonist. A Rebel cavalry company while on a scouting expedition
in the fall of 1861 surprised a group of Yanks and took several prisoners,
including a lieutenant in his late 'teens. The leader of the Confederates wrote
his wife the next day that he could have killed "the handsome little fellow,"
but that he had not the heart to shoot him when he saw his beardless face.
So he pulled his youthful prize up behind and as they rode along they "got
to be quite good friends." When this officer overtook his company he found
to his surprise that the other prisoners had likewise captivated their captors,
for "every rascally Yankee was mounted and my men on foot." And thus
they proceeded to camp.

During the second battle of Bull Run in 1862, W. F. Jenkins, a seventeen-
year-old private of the Twelfth Georgia Regiment, was severely wounded.

At nightfall two of his comrades came to take him to the field hospital. As they struggled along through the darkness, they were halted with the query, "Who are you?"

"We are two men of the Twelfth Georgia, carrying a wounded comrade to the hospital," they replied.

"Don't you know you are in the Union lines?" asked the sentry.

"No," answered one of the Rebs.

"You are. Go to your right," said the Federal.

"Man, you've got a heart in you," said the second Reb as the little party turned to the right and headed for the Confederate lines.

In other instances Federals were the recipients of kindnesses. At Vicksburg, at Fredericksburg and at Cold Harbor, Yankee wounded who cried piteously for water as they lay between the lines were given succor by Rebs who dared to run a gantlet of fire to fulfill errands of mercy. During the engagement at Kenesaw Mountain in June 1864 a copse which sheltered some wounded Federals caught fire, threatening the helpless soldiers who lay there. Colonel W. H. Martin, of the First Arkansas Regiment, immediately jumped to the parapet, waved his handkerchief and cried out to the enemy, "We won't fire a gun until you get them away." Shooting on both sides ceased instantly, and the wounded men were removed from danger. At the end of the brief truce a Federal major gave his own fine pistols to Colonel Martin in appreciation of the humane action. . . .

In Virginia in 1862, and in Mississippi the next year, informal truces were called to give soldiers opportunity to pick the luscious blackberries ripening on the no man's land that lay between the lines.

Occasionally the spirit of mutual helpfulness was carried to amusing extremes. During the Georgia campaign of 1864 Rebel soldiers on picket, lacking digging implements to make rifle pits, were forced to beg spades of Yankee vedettes opposite them; and the Yanks were graciously accommodating. This politeness had a parallel on the Virginia front, but with the men in gray filling the role of lenders. . . .

The spirit of friendliness that sprinkled Yankee-Rebel relations had no more eloquent expression than the musical fetes in which the two armies occasionally participated. Sometimes Federal bands played for the Rebels, as at Fredericksburg during the war's second winter when a crack group of Union musicians posted on the Northern bank of the Rappahannock staged a concert unique in the annals of war. The program began with a medley of Northern airs — patriotic tunes and war songs. This was well enough for the listeners in blue, but not to the complete liking of that part of the audience stationed on the Southern bank.

"Now give us some of ours," shouted Confederates across the river.

Without hesitation the band swung into the tunes of "Dixie," "My Maryland" and the "Bonnie Blue Flag." This brought forth a lusty and prolonged cheer from the Southerners. Finally the music swelled into the tender strains of "Home, Sweet Home," and the countryside reverberated with the cheers of thousands of men on both sides of the stream.

At other times bands of the opposite armies participated in unpremeditated joint concerts. At Murfreesboro, for instance, on the night before the great battle, a Federal band began just before tattoo to play "Yankee Doodle," "Hail Columbia" and other tunes popular in Northern camps. After a little while the Union musicians yielded to the Rebel band which played a group of Southern favorites. These voluntary exchanges had continued for some time when one of the bands struck up "Home, Sweet Home." Immediately the other band joined in, and in a few moments the tune was picked up by a multitude of voices of both camps. For the brief period that the countryside reverberated with the notes of Payne's cherished song the animosities of war were lost in nostalgic reveries, and the fading away of the final notes found tears on the cheeks of scores of veterans who on the morrow were to walk unflinchingly into the maelstrom of battle.

The element of competition was occasionally introduced into these informal concerts. A Confederate band would run through a tune. Then a Federal band would attempt to give a better rendition of the same piece. In these contests — forerunners of present-day "battles of bands" — the Yankees usually came off with the honors.

In the absence of bands the joint fetes often took vocal form. Men on opposite sides of rivers bordering the Confederacy on several occasions united in the singing of "Home, Sweet Home." When in less mellow mood, their efforts were inclined to greater levity. In January 1863, for instance, Lieutenant W. J. Kincheloe of the Forty-ninth Virginia regiment wrote to his father: "We are on one side of the Rappahannock, the Enemy on the other. . . . Our boys will sing a Southern song, the Yankees will reply by singing the same tune to Yankee words." The lieutenant's observation is substantiated by the fact that several Civil War songs had both Yankee and Rebel versions.

One co-operative venture on the Rapidan was of a religious character. Private Goodwin of a Southern regiment, following the example of many of his fellow soldiers, "got religion" during the war, and a group of about fifty of his comrades escorted him down to the river's edge to be baptized. The procession attracted the attention of the Federals, and a considerable number of them came ambling down to the opposite bank to view the proceedings. Presently the Confederates launched into the hymn, "There is a Fountain Filled with Blood." This was a tune familiar to soldiers of both armies, and many of the Yanks joined in the song. Private Goodwin was duly dipped to the satisfaction of all.

This religious collaboration had an unhappy counterpart in interarmy gambling and drinking. There was a little island out in the middle of the Rappahannock where soldiers from both banks were wont to meet now and then to drown their woes in a draught of liquor. Gaming between pickets, and between other troops, was rather frequent. A Rebel officer making an unexpected tour of inspection one night on the Petersburg lines was shocked to find a considerable stretch of the trenches devoid of men. On close inquiry he discovered that the absentees were, by previous arrangement, in the Federal ditches playing cards.

Joint swimming parties were sometimes indulged in by troops stationed along rivers. These were apt to be accompanied by a great deal of "ducking" and banter. In fact, in whatever circumstances Rebs and Yanks came into proximity, there was usually not a little of "smart talk" or "jawing."

The boys in blue would sometimes shout across a Virginia river to inquire how "old Jeff" was getting along. The Rebs would retort by inviting the Yanks to come to Richmond and see, reminding them of several previous unsuccessful efforts to reach the Confederate capital. At Vicksburg the Federals would yell out, "Haven't you Johnnies got a new general — General Starvation?" The men inside the works would come back with the queries, "Have you Yanks all got nigger wives yet? How do you like them?" Before Atlanta the Federals would cry out from their trenches, "What is Confederate money worth?" or "How much do you ask for your slaves?" From the Rebel ditches would come the taunt, "What niggers command your brigade?" or "Have the niggers improved the Yankee breed any?"

A Yank who placed himself in a vulnerable position by shouting to a bedraggled Reb, "Hant you got no better clothes than those?" received the pungent answer from Private Tom Martin: "You are a set of damned fools — do you suppose we put on our good clothes to go out to kill damned dogs?"

On yet another occasion a Federal holding confab with an antagonist between the picket lines said sentimentally, "Why can't this war stop? I love you like a brother." The Reb's reply, in the words of a comrade, was: "You can say more for me than I can say for you for I haven't a dambed bit of love for you."

Good-natured raillery might be provoked by the most unexpected occurrences. One morning early in 1865 a large hawk came flying along over the lines before Petersburg. Soldiers from both sides immediately forgot their potshooting at each other and opened fire on the bird. It became bewildered by the cross fusillade and lit in a tall poplar tree halfway between the trenches. When finally it was shot down, both Yanks and Rebs let out a tremendous whoop, each side claiming the honors of marksmanship and demanding possession of the prize.

By far the most common form of fraternizing was the exchange of small articles of various sorts by men of the opposing camps. Throughout the war, in all portions of the armies, traffic flourished, and this despite the efforts of superior officers to put a stop to it. The usual method of procedure was for the men to meet at some intermediate point between the lines and there to swap tobacco for coffee, peanuts for pocketknives, pipes for stationery, and Southern for Northern newspapers. A Mississippian wrote his sister in 1864 from Petersburg, "We read each other's Papers in 15 minutes after the News Boys bring them from the Office."

These barter sessions were frequently the occasion of mutual cussing of "bombproof" generals, or grousing over troubles — which were very much the same in both armies — of talk about home affairs, of display, with polite comment, of daguerreotypes of sweethearts, and of expression of hope for a speedy end to the war. Now and then the parley would end with a generous snort of "tanglefoot," drawn perforce from the Yankee canteen. In more than one instance the participants in these get-togethers were members of the same family — brothers, or father and son, drawn to different allegiance by the fortunes of war.

Serious-minded Rebs were sometimes conscience-stricken as a result of these interminglings. A Mississippian who wrote his family of "our boys and the Yankees mixing up and talking together on friendly terms," remarked apologetically, "I threw an old dirty Yank a piece of Tobacco and He threw me a little sack of Coffee — I did not have any chat for them."

A Tar Heel who had trafficked recently with the Feds confided to his father:

> I tell you the Yankees assembled around me like a parcel of buserdes [buzzards] would around a lot of dead horses I chatted [with] them about ½ hour and left I tell you I dident feel rite no way.

Rebs and Yanks separated by narrow rivers developed an ingenious device for carrying on trade. Little boats, some two or three feet long, were made of bark or of scrap lumber, fitted with sails, loaded with coffee, tobacco and papers, and the sails set in such fashion as to carry the craft to the opposite shore. The recipients of the cargo on the other side would in turn load the vessel with items of exchange and head it back to the port of origin. A soldier in Lee's army records the fact that on pleasant days during the spring of 1862 the waters of the Rappahannock near Fredericksburg "were fairly dotted with the fairy fleet."

During the war's last winter, pickets facing each other along the lines before Petersburg, when denied the privilege of trade and communication, resorted to the expedient of tying small articles and messages to grapeshot or shell fragments and tossing them over to the rifle pits of their opponents. In this way they "flanked" the interdiction laid down by superiors.

Now and then a couple of Rebs would go over and spend the night in the Yankee camps, returning just before daylight. In such instances the Yanks might give expression to their good will by filling the haversacks of the parting visitors with coffee and other delicacies rarely seen by men in gray. Rebs likewise played host on occasion. A Delaware lieutenant who made a "hollering" acquaintance with a group of Confederates on picket was invited by them to a party behind the Southern lines. The Rebs called for their guest in a boat, outfitted him with civilian clothing, escorted him to the dance, introduced him to the country girls as a new recruit, and before dawn deposited him safely back on the Federal side of the river.

It would be easy to exaggerate the significance of the fraternizing that dotted the Confederate war. Hatred and fighting far outweighed friendliness and intermingling. But the latter always existed in such proportions as to worry high officers. The fact that the men on both sides spoke for the most part the same language, plus the fact that many had mutual acquaintances or relatives, tended to draw them together. This, coupled with curiosity, war-weariness in both camps, failure to comprehend clearly the issues of the conflict, and the desire to trade, made it increasingly difficult to maintain a definite line of demarcation between the two camps. In the last months of the war, as defeat became more and more apparent, Rebs who went out to swap or to parley with the Yankees failed in increasing numbers to return to their side of the lines.

This inescapable urge of blue and gray to intermingle and to exchange niceties suggests that — grim war though it was — the internecine struggle of the sixties was not only in some aspect a chivalric war but that it was in many respects a crazy and a needless war as well. There is some point, at least, to the observation made by a Reb after a conference on a log with a Yankee vedette. "We talked the matter over," he said, "and could have settled the war in thirty minutes had it been left to us."

STUDY GUIDE

1. In the opening of the selection, Wiley describes the hatred of some southern soldiers for the Yankee enemy. What reasons does he give for this hatred? What role might the following factors have played in the soldiers' letters: impressing the folks back home; bolstering their own morale; providing a psychological defense for participating in the horrors of war?

2. Aside from the denunciation of Yankees, the letters that Wiley quotes reveal an extraordinary boasting about the virtues of the South. Find instances in the selection that illustrate the Southerner's conception of women, chivalry, bravery, and so forth. In what ways is there a disparity between their words and their actions?

3. Wiley notes that the Civil War has been called a "polite war," in contrast to twentieth-century wars. What evidence does he give to support this characterization? Does this evidence consist primarily of individual acts of kindness and compassion, or does the official policy of the two armies in conducting the war also reflect humaneness?

4. Consider the following aspects of warfare, and indicate how wars in our time differ from the Civil War in each respect: treatment of civilian populations; individual atrocities; personal confrontations of infantry soldiers

in battle and in picket-line duty; how soldiers are killed; the degree of personal responsibility and concern that higher officers feel for their armies.

5. Compare the feelings described by Wiley with the animosities that are described by Wallace Brown in his essay on the Loyalists during the American Revolution (Reading No. 6). What differences and similarities can you think of in the relations of the two opposing forces during these two wars? Why were the Loyalists in a more difficult position with respect to confiscation of property and such personal abuse as tarring and feathering than were the enemy forces during the Civil War?

BIBLIOGRAPHY

There are more books and articles on the American Civil War than on any other aspect of American history. Much of this material deals with the causes of the war and the military campaigns; to discover some of this literature, you can examine James G. Randall and David Donald, *The Civil War and Reconstruction,* 2nd ed. (Boston, 1961) and Thomas J. Pressly, *Americans Interpret Their Civil War* * (Princeton, N.J., 1954). A good many other aspects of army life are treated in Wiley's *Johnny Reb* and its companion volume by the same author, *The Life of Billy Yank: The Common Soldier of the Union* * (Indianapolis, Ind., 1952). The attitudes of contemporaries toward the war are described in Henry S. Commager, ed., *The Blue and the Gray: The Story of the Civil War as Told by Participants,* * 2 vols. (Indianapolis, Ind., 1950). Among the many general treatments of the war, the best are: Allan Nevins, *The War for the Union,* 3 vols. (New York, 1959–1971); Bruce Catton, *This Hallowed Ground: The Story of the Union Side of the Civil War* * (Garden City, N.Y., 1956); and a three-volume series by Catton, of which the best volume is *A Stillness at Appomattox* * (Garden City, N.Y., 1953). George W. Smith and Charles Judah, eds., *Life in the North during the Civil War: A Source History* (Albuquerque, N.M., 1966) is a collection of writings from the period of the Civil War that will give you an idea of life behind the lines. One of the best secondary works on the same subject, but limited to the capital, is Margaret Leech, *Reveille in Washington, 1860–1865* (New York, 1941). Conditions there, of course, were considerably different from life in the Confederate capital, which is studied in Alfred H. Bill, *The Beleaguered City: Richmond, 1861–1865* (New York, 1946).

For a number of reasons, there are more good works on social conditions in the Confederacy than on wartime life in the North. A general work on the Confederacy, with several chapters on economic and social conditions, is E. Merton Coulter, *The Confederate States of America, 1861–1865* (Baton Rouge, La., 1950). Charles W. Ramsdell, *Behind the Lines in the Southern Confederacy* (Baton Rouge, La., 1944) is an excellent work more strictly confined to the home front, while Mary E. Massey, *Ersatz in the Confederacy* (Columbia, S.C., 1952) is a fascinating study of the substitutes that were used for food, clothing, and other necessities of life.

Bell I. Wiley also has works on southern whites and blacks in the Confederacy: *The Plain People of the Confederacy* (Baton Rouge, La., 1943) and *Southern Negroes, 1861–1865* * (New Haven, Conn., 1938). The latter work should be read in conjunction with the study on Negroes in the North by Benjamin Quarles, *The Negro in the Civil War* * (Boston, 1953). Chapters 7 and 8 of Quarles's book give an interesting picture of the reaction of blacks to emancipation.

* Asterisk indicates book is available in a paperback edition.

To the student:

We, as publishers, realize that one way to improve education is to improve textbooks. We also realize that you, the student, have a large role in the success or failure of textbooks. Although teachers choose books to be used in the classroom, if the students do not buy and use books, those books are failures.

Usually only the teacher is asked about the quality of a text; his opinion alone is considered as revisions are written or as new books are planned. Now, Little, Brown would like to ask you about this book: how you liked or disliked it; why it was successful or dull; if it taught you anything. Would you fill in this form and return it to us at: Little, Brown and Co., College Division, 34 Beacon St., Boston, Mass. 02106. It is your chance to directly affect the publication of future textbooks.

Book title:_____   _____ School:_____

Course title._____   _____ Course enrollment:_____

Instructor's name: _____   _____

1. Did you like the book?_____

2. Was it too easy?_____

   Did you read all the selections?_____

   Which did you like most?_____

   Which did you like least?_____

3. Did you like the cover?_____

   Did you like the size?_____

   Did you like the illustrations?_____

   Did you like the type size?_____

(over)

4. Were the study questions and bibliographies useful?_____

   How should they be changed?_____

   _____

5. Are the introductions useful?_____

   How might they be improved?_____

   _____

6. Do you feel the professor should continue to assign this book next year?

   _____

7. Will you keep this book for your library?_____

8. Please add any comments or suggestions on how we might improve this book, in either content or format.

   _____

   _____

   _____

   _____

   _____

9. May we quote you, either in promotion for this book, or in future publishing ventures?   ____yes   ____no

   _____   _____
   date   signature